WILLIAM RANDOLPH HEARST

AMERICAN

By

MRS. FREMONT OLDER

With a Foreword by Fremont Older

ILLUSTRATED

D. APPLETON-CENTURY COMPANY
INCORPORATED
NEW YORK   1936   LONDON

WILLIAM RANDOLPH HEARST

To the valiant soul of

FREMONT OLDER

this book is dedicated

by Cora Baggerly Older

FOREWORD

WILLIAM RANDOLPH HEARST came back to San Francisco from Harvard in 1887, a gay, laughing, fun-loving youth and took charge of the San Francisco *Examiner.* Who could have prophesied that in a few short years he was destined to change the attitude of mind of millions of people?

When he began his career I was already on my way to become a fairly competent reporter, and agreed with other newspaper men that this young Harvard man was not to be taken seriously. Of course, he was nothing more than the son of a millionaire who thought it would be good fun to "take a fling" at journalism. In a month his drowsy competitors were blinking their eyes before the startling, sparkling pages of the new *Examiner.* There was born a fear that never left them. Their only hope was that young Hearst's wealthy father, Senator George Hearst, would put a stop to the wild extravagance of his son, who, if allowed free rein would wreck his fortune.

Within six months that slender hope disappeared, for the *Examiner,* increasing in circulation and advertising, was showing alarming signs of meeting expenses. During this time young Hearst had discovered that the government of the State of California was in complete and undisputed control of the Southern Pacific Railroad. Even the powerful political sub-bosses, Bill Higgins and blind Chris Buckley, representing both the Republican and Democratic parties, cooled their heels in the anteroom of the Southern Pacific Building at Fourth and Townsend Streets awaiting orders.

Every newspaper in California was more or less controlled by the railroad. During seventeen years this great corporation not only dominated both houses of the Legislature, but the courts as well. Mayors of cities, supervisors of counties, even the coroners and constables were members of this happy family. I had seen Justices of the Supreme Court shamelessly display their annual passes to railroad conductors. When I was a legislative reporter in Sacramento and while the Senate was in session, a blue ticket, good for a free ride to and from San Francisco, was left every Friday on each desk. The same thing happened in the Assembly. It was a thoughtful week-end provision for the comfort of the railroad's slaves.

As an illustration of the frankness of bribery in those days I quoted in one of my articles a prominent citizen as saying: "You couldn't pass the Lord's Prayer in this Legislature without money."

This statement aroused the ire of the Speaker of the House who promptly appointed a special committee to investigate the charge. I was put on the witness stand, solemnly sworn, and asked to name the prominent citizen.

"There he sits," I said, pointing to Mayor Glasscock of Oakland. The Mayor followed me on the stand, frankly admitted that he had said it, and assured the chairman that he could amply substantiate the remark if the committee wanted to hear the evidence. But the committee, not knowing just how much Mayor Glasscock knew, abruptly adjourned the meeting. Nothing more was heard of the threatened investigation.

When William Randolph Hearst assailed this entrenched power his competitors smiled hopefully. Surely the mighty Southern Pacific would make short work of this audacious youngster. But again came disappointment. The *Examiner's* circulation mounted. Advertising covered more pages.

Hearst not only attacked the powerful C. P. Huntington, and eventually defeated his long-cherished Funding Bill, but he exposed the corruption of the minor bosses, Higgins and Chris Buckley, and made it so unpleasant for "blind Chris" that he fled to Canada, there to reside until the storm subsided. Nor did this young crusader overlook the minor grafts of the public utility corporations. The gas and water rates were too high, and he threatened that if the Spring Valley Water Company didn't show more consideration for the common man the city would go to the Sierras for water. This statement was made years before the acquisition of the Hetch-Hetchy water supply. With all of Hearst's campaigning for cheaper water, which was persistent, it took forty years to break the power of Spring Valley, with its active lobby in Washington blocking the city's efforts to acquire those mountain rights. It was not until November, 1934, that the Sierra water came pouring into San Francisco, and the householder's rates were cut 10 per cent.

What were the other newspapers doing while this young editor was engaged in washing the dirty faces of his native state and city? In order to survive they were compelled by the example set them, not only to change their social and political policies, but also their treatment of the news. Not content with overhauling the state and city government, Hearst was publishing the most attractive newspaper west of the Mississippi River.

Up to the time of this revolution in San Francisco journalism, I had developed no particular ambition in life, and was content to be regarded as a capable news gatherer, following life's daily routine, self-satisfied and unimaginative. The policies of the new *Examiner* awakened in me an interest and an enthusiasm that I didn't know I possessed. I found myself longing to become the editor of a newspaper where I would be free to develop some of the same policies. But there were years of plodding ahead of me. Meanwhile, after Mr. Hearst had made a success of the *Examiner* he went to New York and accomplished there, on a much larger scale, what he had done in San Francisco. By pursuing the same policies that had made the *Examiner* the leading paper of the West, in a few years the New York *Journal* had passed Joseph Pulitzer's successful *Evening World*.

In 1895, I became editor of the San Francisco *Bulletin* and gradually secured sufficient control to swing the policies of that moribund newspaper toward the rights of the common man, and away from its old, smug, conservative attitude of "Business is fine. Leave things as they are."

The event which changed the entire current of my life occurred in July, 1916. It was the Mooney case. For two years I continued to expose the perjury of the prosecution's witnesses. This caused great antagonism among the powerful people of the city, and the owner of the *Bulletin*, threatened with the loss of his advertising, gave me orders to drop the Mooney case. I had given twenty-four of the best years of my life to the establishment of the *Bulletin's* social policies, and now the end of my work had come.

Just at my moment of deepest despair William Randolph Hearst asked me to come to his evening paper, the *Call*, and bring the Mooney case with me. That was in August, 1918.

My acquaintance with him was slight, but after I came to work for him, and got rid of the biased point of view that a competing editor invariably has, I became aware that my earlier impressions of the *Examiner's* policies were rather vague and undefined. As I realized the deeper meaning of them I was enthusiastic over the gallant, lonely fight he had made for more than thirty years. I saw him as the most misunderstood man in America. As familiar as I had been with his newspaper crusades, I had failed to realize what a colossal job he had done in America. Under his direction, he had taught millions of people to read and think about their government. In fact there had been such a complete awakening that there was no possibility of America ever again tolerating the sodden conditions that existed when young Hearst first stepped into the *Examiner* office in 1887.

For years I wondered why his life and achievements had never been written. He had been subjected to so much bitter criticism from hostile competing newspapers that the average person had no conception of him. I became more and more eager to have the American people know this man.

Three years ago a friend of mine, knowing that I had lived

through Mr. Hearst's early years, suggested that I was the one to write a book about his life and accomplishments. It would have been a pleasure to do it, but a great part of my life had been spent in directing writers instead of writing. Fortunately for me, while I was supervising the work of other writers, my wife had written several books, and she has done the writing of this volume. I helped her with the research. Together we have accumulated a history not only of Hearst's life, but of the crusades he has made throughout America that have resulted in changing for the better the habits and characters of the greatest people on earth. We feel that the activities of William Randolph Hearst during his forty-seven journalistic years really constitute a history of the reform movement in America.

We are deeply indebted to many people both in and out of the Hearst organization, for our information. In London, Alice M. Head. In New York, Arthur Brisbane, Edmund Coblentz, S. S. Carvalho, George Pancoast, Frederick Burr Opper, Charles Edward Russell, Morrill Goddard, William A. Curley, Joseph V. Connolly, ex-Mayor Hylan, Bradley Kelly, Charles M. Palmer, F. H. L. Noble, Karl Decker, George d'Utassy, Robert Morris. In Chicago, Victor Watson and Ashton Stevens. In San Francisco, Eugene Lent, Mrs. W. B. Bonfils, Edward Clark, William Murray, Ethel Whitmire, Janet Peck, Mrs. Richard Carroll, Julia Morgan, Andrew M. Lawrence, Senator Hiram W. Johnson, John Francis Neylan, Frederick S. Moody, Sr., Katherine Soulé, and the late John Spring. In Los Angeles and Oakland, Evelyn Wells Podesta, Lucylle Walsh, Salome Holliday, Mary d'Antonio, Dr. Frank Barham, George Young, Harry Crocker, Joseph Willicombe and Carl Hoffman.

Other volumes will be written about William Randolph Hearst. A volume could be written about Hearst, builder of San Simeon. A larger volume could tell of Hearst, collector of art. Another volume could show Hearst, prophetic statesman who opposed the World War, foresaw the inevitable disaster following, even debt repudiation, the rise of revolution and Communism.

Only America, whose free air encourages the highest development of the individual, could have produced Hearst. He is as American as Plymouth Rock, as Washington, Franklin, Jefferson, Jackson, Lincoln, Edison and Ford. To America he has devoted forty-nine years of his life—the America of inarticulate millions. For them he has crusaded against privilege and corruption in high places. For them his work has made life less harsh, less unjust. Those millions have been inspired by him with confidence and hope for the future. Although he is the journalist with the greatest power in history, and the creator of the second greatest fortune, he will be remembered especially as William Randolph Hearst, American.

FREMONT OLDER

CONTENTS

CHAPTER VIII

CHAPTER IX

CHAPTER X

CHAPTER XI

CHAPTER XII

CHAPTER XIII

Hotel Del Monte fire. New business office. Employs Gertrude
Atherton. Makes first balloon flight with Harry B. McDowell.
Sends special train to Los Angeles with *Examiner*. Publishes
Thayer's *Casey at the Bat*. Opposes prize-fighting. Tries to improve schools. Attacks house of correction. Demands annexation
of Hawaii. News scoops. Monarch of the Dailies. Employs
George E. Pancoast as secretary. Interested in amateur photography. Goes to Europe with Pancoast. Photographs the Nile
and tombs of Egyptian kings. Buys mummies.

CHAPTER XIV

CHAPTER XV

CHAPTER XVI

CONTENTS

CHAPTER XLV

CHAPTER XLVI

CHAPTER XLVII

CHAPTER XLVIII

CHAPTER XLIX

CHAPTER L

CHAPTER LI

CONTENTS

Rebuilds Hearst Hall. Letters to and from William Randolph Hearst, Jr., and John Hearst. Doctor of Laws from Oglethorpe University. Telegram to Randolph and David Hearst. Letter to Mrs. Hearst.

CHAPTER LII

CHAPTER LIII

CHAPTER LIV

CHAPTER LV

ILLUSTRATIONS

CHAPTER I

INFANCY

IT was a dueling, shooting, lynching, young, joyous, fantastic, golden San Francisco into which William Randolph Hearst was born. Eighteen hundred and sixty-three—the year of Gettysburg and Vicksburg and the Emancipation Proclamation, with the living presence of Abraham Lincoln defending the life of the imperiled Republic. Perhaps even the child sensed these last supreme years of the martyred President, and that is why Lincoln has always been to Hearst a prophet.

William Randolph Hearst came into being in the most picturesque city, in the most romantic State and at the most dramatic moment in the history of the Republic. Invisible forces emanating from these moving conditions and circumstances made him the man he is, and stirred him, the offspring of luxury, to a long life of action. One cannot understand Hearst without understanding California, and San Francisco on the Bay of San Francisco, and the pioneers that bore him.

The voice of Sir Francis Drake was the first English voice ever heard in California, the northern outpost of the Spanish Empire of Philip the Second. During the sixteenth century Drake sailed into the Bay of San Francisco and strode over its drifting, cool, white sandy shores. In the centuries that followed, Portolá and Anza came by land from Mexico. In 1776, birth-year of the great English-speaking Republic on the Atlantic, there prayed at the Mission Dolores, one league distant from the bay, the saintly Padre Junípero Serra. In the gold-intoxicated fifties, before the altar of this crumbling Franciscan house of God, Lola Montez—she who looked like a golden poppy shining in the sun—after loving and wrecking Ludwig, King of Bavaria, wedded and wrecked Patrick Hull.

1

In the marts of San Francisco delved Sherman before he marched to the sea, and in these streets the avenging Murietta flashed his ruthless steel. In San Francisco still lived dark, saturnine Judge David S. Terry, who four years before Hearst was born had shot dead in a duel the bold, valiant Senator David C. Broderick. In the San Francisco of Hearst, the child, lived Bret Harte, Mark Twain, and that bearded poet of the Sierras, Joaquin Miller, and John C. Frémont, the Pathfinder, who opened up the American West. In its streets, great Dons with sweeping sombreros, like Vallejo of the North and Pio Pico of the South, clanked silver spurs. And that unbelievable, beloved madman in epaulets and carrying a sword, Emperor Norton, who fancied himself ruler of the United States and of Mexico, wandered over the plank sidewalks of the city with his two dogs, Bummer and Lazarus.

Since 1848, when Marshall found gold near Sutter's Mill and America roared westward, San Francisco had held the eye of the world. It was the heart of California, and California was the heart of the Pacific West. Here life was deep and intense. San Franciscans scarcely knew that an Italian-Spanish-American named Adelina Patti had just enchanted Paris and was receiving a salary of four hundred dollars a night. Nor did it matter to them that Albert Edward, Prince of Wales, was soon to marry the beautiful Princess Alexandra Caroline of Denmark; nor that the French were laying siege to Puebla, Mexico. The Vigilantes, bearded miners with heavy watches and gold nugget chains, these gamblers and dandies, were centered on America. The Republic might end at any hour. Battles raging on the southern front were daily refought in San Francisco's streets while there looked on American beauties in wide hooped skirts; and dark-eyed, slow Mexican señoras with rebozos over their heads; and velvet-footed Chinese, queues hanging down over gay brocade coats.

Another excitement! Work had been begun on the first railroad connecting East and West. Four promoters, Huntington,

Hopkins, Stanford and Crocker, with only a hundred thousand dollars among them had launched the Central Pacific.

Sixteen years previously San Francisco, now a restless city of eighty thousand, had been a dreamy Spanish-Californian pueblo, Yerba Buena. Overnight the pueblo in 1849 became a swaggering young city in a swaggering young State. With the arrogance of sudden power California repudiated "greenbacks," the legal tender of the United States, and demanded tender of gold.

During the two years preceding the birth of William Randolph Hearst, two hundred million dollars in gold had been sent by California to sustain the credit of the Republic. This gold saved the Union, and Abolitionists loudly acclaimed the glory. In this godless hour Abolitionists and slavery sympathizers warred even before the altars of San Francisco churches. One clergyman was hanged in effigy for declaring that Jefferson Davis was no more traitor than George Washington. The clergyman was driven away to Europe. Newspaper offices were sacked. Among them was the year-old *Examiner*, the first newspaper to be owned by William Randolph Hearst, who was born April 29, 1863, in the Stevenson Hotel on the southwest corner of California and Montgomery Streets.

George Hearst, father of the fair, blue-eyed baby, called his first born "Sonny." Phebe Hearst, the nineteen-year-old mother with a Madonna face and far-seeing gray-blue eyes, silently prepared to make her son the kind of man she desired him to be.

When Sonny was one year old the man who was afterwards to become one of his guiding stars, Abraham Lincoln, was re-elected President of the United States. There was a characteristic San Francisco celebration. Under a brilliant moon in an unclouded sky were bonfires, torches, Roman candles, rockets, illuminated windows, while four thousand men with flags and bands marched twenty abreast in the streets singing *John Brown's Body*. What cheering of newspaper offices! What serenading of dwellings of good Republicans! At the head of the procession cannon thundered. The war would soon be over. The crowd burst out singing, *The Battle Cry of Freedom.*

The war ended. From every housetop waved starry banners. Then suddenly banners drooped and lowered. Bells tolled. Brave San Franciscans grasped each other's hands, looked into each other's eyes, not voicing the terrible words— Lincoln was dead.

All this which happened while the boy Hearst was too small to understand, was to be for him of the gravest import, and perhaps was to mold his life. No crisis in the nation's existence ever seemed to him of such profound tragic significance.

Sonny was named William for his grandfather, William G. Hearst of South Carolina and Missouri. Randolph, a family name, was for his mother's father, Randolph Walker Apperson of Virginia and Missouri. Both Appersons and Randolphs were English. The Hearsts were Scotch and English, with a trace of Irish from Elizabeth Collins of Georgia, William Randolph Hearst's paternal grandmother. All the families had been in America for nearly two hundred years, sturdy pioneers of unresting energy, ever trying to better their condition, always seeking a new frontier.

Sonny was fortunate in both parents. From his father came driving force, quick decision, readiness to venture, interest in large affairs, understanding of the common man. From his mother came desire for culture with an æsthetic sense and passion for beauty which made him the greatest private collector of art that the world has ever seen. From both George Hearst and Phebe Apperson Hearst was inherited by William Randolph Hearst a spirit sensitive to suffering and eager to aid the unfortunate.

Phebe Apperson Hearst was only nineteen when her son was born, but she was hungry for knowledge, athirst for travel, avid for the finer things in life. As a young girl on the Apperson farm in Missouri she held in one hand a study-book, while with the other she performed household tasks. She remembered the difficulties of obtaining an education in Missouri, and

Phebe Apperson Hearst determined that what was achieved
by her with such effort should come easily to her son. In her
quiet grave way she resolved that he should have every advantage, every incentive and aid to go forward.

George Hearst was more than twenty years older than his
wife. In 1820, when he was born, there were only scattered
schools in Missouri. As a child in Franklin County he played
in the primitive neighborhood lead mines. From his father and
the French mine owners, he had his first lessons in practical
geology, exploring with them the mysteries of the earth.

Finally books came to him when he was fourteen. They dealt
mostly with geology and mining. He devoured them with an intensity and concentration that astonished his teachers.

But school soon ended. At his father's death young George
Hearst assumed the burden of supporting his mother, sister
and invalid brother. He kept a store, mined, farmed and found
time for local politics. In 1850, when the world went gold-mad,
he and some of his relations set out for California. Hearst was
on horseback. When he reached Fort Laramie he was stricken
with cholera. There was no shelter. Emigrants slept in the
open in the rain. Hearst sank into the mud with rain beating
upon him. He wanted to die.

But death turned back from George Hearst. He recovered
and pushed forward in spite of the vicissitudes that broke
many spirits and killed many argonauts. When he reached
California he had only a five-franc piece given him by a French
miner.

Conquest of fortune was not easy for George Hearst. For
ten years he followed the gold trails of California and Nevada.
In 1860 he became sixth owner of the Ophir silver mine—the
first great discovery on the Comstock Lode, Virginia City,
Nevada—the Lode that made Mackay, Fair, O'Brien and
Flood multi-millionaires. For the first time in his life George
Hearst was free from the weight of poverty.

There were Indian outbreaks in Nevada. Hearst shut down
his mine and returned to Missouri. He found his mother dying

and his sister dead. At this time he met Phebe Elizabeth Apperson whom he had carried on his shoulder as a child. Now she was eighteen and a school-teacher who spoke French well enough to desire to speak it better. She was eager to go to California, to see what the world was like in the alluring new Eldorado of the Sierra. Phebe Apperson did not know that her suitor was what would be called rich. The inexperienced girl was fascinated by his adventurous life. He was gentle and tender, tall and bearded, with a large high forehead and confidence begotten of inner power and success—different from all other men she knew. She fell in love with him.

The Apperson family protested that Phebe was too young to marry a man of forty. But George Hearst seemed touched with the miracle land of the West. Phebe Elizabeth Apperson married him at Stedville, Missouri, on June 15, 1862, and they set out for California.

Phebe Hearst enjoyed every minute of the way. Noisy Chicago, smart New York, the first sight of the Atlantic, going aboard the steamer, the strange-jungle vegetation at Panama, and brilliant tropical flowers, high waving palms, vines festooned from lofty tamarind and dyewood trees, gorgeous plumed parakeets in cocoanut trees; eating oranges plucked from trees—to the Missouri girl everything had an enchantment. With her instinctive historic sense it was all the more wonderful to Phebe Hearst because she was passing the way that Balboa had passed in 1513. She delighted in the coloring of the Pacific, in the coast of California.

Phebe Hearst's mother had taught her daughter to be a dexterous needlewoman, and all the way the bride sewed on a brown merino dress. She wished to be economical and help George. Brown merino she thought would suit a miner's wife. Her husband was amused.

So long as she lived Phebe Hearst never forgot the view as the ship from Panama sailed through the Golden Gate. She looked at the poppy-covered hills and said, "I intend to live on those hills where I can always see the bay."

George and Phebe Hearst drove from the wharf in a hack to the handsome new Lick House with its mahogany and red-plush furniture. Later they lived in a quiet family hotel, the Stevenson House.

Soon George Hearst delighted his bride by sending her to Davidson's, a fashionable French shop, where her measurements were taken for a black silk dress. To her it seemed a trifle extravagant, but the black silk was becoming to her clear, girlish skin. She caressed her first silk dress like a child, and looked at it many times a day. To her great astonishment one week later came a gray silk dress and another of blue. With the gowns were gloves, bonnets, jewels, everything that a fashionable young woman needed. Most precious of all to Phebe Hearst was her husband's gift of "real" lace. She had an appreciation of fine lace. She always cherished and guarded that first lace bought by her husband. Now her son guards it. To-day William Randolph Hearst's mother's first lace is carefully stored at San Simeon.

Phebe Hearst was overwhelmed by the gifts that continued. She looked at the brown merino dress. Why should she have so many costly clothes? George Hearst did not explain to Phebe that he had a very considerable fortune. The young wife sought counsel of Mrs. David Peck whom she had met on the steamer.

Mrs. Peck explained to the young wife that George Hearst was part owner of the richest mine on the Comstock Lode. Suddenly Phebe Hearst seemed transported on a magic carpet to Bagdad.

Soon after the birth of his son, George Hearst was obliged to return to Virginia City. The Indian outbreaks had been quelled, but he knew that Nevada mining-camp life was unsuited to Phebe and Sonny. He bought for them a comfortable brick dwelling on Rincon Hill where were many charming houses, each with a garden and long French windows opening on a gallery. Here lived fashionable San Francisco. After thirteen years of sleeping on the plains, in rain, in mountain cañons, in cabins, on floors in cheap hotels, at last Hearst had a home with wife, son and servants. For a few weeks he remained in the spacious house with his little family before returning to the turmoil of Nevada.

Eliza Pike was Sonny's deep-breasted nurse and second mother. She adored the fair-haired cherub. She herself was a devout Roman Catholic, but the baby had not been baptized. It worried her. Mrs. Hearst smiled at her anxiety for the soul of Sonny. She assured Eliza there was plenty of time for baptism.

George Hearst had reopened the mine, and the Ophir mills were crunching out silver and gold. Phebe Hearst filled her life with dreams of the future of her son. She would go ahead of him and light the way. In these early years of Sonny's life she plunged into studies that she never before had been able to pursue. Educators outlined for her courses of study and became her best friends. Other highly placed young women in San Francisco were content to divert themselves with dinners and balls, but when Phebe Hearst entered frivolous society she always seemed a little remote.

She never failed to go to the opera. She saw all the great art brought to San Francisco. She studied painting. She made the acquaintance of artists and critics. She bought a few pictures. She helped painters. Orrin Peck, small son of her steamer friends, Mr. and Mrs. David Peck, delighted her with his talent for drawing. She helped not only artists, but her bountiful table was always shared with some lonely person, usually a woman. A rare rich life early began for Phebe Hearst.

The young mother had never been long separated from her parents and she wished them to come to see her and her son. Soon the Randolph Walker Appersons arrived from Missouri. California was even more wonderful than the Appersons imagined, and as for Sonny—the Appersons quite agreed with the big, motherly nurse Eliza Pike, there never was such a baby.

PHEBE APPERSON HEARST AND WILLIAM RANDOLPH
AT THE AGE OF SIX MONTHS

Phebe Hearst would not permit her parents to return to Missouri. She spent days with the Appersons looking for a ranch to please them. She found one, a pear orchard, not far from Alviso and near the old Mission town of Santa Clara. The roomy ranch-house had large pines at the entrance, and was approached by an avenue of poplar trees. A sunny court-yard formed by an L-shaped rear wing and the living- and dining-rooms, looked out on both eastern and western foot-hills. In this courtyard were geraniums, pinks, carnations, hollyhocks, lilacs, and lemon verbena. White, pink and yellow cacti climbed to the second-story window. Duchess roses were everywhere, and white and yellow banksia roses twined themselves round and were visible in pepper and cypress tree-tops. It was a garden that Sonny Hearst never forgot—nor did he forget Prince, the soft-eyed, big Newfoundland dog that was his companion in this paradise.

While ranch-seeking in Santa Clara County Mrs. Hearst left her son with his devoted nurse, Eliza Pike. One day when she returned Eliza, greatly excited, met her at the door. Something extraordinary had happened, the mother knew. She was agitated when Eliza explained, "Madam, I love the baby like my own flesh and blood, and I couldn't sleep nights for thinkin' he might die— There is always maysles and dipthayria, and scarlet fayver—"

"Eliza! Eliza, what's the matter?" asked Mrs. Hearst in alarm. "Did you let the baby fall?"

"The baby is all right, madam, but he might have died. So I took him down to my own church to-day. Blissed, dear, good Fayther baptized him—"

"But, Eliza," protested the mother, "I am a Presbyterian."

"No matter, madam, the baby is a Christian!"

Phebe Hearst had a rare sense of humor, and she laughed in great relief.

When Sonny grew older he was sent to a Presbyterian Sunday school. Later he attended Doctor Coit's St. Paul's school in New Hampshire and became affiliated with the Episcopal church, but he has received the blessing of every Pope since Pius. IX. His favorite Pope was Leo XIII, who appealed to his æsthetic sense. Hearst describes him as looking as if made of alabaster.

CHAPTER II

BOYHOOD

PHEBE HEARST always sought to better her living conditions. The memory of the flowery hillside as she came
into San Francisco followed her. She wished to live where she
could see the bay. In Missouri the Appersons had slaves, and
she had a friendly feeling for Negroes. She had no carriage,
but when she drove she engaged a hack with a colored coachman.

The young mother often took Sonny and his nurse, Eliza
Pike, and drove from Rincon Hill through the fashionable
promenade of Montgomery Street. Here were inviting shops,
bustling hotels and excited, noisy, brokers' offices filled with
clamorous gamblers whose fortunes rose and fell with the fluc-
tuations of the Comstock. She drove into the newly widened
Kearny Street which was more level than Montgomery Street
and free of shouting speculators. She passed Portsmouth
Square, the old Plaza of Yerba Buena where the Mexican
Eagle fell and the Stars and Stripes were first raised in San
Francisco. From there she went toward Meiggs' wharf to catch
a glimpse of the bay and the picturesque bluffs near the Golden
Gate which had enchanted Phebe Hearst, the bride.

Here was what San Francisco called "the country." When
she drove with her son and his nurse along the old Toll Road
toward the Presidio, she looked at the scattering houses on the
hillside of Chestnut Street. High on the right of the hill lived
the French Consul Le Breton in a spacious dwelling that had
been brought around Cape Horn and erected in 1852. Lower
on the left was a rambling one-story house in a tangled garden
belonging to Senator Frank Soulé. Nearer the foot of the hill
was a double chalet built by a Frenchman and furnished with

French furniture. This house nestled in a semi-tropical cup of sunshine.

Once Phebe Hearst left her carriage and climbed the stairs leading like an S to this place. Since coming to San Francisco she had longed to dwell here. George Hearst never said "No" to his wife, and soon Phebe Hearst was the possessor of this hillside and happy as a bird mothering one birdling in a sunny tree-top nest.

William Randolph Hearst's first home memory is of this house—the steps leading up to it, the library, the living-room, the carved rosewood furniture. He remembers the English holly tree and the English ivy on the bank concealing the scar where the hill had been cut into for leveling. He recalls the fragrant boxwood, the lilies of the valley, the geraniums, the hollyhocks, the oranges, the lemon verbena, and the intoxicating *señoras de la noche* strayed from old Spain. From this high hanging garden the boy drank in beauty—still ships sleeping on the great blue diamond of a bay with its Island of the Angels, Yerba Buena, grim Alcatraz and beyond, the Contra Costa hills. To the westward at sunset burning clouds hung over the Golden Gate. To the north Mount Tamalpais sat like the Indian Chief Tamalpais in purple robes enthroned.

In these sentimental sixties lovers from the city at twilight strolled over the hills near the shore. As Sonny grew older he never tired of the gently plashing waters, nor of watching the high tide when the wind drove the majestic waves wildly upon the beach. Best of all he liked to hear the bugle of Fort Alcatraz sounding good night at the end of day. He wished that his mother would never take him to pay visits with her. The boy dreaded Wednesday, her reception day at home. Once he spilled castor-oil on her best moiré gown so that she had to dress twice. He was happiest when Eliza Pike took him adventuring to the edge of the water. He enjoyed playing with his bucket and spade, but he paused to stare childishly at the seagulls slanting their wings on their way to meet a storm. Better than seagulls or even pelicans he liked those

PHEBE APPERSON HEARST

great birds, the ferries going to Oakland, or the greater birds going out of the Golden Gate to the Orient.

When Sonny was a little more than two he took his first voyage on one of those birds. He went by boat with his father and mother to Sacramento on the Sacramento River steamer.

George Hearst had always been interested in politics and public affairs. In his twenties he was a delegate to the Missouri State Convention. In California he had been a member of the southern party of Lecompton. Hearst lived at the mines in Nevada most of the time, but during his absence he was nominated in San Francisco for the Assembly. Although a comparative stranger in the large city George Hearst's friendliness and generosity made him popular. He was easily elected.

It took young Mrs. Hearst two days to get her big trunks ready for Sacramento. With a flutter of pride, accompanied by her friend Miss Camilla Price, she set out with her small son and husband for a winter at the Capital as the wife of a legislator. The sailing of the Sacramento steamer, the excitement attending its departure, and the evening chatter on the boat were all delightful. The Capital with its imposing buildings of state impressed the young matron. Sonny did not like Sacramento because dinner at the Brannan House where they lived was at six instead of at five. Besides, he missed his playroom at home and Prince, the dog at the Apperson ranch.

To make matters worse, rain began. What rain! There had not been so much rain since the floods of the fifties. The storm seemed to stir the slumbering war spirit of the legislators. Lawmakers battered home their arguments with ink-wells and canes. George Hearst and his wife were glad to return to their quiet, tropical hillside nook in San Francisco. It was a relief to take "Billy Buster," as his father now called Sonny, off the boat. On the return journey to San Francisco the boy wandered from his mother and Eliza Pike, and nearly fell overboard.

The family had not lived long in the new house when the Hearst fortune altered. The great Ophir bonanza seemed to

give out, the Comstock threatened to fail. James G. Fair, foreman of the Ophir, was disheartened. If the Comstock failed,
what was left on wind-swept, stark, yellow-brown Mount
Davidson? George Hearst turned his back on Nevada. He had
done with mining, he said. He returned to San Francisco and
the happiness of home.

Hearst became associated with William M. Lent who dealt
in real estate. At this time San Francisco real estate was the
new Mother Lode. Harry Meiggs was making fortunes overnight. Larger and larger grew his investments. He plunged,
bought, sold. Then he bought, bought and bought. He borrowed and bought. He could not meet his obligations. In secret
he forged. He gambled. He forged again. After the superman
of real estate was exposed, he dared not face San Francisco.
He thought of plunging into the bay, but he loved life too
well. On the eve of the exposure of his disgrace "Honest
Harry" Meiggs chartered a steamer, took aboard his family
and supplies, sailed out of the Golden Gate, and never stopped
until he reached Peru where he made another fortune for
himself as a railroad builder. He was knighted by a European
king, and he died a millionaire.

Even mirific Meiggs's flight did not check the real-estate
boom in San Francisco. George Hearst had the land hunger
of his English ancestors. He began buying California land by
the thousand acres. Among other purchases was that of the
Santa Rosa ranch, the nucleus of the San Simeon principality
in San Luis Obispo County.

Through his father's associations in buying and selling real
estate, Billy Buster gained his first boyhood friend, Eugene
Lent. This friendship was to endure through all the years. To
Eugene Lent, William Randolph Hearst is always "Will." Mrs.
Hearst and Mrs. Lent became friends, for the boys were like
brothers. Another of Willie Hearst's boyhood playmates, older
than he, was Orrin Peck who came with his family on the ship
that brought the Hearsts to California. The Pecks lived far
from the Hearsts near the Mission Dolores which was reached

by the Toll Road from San Francisco. Orrin Peck later became a remarkable portrait painter and traveled much with Hearst until he died a few years ago.

Other boys in the neighborhood of Chestnut Street were Walter Carey, son of Judge James Carey; John Spring, son of Francis S. Spring, and Frederick S. Moody, later father-in-law of Helen Wills Moody, the tennis champion. Fred Moody was Willie Hearst's closest neighborhood chum. John Spring's brother was drowned in the bay, and for a time ghosts seemed to haunt Chestnut Street. The children were warned against the bay, and they did not stray from each other's gardens. They lived mostly in Willie Hearst's playhouse which was filled with toys. He had a Punch and Judy show, the first one owned by a boy in San Francisco. It was almost as much fun as a circus. Then there were Willie's two black dogs, Cæsar and Pompey.

The late John Spring said that once when Willie was playing with the boys on the stairway winding up to the Hearst house, George Hearst appeared in the doorway, tall, erect with aquiline nose, broad brow and long graying beard. He wore the usual cutaway coat, high top-boots and slouch hat. Would Willie ask his Dad for ice-cream money? Emphatically Willie would. Anxiously the boys watched George Hearst's hand enter his right pocket. Would Willie get "two bits" or "four bits"? Neither, George Hearst gave his son twenty dollars.

That glittering coin made history for the Chestnut Street boys. Willie led them to a little shop where they banqueted like young Luculluses on cake and more cake, and ice-cream and more ice-cream, and watermelon and more watermelon, until the twenty dollars vanished. From that day George Hearst was to the Chestnut Street boys the grandest man in San Francisco.

But this gift was only an incident to the miner. When he strolled down Montgomery Street his pockets were filled with twenty-dollar gold pieces. He distributed them among his less fortunate friends lying in wait for him.

Phebe Hearst began teaching her son almost as soon as he could walk. His first riding lesson was given him by his mother while he was still a baby; she held him on a horse at the Apperson ranch. Even before his kindergarten days Willie could read a few words. When he was about six his father tried to make him understand that the last spike, the golden spike connecting the tracks of the Central Pacific and the Union Pacific Railroads in Utah, had been driven. Later George Hearst took his son to see the first train arrive at the Bay of San Francisco.

Willie Hearst greatly enjoyed the long visits to his Apperson grandparents. Often he went with his father and mother. Sometimes they stopped for the night at the ranch of the Martin Murphys, who lived in the spacious house that had been brought around Cape Horn in 1849 and erected in a great oak-studded park covering leagues of land. These tarryings always brought a protest from Willie Hearst. "If we stay here overnight we won't be in time for grandma's apple dumplings and fried chicken."

There was no one for whom Mrs. Apperson liked so well to cook as she did for her stocky, blue-eyed little grandson who arrived from the city wearing black velvet jacket and knickers and white blouse. Perhaps it was because Willie was appreciative. Even as late as 1899 he wrote to his mother after visiting his grandmother: "We had fried chicken for dinner, of course. It is the most remarkable thing that nobody on this earth can cook fried chicken but my grandmother. I have been from here to Egypt, and I never tasted any other fried chicken. I am perfectly willing to bet that I could have continued my route around the world without having tasted fried chicken till I got back to grandmother's. When she dies she will take the secret with her, and the cooking of fried chicken will be one of the lost arts."

There was much more fun for a boy in the country than in the city. Grandmother and grandfather had fewer DON'TS than father and mother. Willie thought he helped milk and make butter. Then he liked the canaries singing in pretty yellow cages in the courtyard back of the house, but he also liked Grandpa Apperson's pet squirrels. Sometimes at night coyotes stole through the valley from the western hills and wailed around the ranch-house. Often the boy slept so soundly that he did not wake. Then he said, "Please wake me next time the coyotes come."

The Newfoundland dog followed the lad everywhere. The two raced through the hay-fields where the men were at work. Once the boy grew tired, lay down on a haycock, the dog at his side. When Willie woke, Prince was fighting a strange dog who had approached the sleeping boy. This Newfoundland was the first of Willie Hearst's great dog friends. Years later at the Casa Grande of San Simeon when the Chief arrived there was a scurrying to see that Buddy, another favorite dog of Hearst's, was spotless and bathed. No matter how long the Chief was absent, Buddy even when half-blind was always the first to greet his master.

Once at Grandma Apperson's Willie had a memorable adventure with the Newfoundland. A few miles away lay the old fishing town of Alviso on San Francisco Bay. Willie set out to see the world with the dog.

When they were missed there was hurrying from ranch to ranch. "Willie is lost!" was the cry.

No one waited to harness a horse. The Appersons rode bareback in all directions. One man went toward Santa Clara, another toward Murphys, another toward Saratoga. Grandpa Apperson rode frantically toward the bay. The small boy and large dog were found trudging blithely down the road miles from home.

Early Phebe Hearst impressed upon her son that when he had done wrong or been disobedient, he should always confess, and then he would never be punished. This day Willie hurried to his grandmother. "I was a bad boy. I ran away."

As usual he was spared punishment.

CHAPTER III

FIRST LOVE

HIGH up on the Chestnut Street hill and separated from the Hearst garden by a board fence at the top, was the garden that held Willie Hearst's first romance, little Katherine Soulé. The rambling one-story house of her father, Senator Frank Soulé, seemed to have dropped down casually into the old-fashioned garden. Katherine Soulé was called "Pussy" by the children. She was two or three years older than Willie. She had large blue eyes like his and his own fair hair. Her mother was gentle like Mrs. Hearst. The Hearsts and the Soulés enjoyed the "country," as North Beach was called. They had a common love of gardening and exchanged plants and shrubs.

Pussy Soulé's father was a Forty-Niner, a poet and founder of the first *Chronicle* which was suppressed in 1856 for criticizing the powerful Vigilantes. At this time he was editor of the *Morning Alta,* and he and George Hearst had long friendly discussions of public questions.

Daily Willie Hearst climbed the ladder from his garden to the top of a high board fence, and went down to the Soulé garden by another ladder. Everything in the Soulé garden fascinated Willie. There was a tree where the children played Indian warfare. Then Pussy's father rescued abandoned animals. Thirty stray cats were brought home by him. Pigeons were in the barn, and the children trained a white rabbit to ride on the back of a black Newfoundland dog. Rabbit and dog vanished. Frank Soulé offered five hundred dollars' reward for the dog, but it was never returned. The rabbit's hide was found tacked to a neighbor's garden wall. Willie Hearst was fond of pets, and his tears mingled with those of Pussy Soulé.

Recently she recalled his boyhood. She still sees the broad-headed, tow-haired lad rise above the fence on the ladder. She hears his lisp, "Mitheth Soulé, pleath, can Pussy come over to my house and play?"

The Hearst place with its immaculate garden, its tropical conservatory abloom with passion vines and blue solanum was always paradise for Pussy Soulé. She liked also pretty Mrs. Hearst with her dark hair demurely parted in the center. Willie's mother was always busy directing her garden, taking piano lessons, studying French and painting, or instructing her son.

Willie Hearst was conscious of all beauty. When his mother bought new French dishes he pointed out the rose buds to Pussy. One day his head appeared at the top of the fence and excitedly he called, "Pussy, come and see the 'La France'!"

Pussy had never heard of a La France, and so she hastily climbed the ladder to see this new exciting object.

"Why," she exclaimed, "it's just a rose!"

"It's a La France," corrected the boy.

A large pale pink rose was in bloom, and it must have been one of the first of that variety in California, for the La France rose was introduced in France by Guillot in 1867. Round and round the La France walked the two children.

"Isn't it lovely?" exclaimed Pussy. "I can't believe it's real."

"Pussy, if I wasn't afraid my mother would be mad, I'd cut the La France and give it to you."

Katherine Soulé recalled that when Willie Hearst was a small boy he liked to sing, and he sang well. One day when they were fighting Indians he began singing, but the boys laughed. He would never sing again when the boys were near, but he often sang for her. With a smile she said, "I was his little audience."

Pussy Soulé recalls one of Mrs. Hearst's reception days.

Willie was dressed immaculately in white. He stole out of the front door and down into the street. Some strange rough boys were coming up from the Toll Road muddy and grimy from boisterous play. They sighted the clean little boy in white. Such neatness and whiteness were offensive. The boys called Willie names. He called them names. In a flash the North Beach boys were on top of Willie Hearst. Like one of them he fought, striking and kicking his way out of the gang, ran up the hill, back into the house. Mrs. Hearst looked at the boy, muddy faced, muddy handed, mud from head to foot. Reception guests were coming up the hill. She seized a hair brush and spanked her muddy boy. He cried, but Pussy Soulé cried louder. Up the ladder she went and down, home to her mother still crying.

"What's the matter, Pussy?" asked Mrs. Soulé.

"I can't stand it," answered Pussy. "Mrs. Hearst is spanking Willie."

The next day when Willie went to see his little friend, he said, "Pussy, don't cry any more when I get spanked. It makes it hurt more."

When Willie was disobedient or got into mischief his mother punished him by not allowing him to see Pussy Soulé. On one of these occasions he seized a hammer and beat all the knots out of the board fence separating the two gardens. Like Thisbe and Pyramus the children talked through the openings.

When Mrs. Hearst's displeasure was appeased she gave a children's party of two, for Pussy and Willie. Ice-cream and cake were served at a little table in the ferny conservatory. Mrs. Hearst came in to see how the children were enjoying themselves. Willie looked up at his mother and said, "When I grow up I'm going to marry Pussy." Mrs. Hearst laughed.

But life was to be very different. Shortly after this incident Mrs. Hearst decided to increase the size of her garden, build a stable and keep her own carriage. George Hearst bought the Frank Soulé place. The Soulés moved to another part of town, and only once did they go back to see their old garden.

Willie Hearst never met Pussy Soulé again, but her brother became a distinguished professor at the University of California to which Phebe Hearst gave millions. Still unmarried Katherine Soulé lives alone with her eight cats and dogs. Her face lights up when she says, "There never was a nicer, kinder, more sensitive boy than Willie Hearst."

CHAPTER IV

SCHOOL

AFTER Mrs. Hearst taught Willie his letters and a few words she sent him to a kindergarten kept by Miss K. Mullens in her cottage about two blocks from the Hearst dwelling. The teacher was an Englishwoman of culture who lived with her mother.

Mrs. Hearst always befriended teachers, and a close tie was formed between her and Miss Mullens who later closed her kindergarten and taught in the North Cosmopolitan Grammar School. Willie entered the North Cosmopolitan. Many of his schoolmates came from humble homes. Some were sons of seamen. Rough men they were, and their sons were rough boys. Their faces were not always clean, and their manners left much to be desired, but both George and Phebe Hearst wished their son to have the benefit of a democratic public-school education. Miss Mullens, the teacher, was fond of Willie, and she had him sit near her desk.

This preference outraged the school "gang." They could stand Willie's clean face, his gentle voice, his pleasant manners, but to be a teacher's pet! They taunted him. He was stuck up! His mother didn't even cook! He was a mother's boy. They threatened to knock his block off.

"We were going to lick that kid," recently said one of the gang to the writer. "Gosh, he was smart. He found it out, and what do you think he did? He invited our 'gang' leader up to his big house and stuffed him with jelly, ice-cream and cake. After that, we laid off him."

Mrs. Hearst found out that the boys threatened to beat her son. She was apprehensive. She sent her new carriage driven by a colored coachman to fetch Willie from school. One day her son came to her and said, "Please don't send a carriage for me. The other boys haven't carriages."

From that time Willie Hearst walked home. He tried to lessen the apparent worldly difference between his schoolmates and himself. During his grammar-school days rather shyly he approached his mother saying, "I wish you could sew."

Mrs. Hearst was an excellent needlewoman, and she said somewhat testily, "I can sew, but I think it's more important to spend my time reading and studying. What do you want made?"

The boy hesitated, "I'd like to have patches sewn all over my trousers, so I'll look like other boys."

In spite of the handicap of the Hearst carriage, and good clothes and gentle manners, Willie's democratic spirit, his friendliness, his generosity, his desire to share his toys, but above all his talent for devising novel and unique mischief, established his popularity at school. Eugene Lent told the writer that when he himself thought of something mischievous, Willie always went far beyond, elaborated and developed the prank until it became a bold adventure that he hardly recognized.

The late Frederick S. Moody, Sr., related how Willie and he took a stand together against going to dancing school. A neighborhood dancing class was organized by the Bolton family, pioneers of 1846, who lived a few blocks from the Hearsts. The instructor was a serious Italian named Galivotti. Willie Hearst and Fred Moody could not endure his monotonous "one, two, three." They deserted and hid in the neighborhood nursery garden of Thomas Saywell. They were helping Saywell water plants when their happy play was interrupted by Miss Estrada, aunt of the Bolton children, who appeared to bring the truants back to dancing class.

Willie Hearst defied Miss Estrada. He stuck out his tongue. "I won't go!"

"You bad boy!" replied Miss Estrada.

He showered her with the hose. Miss Estrada had on a

fashionable afternoon dress, and when she returned, dripping, to the dancing class and reported what Willie Hearst had done, it was agreed unanimously that he was the "worst boy in the neighborhood."

Willie Hearst almost lost his reputation through his rebellion against dancing lessons. At that time Lunt's Dancing Academy was an institution in San Francisco. Professor Lunt was a tall, military-looking gentleman with fierce mustaches and definite ideas as to the behavior of young people learning to polka, schottische and waltz at his dancing academy. Mrs. Hearst decided that Professor Lunt should teach Willie dancing. The boy collected a group of his playmates, and they went to the dancing school and threw rocks at the building. The Professor discovered Willie was the ringleader, and when Mrs. Hearst asked that her son be admitted to Lunt's Dancing Academy, the professor with continental politeness, but the firmness of adamant, denied her application. Willie rejoiced.

Fred Moody's mother, the late Mrs. Joseph L. Moody, at ninety years of age recalled how one day when Willie was obstreperous and mischievous she said to him, "I don't want you to play with Fred any more. Go home, Willie."

Crestfallen, Willie disappeared. To her surprise a few hours later she found him hat in hand at the sitting-room door. "Mrs. Moody," he said, "I am sorry I was a bad boy. If I'm not bad any more, will you let me stay and play with Fred?" Mrs. Moody was charmed by his prompt manly apology.

As Willie grew older he became inventive in mischief. Squirrels appeared in his pockets. When he was expected to be decorous and reverential he always had a perverse desire to be the opposite. On reception days he gravely snapped a mechanical mouse among the ladies. Mrs. Hearst and her cultured group of women friends grew to be a little apprehensive if Willie entered the room.

When George and Phebe Hearst had been married ten years they bade all their friends to a large tin wedding. Among the bizarre gifts was a tin watch chain of huge dimensions and a tin horn five feet long. Willie fell heir to them. Long afterwards he called on his friends wearing the watch chain and announcing his arrival by blowing the horn.

By this time Mrs. Hearst was deeply appreciated in San Francisco. The forlorn and unhappy ever had her ear and aid, and she blended the warm hospitality of the old South with the easy grace of Spanish California in a manner so generous and delightful that it has come to be classified as distinctly Californian.

During these first ten years in San Francisco, Mrs. Hearst saw all the art objects in the city. Some excellent pictures had been imported from Europe in the fifties, but they perished in the flames that twice consumed San Francisco.

J. C. Duncan, father of the great Isadora, the dancer, was one of the earliest to introduce and encourage art in a liberal and critical spirit. He imported the "Taking of Samson by the Philistines," by Jacobs of Dresden. He owned a fine "Prometheus" ascribed to Andrea del Sarto. He imported hundreds of Flemish paintings, some by Calame and Verboeckhoven. He had originals by a member of the Peale family. These paintings meant much to Mrs. Hearst. She also gleaned an unsatisfactory glimpse of what the great masters were like from the public gallery of R. B. Woodward of Woodward's Gardens on Mission street. Woodward had commissioned Virgil Williams, a painter schooled in Europe, to make more than a hundred reproductions of Titian, Tintoretto, Leonardo and Botticelli. Mrs. Hearst liked to go to this gallery and dream of the time when she could see the originals. Willie enjoyed these trips to Woodward's Gardens with his mother because there were barking seals and sea-lions in the large tank, and he could toss bread to the swans on the artificial lakes in the gardens surrounding the house.

He never wearied of the drive from Woodward's Gardens back through the town. He envied especially the boys riding in the omnibuses for twenty-five cents. He thought it a good deal of a nuisance to drive in a private carriage with a coachman. He would have preferred to pause and buy peanuts and watch the patent-medicine vendor delivering his fantastic lecture on a street corner, or to be one of the group surrounding the hand-organ grinding out *The Star-Spangled Banner*.

George Hearst was essentially an out-of-doors man. Before he lived in a city he was more than forty. Now he was making a handsome income in real estate. Many would have been satisfied with his profits, but for Hearst money gained in real estate had not the charm of money that came from mining. Before three more years he had his own mining office in San Francisco. Again he was buying and selling mines. Everywhere his judgment was sought. Scrupulously honest he frequently received fifty thousand dollars for his opinion of a mine. During the first ten years of his son's life George Hearst became the greatest mining expert of his time, but he never gambled in stocks and never had his mines listed on the Stock Exchange. Men followed Hearst not only because of his excellent judgment, but because of his quiet, talismanic power. Luck seemed to follow him. Wherever George Hearst mined there was copper, silver, gold.

In recent years while William Randolph Hearst was traveling in Texas, a stranger boarded his train and said, "Your father made my fortune. I want to talk with his son."

"How did my father help you?"

"A long time ago I had a mine that seemed a wonder," answered the Texan. "I consulted your father. He looked it over and shook his head. 'No, don't waste another blast on that prospect. Sell it for anything you can. Get out.' I did. It was the beginning of my fortune."

When George Hearst finally resumed the fascinating game of mining the entire Pacific coast became his operating ground. He rode thousands of miles on horses and mules over burning deserts, through hot cañons and up heat-seared mountains. He loved the out-of-doors, the nervous excitement of setting out, the suspense, the thrill of discovery, the triumph over nature. For he did triumph. He bought, he sold. He bought

GEORGE HEARST

again. His son recalls him always coming and going with handbags of samples of ore. He hoped that the time would come when his father would not again leave home.

George Hearst had two large mines to develop, the Ontario and the Daly. For a year he could be very little in San Francisco, and so he told Mrs. Hearst that she and ten year old Willie might go to Europe.

Phebe Hearst was delighted. Willie looked forward to one long, grand, new school-less lark. Frederick S. Moody, Sr., recalled the farewell parties Willie gave, the longest remembered series of children's parties ever held in San Francisco. Fireworks every night! Each party was such a success that Willie thought he must have another, and another. Ten days of farewell—ice-cream, cake and fireworks.

When Willie Hearst finally set out for Europe with his mother, life was very cheerless for Fred Moody and the other neighborhood boys. Willie fancied that in Europe there would be plenty of fireworks and frolic, but the journey was not to be quite so jolly as he hoped. School was not to be abandoned. Mrs. Hearst was taking along a tutor for her son, a young man named Thomas Barry, with a classical education. Mrs. William M. Lent and her son Eugene had already gone to Europe and Willie looked forward to meeting Eugene in Paris.

On their way to Europe Mrs. Hearst stopped with her son to visit friends and relations at Sullivan, Missouri. Willie did not like Missouri. Bacon he abominated. He told his mother if he had to eat any more bacon he was going back to California. But he enjoyed his first playing in the snow. Then the roads were so muddy that the wheels came off the carriages. He liked that excitement. He saw the great bridge at St. Louis. Spinal meningitis broke out among children, and Mrs. Hearst departed quickly with her son. At Bloomington, Illinois, they visited nurse Eliza Pike. They sailed from Boston on the *Adriatic*.

Mrs. Hearst's diary and letters to her husband still exist, and they record that in Ireland there was so much poverty that Willie wanted to take off his clothes and give them to the poor children. He was pained by the sight of barefoot working women and overworked horses. At the Queen's Court in Dublin where the judges wore robes and curled wigs Willie was greatly amused, and he laughed aloud.

Edinburgh saw him with whooping cough, but his mother recorded that he was unusually interested in old ruins, and he was "picture-crazy." He wanted to take drawing lessons. "I shouldn't want him to be an artist, unless he could be a great one," wrote Mrs. Hearst.

He saw the Bloody Tower in London and Westminster Abbey. When he drove with his mother through the park at Windsor Castle he said, "I would like to live there." He enjoyed feeding the elephants in the Zoological Gardens, but his whooping cough persisted, and he could not hear the great Patti with his mother. He was quiet and good, instead of full of pranks, and that made Mrs. Hearst sad.

"I can never enjoy Woodward's Gardens again," he said, "but I'd like to see everything at once and go home to San Francisco."

But they did not go home. They went to Germany where they had a daily lesson in German at Dresden and spoke German at meals. He went down the Rhine reading German legends. At Hanover he fought the battle of Waterloo with tin soldiers. With much earnestness he wished he had a brother. Phebe Hearst wished he had six brothers. He longed to buy the royal horses at Hanover, and he climbed the statue of Hercules. In Vienna no one under seventeen was allowed to enter an important museum. He bribed the keeper to permit him to look at three rooms.

"He has a mania for antiquities," wrote Phebe Hearst to her husband. "Poor old boy, if you could see him studying, prying into everything, birds, fishes, books." The ten-year-old boy read five books a month aside from his studies and sight-seeing. His mother said it was too much, but he had no one to play with, and his energy demanded action. He tried to write to his father, but he was not satisfied with his letter. His mother urged him to keep on trying.

In Switzerland he was fascinated by the watches and wood carvings. He wanted to buy them all. He read about Pompeii and he wished to go there to explore.

Phebe Hearst did not realize it, but she was training a boy to be a great collector. She had thirsted for beauty, and no one ever enjoyed slaking that thirst more than she did in her late twenties on her first journey to Europe. What blessed joy to pose for her portrait, to have money for purchasing paintings and sculpture. In her later years she financed archæological expeditions and patiently sat in the heat of Egypt while scientists unearthed objects of prehistoric times. She lived to be nearly eighty, but she was never too old, nor too weary to visit an art gallery or museum. Her desire for beauty was never wholly satisfied. Into the ten year old mind of her son she poured the best of herself and the best of all that there was in Europe.

But after all Willie Hearst was not quite eleven and he shouted with joy when at last in Paris he found his chum, Eugene Lent, who was stopping with his mother and an English tutor at the Hotel d'Albe.

CHAPTER V

EUROPE

THE Hotel d'Albe realized that young America had arrived. All the play that had been bottled up in Willie Hearst and Eugene Lent while they were piloted through museums by their mothers effervesced when they met in Paris. They had come from a country where war was still in the air, and now they were invading a foreign land. They marched, countermarched and waved the American flag. A needle-gun with a ramrod was fired off by them. The ramrod drove into the ceiling of the Hotel d'Albe.

Mrs. Hearst and Mrs. Lent were in despair. Then the boys settled down for a time. Semi-seriously they studied French. They had lessons in fencing at a gymnasium. Their tutors took them to see Paris. Tutor Barry had two heroes; Charlemagne, who founded the Holy Roman Empire, and Napoleon, who a thousand years later dashed it to pieces. Barry loved Napoleon, the most picturesque man of history. He told the boys the story of this poor boy from Corsica, the laughing stock of a military school who later as a man with a handful of soldiers conquered Italy, made himself First Consul, and then Emperor, finally shorn of glory to die on a rock in the sea. Tutor Barry made expeditions with the boys to all the palaces occupied by Napoleon, in Paris and in the faubourgs, and at last to his tomb where with reverence they removed their hats.

Already Willie Hearst had seen Charlemagne's tomb at Aix-la-Chapelle and had sat in his chair. Barry drove with the boys to St.-Denis where Charlemagne was crowned. Here was the hero of his heart—Charlemagne, the fair, blue-eyed, soft-voiced, big-boned, iron-muscled, hard-hitting, fighting giant

30

king of the Franks. Barry's eyes glowed as he dwelt on this astounding man who first of all rulers saw peasants as human beings. Nothing was too great nor too small for Charlemagne. He catalogued the plants in his garden, collected books, wrote music, patronized arts, established the first schools, reformed the monetary system, swiftly organized masterful campaigns, fought holy wars, and had a magnificent amplitude of soul to which revenge was alien. He was the greatest man since Cæsar, and greater than Cæsar. Charlemagne made pitch-dark Europe advance a thousand years. After him there lived among plain folk the hope of equality, the dream of justice. Modern democracy was born.

More than eleven hundred years in his tomb Charlemagne became very real to Willie Hearst. In time to come the boy followed his hero's footsteps over Europe, read all that had been written of him. He studied the battlefields of Napoleon and Charlemagne, and figured out how these rulers lost or won in conflict. The spell of Napoleon has largely vanished from Hearst, but Charlemagne is still a potent force in his spirit. Hearst thinks of him as the one ruler who wielded vast power without allowing his head to be turned. To Charlemagne's genius, but especially to his elevated, civilized spirit Hearst pays homage. A few years ago he asked Charles Edward Russell to write for the *Cosmopolitan* magazine Charlemagne's biography, which was published both in magazine and book form.

At Phebe Hearst's request Tutor Barry taught Willie Hearst history. To-day Hearst thinks that his mother's method is the best. She stirred his imagination by acquainting him with dramatic, spectacular events. Hearst's idea is that after the interest of children has been aroused by significant historical events, young people will fill in for themselves the neutral and less interesting background.

Willie Hearst's scholarly tutor, Barry, and Eugene Lent's English tutor kept the boys well controlled for a time while their mothers shopped and visited historic spots.

Willie entertained Eugene by showing him his collections that he had made on his journey. He had stamps, coins, pictures of actors and actresses, beer steins and a porcelain collection. Most significant of all he had collected comic pictures in Germany. He bought all that he could find of amusing *Bilder Bücher*. Already the boy was taking his first steps toward vast collections, but he was also laying the foundation of one of the most popular features of his newspapers, the comic strips.

More than twenty years after Willie Hearst began this collection of *Bilder Bücher*, after he had acquired the New York *Journal*, he found them of great commercial value. He brought forth his collection and showed it to Rudolph Dirks, the cartoonist, who after studying it finally created the "Katzenjammer Kids." The success of the Katzenjammer Kids was the beginning of a valuable new commercial field in American journalism. From that time Hearst made it a point to have the best comics obtainable. He was first to realize that the quickest, most immediate large circulation comes from comic pictures. Without this trip to Europe, and without this accidental collection of *Bilder Bücher*, Hearst might not so quickly have realized the value of comics. This first boyish collection of *Bilder Bücher* is still in Hearst's possession.

Willie Hearst and Eugene Lent could not long be held in subjection by tutors. Eugene bought a graceful toy sailboat. What could be more harmless? It was harmless until he got the idea of having a fire at sea in a wash basin.

"*Magnifique!*" applauded Willie Hearst with his newly acquired French and a newly acquired gesture of the boulevards. They launched the boat on the water-filled basin. Then they saturated it with alcohol and set fire to the boat. It was almost as much fun as a shipwreck.

The success of this exploit fired Willie Hearst's imagination. Why not a bigger fire? "*Épater tout Paris! Magnifique, eh?*"

They brought straw into the room, dampened it so that it would not burn, but would make a smudge. Then they bought red lights at a drug-store and touched matches to the wet straw. Smoke filled the hall. Red lights flashing from the window caused the proprietor to turn in the fire alarm. *"Au feu! Au feu!"*

More alarms were turned in, and to the horror of Mrs. Hearst and Mrs. Lent the Paris fire department arrived in their rooms. The boys were charmed to be the center of so much attention. Mrs. Hearst and Mrs. Lent left Paris for Italy wondering how boys so carefully reared could be capable of such misconduct.

In Florence Willie Hearst took lessons in art, and he learned to strum on the guitar. He went to Verona reading *Romeo and Juliet* and was sad to find that Juliet's dwelling was only an inn.

The travelers arrived at Rome in time for the Carnival preceding Lent. They found the Eternal City in fiesta. The gaiety, the fantastic comedy, the buffoonery of the Roman Carnival delighted the youngsters. The boys dressed themselves in grotesque costumes, and entered into the spirit of play. Even the staid tutors lost themselves in the revelry in the Roman streets. Songs, laughter, dancing, pranks, the tossing of flowers, the lightning flirtations, made of somber Rome a new enchanted city.

Tutor Barry told Willie Hearst the story of the Carnival. Rome was its inspiration. Many of the Popes were patrons and promoters of carnival gaiety during the last three weeks preceding Lent. In reality, the Roman Carnival was the hybrid of a pagan festival and a Roman Saturnalia.

After the austerity of Lent began Tutor Barry took the boys about Rome. He showed them the Corso where in ancient days races were held as part of the Carnival festivities. He drove with them to the Forum and related that in ancient times during the Carnival period bull-baiting was here practised. The Popes determined to suppress lawlessness and crime during the Carnival, and they set up gibbets and whipping posts warning robbers and cutthroats against misconduct.

And so Willie Hearst learned history. Young as he was, the boy deeply enjoyed Rome. He delivered Cicero's orations on the site where they were spoken. He visited the Colosseum by moonlight and clambered over it carrying a torch. In comparison Paris seemed a playground. Willie was glad that his mother was sending home sculpture. He was stimulated to begin another collection in Rome, and with the greatest enthusiasm he purchased Papal medallions.

Before they left Rome Mrs. Hearst and her party had a special audience with Pio Nino and received the papal blessing. During Willie Hearst's first visit to Rome, according to Eugene Lent, the boy revealed what later became one of his chief characteristics, an inability to be awed. A light was pointed out to him that had burned for a thousand years in Rome without being extinguished.

"Eugene," said Willie, "I'd like to put out that light. Isn't there some way it can be done?"

During his remaining days in Rome Willie cudgeled his brain trying to devise a method for extinguishing the light. The lamp was too well guarded, and regretfully Willie Hearst left Rome with the light still burning.

CHAPTER VI

FIRST HERO

GEORGE HEARST was glad when his wife and son came back from Europe in 1874. Mrs. Hearst and Will had gifts for every one. From each country visited the boy brought something for his grandparents. The Appersons always cherished a mechanical clock bought by him on this journey.

After the excitement of homecoming was over Phebe Hearst discovered that prosperous, booming America had disappeared. There was a new, frightened, paralyzed America, just emerging from the nightmare of a panic. People who had been rich in 1873 were now dazed to find themselves counting nickels in 1874. It was said that Mackay, Fair, and even Con Virginia were tottering.

George Hearst was weighed down with the development of two mines, the Ontario and the Daly. Hearst knew that if the work could go on the mines would prove rich. Where could he get money to develop them?

Mrs. Hearst aided as best she could. With many heartaches she sold her gracious house on Chestnut Street, the house that looked out on the gate of gold and the purple mountain of Tamalpais. She gave up horses and carriages and went with her husband and son to board with some old friends, the Winns.

Will Hearst missed his playmates, the horses, the stable, the delightful garden in Chestnut Street, the conservatory where rare plants were always in bloom. When he left that garden of his boyhood he seemed to move out of a shimmering rainbow. As compensation he spent more time at the ranch of his grandparents in the Santa Clara Valley. More than any other

35

place this ranch in the changeless sunshine seemed his permanent home.

In San Francisco Will attended both the Lincoln and Washington Grammar Schools. When not in mischief he excelled in the class-room. Even at that time he showed extraordinary power of concentration.

After twelve months passed money circulated freely once more. There flowed to George Hearst a stream of gold from the Ontario mine. He had been rich before, but this was the beginning of a vast fortune. From this time money ever surged toward him in high tide, and lordly domains spread out under his feet as if he were a king.

When the Hearsts had been obliged to sell their Chestnut Street fairyland Phebe Hearst was somewhat anxious. No fortune was permanent, she realized, and so she determined to guard against future ebbs and floods in their finances. George Hearst was setting out to inspect what later became the great Homestake mine, but its value was still unknown. Phebe Hearst said to her husband as he was leaving, "Whatever this mine proves to be, let's keep it as a home stake."

"All right," answered George Hearst. "We'll name it Homestake."

The Homestake mine yielded millions, and after more than fifty years, even during the depression beginning with 1929, its shares rose above three hundred. After developing the Homestake mine George Hearst took over the Anaconda mines in Mexico, the million-acre Babicora ranch, and the Campeche.

During these prosperous days the Hearsts bought the Graves house on Van Ness Avenue and added an art gallery. Each year Mrs. Hearst acquired more sculpture, paintings and tapestries. A salon naturally formed. Mrs. Hearst opened her house for charity. She had some famous *tableaux vivants* which were witnessed by Lord Rosebery and his distinguished English friends.

It was in 1876, when Will Hearst was thirteen, that he recalls meeting his first political hero, Samuel J. Tilden, Democratic candidate for President. If George Hearst had not given his immense energy and talent to mining, if he had not been fascinated by the game of making millions, naturally and instinctively he would have dominated California politics. He had been greatly indignant over and had felt as a personal shame the scandals of President Grant's Administration. He believed that the nation was aroused to a sense of shame like his own. With Tilden nominated the Democratic Party had an excellent chance to return to power.

Samuel J. Tilden was a statesman with a remarkable record for reform. He had impeached the corrupt judges of the New York "ring." By unearthing concealed bank accounts he revealed how spoils had been divided. He denounced those plunderers, the "Canal Ring," made up of members of both parties who had systematically robbed New York through maladministration of its canals. Tilden's fame as a reformer had made him Governor of New York in 1874, and now in 1876 the Democrats felt that he was the one to restore Democracy and rescue the political reputation of the United States.

The Republicans opposed Tilden with the honest, but colorless Rutherford B. Hayes of Ohio who made a "sound money" campaign, advocating the speediest possible resumption of specie payment. Tilden couldn't help being elected, argued George Hearst. Will Hearst boyishly shared his father's faith and excitement over the approaching election. In the autumn of 1876 he was delighted when his mother announced that she was going to the World's Fair in Philadelphia, a celebration of the centenary of the Declaration of Independence. They would pass through New York and would probably meet Tilden. Will even named his dog Governor Tilden.

When Mrs. Hearst and her son arrived in New York City the Hayes-Tilden campaign was at its height. Flags were waving, the air was electric. New York City had never elected a President. At night there were parades, colored lights, glittering uniforms and campaign music that made the boy's feet dance as the bands went up and down Broadway. "Hurrah for Tilden! Hurrah! Hurrah! Three cheers for Tilden, the next President!"

For Will Hearst this was better than those great imaginary dramas in Europe; better than Dickens's foggy London with its grim Tower; better than Fontainebleau of the magnificent Louis and Napoleon; better than even St.-Denis where Charlemagne was crowned; better than the gay Carnival of Rome; the Forum; or the Colosseum. This music, these uniforms, these moving men were a new carnival to Will Hearst. Here was the drama of life. Looking down on it all with his mother from the hotel window he had never felt so alive, so uplifted. Did the thirteen year old boy have a premonition that one day he himself would march up and down these streets, and that he would listen to such cheers?

When Mrs. Hearst told Will that they were to go to pay their respects to Samuel J. Tilden the boy felt as if he were going to call on Napoleon, or Charlemagne, or Cæsar. Mother and son went up the steps of that pleasant, old brick house looking out on Gramercy Park to which the surrounding property owners alone had the key. Trembling the boy stood in the presence of his first flesh and blood hero and gazed up at him. What would this distinguished-looking man say? How would he speak? Could a boy possibly understand? His hero talked with Mrs. Hearst and her son about their trip to Europe and about the chances of the Democrats carrying the West. Mrs. Hearst was certain, her husband was certain, she said, that the Democrats would sweep the country.

The boy was relieved. His Charlemagne spoke language that he understood. The hero placed his hand on Will Hearst's head and told him to be sure to be always a good boy and a good Democrat like his father. It was as easy to talk with hero Tilden as with his own father or Tutor Barry. Will regained equipoise and looked about the room with his keen blue eyes desirous of seeing what kind of house his hero lived in. The drawing-room had a high ceiling, a polished inlaid floor and choice art objects. To his joy Will espied an old friend

in marble, "Flora," by Ansiglioni. To-day he smiles as he recalls that when he saw "Flora," that devastating goddess of
flowers, he was so happy that he could not refrain from exclaiming, "Mr. Tilden, you have a 'Flora' just like ours at
home!"

Phebe Hearst was somewhat disconcerted, perhaps because
she discovered that Samuel J. Tilden was disconcerted. When
they left the house she gave her son a suggestion, "Never tell
people that you have something like theirs. They don't like
it." The boy always remembered.

Will Hearst's hero, Samuel Jones Tilden, the statesman he
had talked with and shaken hands with, was declared elected
in all the newspapers the day after election. How happy the
Hearsts were! Tilden had a quarter of a million majority over
his opponent. Then the Republicans claimed the victory. South
Carolina, Florida, Louisiana and Oregon were close. An Electoral Commission was appointed by Congress, and for months
the nation lived in suspense and heated battle awaiting the
report.

The Commission's decision was taken on strict party lines,
and two days before the fourth of March all four States were
given to the Republicans. Public indignation flamed. With a
high sense of patriotism Tilden acquiesced in the decision and
requested his followers to do the same. George Hearst was as
unhappy as if Tilden had been his own brother, and Will
shared his father's sadness. He had met his first political disappointment, and young as he was he seemed to die a little.
At fourteen he learned that the way of the reformer to office
is hard.

CHAPTER VII

FIRST ENGAGEMENT

WHILE Will Hearst was in the Lincoln Grammar School a great, new, permanent influence came into his life, Charles Dickens, his first literary hero, and his literary hero for all time, the one writer that has most completely satisfied Hearst. During this same period the wit 'of Thackeray and the pageantry of Sir Walter Scott attracted and interested him, but he always returned to Dickens. In this novelist Will found richness and variety of humor, riotous fancy, unequaled genius for characterization, sympathy for humanity and a desire to better the conditions of the world of which he never tired. *Dombey and Son* was his favorite novel, and Captain Cuttle one of his best-liked characters. Again and again he reads the English novelist, and he is always astonished and delighted by his variety, humor and understanding. In Hearst's conversation there are frequent references to Dickens. To-day the favorite writers of his own staff are those who have come under Dickens's sway. Many of the crusades sponsored by the Hearst newspapers have been inspired by the spirit of Charles Dickens.

Like Dickens, Will Hearst delighted in the theater. Here were romance, poetry, color, action. Will was a school-boy when he began haunting the splendid, new California Theater in San Francisco. This theater was a fascinating place with its mirrors and tessellated floors, and its stage where appeared the best actors of the day. He never forgot Booth's repressed, slim, burning, black velvet Hamlet, nor Jefferson's whimsical Rip Van Winkle, nor Clara Morris's Camille shedding real tears, making her audience suffer the sorrows of the wasting demi-mondaine. He never forgot the white camellias in her hair. To-day at San Simeon one of Hearst's favorite flowers is the camellia. There lingers in the word itself some of the aroma of Dumas's deathless romance. And as for Adelaide Neilson with her magnolia skin, the first time Will saw her in the pearl-festooned robes of Juliet, he was minded to walk straight over the heads of all the people to her. For two nights he did not sleep after he saw the incomparable Neilson. This new joy, the theater, richly enhanced the absorbent nature of Will Hearst with poetry, action, color, intensity. When he saw these great dramas with their background of ancient castles, sylvan scenes and Roman Forums he fought the battles with the soldiers on the stage, he loved with the lovers, and in the dark, splendid tragedies, he died a hundred deaths. The greatest tragedy was one of reality. Adelaide Neilson, the goddess of the youth of the world, died suddenly in Paris in 1877. Will Hearst was fourteen, but for a time life went gray.

Life cannot remain long gray to youth. Minstrel Billy Emerson was singing,

> The ladies sigh as I go by,
> "Are you there, Moriar-i-tee?"

Will Hearst was charmed by the humor and grace of Emerson, and his rich voice. Often he sat in the theater, chin on chest, watching every motion of Billy Emerson, absorbing the nuances of his dialect, registering each word, tone and note, like a recording machine. He himself had a good singing voice, and he learned Billy Emerson's songs. He knew most of the popular songs of the day. The theater stimulated Will's desire to dance. He forgot the days when he threw rocks at Lunt's Dancing Academy, and became an excellent dancer. After the Hearsts sold the Graves house on Van Ness Avenue they rented the imposing white stucco Spanish-looking residence of their friends, the Heads, in Taylor Street. Will Hearst enjoyed the Head house, for he and his friends fitted up a theater in the stable and produced plays and gave minstrel shows.

Mrs. Hearst and the parents and relations of the young

players attended the performances in the little theater. Will Hearst had such a great gift of mimicry that his talent seemed at times to cease being amateur and approach professionalism. Mrs. Hearst feared lest her son might go on the stage, but he never thought of this. He was passing through a phase, living intensely a dramatic mood.

Often during his school-days Will Hearst and his friends dined and supped in the courtyard of the new Palace, the most magnificent hotel at that time in the United States. Its erection wrecked the life of William Ralston, San Francisco's first promoter prince who ended his financial trouble and his existence in the Bay of San Francisco. Will Hearst and his coterie of carefree friends were laughter-loving like the city that bore them. In the courtyard of the Palace they feasted together near the huge braziers filled with glowing charcoal below the white marble galleries. In these joyous evenings they often glimpsed the magical men and women of the theater when they entered or stepped down from their carriages on their way to and from the green room of the California Theater.

At this time Will Hearst had no serious ambition. Affairs of state, direction of public opinion, or accumulation of a vast fortune held small place in his thoughts, but he showed a capacity for leadership. Wherever he went he was the center of a large group and of its activity, but it all resulted in play.

When George Hearst came back to San Francisco from his mines for a holiday often he strolled through the streets with his son, the two eating peanuts as they walked, the father talking with his son of serious affairs. Sometimes Hearst, the elder, took Will and his young school friends to the San Simeon ranch of forty-five thousand acres in San Luis Obispo County. San Simeon spread out over the Santa Lucia Mountains down to the ocean and the Bay at San Simeon, a gentle sapphire indenture in the Pacific. Don "Pancho" Estrada, who now lives at San Simeon, taught Will Hearst to toss a reata like a vaquero.

In these early days Phebe Hearst did not go to San Simeon, for the journey was rough even for men. Sometimes father and son went on a coast steamer. At San Simeon Bay they were met by a small tug. The transfer from the steamer to the small boat was hair-raising, but the excitement of landing in the tug delighted Will.

Sometimes George and Will Hearst traveled by train to Paso Robles. Often Will played games on the train, but his father said to him, "When you travel don't play games. Look at the landscape. Study the soil and the conformation of the earth. Always learn what you can." In the brain of the great mining expert were preserved photographs of miles of mountains, cañons, deserts and valleys, just as later his son held images of objects of art.

When the Hearst party arrived in Paso Robles they were met by vaqueros with saddled horses. Then back they rode over the mountains by way of Cayucos and up the coast to the ranch-house. Will Hearst had at San Simeon handsome silver-trimmed Mexican saddles. They were the nucleus of his collection of Mexican saddles, the most complete in the world to-day.

At times Will Hearst and his friends chose the wildest route to San Simeon along the coast over the mountains from Monterey. They camped by night looking out on the Pacific. On one of these journeys their supply of butter gave out and Will rode into the camp of a man named Pringle who had a gold-mine on the coast. He asked for butter. Pringle stared at him and replied, "Butter! What in hell is that? I haven't seen any in twenty years."

In 1878, George Hearst erected a wharf at San Simeon, and soon he began building a spacious, comfortable, white ranch house with green shutters, the first Hearst country place. This house still stands at the foot of the enchanted hill in a grove of cypress, magnolia, Eugenia, laurel and oak. With landing at San Simeon facilitated by the new wharf Phebe Hearst could join her husband and Will at the ranch.

The Lents and Heads were often the Hearsts' guests. Phebe Hearst had learned to ride in Missouri, and often she and her friends went on camping trips into the mountains. They frequently stopped on what to-day is known as *La Cuesta Encantada,* or "The Enchanted Hill." George Hearst especially liked the thicket of oaks on the crest of the elevation, and he never tired of looking at the sea from this point. The camping place was called Camp Hill.

No one ever had a happier boyhood than Will Hearst on the sunny Pacific coast, and that was why it was a dark moment for him when his parents decided that he was to finish his preparatory course in the East in order to take entrance examinations for Harvard.

Another trip was made by him to Europe with his mother when she went to take the baths in Germany. In 1880 he returned with Tutor Barry leaving Mrs. Hearst in Europe. Will entered St. Paul's, Doctor Coit's Episcopal School at Concord, New Hampshire, and roomed with Will Tevis of San Francisco. There were two hundred and fifty boys at St. Paul's, but Will was homesick for California, for his father, the wonderman of the mines, but especially for his mother. He wrote to her at the baths in Germany, "If you get well, you shall never have anything to make you sick again, if I can help it....I often think how bad I have been and how many unkind words I have said, and I am sure that when you come back I will be good and never be so bad again."

Newspapers already were playing an important part in his life, and he asked Mrs. Hearst to subscribe for the London *Times* for the fifth form reading-room at St. Paul's. He was especially irked by the compulsory church attendance at St. Paul's. Three times a day he went, and on Sunday the services were each an hour and a half long. He called it "Camp Meeting." He said he believed every old minister in the country came there to practice on the boys. "The Doctor preaches pretty well," he wrote his mother, "but he hollers too much."

Will enjoyed being captain of his baseball nine, and he survived weather that was twenty-five below zero, although it made the Californian despondent and lonely. To his mother he wrote, "The only thing that comforts me is that the time is getting shorter every day till you will be here."

Occasionally he escaped to New York to visit his guardian, Mr. Hughes, an uncle of Orrin Peck's. Once he wrote Mr. Hughes, "May I be invited to New York for the holidays?" Mr. Hughes was busy and neglected to send the invitation. "For God's sake," came a telegram, "please ask me to New York." He was invited.

Finally the dreary year at St. Paul's ended. Once more he was in California enjoying his glowing home life and sitting up until two in the morning talking politics with his father, or strolling up and down Kearny Street with him. Often he said, "Father, it is too bad eastern people don't know what a wonderful state California is."

"Billy Buster," answered the pioneer, "if they knew, they would all come out here and crowd us old Californians into the Pacific Ocean. If the eastern coast had not been settled first, it would never have been settled at all. It's lucky for the East the Pilgrim Fathers never saw California."

For several years George Hearst had owned the San Francisco *Examiner*, the most influential Democratic paper in the state. It was edited by George Penn Johnson, who had shot and killed Senator William Ferguson at a distance of ten paces in a duel on Angel Island in 1855. The paper was first published June 12, 1865, by William Moss, editor of the *Democratic Press*, which had been suppressed a few months previously by the Government. After Captain Moss's death the paper passed through many hands and in 1880 was bought by George Hearst, who made it a morning paper. Already Will looked at the *Examiner* with interest. Changes, he read, were probable in the life of his father. Hearst was one of the leaders of the Democratic Party in California, and often mentioned for Governor. In 1882, his name was presented to the Democratic Convention in San José as candidate for Governor, but Hearst's friend, General George Stoneman, was selected.

Will Hearst had several months of intensified tutoring in order to enter Harvard, and before leaving San Francisco he became engaged for the first time. Sybil Sanderson, daughter of Judge Sanderson of the Supreme Court of California, was the girl who captivated his fancy. Everything about Sybil Sanderson, her soft limpid eyes, her ravishing figure, her impetuous charming manner, her joy in living, but above all her voice that was like a high clear bell had entranced San Francisco, and now threw their spell over Will Hearst. The Sandersons lived in a large white house overlooking the bay in the western part of the city, and they were all happy to serve dear, delightful Sybil. Mrs. Sanderson and her older daughter, Jennie, were both certain that Sybil had more beauty than Adelaide Neilson, and that her voice was lovelier than Patti's. Already they planned that she should go to Paris and enter the Conservatoire. Will Hearst met Sybil at the Hotel Del Monte after he came home from St. Paul's. He was enthralled.

It was at a time when the beauty of Monterey, the old Spanish Capital of California, was most glamorous. Robert Louis Stevenson had lived there a few years before, and in the streets one still saw grave, sad-eyed, brown-skinned men and women who were born under the red, white and green of Mexico, and whose spirit still paid allegiance to the fierce eagle and thorny *nopal* as their national emblem. Will Hearst and Sybil Sanderson strolled up and down these streets of romance. They boated, they swam, they rode, they wandered on the white sands by day, and under the pale moon they were betrothed.

Mrs. Sanderson, and especially Miss Jennie, had other plans for Sybil. The girl herself felt the lure of Paris. Across the sea in the art capital of the world was a great place waiting for her, and so the engagement ended with the summer.

Sybil Sanderson was whisked away to Paris by her worshipful mother and sister. Will wished to follow, but he was shy.

He felt unable to cope with the Sanderson family ambition and opposition, and so he entered Harvard in 1883.

Will Hearst and Sybil Sanderson never again walked on the beach at Del Monte. She became a student at the Conservatoire. Massenet wrote for her *Thaïs* and *Manon*. Her exquisite art, her high notes of "Esclarimonde" utterly enchanted Paris. At times on his trips to Europe Will Hearst met Sybil Sanderson. When she came to New York City to make her début at the Metropolitan Opera House, the San Francisco *Examiner* published a page of the event. In 1903, when William Randolph Hearst arrived in Paris with his lovely bride, Millicent Willson Hearst, he found that "La Belle Sanderson" had died that week.

CHAPTER VIII

HARVARD

WILL HEARST entered Harvard at a time of cutaways, derbies, walking-sticks, and vandyke beards. In this same year Joseph Pulitzer of Magyar-German-Jewish descent, a restless, driving editor who owned the St. Louis *Despatch*, went to New York and bought the *World* from Jay Gould. Mrs. Hearst accompanied her son to Cambridge and had his room in Matthews Hall handsomely re-decorated, equipped with a complete library and fitted out with enameled smoking sets of Harvard red.

From the beginning Hearst was unhappy at Harvard. He did not like the pretty New England scenery. He wrote to his mother, "I long to see our own woods, the jagged rocks, the majestic pines, and the towering mountains."

About this time business losses threatened George Hearst and Phebe Hearst wrote Will concerning them. His reply was, "I hope Papa will understand that I know I may have to work my way in the world, and I do not feel terrified at the prospect." But fortune again smiled for George Hearst and Will's allowance was increased.

At Harvard, Will was happy to be with his friend, Eugene Lent, who for a year had been business editor of the *Lampoon*, a brilliant comic weekly which produced such writers as E. S. Martin, Judge Robert Grant, Barrett Wendell, Edward Everett Hale, Jr., Owen Wister, author of *The Virginian;* William Roscoe Thayer, the historian; and George Santayana, the philosopher.

The *Lampoon* was peculiarly of Harvard including its red cover, and it was affectionately called "Lampy." From 1876 to 1880 it had a brief dazzling career and expired. It was resuscitated in 1881. Invariably "Lampy" lost money. No business editor could afford to accept the position unless he had an independent fortune, because it was understood that he must balance the budget. When Will Hearst arrived at Harvard he found Eugene Lent slowly sinking for the last time in a sea of "red ink." What could he do to aid? Recently Lent said, "Perhaps if I hadn't been in a hole and Will hadn't tried to help me out, he might never have taken up journalism."

Will became business editor of "Lampy," and with it assumed responsibility for the red ink. He knew nothing of newspaper work. All his life had been spent trying to have as much fun as possible. The position of business editor of the *Lampoon* was just another kind of lark. With his large allowance he bought haberdashery, clothing, and porcelains at the Cambridge shops. He solicited advertisements of the shopkeepers for "Lampy." He obtained advertising, but each inch cost him personally several times what it was worth.

Will Hearst was not satisfied with being that kind of a business editor. He abandoned the methods of an amateur. He determined to make the paper self-sustaining. He did not realize it, but his life work had begun.

Eugene Lent discovered this when he entered the *Lampoon* office and found his chum with all the college weeklies spread out before him on the floor. The pleasure-loving, prank-provoking Will Hearst was making a list of the advertisers in all of the college weeklies. None of "Lampy's" other business editors had thought of this method. Later Will visited as many advertisers as possible. He sent student-solicitors to see other business men. Lent has a copy of the *Lampoon* of 1883 showing written in Hearst's handwriting the amount paid by each firm for advertising. New business came to the *Lampoon*.

Hearst did not overlook subscribers. His mother in San Francisco was engaged by him as a solicitor. "Perhaps Mr. Head, Mr. Robertson, Cousin Joe, and Harry Tevis might like to subscribe. At any rate, we will give them a chance...."

The *Lampoon* ought to be supported by Harvard men with contributions and subscriptions."

In 1901, George Santayana wrote of the methods of the group responsible for the college paper when he and Hearst were in the same class at Harvard: "The business editor [Hearst] alone took a serious, responsible view of the situation. The rest of us cultivated a philosophic disbelief in Space and Time."

To his mother Will Hearst wrote in 1885 the result of his two years' work on the *Lampoon:*

We took up the *Lampoon* when the subscription list numbered three hundred. Nine hundred a year came from subscribers and three hundred a year from "ads" making a grand total of twelve hundred. As it takes fourteen hundred to run the thing, we scoured the county for ads. We ransacked the college for subscriptions. In fact, we infused energy into the *Lampoon,* and now we stand on a firm basis with a subscription list of 450 with $900 in advertising making a grand total of $2,250 and leaving a profit of $650 after the debt is paid.

Then followed the first record of Hearst's desire to manage the *Examiner,* for he added, "Show this to Papa, and tell him just to wait till Gene and I get hold of the old *Examiner* and run her in the same way."

To the students at Harvard the success of the *Lampoon* seemed incredible. The staff of the paper purchased a punch bowl and had an oyster supper. They gave a dinner for all the *Lampoon* ex-presidents. The students thought the young waster, Will Hearst, had the touch of Midas.

Will did not try to write articles for the *Lampoon.* He made several sketches for cartoons and wrote comic verses, but he did not sign his name. He took a great interest in baseball and was vice-president of a baseball organization at Harvard. He was successful in planning and directing parades. He cooked Welsh rabbit and baked potatoes for midnight suppers. Even to-day at San Simeon he occasionally surprises a large house party with a midnight Welsh rabbit cooked by him and served in the great refectory where Gothic tapestries look down from high walls and *palio* banners of Siena flutter.

At Harvard Will Hearst perpetrated unique practical jokes. For a time he kept an alligator in his room. With a quite grave countenance he visited the students with the alligator. So varied were his interests that he studied only in brilliant spurts.

In his Freshman year he had Latin, Greek and German. He stood high in German, but he dropped Latin and Greek. He thought they did him no good. He tried Philosophy, but gave up. To his mother he expressed his reason, "The professor got up and began talking about the as-it-wereness-of-the-sometimes, and I lit out. I have taken English instead." Like his father, Will Hearst was interested in geology and he enjoyed a course under Nathaniel Shayler whose original humor and deep guttural voice as well as his entertaining interpretation of geology, attracted many students. Le Baron Russell Briggs and Barrett Wendell made English enthralling. Best of all Will enjoyed the History of Fine Arts under Charles Eliot Norton, friend of Ruskin. This professor had great personal charm, wide knowledge, and when he taught art he really gave a history of the world. Perhaps Will Hearst was best equipped of his class to assimilate and enjoy Norton's lectures.

During the first years at Harvard Will Hearst's greatest friendship was for a Californian, Jack Follansbee, who was generally beloved by man, woman and child. When Follansbee's uncle, James R. Keene of Wall Street, crashed his nephew Jack was obliged to leave college. This was a distinct personal loss to Will. He wrote long letters to his father entreating his protection for Jack, which resulted in a large gift of land in Mexico. The lives of Will Hearst and Jack Follansbee were always interwoven until they were separated by death.

Other friendships formed at Harvard by Will Hearst were for three men who were to go with him to the *Examiner;* F. L. H. Noble; Fred Briggs, the cartoonist of Springfield,

Massachusetts; and E. L. Thayer, who later wrote *Casey at the Bat*.

Cartooning of the Faculty was not permitted at Harvard. Some of the *Lampoon* art had to be suppressed, a cartoon of Charles Eliot Norton included. Will clashed with the Faculty, but he was permitted to remain.

In comic rôles in college productions he was always a success. His impersonations of Henry Irving and a mock temperance lecture given by him obtained his entrance to a restricted club. In 1885 he took part in the historical burlesque in four acts, *Joan of Arc,* or *The Old Maid of Orleans*. He played Pretzel, the German valet, "an interesting cuss with a penchant for legerdemain." Thayer always insisted that the success of *Joan of Arc* was due to the rôle of Pretzel played by Hearst.

While Hearst was in college his twenty-first birthday came and he wrote to his mother, "I for my part don't see why one should rejoice on entering upon the duties and responsibilities which are supposed to attend the age of manhood. I should prefer to be nineteen again, and twenty-one only when it is necessary to leave college and begin life-work in earnest."

Often he showed impatience of the prolonged routine and class-room restraint. It seemed to him that the four years should be condensed that he might sooner enter the world. When he was twenty-one he cast his first vote for Cleveland and Hendricks. Joyously he wrote his mother that he was carrying Massachusetts for the Democrats, and he asked a contribution from his father.

On election night it was first reported that Blaine was elected, and then came the news of the first Democratic victory since the Civil War. Hearst and the young Harvard Democrats after Cleveland's election flung out the flag with Victory painted in large letters on a strip of canvas at the bottom. A crowd assembled and cheered lustily. Many of the free-trade professors were for Cleveland and most of the im-

WILLIAM RANDOLPH HEARST AS A HARVARD
FRESHMAN

WILLIAM RANDOLPH HEARST AT TWENTY-EIGHT

portant students rejoiced in the defeat of James G. Blaine, The Plumed Knight—the agent of reaction in the United States.

Will Hearst directed the celebration. There was a flag-raising at Holyoke and Mount Auburn Streets. Harvard had never seen such fireworks; tons of rockets. Higgins's band played. They were so hilarious that they faded out. Bands, too many bands. Too much excitement. It was too ear-splitting for Harvard. Will Hearst felt that the Faculty were ungrateful for his celebration of the political millennium. But the students enjoyed the parade. They congratulated Will and hoped he would organize another. That was precisely what he did. The Faculty muttered over the confusion and excitement of the dynamic Californian's celebrations.

In reality, Will was thinking more of action in the world than of Harvard. His father was being mentioned for the United States Senate, and in a whimsical vein he wrote to George Hearst words that were prophetic. On November 23, 1885, he advised the family to buy a house in Washington. "We may one day read in the papers that 'the Honorable George Hearst, having served twelve years as Senator of the United States is about to retire from public life. The loss of such an ardent advocate of their rights will be greatly deplored by the people throughout the Union, but they will be partially compensated by the knowledge that his son has just been elected to Congress and has devoted himself to the cause which the elder Hearst has so nobly upheld!' "

The following year George Hearst was appointed by Governor Stoneman of California to fill a vacancy in the United States Senate caused by the death of Senator Miller. In Washington Phebe Hearst entered a world that had always interested her. She was still young, sympathetic, graceful, with millions at her command and a husband who was liked by the highly placed, by everyday people and by the lowly. The Hearst Washington residence became a cultural center.

Almost with joy Will Hearst and his chum Ben Thayer

were informed by the Harvard Faculty that they had been "rusticated" or temporarily suspended. To-day William Randolph Hearst speaks of the incident with the pleased smile of a mischievous boy.

On his first visit to his parents in Washington, the young Californian suddenly had a new sense of the significance of the capital. The very name Washington suggested the undefeatable strength and idealism of the creator of the city. Wherever Will Hearst turned in these wide, graciously curving streets, in the classical buildings, in the hospitable parks, he felt hovering the spirit of George Washington. The very site of the city had been chosen by him. In the beginning it was called "The Capital in the Woods." The streets had been laid out by L'Enfant under the guidance of Washington. It was almost Washington's garden, the first great garden of the Republic on this forested continent. It belonged to all. Here were centered the hopes of the common man for liberty and justice, for in this vast remote domain of America the common man had become a freer individual and received a greater measure of liberty and justice than the citizens of any other country.

It was Washington himself who gave reality to liberty and justice. He clarified the inchoate and inarticulate aims of the disrupted colonies, inspired them with his own spirit and bequeathed to them the great American dream. In these streets of Washington, Hearst was stirred by a new reverence for America, its past and its hopes. His Americanism became a passionate faith.

The Hearsts were disappointed that their son had been "rusticated," but Phebe Hearst was always glad to have Will with her. Proudly she introduced him to many attractive women moving through her drawing-room. Will Hearst was presented to the First Lady of the Land, lovely, young Frances Folsom Cleveland who, the British Ambassador observed, was so well poised that she sat through even a long dinner without touching her dress, face or hair.

Young Hearst was interested in the passing parade, but he cared little for society. Like his father he found long dinners tedious. Under protest Senator George Hearst attended formal entertainments. He always wore high top-boots, and only occasionally could be induced to put on a frock coat.

The highest moment that Washington had to offer Will Hearst was when he first entered the chaste, classical White House with his father to call on President Grover Cleveland. It was as if he passed over the threshold of a temple. All the men and women who had entered this door came to him in memory. While Will Hearst waited with his father even Washington became shadowy and remote, almost unapproachable. There stood forth the matchless Democrat, Jefferson, and the matchless Republican, Lincoln—brothers in democracy, human, close to him, close to all men and women.

For the second time Will Hearst was in the presence of one of his living heroes, Grover Cleveland. Even after all the years William Randolph Hearst can make Grover Cleveland live again with his impersonation of the great iron paw coming straight toward him like a huge crane about to crush his hand. His own voice becomes the deep Cleveland voice booming, "How are you, son?"

Here was a man Will Hearst thought he would like to resemble. He went out into the streets. They seemed hallowed. Heroes were everywhere. These monuments had been erected to them—for him. Reverently the youth went from national shrine to national shrine. He re-visited Mount Vernon. He made a pilgrimage to Monticello. With that intensity of concentration which has always been so large a part of William Randolph Hearst he absorbed volume after volume on the heroes of American history. He longed to be one of them.

Suddenly he did become a hero—to a woman. And she became a heroine to him. Eleanor Calhoun and Will Hearst fell in love.

CHAPTER IX

SECOND ENGAGEMENT

WILL HEARST first saw Eleanor Calhoun in his mother's drawing-room in Washington. Phebe Hearst loved beauty, and she delighted in filling her drawing-room with attractive young girls. Will saw only Eleanor. So swift, so intense was the attraction between these two that there was something almost mystical in their understanding when they came together. She was a Californian, he was a Californian. The Calhouns were of the Abbeville district of South Carolina where the great John C. Calhoun was born. The Hearsts came from the same county. When Eleanor and Will met it was as if one hundred years before their spirits had missed meeting in South Carolina, had flown to California where again they failed to unite, and now at the end of two crossings of the continent, at last came together.

Eleanor Calhoun was on her way to London to study for the stage. She desired to be a great Shakespearean actress. In California she had starred in amateur theatricals. After one of her performances the youth of San Francisco took the horses from her carriage and themselves drew the girl to her hotel. Already Eleanor had great poise and self-command, with something of the gift of personality that distinguished her great-uncle Senator John C. Calhoun.

Eleanor Calhoun was like John C. Calhoun in height, grace, slenderness, brilliant deep-blue eyes, independence of character, and rich resonant voice. She wore flowing robes when she read Shakespeare and she seemed Rosalind, Beatrice, Portia, Juliet and Cleopatra.

"Whatever she saw in me, I don't know," William Randolph Hearst says to-day modestly. Possibly she saw everything. Two or three years older than he, an artist, with swift understanding, perhaps better than any one she understood the kind of man that he was likely to become. According to his bust by Ansiglioni he looked like a young Roman ruler.

Eleanor Calhoun was a girl of the forests, born in a beautiful California mountain valley. Her autobiography describes her childhood in Tulare County, looking out on range upon range of high peaks. Shut in as she was in these mountains as a child, she prophesied to her mother that one day she would live in London and Paris. Already she knew cities, because her people were cultured, and the book-shelves in her home were filled with Shakespeare, Dickens, Thackeray, Cervantes, Hugo, Schiller, Goethe and Dante. The world of these writers was her world.

No one but Eleanor believed she would live in London and Paris. The girl moved in a trance of day-dreams. Often she climbed to the topmost rock on the topmost peak near her home and called to all space merely to hear the echoes. They were like answers from the great world of London and Paris for which she longed. Sometimes when she stood on a mountain peak calling to space, calling for friendship, fame, coyotes' voices came back like tortured mad souls. Then Eleanor was happy. Space had answered. She looked down through the blue mist, saw the distant mountains, and knew that beyond the desert was a place waiting for her.

Judge Calhoun died, and Mrs. Calhoun moved with her daughter to the pueblo of San José, the first American capital of California. At this time there still lingered around the plaza crumbling adobes, ruins of the first civic settlement in California. At San José Eleanor entered the Normal School. She took part in amateur theatricals, and appeared in a cast that was to become distinguished. Among the members of the company were Frank Bacon, later author-star of *Lightnin'*, and a young man from Stockton who played Negro parts, and was afterwards Governor of California, James H. Budd.

Later Eleanor appeared in San Francisco where the socially

predominant Southern set welcomed this talented, beautiful girl from the mountains. With the Civil War only a few years away the Tevises, Haggins and McMullins adored any one named Calhoun. Delightedly they aided Eleanor to triumph, and she set out for Washington on her way to London and Paris. Then she met Will Hearst.

He wooed with flowers, gifts and ardent devotion, but no wooing was necessary. Eleanor Calhoun was as rapturously devoted to him as he was to her. They had like tastes, a romantic love of the theater and literature. Both were young and handsome. They became engaged.

The Hearsts opposed. In that generation it was unusual, almost a tragedy, for a man to choose a woman a few years older than himself. Besides, in the eighties few well-born girls went on the stage. Phebe Hearst had no desire for a daughter who longed to be an actress. Eleanor Calhoun with her picturesque Shakespearean clothes, her thrilling voice, her desire to hear thousands of people clapping, shouting and stamping for her, was too aflame with genius, too difficult to be domesticated, to please Phebe Hearst. Like all mothers of that day she wished her son to marry a girl younger than himself, a conventional, restrained girl, who desired to settle down. Her wishes were stated to her son, and to Eleanor Calhoun. The two agreed to a separation until Will should leave college. They were willing to test their love. Nothing could ever happen that would make them give each other up; so they vowed. Eleanor Calhoun went to London to study for the stage, and Will returned to Harvard.

After a year and a half the engagement was broken by mutual consent. During nearly twenty years thereafter William Randolph Hearst did not consider marriage.

In London Eleanor Calhoun fulfilled her dream. The James Russell Lowells made a great pet of the beautiful Californian. Over night she became an assured success when she played Dora in *Diplomacy*. The Prince of Wales, afterwards Edward the Seventh, went behind the scenes to tell her how charming she was. Most actresses thought it sufficient to be called charming by the Prince of Wales, but not Eleanor Calhoun, kinswoman of the great Calhoun. Her answer was, "Thank you, Sir—and what does the Princess of Wales think of me?"

This response from the young American beauty delighted the Prince and he answered, "She thinks you are enchanting. May I not present you to her next week? She will tell you herself."

Mrs. James Russell Lowell, wife of the American Ambassador, promised to present Eleanor to the Princess. Characteristic of Eleanor, and not unlike John C. Calhoun, was her remark to Mrs. Lowell, "I want to see everything and every one, but even if I am presented to Queens and Princesses, I'll not curtsy."

Mrs. Lowell explained to her young protégée that a curtsy was only a manner of greeting, superficial like shaking hands. Why combat the custom of the country?

Eleanor Calhoun grasped Mrs. Lowell's point, and she agreed to observe the custom of the Court. Her difficulty was not one of manners, but of money. She had no suitable dress to wear. She went to her apartment, and aided by her maid she fashioned a white muslin dress for the occasion. Among the costly gowns of the great ladies of Victoria's Court this white muslin frock stood out like a forget-me-not in a big bowl of orchids. Such simplicity especially attracted the admiration of the Princess who was famous for her gowns. She sought out the young Californian in the gathering, complimented her on her frock, and told her that it made her look like a white rosebud. Eleanor frankly explained to the Princess that she had made it herself. The Princess answered that when she lived in Denmark she used to make many of her own gowns, and she and the Californian then had a pleasant chat about dressmaking.

The Princess of Wales made Eleanor Calhoun the London fashion. Royalty called, then the peerage. The girl became the friend of Browning, Lady Dorothy Nevill, Bernard Shaw, Oscar Wilde, Joseph Chamberlain, Whistler and Henry James. She made the first out-of-doors production of *As You Like It,* and played Rosalind. She went to Paris where she met Coquelin and Mounet-Sully. She studied French, and so perfected her accent that she appeared with Coquelin in leading parts of some of Sardou's plays.

In 1903 Eleanor Calhoun became a Princess herself, for she married Prince Stephen Lazar Eugene Lazarovich-Hrebelianovich, a Prince of the Royal House of Serbia which had not reigned for centuries. The Prince has written a history of Serbia. The Prince and Princess live most of the time in Paris.

William Randolph Hearst and the Princess Lazarovich have met only occasionally, but of such enduring loyal substance was his devotion to her that by the alchemy of the years it was transmuted into an imperishable friendship. During the Great War he heard that she and her husband were in peril in Serbia. So touched was he by this information that he sent a messenger all the way from London to the Balkans to see what aid he could offer.

CHAPTER X

LEAVES COLLEGE

WHEN Will Hearst's term of rustication ended he returned to Harvard, the same rollicking youth. Again he majored in jokes, pranks and sociability. He was the leader of a group bent on converting Harvard into a play world. He himself seldom drank even beer, but his friends were Harvard's merriest roysterers. More and more were their misdemeanors held to be a violation of discipline and order.

In the midst of this merry life Will Hearst was collecting fine books. He telegraphed his father requesting three thousand dollars to pay for a rare edition of Alexander Hamilton's *Federalist*. He obtained a letter of introduction to General Taylor of the Boston *Globe* and inspected that newspaper plant. He was fond of watching machinery and deciphering its processes. He had talent for mechanics. The more he read and studied newspapers, the greater grew the glamour of newspaper life. The sound of whirring, speeding presses; the excited boys rushing into the street crying out the latest news; the suspense of never knowing what was to happen next; the drama of living behind the scenes of sudden throbbing tragedies; the secrets that were discovered but never published; the power of molding political destiny; the power to better conditions of the race—everything about newspaper life fascinated Will Hearst. He must have the *Examiner*.

Although three thousand miles away from his father's little paper frequently he offered suggestions. In a letter to Senator Hearst two years before he left college when he was twenty-one he commented on the illustrations appearing in the *Examiner*:

I believe the *Examiner* has furnished the crowning absurdity of illustrated journalism, in illustrating an article on the chicken show by means of the identical Democratic rooster used during the late campaign. In my letter to the editor, however, I did not refer to this for fear of offending him, but I did tell him that in my opinion the cuts that have recently appeared in the paper bore an unquestionable resemblance to Cuticura soap advertisements. I am inclined to believe that our editor has illustrated many of his articles from his stock on hand of cuts representing gentlemen before and after using Cuticura. In case my remarks should have no effect, and he should continue in his career of desolation, let me beg of you to remonstrate with him and thus prevent him from giving the finishing stroke to our miserable little sheet. I have begun to have a strange fondness for our little paper—a tenderness like unto that which a mother feels for a puny or deformed offspring. I should hate to see it die after it has battled so long and so nobly for its existence. To tell the truth, I am possessed of the weakness which at some time or other besets most men—I am convinced that I can run a paper successfully.

Now if you will let me take over the *Examiner*—with enough money to carry out my scheme—I will tell you what I will do. In the first place I would change the general appearance of the paper and make several wide columns where we now have nine narrow ones. Then I would have the type spaced more, and these two changes would give the pages a cleaner and neater appearance. It would be well to make the paper as far as possible original. Clip only when absolutely necessary. Imitate only some leading journal like the New York *World* which is undoubtedly the best paper of that class to which the *Examiner* should belong —the class which appeals to the people and which depends for its success upon enterprise, energy and a certain startling originality, and not upon the wisdom of its political opinions, nor the lofty style of its editorials.

To accomplish this we must have—as the *World* has—active, intelligent and energetic young men. We must have men who come out West in the hopeful buoyancy of youth for the purpose of making their fortune, and not a worthless scum that have been carried there by the eddies of repeated failures. We must advertise the paper from Oregon to New Mexico, and must also increase our number of advertisements if we have to lower our rates. We can put on the first page that our circulation is such and our advertisements are so and so. Illustrations are very important. They embellish a page. They attract the eye and stimulate the imagination. . . .

Another detail of unquestionable importance is that we actually or apparently establish some connection between ourselves and the New York *World*, and obtain a certain prestige in bearing some relation to that paper. We might contract to have important private telegrams forwarded. Understand that the principal advantage we are to derive is from the attention such a connection would excite and from the advertisement we could make of it. Whether the *World* would consent to such an arrangement for any reasonable sum is very doubtful, for its net profit is over one thousand dollars a day. No doubt it would consider the *Examiner* beneath its notice. Just think, over a thousand dollars a day, and four years ago it belonged to Jay Gould and was losing money rapidly.

And now is the most important suggestion—all these changes should not be made by degrees, but at once so that the improvement will be very marked and noticeable and will attract universal attention and comment.

The Harvard Junior apparently was thinking more about owning a newspaper than about his college course, for he closed his letter by adding, "There is little to be said about my studies. I am getting on in all of them well enough to be able to spend considerable time in outside reading and in journalistic investigation."

Senator Hearst was firm in his refusal to consider his son's desire to take over the *Examiner*, but Will Hearst had no other thought for his life career. His mind was fixed on Ballard Smith, formerly of the New York *Herald*, as editor of the *Examiner*. His mother was in Paris and a cablegram is in existence saying to her, "Please see Ballard Smith in London and ask him if he will be editor of the San Francisco *Examiner*."

At this time salaries generally were low, and editors' salaries were lowest of all. Ballard Smith had been paid the unparalleled sum of seven thousand a year by the *Herald*. It did not daunt Will Hearst, but his millionaire father thought it was folly. Another letter about this time was written by the Harvard student to his father:

I will give you the benefit of my large head and great experience on this subject—and not charge you a cent. The objection to Mr. Ballard Smith is, that he is high-priced. You must reconcile yourself to paying the salary or give up the *Examiner*. It has been conclusively proven that poor wages and mediocre talent will not do, and the only thing that remains to be tried is first-class talent and corresponding wages. You could not even sell the paper at present, so I think this is the only thing to be done. Mr. Ballard Smith will state his terms and I would say, "Mr. Smith, I guarantee you this amount and I promise you a certain interest in the paper in case you make a glittering success. You are to have entire control of the paper, Mr. Smith, with the privilege of employing whomever you please."

Senator Hearst feared the worst for his son. Will was taking a newspaper seriously. He was genuinely alarmed when Billy Buster appeared before him from Harvard and asked for the *Examiner*.

"What a fool idea!" exploded the Senator, "the *Examiner* is losing money. It never earned a cent. A losing paper is as bad as a losing gold mine. I keep the *Examiner* only to help the Democrats. No one would ever take it off my hands."

"The *Lampoon* was losing money," replied Will. "I made that succeed."

"I wouldn't spend two bits on the *Examiner*. Newspapers aren't a business. They are deficits. Let's go down to Chihuahua and see the Babicora ranch. That's a business for you. Forget about the *Examiner*."

Senator Hearst took Eugene Lent and Jack Follansbee to Mexico with Will. In Mexico they traveled like grandees. They rode for several days over the long leagues to the Babicora ranch, lying on four vast plateaus separated by four ranges of mountains eight thousand feet high and extending over a million acres. The Babicora ranch had a huge adobe house surrounding a large courtyard with many Mexican servants. The Hacienda was a community in itself. Outside hundreds of vaqueros guarded great herds of thriving cattle.

"Take the Babicora," said Senator Hearst to his son. "I will give Jack Follansbee a hundred thousand acres so you can be neighbors. President Diaz is friendly. Live here. Keep away from newspapers."

Will Hearst thanked his father for the ranch, but the Senator might as well have given him darkest Africa. Life in the sprawling, gray adobe ranch-house with an army of vaqueros was unthinkable. On these mountaintops with their violent storms, deprived of human contacts that he most desired, in a foreign country, young Hearst felt exiled. Senator Hearst was a man of mountains, deserts and plains. The million-acre Babicora was to him a comfortable breathing place. And as for storms—what was life but a storm? Cattle were a real business. No nonsense about them. He couldn't understand why Will wouldn't live there. He would have him meet the President.

The Señor President Diaz as usual was seated on a volcano, but he enjoyed it. He received the Señor Senator from the United States as his own brother. The son of the Señor Senator as his own son. The Señor President toasted the Señor Senator with imperial Spanish hospitality in the Señor President's palace at Chapultepec. Will Hearst boated among the floating gardens at Zochimilco. He visualized the City of Mexico during the reign of Montezuma before the Fair God came. He relived the bloody invasion of Cortez. He brought back the horror of that ruthless, slow destruction of the Venice of this continent, the filling in of the canals upon which the city was built, the razing of the noble Aztec buildings. He saw a highly complex civilization strangled. He listened to the self-justification of the Conquistadors. They had wiped out the bloody sacrifice of human life on which the old religion was founded. No longer were vast numbers of victims slain at one ceremony to appease the gods of the barbarian. A new civilization, a new empire had been built. Here was a university established in 1551. Here was a cathedral founded in 1573. Here were paintings by Rubens, Murillo, Guido Reni, and paintings by the masters of Mexico. Will Hearst saw, felt and understood Mexico, but life had another summons.

Senator Hearst would have liked to linger in Mexico. Wherever there was gold the earth talked to him as a man, as the Indians said it did when he was a boy. He sensed that he was in a country where ancient Aztec nobles had worn golden cuirasses and ornaments of precious stones, and where gold in millions lay buried in the ground. Reluctantly he went north. Sadly he heard his son say, "Mexico is a great country with a splendid future. The Babicora is a grand ranch, but I'd like to have the *Examiner*."

Jack Follansbee, genial, jovial, in his happy-go-lucky way accepted his hundred thousand acres and for years lived on the Babicora ranch. He became a Mexican grandee, and pleasantly varied his life by long visits to the United States.

Will Hearst could not be induced to remain in Chihuahua, but he was only twenty-two. The Senator did not give up hope. Senator Hearst was in the late sixties, and he looked forward to having his son assume some of the burdens of his many business activities. The western world of affairs belonged to the Senator. Mines and ranches from Mexico to Canada. California, Nevada, Utah, Montana, Dakota and New Mexico, all knew him, had given him of their riches—fifteen millions in fifteen years. The favorite of the Senator's ranches was beautiful San Simeon lazing on the tawny hills and Santa Lucia Mountains near San Luis Obispo. The Senator visualized his son as living in his great garden of forty-five thousand acres. There was not a more beautiful ranch in California. He offered it to Will, and so was astonished and disappointed when his son reiterated, "Father, may I have the *Examiner?*"

The Senator was in despair, but he determined to show Will a mine instead of a ranch. He took him to the Anaconda in

Montana, a property bought by him from Marcus Daly as a silver-mine, but which proved to be one of the richest copper-mines in the world. Will Hearst realized that a copper-mine of the richness and depth of the Anaconda meant great wealth, but there was no excitement in prosaic money-making. Copper did not interest him. He desired a fluid life. He longed to deploy his energy in a totally different manner, and so with gentle, but unbending decision he answered, "The Anaconda is a great mine, but I'd rather own the *Examiner*."

The Senator thought that Will's fixed idea was growing worse, and so he reserved till last the Homestake in Dakota. "Now there is a great mine. Its very name is lucky. Your mother named it. Take the Homestake, the most dependable thing I have."

"I know," replied Will, "it's a wonderful mine, and you are very kind, but I'd rather have the *Examiner*."

Senator Hearst could not understand his son's determination to possess a little daily paper deeply in red ink, with a few thousand subscribers, and as a serious business, a joke. He sent him back to Harvard to see if he couldn't learn better sense.

But Harvard was no more for Will Hearst. He was thinking of the *Examiner* and of the thrill he would have in building it into a great successful paper. Before he took his degree he left Cambridge never to return and went to work on the New York *World* as a reporter under the late Ballard Smith.

Senator Hearst thought Will over. The boy didn't drink like so many rich men's sons. He didn't gamble. He wasn't lazy. He had plenty of energy. He had put the Harvard *Lampoon* on a paying basis. The *Examiner* would educate him in business, and the boy would never want another newspaper. After a few years of the *Examiner* Will would be glad to have the Babicora ranch in Mexico, or the Anaconda mine, or the Homestake, or even the San Simeon ranch. The Senator decided to let Will play with the *Examiner* for a few years.

When Will Hearst heard the news he was the happiest reporter in New York City. To-day he says that Ballard Smith was the greatest editor he ever knew. Smith never failed to have on his front page one striking dramatic story. If he couldn't find it in New York, he dragged it out of the mountains of Kentucky, or the prairies of the Middle West. It was a bait to the reading public. Hearst admired Smith to such an extent that when he left the *World* to return to San Francisco he said to him, "I have the San Francisco *Examiner*. Will you be its editor?"

Ballard Smith thought the matter over. "Thank you, I am well satisfied here. I will remain with the *World*. Do you mind if I give you some advice? Don't employ any of these expensive New York editors. You understand the work pretty well. Be your own editor."

Senator George Hearst was in the turmoil of a political campaign endeavoring to be returned to the United States Senate when he received a letter from his son. It was significant because Will Hearst was not yet twenty-three, but he definitely outlined the direction to be followed by his newspapers for forty-nine years in these words:

DEAR FATHER:

I want to see you about the paper. I shall be through here on the 10th of February, and I shall go immediately to San Francisco if I can catch you before you come here. I am anxious to begin work on the *Examiner*. I have all my pipes laid, and it only remains to turn on the gas. One year from the day I take hold of the thing our circulation will have increased ten thousand.

It is necessary that the *Examiner* destroy every possibility of being considered an organ. I know it is not an organ exclusively devoted to your interests, but there are many people who do not know this, and so, the influence and accordingly the sale of the paper is thus largely affected. . . .

We must be alarmingly enterprising, and we must be startlingly original. We must be honest and fearless. We must have greater variety than we have ever had. We must print more matter than we have printed. We must increase our force, and enlarge our editorial building. . . .

There are some things that I intend to do new and striking which will constitute a revolution in the sleepy journalism of the Pacific slope and will focus the eyes of all that section on the *Examiner*. I am not going to write you what these are, for the letter might get lost, or you might leak. You would be telling people about the big things that Billy Buster was proposing to bring out in the paper, and the first thing I knew somebody else would have it. No, I will tell you when we meet, but cut this out and paste it on Pickering. [Owner of *Call*.] In a year we will have increased at least ten thousand in circulation. In two years we will be paying. And in five years we will be the biggest paper on the Pacific slope. We won't be paying for two years because up to that time I purpose turning back into the improvement of the paper every cent that comes in.

Your affectionate son,
W. R. Hearst

So it happened that in February, 1887, Senator George Hearst gave the San Francisco *Examiner* to his tall, slender, blond son with a head like Charlemagne, and a silky voice, and a gentle manner, and a knowledge of porcelains, Persian pottery, tapestries, archæology, the theater, and a dream of America. Senator Hearst was a realist. He also gave his son several hundred thousand dollars to pay the newspaper losses.

On the day that Senator George Hearst took the oath of office for the second time in Washington, W. R. Hearst published his first edition of the *Examiner* in San Francisco.

CHAPTER XI

EDITOR OF THE *EXAMINER*

ON March 4, 1887, "W. R. Hearst, Proprietor," appeared for the first time on the editorial page of the *Examiner*. A few days later were added the words "& Publisher."

W. R. Hearst took possession of the *Examiner* when the newspapers wrote most about Edwin Booth, James G. Blaine, Lillian Russell, "Czar" Reed, Frances Folsom Cleveland, Ellen Terry, Lily Langtry, Gladstone, Sarah Bernhardt, walking-sticks, bangs, bustles, hoop-skirts and "Little Annie Rooney."

Young Bob La Follette was in Congress from Wisconsin. Young Theodore Roosevelt had just been overwhelmingly defeated for the mayoralty of New York City. Young William Jennings Bryan, who had been practicing law at Jacksonville, Illinois, had just removed to Lincoln, Nebraska. Young Woodrow Wilson was an obscure professor at Bryn Mawr. None of these men had ever met, nor had they heard of the young Californian W. R. Hearst, but all were destined to mold the progressive political thought of their time in the United States.

When W. R. Hearst became proprietor and publisher of the *Examiner*, Tammany ruled New York, and Chris Buckley, the Democratic blind boss, and Bill Higgins, ruled San Francisco. The Southern Pacific Railroad Company ruled all the bosses in California.

Hearst brought with him a group from Harvard to work on the San Francisco *Examiner*, Eugene Lent, E. L. Thayer and Fred Briggs, the cartoonist. He ordered expensive machinery, and sent the bills to his father. San Francisco prophesied that even Senator Hearst would go bankrupt.

The Senator paid the bills. He was educating his son in business. Besides he had faith in the unlimited gold supply yet undiscovered, and all his life he had taken chances. The plains, cholera, Jackass Canyon, Grass Valley, Nevada City, Virginia City, San Francisco, Utah, Dakota, New Mexico, Montana, Mexico, all had been a chance, but all had swept him onward toward his flood of fortune. The Senator hoped that Will had the intuition, or guiding star, or genius that led George Hearst, an obscure man from Missouri—one in a half million—to fame, and gave him the cleanest, kindliest millions ever accumulated in the West.

E. B. Henderson, managing editor of the *Examiner*, could not imagine that the Senator's son with his bright college clothing and unusual methods knew precisely the kind of paper desired by the public. Henderson liked to place editorials and special articles on the front page—let the news take care of itself. That was not Will Hearst's kind of a paper. The *Examiner* should blaze with news. It should draw its life blood, the news, from every block in the city, every hamlet, the heart of the jungles, the vastness of the desert, the white bleakness of the Polar regions, from under the sea and from the sky. Every industry, every laboratory, every romance should give the *Examiner* news. The paper should throb with life white-hot. Above all, it should reflect every facet of the progress of civilization, and its spirit should always beat with and battle for the common interest of the common people.

Like all San Francisco papers at that time the *Examiner* was published in rickety, shabby quarters in the oldest business section of the city. A. M. Lawrence of San Francisco, for many years an executive of William Randolph Hearst, is the only survivor of the staff that served Senator Hearst. Lawrence describes the office in Sacramento Street between Montgomery and Leidesdorff Streets across the way from the old "What Cheer House."

The paper was a "blanket" sheet of four and six pages published daily with eight pages on Sunday. The circulation of twenty-three thousand, nine hundred and fourteen was rapidly declining. Advertising was meager, and the *Examiner* had an unbroken record for losing money. The reportorial and editorial staffs were inadequate and, as was usual in those days, poorly paid. The art department consisted of two or three men working with the antiquated plate chalk process, over a coal-oil stove. The composing-rooms were overcrowded and uncomfortable. A single press drearily clacked off the declining circulation.

Managing Editor Henderson who had edited the paper for Senator Hearst, as the new proprietor soon found out, was as different from Ballard Smith as could be imagined. Henderson considered himself still responsible to the Senator, and so he dictated his plans for the day's paper to the twenty-three year old youth from Harvard. Henderson kept a copy of each dictation in order to clear himself of any blame in the eyes of Senator Hearst when disaster inevitable should befall the paper. Henderson only reflected the spirit of San Francisco in assuming that the *Examiner* was foredoomed.

Will Hearst and his friends Lent, Thayer and Briggs, the cartoonist, were gaily unconscious of the attitude of Editor Henderson and of San Francisco in general. They behaved as if publishing the *Examiner* were a Harvard flag raising.

Hearst ordered a new telegraph service from the New York *Herald*. He watched the installation of modern machinery— he could have assembled it himself. The first day he read all the articles in manuscript, and he criticized the headings. How would Ballard Smith have arranged them? Hearst was everywhere, in the local room, in the art room, in the greasy press-room. The hum of the machinery was like music. He sat up all night to see his first paper published.

Tenderly he looked at that *Examiner* of March 4, 1887, fondly as a mother looks at her first-born. Before he went home in the morning he made his plans for the next day's paper. He did not wish to drive home. Joyously he walked up the high hill of California Street and over to the family residence in Taylor Street. He scarcely realized that he was walking. His *Examiner* was born. It was one day old. So happy was he in the fulfilment of his dream on March 4, 1887, that to-day Hearst says that since that time "nothing else has ever seemed utterly important."

CHAPTER XII

LEARNS POLITICS

SAN FRANCISCO read Will Hearst's *Examiner* with curiosity and amusement. The only child of the millionaire Senator was playing with his newest toy. San Francisco did not realize—perhaps no one realized—that on March 4, 1887, a new journalism was born. In England a Northcliffe would follow. Even the impregnable London *Times,* governments, and to a certain extent civilization, would be transformed by the new journalism.

Did young Hearst know how immeasurably he would influence public opinion with his forty-one newspapers and magazines? Did he foresee that statesmen and Presidents would ask his favor? Did he imagine that art collections and palaces would be his, as splendid as those of royalty? Did he foresee that he would be feared and hated by the predatory rich, and hailed by the plundered poor? Whatever he thought, that first day at the age of twenty-three he looked not unlike another pale youth of twenty-five when his eyes from the summit of the Alps swept over the unknown Italy he was to conquer.

Least of all did the owners of the *Morning Call* and *Evening Bulletin,* the *Chronicle,* the *Alta,* the afternoon *Report,* and the *Evening Post* realize that there was a revolution in journalism in San Francisco. This first year that Hearst owned the *Examiner* was the most significant of his journalistic life. It revealed his attitude on political and social questions. It made clear what his methods would be, and forecast the years to follow.

Two weeks after Hearst became proprietor of the *Examiner,* in both editorial and news columns he attacked the proposed new charter. Hearst opposed the charter because it had been written by Bill Higgins, the lumbering Republican boss, and by Chris Buckley, the blind Democratic saloon-keeper boss. These bosses were agents for another higher boss, Bill Stow, who was the right hand of that cold, crafty Colossus of a Republican boss, Collis Potter Huntington, railroad builder.

At the time Hearst took over the *Examiner* the actual government of California was not at Sacramento, but in the Central Pacific office at Fourth and Townsend Streets, San Francisco, where the spirit of C. P. Huntington presided. Two or three times a year he appeared from New York in the flesh, a slouch-hatted, snowy-bearded giant, to plan public policies, decide public questions and determine political appointments not only for San Francisco but for California.

Huntington had been a Sacramento hardware dealer. He treated men as if they were shovels and plows to be used by his company. If a young man wished to go into politics he called at Fourth and Townsend Streets. Here Judges of the County, State, and even the United States were named. Editors criticizing the Southern Pacific Company were bankrupted, if possible, by a suggestion to local merchants to withdraw advertising. Some newspapers were owned by the company, but their most effective journals were subsidized. Railroad passes were distributed among sheriffs, editors, judges, university professors, teachers, even clergymen—all people who had any kind of power. California was called "Huntington's plantation."

Hearst had been absent from San Francisco for several years before he took over the *Examiner,* but during the first few weeks of the fight against the charter written to further corporate greed, he rapidly learned local politics. Bill Higgins and Chris Buckley were panic-stricken to find that the new *Examiner* was battling them. The bosses united forces, but for the first time they knew the humiliation of defeat. The charter was beaten. At twenty-three Hearst drew blood of the Southern Pacific bosses. He had the first thrill of victory.

In the same year he began a campaign for a new charter, and the battle did not end until 1898, when to the great rejoicing of San Francisco the charter was obtained. Early the public learned that in matters not vital, Hearst was gracious and inclined to concession, but in essentials such as politics and principles he was inflexible. Behind his smiling gray-blue eyes is a memory that never forgets, and an iron will to enforce that memory.

Hearst soon found that California was being asphyxiated by high railroad rates. The Southern Pacific absorbed the profits of orange growers. Frequently fruit rotted on trees because it could not be shipped to market. Owing to high freight rates wheat could not be distributed in the East. California was a glorious garden, almost as large as France, but owing to the cost of travel, it had but a twentieth of the population of France. Hearst's first great crusade was to try to capture freedom from the Southern Pacific for California.

The publisher realized that he could succeed only by having the best equipment of machines and the ablest men. He sought the most gifted writers on the Pacific coast, and from the beginning he revealed talent in discovering them. There came first to his attention Ambrose Bierce, a writer of genius. Bierce had attracted attention on the weeklies, the *News Letter, Wasp* and *Argonaut*. The circulation of those papers was limited, but Hearst foresaw that the Bierce column would be vastly effective in the *Examiner*. He set about trying to engage the writer for his own editorial page.

Bierce, who was a sufferer from asthma, usually lived in the hills remote from San Francisco. Occasionally he came to Oakland for a few weeks. His friends called him the "blond god of the mountains." Hearst made it a point to know when he arrived. Bierce's biographer, Carey MacWilliams, describes this meeting of the great satirist with Hearst in the "blond god's" own language:

I heard a gentle tapping at my apartment door. I opened, and I found a young man, the youngest young man, it seems to me, that I had ever confronted. His appearance, his attitude, his entire personality suggested extreme diffidence. I did not ask him to come in, install him in my better chair (I had two) and inquire how we could serve each other. If my memory is not at' fault, I merely said, "Well?" and waited results. "I am from the San Francisco *Examiner*," he exclaimed in a voice like the fragrance of violets made audible, and backed away a little. "Oh," I said, "you come from Mr. Hearst." Then that unearthly child lifted his blue eyes and cooed, "I am Mr. Hearst."

That day was important in Bierce's life, for the contract obtained by him from the *Examiner* was so remunerative that he had leisure and time to create his short stories. It made possible the development of a consummate artist in American letters.

In going to the *Examiner* Bierce made two conditions. His column "Prattle" was to appear on the editorial page adjacent to the editorials, and it was to be published precisely as written. He was to write two columns for the Sunday edition, and if he did any extra work during the week, it was to be paid for at space rates.

Bierce added much distinction to the editorial page of the *Examiner*. Frequently his opinion expressed in "Prattle" opposed the *Examiner's* policies, but Hearst, who above all men appreciates wit, never interfered. He especially enjoyed the great satirist's column. When Bierce went to the *Examiner* he abandoned the bludgeon used by him on the weeklies and took up the rapier, thereby adding a new, subtle sting to his work and immeasurably increasing his power. Carey MacWilliams says that in his neurotic, invalid moods Bierce offered many spirited and periodic resignations to the *Examiner*, but at all times he was "pampered, mollified and befriended by Hearst."

During the first month after the rebirth of the *Examiner* a twelve-page paper was announced. That month was historic in San Francisco. It saw an attack by Hearst on the Spring Valley Water Company, demanding lower rates of the railroad-controlled Board of Supervisors. This was the beginning of the struggle long carried on by the *Examiner* for cheaper water rates for the city. The Spring Valley Water Company was paying dividends of millions yearly. The *Examiner* urged the Company to reduce rates. Three pertinent questions were asked by the paper: "Are water rates excessive? Do the meters register correctly? Shall small consumers be charged twice as much as large ones?"

Hearst predicted that the Spring Valley Water Company would oblige the people of San Francisco to bring their own water supply from the Sierras. San Francisco taxpayers were soon in a fighting mood. The corporation-controlled Supervisors were forced to reduce water rates 16 per cent. Hearst urged San Francisco to plan for public ownership of water, but obstacles were continually placed in the way of the city's project.

Years rolled by, and the defective water mains broken by the earthquake caused the destruction of San Francisco by fire. Then the people voted seven to one in favor of the municipally owned Hetch-Hetchy water project long advocated by the *Examiner*.

Corporations tried to revoke the Hetch-Hetchy right to use the reservoir site in the Hetch-Hetchy valley by appealing to Congress in 1909 through Secretary Ballinger. Hearst in the *Examiner* caused a petition of twenty-three thousand names to be signed. It was carried to Washington on November 19, 1913, by Mayor Rolph, later Governor of California. While he was in Washington a sixteen-page special Washington edition of the San Francisco *Examiner* devoted entirely to the Hetch-Hetchy Bill was published and laid on the desk of each member of the Senate. President Wilson used his influence in Congress, and the measure was passed.

San Francisco now has in use the Hetch-Hetchy water supply, and the city need never be apprehensive of burning as it did in 1906, through the inadequate maintenance of a privately owned water company.

CHAPTER XIII

CRUSADES

DURING Hearst's first few months as owner of the *Examiner* he enlisted in a half-dozen crusades. He campaigned to compel the electric company to place their wires underground in the downtown district. He tried to prevent Postmaster General John Wanamaker paying more than a million dollars for a bog called the "Pipesville swamp" to build the United States Post-office on, but he failed. Wanamaker refused to be interviewed on the subject, saying, "I never give interviews on Sunday."

"He is a truly good man," scoffed the *Examiner*.

The post-office was erected on the bog, and the earthquake of 1906 proved the wisdom of the *Examiner's* opposition.

In April of 1887, Hearst began a crusade that he still continues, the effort to suppress narcotics.

Action was swift in the *Examiner* office in these early months of 1887. Hearst was the steam of the organization, and the staff had difficulty in keeping abreast of the proprietor. Managing Editor Henderson, who came with the paper from the dusty past, was dazed when he saw the ritual of the sacrosanct journalism of the sixties and seventies swept aside by the new master of the eighties.

In a letter to his mother written at this time Hearst revealed that he had no idea how difficult a task he had undertaken when he became editor:

I don't suppose that I shall live more than three or four years if this strain keeps up. I don't get to bed until two o'clock and I wake up about seven in the morning and can't get to sleep again, for I must see the paper and compare it with the *Chronicle*.

If we are the best, I can turn over and go to sleep with quiet satisfaction, but if the *Chronicle* happens to scoop us, that lets me out of all sleep for the day. . . .

Thank Heaven for one thing, our efforts are appreciated. The great and good people of California want the *Examiner*. They don't want it very bad; they don't want it much harder than at the rate of thirty additional copies a day, but in time this will count. If we can manage to keep ahead we will have in a year from thirty to thirty-two thousand subscribers. That will put us well ahead of the *Call,* and well up with the *Chronicle.*

On the morning of April 1st, of that year, Hearst discovered from the early editions of the *Chronicle* and *Call* that he had been "scooped." The fashionable Hotel Del Monte was burning to the ground. Hearst was stunned. What should he do? How could he turn the "scoop" of the burning Hotel Del Monte into victory? To-day he says that a "scoop" does not necessarily matter greatly. Frequently the handling of second day's news is more important.

Before he slept he engaged a special train to go to the fire, the first time a train was used in California to cover news. On the train was a swarm of *Examiner* writers and artists. While the conflagration was still roaring they arrived and caused almost as much commotion as the fire itself.

The *Examiner* of April 3rd, devoted the entire first, and half of the second page to well-written and completely illustrated articles on the fire. Hearst himself wrote the legends of the hotel and headings of the articles. Such newspaper pictures had never before been seen in California, three and four columns wide. For a daily paper the size was unparalleled—fourteen pages. To supply the demand for the *Examiner* three editions were printed. San Franciscans ceased being amused by the toy of the millionaire's son. They realized they had a newspaper, but it was predicted that special trains would ruin even Senator Hearst. Will Hearst could not last long.

Will Hearst intended to last. In April, 1888, he was twenty-five, but in his festive clothing, with his boyish manner he looked younger. He had a new game, work, and he was playing just as hard as he could play. He went through the offices humming a cowboy lament, dancing a jig, mimicking the doldrums of the prophets who said the *Examiner* would fail. He drew sketches for cartoons in the art department. He made notes for editors. He suggested headings for news stories. He selected new type for printers. He supervised the stereotypers.

Briggs drew his best cartoons. "Phinney" Thayer wrote his most humorous column. Eugene Lent supplied stories of the financial, club and social world. Joe Ward was a brilliant city editor. Hearst leased commodious quarters for the editorial, art and printing departments. New mechanical methods were introduced.

Nor was the business department overlooked. The *Examiner* business office was established on one of the most important corners of the city, at Grant Avenue and Market Street. Forceful and tactful advertising solicitors, and businessmen with new ideas were engaged under contract.

From childhood trained to observation and discrimination, Hearst turned to minute criticism of his own paper. He became meticulous as to type, printing, pictures and vivacity of style. He offered prizes for the best-written news items, for "scoops." Above all—news. The *Examiner* must be first! Get the news! It will not drop off a tree into your lap while you sleep. Work! Each big story must be in the *Examiner* first, in the most attractive type, with the most alluring pictures, and written by the best writers. Never be dull. Never be dreary. Hearst could not endure bores. He would not permit his paper to be boring. It must be instructive, interesting, witty. The man on the street must be appealed to, youngsters, professional men, business men, scholars, but especially women, must like the *Examiner*.

For lovers of fiction Hearst published a serial called *Guilderoy* by Ouida (Louise de la Ramée) and *Mystery Tales* by Anna Katherine Green. Gertrude Atherton, just beginning her career, wrote for the *Examiner, Monterey—Then and Now*.

A popular song by Ned Harrigan and Dave Braham from *McNooney's Visit,* was the first music ever printed in the West by a daily paper. When Henry Ward Beecher died the *Examiner* had the most complete story.

Hearst sent up a big balloon labeled the *Examiner* in staring letters. His first flight into the air was in this balloon with Harry B. McDowell, son of General McDowell, a photographer, and a flock of homing pigeons. The next day San Francisco read a description of the city viewed from the sky and enjoyed drawings of large photographs taken from the air illustrating the scene.

The *Examiner* went out into the State. A balloon was sent up in Los Angeles. California was just discovering the climate of the South. Startling and sudden rises in real estate and an immense increase in population came to Los Angeles. Hearst sent a special train from San Francisco with a twenty-eight page edition of the *Examiner*. A balloon floating over Los Angeles told of the paper's arrival.

Sports were given new importance in the *Examiner*. The horses of Keene, Baldwin, Ashe, Senator Stanford, and Senator Hearst were gaining great victories on the Atlantic coast. The *Examiner* published a full account of the *Coronet* winning the transatlantic yacht race. At Harvard, Hearst had been devoted to baseball, and he was especially interested in stories of the great American game. On the first page of the *Examiner* was news of George Vanhaltren then pitching for the Chicago Cubs, and of Kelly "The Ten Thousand Dollar Beauty of Baseball."

About this time Ernest L. (Phinney) Thayer, one of Hearst's Harvard chums, because of illness, returned East, but he sent a weekly column published Sunday morning. For this column he wrote *Casey at the Bat.*

Thayer recently said at Santa Barbara, where he now lives, that Archibald Clavering Gunter, a popular California novelist, liked the poem so much that he gave it to De Wolfe Hopper to recite on a New York program entertaining baseball people.

Hopper's recitation made such a great success that he continued giving it for forty-seven years, until he died in 1935. Many thousand copies of *Casey at the Bat* have been sold, and it has become an American classic.

As much as Hearst liked baseball he loathed prize-fighting. The Queensberry rules had been accepted in the ring, but there survived stories of bare-fisted, bloody battles. John L. Sullivan was champion, and Corbett was still an amateur boxing bank clerk in San Francisco. Hearst was discouraged by the widespread interest in contests between well-trained specimens of the human brute. In those days he campaigned against prize-fighting, and on November 13, 1914, it was declared illegal in California. Hearst would like to see prize-fighting abolished in the United States.

Early Hearst defined his attitude on Prohibition in an editorial on the South Carolina Dispensary Law: "The law has not had long enough nor fair enough trial to pronounce upon its merits. . . . It does not, like prohibition, deprive the citizen of the opportunity to buy liquor if he wants it, and it makes easy the strict regulation of the traffic. . . . The system opens the way to deal with the most evident evils of the liquor problem, without attempting to interfere with the appetites of the people. Whether it has features that will make it more objectionable than the evil against which it is directed has not yet appeared."

Three years after Hearst took charge of the *Examiner* he had a sympathetic page interview with Henry George who at one time owned the San Francisco *Evening Post* and tried to establish a penny paper for workingmen. George's theory of Single Tax interested Hearst. During the Bryan campaign Hearst employed George to write articles. At thirty, came Hearst's first editorial favoring a tax on all incomes over a thousand dollars, although such a tax would have meant heavy payments by his family.

Phebe Hearst had inculcated in her son interest in the public schools. He advocated free school-books, better school buildings, increase in salaries for teachers, and civil service in appointments. Early Hearst became interested in developing the University of California.

A series of excursions and outings on San Francisco Bay was given to children of *Examiner* subscribers. Management of the House of Correction was investigated. Bad food and unsanitary living conditions were revealed. The institution was reformed. Corruption in the Police Department was investigated, and long lists of gambling houses and fan-tan places were closed.

Terence Powderly, chief of the Knights of Labor, felt the strength of the *Examiner's* support. In the editorial department Hearst branched out nationally. He demanded the annexation of Hawaii, and his demands continued until the island kingdom was a part of the United States.

In the *Examiner* Hearst always balanced crusades for causes, politics and reform with humorous stories deftly written and ever increasing caricatures and cartoons. Wherever there was news the resourceful *Examiner* reporters were to be found. No matter what the event, the assassination of Judge David Terry by Nagle, the bodyguard of Chief Justice Field, the dramatic chase of a murderer, or the Sullivan-Felton Congressional contest, the interviewing of the svelte Bernhardt as she came into Nevada on her visit to California, or the confession of a murderer, *Examiner* men were usually first. They brought into the office the confession of Benhayon, which freed Dr. Bowers condemned to hang for murdering his wife for life insurance. Benhayon killed himself after writing his confession of murdering his own sister, wife of Dr. Bowers, but it was generally believed that Bowers in his cell had Benhayon also murdered. The public was chilled with horror, but Bowers was saved from the scaffold.

Service of the *Examiner* was always being improved. Sunday morning special trains carried the paper to subscribers one hundred miles distant. These trains steaming up and down the State gave very different delivery of the paper from the early

days after Senator Hearst bought the *Examiner*. Then one
man trundled a bundle of papers over the cobblestones to the
post-office. Another carried the bundles to the water-front,
where two sturdy oarsmen in a rowboat crossed the bay to
Oakland and connected with stages and steam trains.

Soon people began thinking that if they did not read the
Examiner they were missing the news. And they were. The
size of the paper kept on increasing. Circulation poured in, a
thousand a week. Rival papers said it couldn't last. They hoped
and prayed it couldn't. In confidence and pride the *Examiner*
christened itself the Monarch of the Dailies.

Not only was no money spared in obtaining the news, but
public questions were discussed with freedom and ability never
before known in the West. Feature after feature was added.
The *Examiner* became the Mecca for underpaid newspaper-
men. Salaries mounted to a degree unheard of on the Pacific
coast. Hearst surprised his staff with gifts and promotions. In
the office the best stories were told. Laughter rang out. Hearst
lived in the editorial rooms, printing office and art department.

New men were employed: Samuel E. Moffett, scholarly editorial writer, nephew of Mark Twain; Allen Kelly, nature
writer and animal lover; T. T. Williams, scintillating writer
who later became business manager; E. H. Hamilton, who
never wrote a dull line; A. M. Lawrence, dynamic assistant
city editor; and Charles Michelson, at present manager of
publicity for the Democratic Party.

In 1888, Hearst selected from the composing room one of
the most valuable men in his employ, George E. Pancoast. This
man had unique talents, and following the suggestions of
Hearst, they were developed until he made from his inventions
of color presses, millions for his employer and large sums for
himself.

Pancoast came from Cambridge, Massachusetts, where he
had served his apprenticeship at the University Press. His
talent was called to Hearst's attention through his sense of
humor. Pancoast was filling temporarily a vacancy in the tele-

graph department. Ike Allen, telegraph editor, corrected a heading written by Pancoast, and changed it to read: IT'S ALL RIGHT NOW.

Vexed but amused Pancoast set up a poster reading:

IKE ALLEN'S PATENT ADJUSTABLE HEAD

WILL FIT ANY STORY BY
CHANGING ONE LETTER

IT'S ALL RIGHT NOW or IT'S ALL RIGHT NOT

Hearst read the poster, laughed and asked, "Who is the comedian?" The publisher met Pancoast and asked, "Can you write shorthand?"

"Only longhand."

"Will you please take some letters for me?" said Hearst.

Pancoast wrote the letters and returned to the telegraph office. A few days later Hearst met him and asked, "Didn't you like that job?"

"It's the first time I knew I had another job."

Pancoast became Hearst's secretary. He kept irregular hours and never bothered much about sleep. Pancoast says he was the first secretary employed by Hearst that could always be found, no matter when the publisher appeared in the office.

Pancoast spent much time on amateur photography, and through him Hearst became interested in and acquired a knowledge of photography that has been of inestimable value in the development of his newspaper plants.

One morning at Sausalito where both the publisher and his secretary had week-end houses, Pancoast photographed masts of ships, the top of Angel Island, and Belvedere rising above a fog bank over the bay.

It was a unique picture and Hearst immediately became an enthusiastic photographer. In twenty-four hours he had bought the best photograph apparatus in San Francisco, and had wired East for more. He worked in the dark-room until his hands looked like mahogany. He made lantern slides. He bought another house in Sausalito, gutted the second story and made a hall to show his pictures in. Pancoast says that when Hearst takes up new work he is not satisfied until he can do it better than it has ever been done.

In 1891 and 1892, when Hearst and Pancoast went to Europe, it was difficult to buy photographic apparatus. They traveled with duplicates of all cameras and their parts. Hearst had trunks of plates. He photographed the Nile. To his mother he wrote, "The Nile is pretty fair, but a little too much like the Sacramento. I don't think I'd enjoy it much if it were not for the queer types of people and the opportunity it gives me for photography."

The tombs of the Kings of Egypt and the dark chambers of the temples of Karnak, Luxor and the Island of Philæ were photographed by Hearst. He made the first flashlight photographs of the carvings in these places. Before that time only drawings by artists had been done. Setting his cameras in the long deep passageways hewn out of solid rock, Hearst took his flashlight pictures. Natives howled like dogs at these flashlights because they thought they were the Evil Eye. So frightened were they that the British Government forbade any more photography in the Tombs of the Kings. But Hearst had already secured the coveted pictures.

The publisher brought from Egypt a collection of mummies still in his possession. Pancoast relates an incident of their journey to Egypt that showed his tendency to take the part of the weak. While photographing a little Egyptian town, Hearst saw a man beating a child. The publisher threw his camera at the man. Pancoast says that Hearst can be brusque with a writer or executive, people strong enough to defend themselves, but he is always considerate of the humble.

It is a curious coincidence that Hearst should have been the first to photograph the Tombs of the Kings of Egypt, for his mother, Mrs. Phebe Hearst, years later financed the Carter Expedition resulting in the excavations that disclosed the Tomb of King Tutankhamen.

While Hearst and Pancoast were on the journey to Egypt they stopped at the Hotel Wagram, Paris. Pancoast was not feeling well. He was born in New England, and he had a great liking for Boston baked beans, clam chowder and codfish. They were not to be obtained at the Wagram. Hearst cabled Ike Allen of the San Francisco *Examiner* for one dozen cans of Boston baked beans, one dozen clam chowder and two codfish.

Allen thought the message was a code of some political event. He went to several banks and asked them to help decipher the message by their code. No light was obtained, and so Allen cabled: "What code are you using?"

Hearst replied: "No code—damnfool—want one dozen chowder, baked beans, codfish."

This journey to Egypt cemented the friendship between Hearst and Pancoast which has lasted for forty-five years with a happy relation on both sides. Pancoast entered Hearst's employ as a printer. He invented the famous Pancoast presses and has now a commanding position. He told the writer that if he ever received a request or order without the word "Please" or "Kindly," he would know that the communication was not from Hearst.

Pancoast insists that he would rather show Hearst a blueprint for a press than he would a manufacturer. In his opinion Hearst reads a blue-print better than most builders of presses.

Hearst smiles at Pancoast's self-effacement. When he discovered that Pancoast had the Yankee genius for invention he realized that he was of too great value to be a secretary. Pancoast was placed in charge of supervising the mechanical part of his papers. Hearst insists that Pancoast overestimates "my own mechanical understanding, perhaps because the ordinary publisher knows nothing about blue-prints or presses. An inventor like Pancoast is always surprised to find that I know a little."

CHAPTER XIV

STANDS WITH WORKERS

D URING the first year that Hearst owned the *Examiner* he disclosed that he could not listen to the story of suffering without trying to give aid. The *Examiner* exposed maladministration of San Francisco jails and receiving hospitals as well as mismanagement of San Quentin prison.

A consumptive was turned away from the San Francisco County Hospital. This pitiless act revealed to Hearst the defects in the city and county hospitals. After investigation he pointed out their incompetent management. "Hospital horrors," they were called by the *Examiner*. Their appliances were out of date, and years previously the term of usefulness of their buildings had ended. As for San Quentin, the *Examiner* said, "Governor Waterman is not supposed to know much, but he knows that the State prison is extravagantly and inefficiently managed."

As a climax to Hearst's campaign for better receiving-hospital conditions, a baby was born in the city prison a few days before Christmas:

It is a pathetic story [the *Examiner* wrote about the little newcomer in the city prison]. To be born in jail, even in that part of the jail which serves the rich but thrifty city as a receiving hospital, is not a promising beginning for life. It is no fault of poor Minnie Fields that her child had so inauspicious an introduction to the world. Left a widow at her time of greatest need, she worked as long as she could, but the fight was too hard.

It is in Christmas week that this pitiful thing occurs. There is not a very merry Christmas in prospect for Minnie Fields and her baby. Cannot this free-hearted city do something to make it a little less dreary?

A public subscription for the boy will lighten the handicap with which he starts in life. Let those who are pouring Christmas gifts upon friends who do not need them add to their lists the name of one in desperate want of some kindness.

The *Examiner* headed the subscription, and during the first two days nearly three hundred dollars were collected in addition to a large amount of clothing for both mother and baby. Out of the total collections after Minnie Fields and child were comfortably provided for, there was left a balance of three hundred dollars which on February 5, 1888, was sent to the editor of the Fresno *Republican* to be invested in lots to be kept until the baby was twenty-one.

During 1887 Hearst took his first step in what was to be a long crusade to force the Southern Pacific Railroad Company to pay its debt of twenty-seven million and five hundred thousand dollars to the Federal Government. The money was due in 1900.

Although Hearst was not yet twenty-four, already he had in mind national influence for his paper. He decided to publish an edition of the *Examiner* on Washington's birthday in Washington, D. C. Half of the San Francisco *Examiner* staff appeared in the capital to publish the Washington edition. Hearst's purpose was to stimulate agitation to bring the Democratic National Convention to San Francisco. The Democratic National Committeemen were meeting at that time in Washington. Hearst thought this a fitting occasion to approach them with the proposal.

Eastern editors protested that expense would be too great to bring telegraphic news from a city so far west as San Francisco. Already Hearst in 1888, had in mind a New York edition of the *Examiner*. He offered to publish his paper in New York and supply telegraphic news of the convention for eastern papers, but St. Louis had regional political advantage and won the prize.

Senator and Mrs. Hearst were delighted to find their son's paper on their doorstep in Washington. The Senator especially rejoiced that Will had settled down to hard work and was already attracting nation-wide attention. The *Examiner's* circulation had mounted from twenty-three thousand, nine hundred and fourteen to forty-seven thousand, five hundred and twenty-six. This gain in circulation and the necessary improvements cost the Senator several hundred thousand dollars, but he was the best authority of his time on gold-mines. Notwithstanding the expense of the first year of the *Examiner*, George Hearst realized that his twenty-four year old son was a new kind of gold-mine. The Senator gladly paid the deficit, and on the evening of March 3, 1888, W. R. Hearst gave the first big birthday party for the Monarch of the Dailies at 508 Montgomery Street. His birthday present to his paper was a swift, shining new press which was much admired by the guests.

A few days later, when Kaiser Wilhelm the First died, the *Examiner* appeared in both German and English. Two editions were brought out on March 9th, to meet the demand.

In this same year Hearst appeared in national politics. When the Democratic Convention was being held in St. Louis he sent a representative of the *Examiner* to Columbus, Ohio, where Judge Allen G. Thurman lived, to ask if he would accept the nomination as Vice-President on the Democratic ticket. Thurman replied that if the nomination were tendered unanimously he would be a candidate. President Cleveland was renominated and Thurman was named as his running-mate. Thurman sent a message to Hearst thanking him for starting a movement that gave him the nomination.

The convention was reported by "Gath" George Alfred Thompson and Ballard Smith, the editor who gave Hearst his first lessons in journalism. R. D. Bogart and A. M. Lawrence reported the convention from the San Francisco point of view. Their telegrams covered a page and a quarter of small type, astounding in those days.

Soon after Hearst became proprietor of the *Examiner* he

discovered that the Central Pacific Railroad was trying to side-track San Francisco. He urged merchants to get solidly behind a new line of steamers from Vancouver to Hongkong subsidized at three hundred thousand dollars a year by the British and Canadian governments. In these earliest days Hearst advocated the Merchant Marine. Frequent, regular and cheap steamer communication was needed to develop profitable trade.

Hearst had owned the *Examiner* one year when he found that defenses of the San Francisco harbor were fit only for a South American republic. He urged modern armament for the fortifications. In 1888, when he was twenty-five, Hearst first proclaimed his foreign policy still advocated in 1936: *Defense on as reasonable terms as possible, with no foreign entanglements among the European nations.*

From the beginning Hearst urged that white labor in California be protected. He had in mind that from 1850 California workers had been threatened with Oriental labor. Millions of unemployed yellow and brown men from across the Pacific, who could live on fifty cents a day and work for starvation wages, drove terror into the hearts of white laborers. In the late seventies Denis Kearney, sand-lot orator, had elected and controlled the Mayor of San Francisco with the slogan, "The Chinese must go!"

The Chinese had been kept out of California by the Scott Exclusion Law, but now fifteen years later a repeal of the Scott law was advocated. White laborers were panic-stricken. Mass meetings protested against the Chinese influx. Chinamen were stealthily creeping across borders, or brazenly entering the ports by bribery. The Federal court of San Francisco was landing Chinese under a writ of habeas corpus in direct violation of the law. Subterranean slave trade was being carried on in Chinatown. Young American boys were smoking opium.

Hearst was one of the first large employers of labor to recognize that high wages bring prosperity. He sought interviews with other employers. With cynical frankness C. P. Huntington demanded Chinese workmen. "Labor cannot be too cheap for me. Let Federal officials alone." The battle went on to break down the Scott Exclusion Law. Finally more drastic exclusion laws were passed and vigorously enforced, but to this day Hearst is watchful of the Orient as a menace to white workmen and to conditions necessary to maintain decent dignity for white labor.

In the late eighties, owing to new inventions there was a labor depression. Ironworkers struck. They demanded eight hours a day. Eleven hundred men stood in line waiting for a chance to exchange their labor at a dollar a day. Thousands were unemployed. The *Examiner* ran three labor trains from San Francisco, Sacramento and Los Angeles. Relief committees were formed. Hearst declared that all must have aid:

San Francisco can better afford to supply any amount of capital to give willing workers a chance than to drive them to begging or stealing. We are not giving money to charity. We are spending it in a way that will give pleasure to ourselves and our children. . . . If every foot of the park should be reclaimed, if roads could be constructed throughout, a lake excavated and a zoölogical garden laid out, the money would all come back in increased value of San Francisco property. Outside lands would boom. Lots out toward the ocean would be as valuable in proportion as the Central Park tract in New York on which Lenox Library stands.

More than a thousand men were given work developing Golden Gate Park. Nine thousand feet of pipe were laid. Eighty thousand trees were planted.

Workers asked for eight hours a day, and Hearst wrote:

The workmen are merely demanding what is reasonable. They should have it at once. . . . If machinery enables one man to do as much as a dozen could have done fifty years ago, it is only fair that one man should take his work a little more easily than he would have had to take it then. There is no reason why his nose should be held to the grindstone of toil, when science has offered him a way to escape. If he could do his share of work under the old method in ten or twelve or even fourteen hours a day, he can certainly do it in eight.... All the people must be supported in some way.

The eight-hour day was granted ironworkers. Rejoicingly Hearst wrote that it created jobs for thousands of unemployed.

Early in Hearst's career he realized that California lagged in industrial and commercial prosperity largely because of high freight rates. They could not be lowered because the State was dominated politically by the railroad. Before he had owned the *Examiner* a year he was trying to loosen the clutch of the Southern Pacific from the throat of the Golden State. He opened a campaign for cheaper freight rates. At that time Senator Hearst was a colleague of Senator Leland Stanford in the Senate. They had been friends from the early fifties in Sacramento. Senator Hearst frequently opposed Senator Stanford's activities in the Senate. His son did not hesitate to attack iniquities in the management of the Southern Pacific.

Thwarted in his efforts to lower freight rates, Hearst's mind turned to the possibility of a canal across the Isthmus of Panama. When he was twenty-five he discussed the Isthmian canal question in an editorial. The time had come to level the barrier placed by nature between the two oceans, the barrier that stood in the way of Magellan. Hearst wanted California to build the canal. He said that San Francisco alone could do it.

So many ideas filled Hearst's mind and so many activities crowded his life that he was scarcely conscious of the launching of the *Maine*, November 19, 1890, the largest and most powerful war vessel at that time ever built in the United States. It was constructed at the Union Iron Works, San Francisco, and the *Examiner* had a first-page article and an editorial on the day of its launching. But no one realized the ominous significance of the grim battle-ship. No one could foresee that the sinking of this pride of the navy in the Havana harbor a few years later would be the immediate cause of the Spanish-American War.

CHAPTER XV

FIRST SUCCESS

HEARST never relaxed in seeking new and able men for his papers and magazines. In the early days of the *Examiner*, whenever he heard of a man of unusual quality or talent he made a mental note of his name. During the second year that he owned the *Examiner*, Hearst was told of Charles M. Palmer, proprietor of the *Northwestern Miller*, a leading paper published in Minneapolis. Palmer also had an interest in the St. Joseph (Missouri) *News*, and in some other trade publications. As publisher of the Minneapolis *Tribune* Palmer had originated novel publicity in promoting circulation and obtained excellent results. Hearst had never met him, but on Thanksgiving Day, 1889, he sent Palmer a telegram asking if he would come to the *Examiner*, when he would begin work, and what salary he would expect.

Palmer soon left Minneapolis to become business manager of the *Examiner*. The position had been held by E. W. Townsend, former secretary of Senator George Hearst. Townsend was a gifted writer. He had gained national renown as the author of *Chimmie Fadden*, but he disclaimed knowledge of commercial matters, and so even he was glad to welcome the new business manager. Palmer was assisted by William F. Bogart, a capable and greatly beloved man who remained with Hearst all his life. During the years of his retirement he was pensioned.

Charles M. Palmer is now a wealthy New York newspaper broker. He describes his journey to San Francisco through blizzards and floods which delayed him five days. He had never seen Hearst before, but he found him one of the most attractive men he had ever met, singularly self-effacing, seemingly deferring to the opinions of others. After Palmer had been with Hearst for some time he says he discovered that he was working for a young man with a strong will who knew precisely what he wished and how it could be obtained, a man with one of the keenest and most active brains ever given a human being. In fact, a genius.

Palmer says that when he arrived there was no paper in the United States presenting the news in a more appetizing way than the *Examiner*. It was the most talked of and the most eagerly read paper on the Pacific coast. Soon Palmer learned that his own task was to take circulation from the conservative *Chronicle*, and classified advertising from the old *Call*, and to convince the merchants that the *Examiner* was the best paper for general advertising. This feat Palmer easily accomplished.

Palmer soon discovered that his twenty-six year old employer not only had as objective the building-up of the *Examiner*, but he had in mind establishing a branch of his paper in New York and Chicago, and possibly other intermediate cities. Hearst's idea was that if he had a paper in Chicago, and another in New York, each could serve the other with news of general interest and editorial and pictorial matter, at a great reduction of cost. Palmer's memory is supported by that of George Pancoast who says that about this time he was crossing San Francisco Bay on a ferry-boat with his employer, and Hearst took from his pocket a railway time-table, drew a circle around the names of several large cities and said, "George, a paper there, and there, and there." The idea of a chain of papers, born when he was twenty-six, never left Hearst.

Under Palmer the *Examiner* advertising steadily mounted. At this time Hearst met by chance in the bar-room of the Hoffman House in New York City a man who later was of great value to the *Examiner*. S. S. (Sam) Chamberlain had been editor of Bennett's Paris *Herald*. An immediate friendship sprang up between Hearst and Chamberlain lasting until the editor's death. Sam Chamberlain had good looks, distinction, a flashing resourceful mind, and was probably the best-dressed man in San Francisco. Soon he became managing editor of the *Examiner*. When Queen Liliuokalani was deposed Chamberlain took the first steamer for Honolulu and obtained from the ex-Queen an exclusive interview, the first ever granted by Her Majesty.

A tall, fair-haired, scintillating, Highlander Scotsman with sandy mustache and goatee, Arthur McEwen, was chief editorial writer. In his early youth McEwen had been deeply religious, and his work had spiritual fervor. When he became a friend of Henry George, his religious tendency was transformed into enthusiasm for Single Tax and a passionate desire to wage the battles of the people. Until his death in 1907, his life was driven and tormented by unattainable ideals. McEwen's wit, humor, irony and idealism flowed into the *Examiner* and gave its editorial page classical distinction.

Joe Ward was still city editor. John C. Klein was a free-lance. Bill Hart was copy reader. Bob Davis, lately arrived from Nevada, was a "cub" reporter. Ambrose Bierce had his biting column, "Prattle."

Hearst frequently made suggestions to the editors in long-hand. He had not begun writing, but outlines of editorials were given with such completeness that they needed few alterations to be published. His suggestions appeared as cartoons executed by Briggs and Nast.

Thomas Nast, the greatest cartoonist of his day, had a Hogarth-like genius. In New York City, Nast had created the famous Tammany Tiger, and was largely responsible for the revolt against Tweed led by Samuel J. Tilden. One of Hearst's best suggestions was given to Thomas Nast shortly after he arrived in San Francisco and began working on the *Examiner*. Hearst was engaged in a campaign to force the cable roads to equip their cars with life-saving fenders. Hearst requested Nast to cartoon the railroad company.

A newcomer in San Francisco, Nast was unfamiliar with the fact that fenderless cars had caused the death of many children and elderly people. Nast's technique was admirable, but his first cartoon was not entirely successful. Hearst early developed tactful direction of men. He praised Nast's cartoon which was to appear the following morning. That evening Hearst asked the cartoonist to join the editorial group at an Italian restaurant.

During dinner he said, "Mr. Nast, the cars have maimed and killed many children. Sometimes when I look at a street-car I seem to see a skeleton as motorman. The little children don't know that death is in control, and so they thoughtlessly cross its path."

That remark was Nast's inspiration. "I have it, Mr. Hearst! Death, the Gripman! I'll draw it! Kill the other cartoon." Nast worked half the night on the picture and made so striking and so dramatic a cartoon that "Death, the Gripman," became a legend in San Francisco.

During the third year that Hearst owned the *Examiner* there joined the staff a young woman, Winifred Sweet, who immediately became recognized as a person of tremendous force and ability. Her statuesque frame, her auburn hair, her brilliant eyes, showed energy, enthusiasm and resourcefulness. With it all she was as wholesome and pink and white as an apple blossom. She appeared at a time when women in the newspaper world were a novelty, but it was not as a novelty that she gained fame. Success came to her immediately because immediately she became uniquely valuable. A daughter of a Colonel in the United States Army, she had her father's executive ability, and an original compelling charm. She knew how to manage masses of children and people. Because her mother always sang the children to sleep with the song, *Annie Laurie,* Winifred Sweet took the name Annie Laurie as a *nom de plume.*

Immediately Annie Laurie was placed in charge of the children's festivities by the *Examiner* editor. Hearst was absent at the time of her arrival, and she tells how she made his acquaintance. She was in Golden Gate Park in charge of a large number of picnicking children. There appeared at this picnic a tall, slender, fair youth with arms full of toys, a stranger to her, but he was not long a stranger to the children. He sat on the ground and joined in their games. He was the most popular man at the picnic. Annie Laurie wondered who he was. It was her first meeting with Hearst.

Soon, Annie Laurie married an able writer, Orlow Black, and when she wrote anything published outside of San Francisco, it was under the name of Winifred Black. Her articles are syndicated throughout the nation, but in San Francisco she continues to be known and loved as Annie Laurie.

When Christmas came she almost changed the name of Santa Claus to Annie Laurie. She collected books and toys and raised large funds for children. She organized the children's Christmas fair and the *Examiner's* Christmas tree. Later she headed a small army of thirty thousand children who were guests of the *Examiner* at the Mid-Winter Fair.

In the early nineties Jimmie, son of an *Examiner* artist, fell hopelessly ill. Hospitals refused to admit him because he was an incurable cripple.

"We must have a hospital," said Hearst.

The editor gave A. C. Schweinfurth, the architect, his own plan—circular, many-windowed rooms with a sun parlor on the top floor. The parlor was to be filled with birds.

The building was erected for the crippled Jimmie. Hearst contributed largely to the hospital, but he asked Annie Laurie to take charge of collecting funds for the Little Jim campaign. Annie Laurie had a son, and to her little Jim seemed her own boy. Annie Laurie called on the women of San Francisco to save the suffering children. She got up a Christmas edition of the *Examiner* and asked the society women to write, edit and publish the paper in the name of Little Jim. Fashionable women accepted editorial and business positions. Funds began arriving for the Little Jim Hospital.

On December 24th, from the City of Mexico came the following telegram to the new editors of the *Examiner:*

Mrs. Frank Pixley,
   Managing editor, the "Examiner,"
   San Francisco.

I wish you and your associates a Merry Christmas, and in anticipation of the brilliant manner in which you will scoop the *Chronicle,* I beg you to promote the entire staff.

(Signed) W. R. HEARST

One hundred and thirty thousand copies of the paper were printed, and more than ten thousand dollars were raised for the Little Jim Fund. Soon the home for incurable children became a reality. The hospital was dedicated December 21, 1895, but Hearst himself was not present. For years he avoided all public occasions on which he might be asked to make a speech. Especially was he reluctant to be present while speeches were being made in which he knew he would be the object of adulation. On the day of the presentation of the Little Jim Hospital Hearst was riding over the hills in Mendocino County with George Pancoast.

Annie Laurie continued with her humane work. Dramatically she pretended to faint in the streets of San Francisco. She was carried to the receiving hospital. She wrote her experiences of the treatment accorded her. The result was a new ambulance for the city. She went to Del Monte and described a pigeon-shooting match. She said that fashionable women of the day glorying in the death of pigeons, were not far removed from women of Roman society watching combats of gladiators. She was the first woman to report a prize-fight. By a ruse she interviewed President Harrison, boarding his train in Nevada. The President was as aloof to the press as an iceberg, but she succeeded in entering the car.

Annie Laurie was the first woman to interview a President except Ann Royal, mother of personal journalism in the United States. Ann owned a newspaper in Washington, D. C., and she found out that President John Quincy Adams early every morning swam in the Potomac River in a state of nature. One morning Ann Royal lay in wait for the President, seized his clothes lying on the bank, and while he was swimming asked him questions. She told him he should not have his clothing until he replied. Ann Royal "scooped" not only the United States, but all history.

Annie Laurie was as resourceful and daring as Ann Royal. She went to Utah, lived with Mormon wives and obtained their story. Mormon women said they would like to see Brigham Young in Congress. Annie Laurie's investigations aided the campaign against Mormonism.

At the suggestion of Hearst, Annie Laurie went with Sister Rose Gertrude to Molokai and lived with the lepers for whom the saintly Father Damien gave his life. On her return from Molokai she stopped at Honolulu and interviewed King Kalakaua. During the silver campaign she traveled with the William Jennings Bryans, visited hundreds of small towns in America, and learned to know the American people, North, South, East and West. During these more than forty years since Annie Laurie began to work for Hearst, when anything of special importance was to be done, a task requiring feeling and courage, he has always asked her coöperation. She is one of his closest friends.

In the early days of his journalistic career Hearst established an *Examiner* Bureau of Claims in Washington. This organization protected the Indians against whom depredations had been going on for more than fifty years with immense destruction of property and loss of life. Soldiers had also been victimized by agents. Through the *Examiner* Hearst offered to secure pensions for soldiers of the Rebellion free of charge. If a soldier had served in the war ninety days and had been disabled for any cause, he had only to apply to the *Examiner* Bureau of Claims. Pensions for widows and children were procured without regard to the cause of the soldier's death. Pensions for fathers and mothers were also obtained. The same bureau procured patents, but no charges were made unless the patent was obtained.

In his enthusiasm for the success of his paper Hearst sometimes did the work of a reporter. Sam Ewing, one of the best newsgatherers in the United States, tells how after he himself failed to obtain advance plans for Stanford University, Hearst would not give up. The proprietor went with Ewing to Senator Stanford, procured the plans of Stanford University and "scooped" his competitors.

After Hearst had owned the *Examiner* three years, through his own resourcefulness the paper obtained one of the most important "scoops" in the history of journalism. The McKinley Tariff Bill was to be introduced in Congress. Congressman Joseph McKenna, later Justice McKenna of the United States Supreme Court, was chairman of the Congressional Tariff Committee. The public was most eager to know about the McKinley Tariff Bill because it would mean drastic changes in business. It occurred to the young journalist that here was an opportunity to get a big "scoop." Hearst was in Washington, the guest of his parents, and he called on Congressman McKenna. The Congressman was pleased to see the California journalist. What could he do for him? The boyish-looking editor didn't want much—only an exclusive copy of the McKinley Tariff Bill for his newspaper. The Congressman was stupefied. What an incredible request! The young man argued gently, but persuasively in the voice described by Bierce as the "fragrance of violets made audible."

As a result Hearst sent to the *Examiner* from Washington the longest telegram which up to that time had ever gone over the wires, the complete McKinley Tariff Bill. It was published in small type, and was a three-page "scoop." The *Examiner* made it public ahead of the Associated Press. The local papers did not understand, nor did the Associated Press. They thought it not authentic, but after two days the Associated Press awoke and published the McKinley Tariff Bill.

The proprietor-reporter felt encouraged. After this "scoop" he wouldn't have hesitated to ask his father for a few thousand more to meet his losses. Only that wasn't necessary. The

Examiner "red" ink had been deepened into maroon, and finally turned into black.

The happiest person in the world was not William Randolph Hearst, but his father, Senator George Hearst. Quietly the Senator exulted in his son's success. Although he himself had been able to make fifteen millions in fifteen years from mines and real estate, so long as he owned the *Examiner* it lost money. Then along came the twenty-three year old Harvard student, Will Hearst, who had never done anything but spend money, and in three years he had made a losing newspaper pay large dividends. Will's success brought back to Senator Hearst the memory of the time when he had bought the Anaconda as a silver-mine, and it turned out to be the greatest copper mine in the world.

CHAPTER XVI

DEATH OF SENATOR HEARST

WHEN William Randolph Hearst gives his attention to a subject for the moment his mind is closed to all else. Lightning decisions are made by him, and he is at the telephone or in the telegraph office. His varied interests have saved him from having a one-track mind.

Hearst has always been fond of animals. In his boyhood he had two dogs, Cæsar and Pompey. His collection of animals grew until to-day at San Simeon he is the greatest non-commercial owner of animals in the world. A statesman or celebrity may bore him, but his face lights up with tenderness when a young spotted deer breaks away from her herd as Bessie does, and at sunset clatters up the tiled terraces of San Simeon. When Diana, the seal, came into port at San Simeon, waddled up to the warehouses and decided to adopt the ranch as her home, Hearst was as pleased as if a distinguished visitor had arrived from Mars. For the moment he abandoned national and international interests, and set his mind to work on Diana's future. By telephone he ordered a shelter to be made for her so that daily she might be fed fresh fish, and at the same time have a daily plunge in the Pacific. Soon Diana became so tame that she tried to live in the house of her keeper.

Once at San Simeon, Hearst kept ambassadors waiting an hour for dinner. He had been sitting with a dying dog. When an animal on the ranch dies, Hearst is so depressed that those close to him have learned not to discuss it.

In the early *Examiner* days on one occasion Hearst ordered his motor-boat, *Aquila*, to bring a veterinarian from San Francisco to Sausalito to set a guinea-pig's broken leg. When Walter

Howey was editor of the Chicago *Herald and Examiner* he received a telegram from Dodge City, signed W. R. Hearst. The publisher was on his way from New York to California with his son William Randolph, Jr., who was ten years old. The telegram said: "In a box-car near a water tank about a mile west of Kansas City is a bawling, black and white spotted calf. Bill wants the darned thing." Howey had the Kansas City correspondent of the *Herald and Examiner* buy the calf. It was consigned to the Hacienda of Mrs. Phebe Hearst. After a long contented life on the hills of San Simeon the animal died.

One of Hearst's former publishers, Charles Edward Russell, says that when he was driving through the country near Rome with Hearst they came upon a peasant beating an overburdened horse. Hearst got out of the carriage, seized the man's whip and said, "If you strike that horse again, I'll beat you." For a long distance Hearst watched the man and then went into Rome. He reported the case to the Society for the Prevention of Cruelty to Animals and left a check for two hundred dollars.

George Pancoast recalls Hearst's devotion to two baby brown bears at the Mid-Winter Fair in 1893. Hearst bought them and asked Pancoast to take them over to the first country home ever owned by him, a stock farm begun by his father across San Francisco Bay near Pleasanton.

Pancoast engaged an express wagon, and with much trepidation and considerable difficulty succeeded in transporting the baby bears to Pleasanton where they were housed in a spacious stockade built around an oak tree. Hearst called the property, "El Rancho del Oso."

A. C. Schweinfurth, the architect, transformed the comfortable old-fashioned ranch-house into a pleasant modern country home where in the early nineties Hearst spent weekends with Eugene Lent, Sam Chamberlain, Ned Hamilton, Petey Bigelow, or "Cozy" Noble.

"El Rancho del Oso" did not long bear that name. In 1892,

while in Europe, Hearst and Pancoast passed a courtyard in Verona, Italy. Hearst peered into the romantic spot and exclaimed to Pancoast, "Look at that well!"

In the center of the courtyard was a beautiful well-head with long iron runways extending to the iron balconies on the second story so that housewives could draw their buckets up the runways to the balcony. Hearst bought the well-head which weighed five or six tons and carted it from Verona to the sea. Several months later it was landed in San Francisco and was installed in the garden of the Pleasanton ranch.

After Hearst took up his residence in New York, Mrs. Phebe Hearst moved to "El Rancho del Oso." She made many improvements and enlargements in the buildings, and changed the name of the ranch to "La Hacienda del Pozo de la Verona."

Hearst's love of animals took many forms of expression. Even in those swirling, rushing days when he remained up till sunrise to establish the *Examiner* on a paying basis he could hardly tear himself away from a visiting circus. Frequently he took members of his staff to look at parrots and cockatoos at Warner's at North Beach. He delighted in feeding fruit to the birds and peanuts to the monkeys.

Hearst contributed the first wild animal to Golden Gate Park. In 1889, he was talking with Allen Kelly, a member of the *Examiner* staff, a plainsman and a friend of animals. An argument rose in the editorial room as to whether the grizzly bear was extinct in the valleys of California. Hearst did not think it was, nor did Kelly. The plainsman made a bet that he could find a grizzly bear in the valleys. He set out to win his wager.

Two months passed before Kelly returned, but he brought back a grizzly bear captured in the valley of San Bernardino. It was named "Monarch" and given a home in Golden Gate Park. A handsome mate from the mountains was obtained for Monarch and the pair had two cubs. Mr. and Mrs. Monarch and the little Monarchs, playing like clumsy puppies, were a petted, indulged bear family. Almost as free as in the forest they lived in a spacious pit. In his sheltered home Monarch later developed cancer, and there was nothing for Keeper Onimus to do, but shoot him. The Monarch had been so affectionately cared for that he did not understand danger when his keeper lifted his gun to take aim. Whatever his friend did was right. Monarch swayed, reeled, quietly covered his face with his great paws and died.

When Hearst had owned the *Examiner* only two years he published editorials several times a month trying to convince the Park Commissioners that a zoölogical garden should be established in Golden Gate Park. Already there was a nucleus for such a garden—bear, pigeons and deer. "The best thing would be to begin deliberately to create a zoölogical garden that would rank with any in the world. The schools could send their classes to it in charge of teachers to gain practical knowledge of natural history."

"It would cost about seventy-five thousand dollars," he wrote. When the Golden Gate Zoölogical Garden was established many years later it cost seventy thousand dollars.

Hearst not only advocated a zoölogical garden for Golden Gate Park, but he urged the establishment of an aviary and an aquarium. Playgrounds in the park should be made accessible to all children. Shortly after Superintendent John McLaren arrived to take charge of Golden Gate Park, the first children's playground in the United States was established.

Development of Golden Gate Park was especially difficult because it was necessary to reclaim the sand dunes foot by foot. Before the era of automobiles the refuse of animals was invaluable in enriching the sand where nothing would grow except a limited number of native sand-plants. The *Examiner* supported the measure which ordered street sweepings deposited on unreclaimed ground.

About this same time Hearst learned of vandalism in the Yosemite Valley. Trees were being lawlessly destroyed. Hearst succeeded in having new commissioners appointed over the valley, and Nature's great cathedral was protected. Later Congress withdrew the Big Tree grove of Tulare from the Public Lands area and immensely extended the boundaries of the Yosemite.

Hearst then began a movement that was the beginning of his forty years' battle for good roads in California and throughout the United States. He urged that the San Francisco supervisors replace cobblestones in the streets with noiseless asphalt, the only material recognized by the East and Europe as suitable for modern pavements. There was much graft in handling the cobblestones and the Supervisors long refused to use asphalt. They insisted on streets paved with stones destructive to wheels and ruinous to animals' feet. After months of resistance the Supervisors agreed to pave Kearny Street with a bituminous rock which made a smooth, noiseless street.

Forty years ago Hearst in an *Examiner* editorial pointed out that preparations should be made for good roads for automobiles. The occasion was the race of horseless carriages for four thousand dollar prizes given by the Chicago *Times Herald*. Hearst wrote:

It will be a small affair in point of endurance compared with the great Paris-Bordeaux competition that suggested it, as the course will cover only the forty miles from Chicago to Waukegan, but as a first important test of automobile carriages in America it has immense significance.... Any sort of contrivance on three or four wheels and propelled entirely by gasoline, petroleum, electricity or steam is eligible. The horseless carriage should be welcomed as a reinforcement of perhaps decisive importance in a battle that has raged with varying fortunes for a hundred years—the contest for good roads.

At first Hearst's advocacy of good roads met with opposition. The new vehicles were called a rich man's hobby. Later they became the poor man's necessity. Wherever Hearst acquired a paper he demanded good roads, and this policy is one widely appreciated. Automobiles have taken millions of shutins, men and women, from their homes, given them fresh air, shown them beautiful scenery, widened their world. Especially is this true in California. There are so many automobiles that the entire population can take to the road and live in their machines.

In all his efforts to better conditions in San Francisco Hearst was opposed by Chris Buckley, the blind boss, who used to walk San Francisco streets led by a guide, seeing nothing, and yet in his world of darkness knowing and controlling everything in the city's political world. Buckley was slow, cunning, corrupt. In the first years of Hearst's activity the *Examiner* declared that Buckley must go. The boss was indicted and he fled. With him went most of his followers. They remained in Canada three years. On their return a meeting was called at the Metropolitan Temple to protest against restoration of Buckley rule.

"When Chris Buckley," said the *Examiner*, "was driven from San Francisco three years ago by an honest Grand Jury backed by an aroused public opinion, he intimated that the clouds would roll by, and he would be back as safe and free as ever. He had the gift of prophecy. He's here again, and out of jail."

Thousands attended the mass meeting of protest against Buckley held January 5, 1892. At that time, in his early thirties, James D. Phelan was elected chairman of this meeting which was the beginning of his political life. Later he served several terms as a distinguished Mayor of San Francisco, and finally he went to the United States Senate. When the meeting was over Buckley entered political darkness as black as the world of his sightless eyes.

In this struggle to improve conditions in San Francisco Hearst was aided by a great cartoonist, Homer Davenport, who drifted into the *Examiner* officer, a gangly youth from Oregon. At first Davenport's genius was unrecognized. His opportunity came when a famous horse died. There was no picture of the animal in the *Examiner* office. Davenport loved horses, and he had seen the animal one year before. He drew the horse from memory. The owner was so pleased that he bought the picture. Hearst recognized that he had found by accident the man that he had been looking for. Davenport began by cartooning Buckley and the local Republican boss, Dan Burns. Later he cartooned C. P. Huntington, Mark Hanna, McKinley and the G. O. P. elephant. Sometimes his cartoons were given more conspicuous place than political articles. A cartoon of Sam Rainey, a political boss, occupied the entire front page of the *Examiner*.

"We know too much to do such things now," said Hearst recently with a smile, "but such things were what made the paper."

Many of the *Examiner* reporters were conspicuous for their daring. Allen Kelly appeared in a gallant exploit in January, 1890. The crew of the seabound tug *Monarch* heard cries of distress and saw a half-naked man clinging to a low, storm-scourged rock near Point Bonita outside the Golden Gate. The matter was reported to the government life-saving station, but the life-savers could not launch their boat. Hearst read of the man's tragic plight and he exclaimed, "Won't some one go to that man's rescue?"

Allen Kelly and H. R. Haxton volunteered. "Take my motor-boat, the *Aquila*," urged Hearst.

The two reporters in the *Aquila* battled their way to Point Bonita. Haxton dove into the lashing sea, carried the line to the rock and brought the half-dead fisherman, Antone Nicolas, safely to land. For this impromptu life-saving the societies of fishermen passed resolutions of thanks for the splendid work of Haxton and Kelly after the live-saving service of the United States had failed.

About this time Haxton again risked his life in order to improve the life-saving service of the Oakland ferry-boats. He fell overboard from an Oakland ferry-boat and exposed the slowness of rescue. From this time there were more life-boats and life-preservers on Oakland ferries. Boat drills were speeded up and travelers on the overcrowded boats were protected from disaster.

J. H. Bromage ventured his life in exposing the activities of the *Montserrat*, a sailing vessel that was dealing in slaves. Bromage shipped to the South Seas on the *Montserrat*, saw the captain entice several hundred islanders from their homes, take them by force to Guatemala and deliver them in suffering hordes to work in the sugar-fields. The *Examiner* made a campaign against "black-birding" steamers.

In the early nineties Sontag and Evans, train robbers and slayers of three men, entrenched themselves in the fastnesses of Fresno mountains. Frank Norris pointed out in his novel, *The Octopus*, that Sontag and Evans held up a train near Clovis after having been evicted by the Southern Pacific Railroad Company with other settlers from land upon which they had been invited by the Government to make their homes. Burning for revenge Evans took to the road. Sontag joined him. They committed robbery after robbery.

Huge rewards were offered for their apprehension. Sheriffs, detectives and posses were on the trail of the outlaws. An *Examiner* reporter, Henry D. (Petey) Bigelow, followed the bandits to their hiding place. Flag of truce in hand he approached, interviewed them, and returned to San Francisco with a story that thrilled California.

Senator George Hearst delighted more in these triumphs of his son than ever he had in his own triumphs. He told his friends that the *Examiner* had fifty-seven thousand, three hundred and eighty subscribers. Then after serving four years of his elected term in the United States Senate, on March 1, 1891, life ceased for George Hearst. For the first time Will Hearst was stricken with grief, deep and poignant, unlike any other, the grief that comes from parting from a beloved parent. He was at his father's side in Washington at the end.

Covered with flags and flowers, George Hearst went home with his family for the last time to the city of many hills on the western sea. High officials also were on that journey, but the widow and son felt utterly alone.

Gold had come to George Hearst like a river, and it was his

happiness to let it flow from him like a river renewing his friends' lives. Some persons give for conspicuous display. Others from a sense of duty. Others are listening to Divine command. Tolstoy gave because he was a great gentleman, and he said it was impolite not to share his possessions. George Hearst had known poverty, hardships and suffering. Through experience his spirit had grown until his greatest pleasure was to lessen the poverty, hardship and suffering for both the worthy and the unworthy. One of the most pleasant memories of William Randolph Hearst is that of seeing his father and mother seated together evening after evening answering letters and enclosing checks in response to requests for aid.

Nor were George Hearst's benefactions entirely of gold. Tears streamed down the cheeks of aged men when the train brought the miner back to those who had been heartened by his pleasant smile, warm handclasp and encouraging words. Alone, obscure, George Hearst, the pioneer, had first come to San Francisco bringing specimens of the Ophir mine on the Comstock Lode, the richest silver-mine the world had ever seen. Now famous, he returned to friends who sorrowed for the loss of the gold in the heart of this miner-Senator.

Later William Randolph Hearst wrote to his mother:

I want to say when I spoke against my father going into politics I was very young and very foolish. There is nothing that I am prouder of to-day than my father's record as Senator and of the high esteem in which he is held and still remembered by men high in place of the nation. That record and that opportunity to show the whole people his fine character is the greatest thing of the many good things he bequeathed us. George Hearst, Senator, is better known and wider known than George Hearst, miner. We share the advantage of that, and I am proud of it and glad to-day that he went into the service of the nation.

To his widow, Phebe Apperson Hearst, George Hearst left his entire fortune, eighteen millions. Already his son owned the Babicora ranch in Mexico, and the highly profitable *Examiner*. Phebe Hearst long afterwards wrote William Randolph Hearst that she had made him her sole heir, and he replied in a letter:

My father never did a better thing than when he made the will he did. I have admired him for it and have been happy to concur in it, and I have never told you how many times I have been advised by fools and scoundrels otherwise. That is the kind of thing for our own kind of people, and I hope to so live that you will have as much confidence in me as my father had in you. I hope too that I will never live to read your will, and that you will live as long as I do and that we both shall be as happy as I am now.

Affectionately and gratefully,

WILL

CHAPTER XVII

FIGHTING THE FUNDING BILL

AS early as 1893, Hearst followed the great art sales of the world. At thirty he was known to dealers as an enthusiastic and judicious collector of art objects. He was advised of the approaching art sale of the great Spitzer collection in Paris, one of the most valuable ever assembled. National museums were allowed by their directors large sums to spend in enriching their galleries from the Spitzer collection. Hearst tore himself away from the *Examiner* and arrived in Paris in time to inspect the treasures before the date set for the auction.

Soon after his arrival in Paris the British Museum asked for a postponement of the auction sale, in order to raise additional sums for purchasing. The time of the sale was extended three months. This delay was too long for Hearst. He could not remain away from his absorbing *Examiner*. So he employed a French agent who understood art to make the purchases.

With the commissionaire Hearst inspected pieces of Tanagra in which he was most interested, naming the highest price to be offered. Then the publisher left for home.

On board ship he became fearful lest his orders might be misunderstood, and so he wrote a detailed letter to the commissionaire closing with, "Of course, I don't want any of the darned old things which will run up to fabulous prices."

The Spitzer sale was held, and in the art world it was of such great importance that a full account of it was cabled to the New York *Sun* and telegraphed to Hearst in San Francisco. Eagerly the young publisher looked at the news columns to see if the commissionaire had obtained for him the Tanagra statuettes that he had ordered.

Hearst was in dismay. The statuettes had been sold, not to

him, and the price paid was less than the one he authorized. Hearst cabled his representative immediately, "Why did you not buy the Tanagras?"

Back came the answer by cable, "Followed instructions explicitly. Am writing."

Hearst recalled those terra-cotta statuettes—so beautiful that they had been placed by the Greeks in the graves of those they most loved. How dull of the French commissionaire to overlook those statuettes showing the daily life of the Greek women. Impatiently Hearst awaited the explanation of the French commissionaire:

In your letter of instructions written from the steamer you said, "I don't want any of the darned old things which will run up to fabulous prices." I did not comprehend the meaning of "darned," but I looked it up in the dictionary and found that it meant *repaired*. All of the Tanagras had been repaired or restored. They date from the third century, B.C.

Hearst realized the danger of using slang with a foreigner.

His mind turned swiftly from art collections to the *Examiner*. The paper had outgrown its plant on Mission Street, and in 1894, he bought one of the most central corners in San Francisco at Third and Market Streets. Specifications for the new building were given to his architect, A. C. Schweinfurth. The publisher desired to have not only the most modern building, but so to arrange its construction that public school children of the higher grades could be shown the actual process of making a newspaper. A lecturer would explain each motion of the production while the children looked down from one end of the U-shaped mezzanine on the top floor.

First was visible the linotype operator taking the "copy." The lecturer showed the children by matrix, assembly bar and molds, how the characters were released, and the machine automatically cast the metal line. Next came proof-printing of those lines, together with the hand-set heads and the sending of copy and proofs to proof-readers. Page make-up tables were in the center of the U-balcony. The children saw how corrections were made, and material passed to the make-up tables.

Starting from the other end of the balcony, the illustration copy was turned over to the photo-engraver. He set up and photographed this copy. In a dark-room directly under the balcony the negative was developed. Through a yellow glass transom the pupils could see the plate assume form. The negative was then put in contact with a sensitized sheet of zinc, printing the design on the metal. This design was powdered with a resinous substance, which when heated became acid-proof, so that, emerged and agitated in nitric acid, the unprotected zinc portion was eaten away. This left the design in relief making a printing surface.

These operations brought the art product back to meet the type at the page assembled. Here the column rules, linotype and cuts were made into page form and locked in a frame. In those days wet mats prepared by pasting together sheets of blotting paper and tissue paper, were placed in their damp condition on the face of the form and subjected to heavy pressure under a roller. Then they were baked on a steam table. This produced a papier-mâché impression of the form.

This "mat" was the focal point of newspaper production combining all the efforts of the editorial, art and advertising departments, so that at this point a school-boy could carry an entire edition of a forty-page paper under his arm. Realizing this Hearst decided, for the first time on record, to split the stereotyping plant, doing the molding in the composing-room and the casting in another room adjoining the press-room.

When the "mat" was finished it was dropped in a chute in the elevator shaft to the casting-room in the basement. The pupils went down in an elevator to a balcony in the basement from which they saw the "mat" put into a curved casting box. They watched hot metal poured in to make curved plates to fit the press cylinders. From this balcony were seen the running presses and the delivery-room.

In unbroken sequence, the mechanical construction of a

paper from "copy" to the street was shown. This progressive routine of the paper resulted in the first "straight line" newspaper plant. Since that time the principle has not been deviated from in any Hearst plant, regardless of physical obstacles. Hearst has carefully studied all plans of new buildings to be certain that "straight line" production was assured. Other publishers have attempted "straight line" production but have seldom realized it.

The publisher always kept in touch with inventions in the mechanical part of his paper. In 1895, Hearst brought to the *Examiner* fifteen linotype machines. In introducing these typesetting machines he promised that no man should lose his position because of the inventions. At his own expense he would give every man an opportunity to learn the linotype. If any workman should prove unable to master the machine, Hearst promised to shift him from text-setting to another position. He predicted that the new machines would increase and not lessen employment. He said that the publisher would be able to give the public more pages for the same sales price. This prediction was an understatement of the increased work that would come to the men as the result of the linotype. In 1895, an eight-page paper was an exception, but of late years the New York *Journal* has frequently printed sixty-four pages.

Although Hearst had potential control of his mother's fortune, he continued advocating the income tax, 2 per cent on all incomes in excess of four thousand dollars a year. Soon after the death of his father he began campaigning for election of United States Senators by direct vote of the people. During a period when a seat in the United States Senate usually cost the holder a large sum, Senator Hearst's selection was free from scandal, but William Randolph Hearst understood the abuses in the election of United States Senators. In his paper he called the Senate, "the House of Lords of the Trusts." Championship of the income tax and election of United States Senators by direct vote of the people was the beginning of Hearst's unpopularity among high financiers. In that day

"Socialist" was anathema, but Hearst heard it applied to him. Then he learned to close his ears and smile as he does to-day when unpleasant comments are flung at him.

Not until 1898, did the House of Representatives pass the Corless Resolution providing for the popular election of United States Senators. In 1903, Hearst charged that Senators were keeping the resolution asleep in committees. For years the Senate prevented a vote being taken by refusing to have the resolution reported out. When it was brought up it was "talked to death." "The Old Guard," led by Senators Root, Depew, Aldrich and Bailey, was always able to defeat efforts to bring about further consideration of the resolution.

In 1911, Hearst addressed members of forty legislatures in session, saying that the people demanded the election of United States Senators by direct vote. Ten years later, after a campaign of twenty-one years, the battle was won and the Constitution of the United States was amended for the seventeenth time.

Hearst's agitation for a new charter for San Francisco crystallized in 1899, when fifteen freeholders were selected to draft a charter calling for the commission form of government. The Mayor had power to appoint all commissioners, making them responsive to him. It was by far the best charter ever proposed to the voters of San Francisco. Into the campaign came several new Democratic political forces, James D. Phelan, the millionaire with a taste for art and letters; Franklin K. Lane, later Secretary of the Interior under President Wilson; and Gavin McNab, long a political leader. Two years after Phelan was elected Mayor, the new charter was adopted.

Hearst early became interested in government ownership of public utilities. The Geary Street Railway franchise, granted in 1878, was to expire November 6, 1903. In 1896, the company tried to extend its franchise another fifty years. Why was there such a hurry for extension of the franchise, asked Hearst in open-eyed wonder. All was clarified—the franchise expired in

1903, but the company's bonds ran until 1921. The franchise must be renewed to protect the bondholders.

Hearst remarked in the *Examiner*, "It is probable that by 1903, the people of San Francisco will be buying up franchises, instead of selling or giving them away."

He pointed out that the new charter soon to be voted on, provided for the acquisition of street railways by the city whenever the people should so determine. The *Examiner* admonished the supervisors, "Do not extend the franchise."

The Geary Street Railway officials were horrified. In their own press they asked, "Do San Francisco people wish to have railroads run by politicians? The city will lose money if they go into business."

Hearst replied that San Francisco possessed sufficient intelligence to operate a street-car line for public interests. The battle went on with Mayor James D. Phelan in command of the field.

In November, 1903, the Geary Street franchise reverted to the city. Hearst in the *Examiner* continued to advocate the city taking over and operating the Geary Street Railway as a municipal enterprise. On May 2, 1905, the supervisors voted three hundred and fifty thousand dollars for the project, but suddenly twelve savings-banks lined up against the Geary Street appropriation. In a suit they united to have the item for the construction of the railroad stricken from the budget. A majority of the voters several times cast their ballots to build the road, but years passed before the necessary two-thirds vote was obtained.

Eventually the railway defeated itself by refusing to extend its lines into outlying districts. This arrogance was resented by small home-owners. Indignation culminated when the United Railways refused to give adequate service for the Panama-Pacific Exposition planned for 1915.

On December 30, 1909, the people voted to take over the Geary Street Road and spend two million dollars for improvements. In 1912, for the first time a great American city had the proud opportunity to ride on their own street-cars. Mayor Rolph took the first car over the Geary line. Hearst in the *Examiner* rejoiced over the victorious end of the fourteen-year battle.

San Francisco has a railway system worth ten millions with only three millions of bonds outstanding. Seven millions represent the profits of the railroad, and they have been used in amortizing the bonding debt and in building extensions. The railroad gives excellent service, and has developed the Richmond, Park, Presidio and Marina districts as well as much of Sunset, and all districts lying west of Twin Peaks. It is said that one hundred million dollars have been added to the assessed value of these districts.

Street-car fares began increasing in the United States in 1918, but the San Francisco municipally owned railway has maintained a five-cent fare. Its two privately owned competitors have been obliged to keep their rates at five cents. Had it not been for the long struggle led by Hearst, to-day the Geary Street line would be a part of the street railway monopoly.

The influence of the municipally owned Geary Street Railroad has extended into the nation. Seattle, Detroit and New York own and operate some of their street railways and subways.

During Hearst's first year in journalism he began a struggle that led to Washington. It was to force the Southern Pacific Railroad to pay its debt of twenty-seven millions, and five hundred thousand dollars due in 1900 to the Federal Government.

"We can pay neither interest nor principal," said the Southern Pacific.

In 1887, the Pacific Railroad Commission was appointed to inquire into the condition of the company and discover what use was being made of its income. The commission held its first session in San Francisco. On the witness stand C. P. Huntington, an unlettered realist, revealed one source of his sinister power over Congress. After much dodging and twisting Huntington admitted that he had spent in Washington, for which he had no adequate vouchers, five million, four hundred and ninety-seven thousand, five hundred and thirty-nine dollars. But he had no money to pay the interest to the Government for money advanced to the railroad.

In the famous Colton letters written by Huntington to one of his partners he revealed his methods and also the sort of men he dealt with in Washington. Congress was called, "the hungriest set of men who ever got together. . . . The devil only knows what they will do." Congressman Luttrell was called a "wild hog." "Don't let him come back to Washington, Colton. Beat him anyway. If he gets the nomination, put up another Democrat to run against him, and in that way elect a Republican. Beat him." Something or somebody changed Luttrell. In six months Huntington wrote to Colton:

Write a letter to Luttrell saying I say he is doing first rate, and is very able, etc. Send me a copy. . . . I believe with two hundred thousand we can pass our bill. All the members in the House from California are doing first rate except Piper, and he is a damned hog. The city of San Francisco shouldn't send a scavenger like him back to Congress. Anyway, we can fix him.

The Sacramento *Union* hurts us very much by abusing our best friends, Roscoe Conkling and [Senator] Stewart. . . . If I owned the paper I'd control it or burn it. Is it not possible to control the agent of the Associated Press in San Francisco? The matters that hurt the C. P. and S. P. most are dispatches that come back from San Francisco.

Huntington revealed great contempt for Supreme Court Justices. "They're sure to do their worst, but my better judgment tells me to take the scamps into camp."

Apparently Congress was insatiable in its demands. Huntington wrote, "Congress will try to pass some kind of a bill to make us commence paying them what we owe the Government. . . . Every year the fight grows more and more expensive. Matters never looked worse in Washington than they do at this time. It seems as though all the strikers [grafters] in the world were there. . . . The boys are very hungry, but it will cost considerable to be saved."

After listening to these many interesting activities, the Pacific Railroad Commission glossed over the offenses of the railroad. Governor Pattison in a minority report urged the Government to forfeit the Southern Pacific Railway's Charter because of fraud and dishonesty. Although the Pacific Railroad Commission failed in its purpose, its revelations furnished material for Hearst's crusade.

The Southern Pacific Company dominated the affairs of ten states and territories. Huntington fixed the freight rate as "all the traffic will bear." The four rulers of the Southern Pacific, Huntington, Stanford, Crocker and Hopkins, held absolute control of the western highways, and out of them had made vast fortunes and had established a railroad empire. In 1890, Hearst took up the lance against the consolidation of the Union Pacific, Southern Pacific, Atchison, and Missouri Pacific, which would have placed about thirty thousand miles of road under a single management and destroyed all hope of the Atchison entering San Francisco with possible relief from the exactions of the Southern Pacific.

In an effort to emancipate California from the Southern Pacific, Hearst supported the People's Railroad which was begun in 1893 by Claus Spreckels. It extended two hundred and thirty miles from Stockton to Bakersfield, and was built at an expense of four million and six hundred thousand dollars. Hearst bought a considerable block of stock himself. The *Examiner* ran a special train through the San Joaquin Valley to gather subscriptions for the new railroad. Hearst matched each ten thousand dollars paid by popular subscription with ten thousand from the *Examiner*. The railroad was built with great enthusiasm, but it was afterwards sold by Claus Spreckels to the Southern Pacific.

In the same year that the People's Railroad was begun, Hearst took up the cause of settlers who had been invited by the United States Government to settle on public lands, but were later evicted as the result of a decision by Federal Judge Erskine Ross, who said that the land must be paid for a second time to the Southern Pacific. Hearst pointed out in editorials that the settlers were more important to the railroad than the railroad was to them. The Southern Pacific was urged to do the fair thing.

For seven years Hearst insisted that the twenty-seven million dollars due from the Southern Pacific Railroad in 1900 to the Federal Government should be paid, but the company refused to meet even semi-annual interest. They obtained from the United States Supreme Court a decision that they might not meet the interest until they paid the principal. This decision obliged the United States to advance the semi-annual interest from the Treasury and charge it to the company. The debt had run up to the very handsome sum of sixty millions.

C. P. Huntington always contributed munificently to the Republican campaign fund, and he formulated a bill that would postpone the payment of the trifling sixty millions to the nebulous nevermore. It was called the Pacific Railroad Funding Bill. Huntington was determined that it should be jammed through Congress. Hearst was equally determined to stop it. He employed Homer Davenport, with his Hogarthian genius as a cartoonist, and Ambrose Bierce, the satirist. From his office Hearst directed the battle.

Bierce penned the biting words:

The worst railroads in the world are in America. The worst railroads in America are in the West. The worst railroads in the West are on the Pacific slope. The worst railroads on the Pacific slope are operated by the Southern Pacific. The worst railroad operated by the Southern Pacific is the Central Pacific. It owes this Government more millions of dollars than Leland Stanford has vanities. It will pay fewer cents than Collis P. Huntington has virtues.

Hearst caused to be circulated a petition to the Senate and House of Representatives for the acquisition of the Central and Union Pacific Railroad by the Government. Even those not approving of government ownership of all railroads were urged to sign the petition to take over the Central and Union Pacific. "Sign the petition! Sign it now!" was the cry. Immediately fifty thousand voters signed. By August 10th, more than one hundred thousand voters added their names. This petition became a great moral and political force and stayed the progress of the bill in the House.

The *Examiner* organized a large meeting of protestants against the passage of the Pacific Railroad Funding Bill. Bierce and his colleagues labored in Washington with members of Congress from Oregon, Washington, Nevada, Idaho and Arizona. From these States more than thirty thousand signatures of protest were obtained to the petition. The Far West realized that the fight against the Funding Bill was not a matter that concerned California alone. All Western States were dependent upon the transcontinental railroad to market their products. The Huntington lobby was actively at work in Washington on members of Congress with plausible arguments and "figures that lied."

Governor James H. Budd of California stated that he would treat the railroad indebtedness as he would that of an individual, . . . "In case the same cannot be paid I will have the government take possession of the roads by foreclosure and operate them."

Huntington caused many telegrams to be sent to Washington by San Franciscans supporting the Funding Bill, but they were of no avail. In the language of Bierce, Congress decided that, "It is not expedient to give a man one hundred years to pay a debt, the past consideration being that already for thirty years he has been engaged in beating you out of it."

On March 28, 1896, the *Examiner* jubilated over the victory, "Ring the bells and fire the anvils! The Funding Bill is practically dead. . . . This is a time for rejoicing. The *Examiner* has had a hand in the fight. Permit us to lead in the cheering."

The Funding Bill was withdrawn and killed. Congress adopted an amendment providing for the collection of the

Pacific Railroad subsidy debts, principal and interest. California cheered. Governor James H. Budd proclaimed a public holiday, and in the name of the State sent a telegram of congratulation to Hearst.

Years later Charles Edward Russell wrote, "This may be held to be as wonderful a victory as was ever achieved by one man's pen, and also one of the most remarkable tributes to the power of persistent publicity."

CHAPTER XVIII

NEW YORK

WHEN George Hearst was thirty and living in Missouri he turned his eyes and saw an Eldorado shining beyond the mighty Sierra in the West. At thirty-two his son, William Randolph Hearst, watched the California sun rise in the East, and there beyond the Sierra he saw an Eldorado. He was still a youth, tall and slender, with a gay laughing mouth, festive clothing and a collegiate manner. Wherever pleasure was to be found there was he, in the theater, on his yacht racing with a Sausalito ferry, riding through the wilds along the coast between Monterey and San Simeon. He had the unresting energy of youth. But even those close to him did not recognize Hearst's genius in his quiet divination of the future, in his steadfast objective, in his unyielding will, in his ability to understand and do well many things, in his refusal to recognize the impossible.

With the expenditure of less than a million dollars Hearst had established the *Examiner* so solidly that it surpassed all other San Francisco newspapers. With one exception it was to give the greatest return on the original investment of any newspaper venture in the United States. Hearst alone realized that his career as an editor and publisher was only beginning.

He thought of Pulitzer in his glittering dome in Printing House Square, New York City. He knew that the owner of the *World* had come to the United States as a youngster from Hungary, not understanding a word of English. By reading newspapers gradually the immigrant lad had taught himself the new language. Although always restrained by the inhibitions of an old civilization, Pulitzer had outdistanced established New York journalists, Bennett of the *Herald* and Dana of the *Sun*.

Heredity, fortune, culture, schools, Harvard, Europe, all had contributed to the making of Hearst. Why should he not outrun the immigrant boy? Why should he not overthrow the entrenched New York bosses? Competition was the food for which Hearst fiercely hungered. Pulitzer, the bosses, the great city challenged.

Every one said Hearst was taking a risk—too great a risk. "Of course," laughed he. Therein lay the charm of his venture. Hearst came of a family, from a city, a state, from a nation of men and women who triumphed because they dared risk all. He followed his vision to the East.

How clear that vision was. For years it had haunted him, Printing House Square—to Hearst the most wonderful center in the world, in the mightiest city of modern times, New York. All the life-blood of the world flowed into Printing House Square. How the *World* dome gleamed! Hearst must build higher than that shining dome erected by Pulitzer.

In 1892, Business Manager Charles M. Palmer of the *Examiner* had been sent to Chicago and New York to interview various newspaper owners. At that time, Victor Lawson of Chicago owned the *Morning Record* and the very successful *Evening News*. He was willing to sell the *Record,* but if he should sell he insisted that he must have returned all spent by him in establishing the newspaper, about two million dollars. This was a prohibitive figure, especially in view of the fact that the paper was in "red" and further investment of a large sum would be necessary.

Then Palmer approached various newspaper owners in New York. At that time the *Times* was in a marked decline from its early history of success and profit as a leading and aggressive paper. Both its circulation and advertising were steadily decreasing. The owners named the price of one million, two hundred and fifty thousand dollars. Palmer decided that this was an excessive valuation. Clearly the amount of money needed to place the *Times* on a paying basis would have been great, since the news requirements of the metropolis were large.

Then Palmer went to the *Recorder*. This newspaper had been established by George W. Turner, formerly business manager of the New York *World,* with financial backing of James B. Duke of the American Tobacco Company and Joseph B. Knapp of the American Lithographing Company. Both were very wealthy men ambitious to control a New York newspaper. The *Recorder* never reached the point where its receipts equaled its expenditures, nor did it win a definite place among newspapers in New York. Duke and Knapp were getting tired, and were trying to withdraw their money from the newspaper business, but they demanded a fantastic sum for the *Recorder.* The negotiations of Business Manager Palmer were frustrated, and for three years Hearst made no further effort to enter the New York newspaper field.

But for three years only. In his twenties Hearst coined the phrase, "The impossible is only a little more difficult than the possible." Again the impossible appealed to Hearst.

In 1895 Business Manager Charles M. Palmer was in Europe on a long vacation. He planned to go into business for himself. Hearst met Palmer in Paris in July and suggested that the business manager go again to New York, look over the newspaper field, and see what could be done in the way of purchasing a daily paper.

Palmer preceded Hearst to New York. When Hearst arrived from Europe the business manager reported that the *Times, Recorder, Advertiser* and *Morning Journal* were for sale. None of the four papers was really desirable. Exorbitant prices were asked by owners of three of the newspapers. Hearst decided that the *Morning Journal* offered the greatest possibility. Some one objected that the *Journal* had the worst reputation of any paper in New York. Hearst's answer was, "I'll change its reputation in two days, and I'll give it the largest circulation in the city."

The *Morning Journal* had been established in 1881 by Alfred

Pulitzer, brother of Joseph Pulitzer. It began as a one-cent paper and attained considerable success, for several years returning annually to its owner one hundred thousand dollars. In 1894, Alfred Pulitzer increased the price of the *Journal* to two cents, and attempted to rival his brother Joseph Pulitzer who had made a great success of the *World* after it was purchased by him from Jay Gould in 1883. The increase in the price of the *Journal* was disastrous to its circulation, which dropped from a hundred and thirty-five thousand to thirty thousand.

By this time Alfred Pulitzer had become virtually a non-resident of New York, and was floating on the shimmering stream of gay social life of European capitals. Alfred Pulitzer returned to New York a few months before Palmer appeared, and sold the *Journal* to John R. McLean, a wealthy resident of Washington, D. C., and owner of the Cincinnati *Enquirer,* a notably successful paper. In his panic-stricken eagerness to rid himself of the *Journal,* Pulitzer forgot to take out of the treasury seventy thousand dollars. McLean had spent that sum and about one hundred thousand dollars more.

McLean was politically ambitious. He had made a large fortune in his business ventures and confidently he had entered New York. He planned to introduce some of the features which made the Cincinnati *Enquirer* a valuable property, but New York did not respond to the *Enquirer* methods. After McLean had wasted a considerable sum, Charles M. Palmer called on him to inquire about the purchase of the *Journal.* McLean was glad to consider any plans to relieve him of the painful experience of writing a weekly check to obliterate his red ink.

When Palmer called, the owner of the *Journal* was occupying the August Belmont house on Fifth Avenue in the lower sixties. Hearst's representative found McLean conducting the *Journal* by telephone from the empty first-floor drawing-room furnished only with an unpainted kitchen table, three chairs to match, and a telephone. McLean was joyous but discreet, even when he saw a life-boat approaching. He showed the restraint developed by business experience. He asked Palmer to approach Hearst and request him to become an equal partner in the *Morning Journal*.

Palmer replied that Hearst had never had a tendency to share his responsibilities with others, and he considered such a request useless. McLean insisted. He explained that he had invested three hundred and sixty thousand dollars in the *Journal*, but he would be willing to sell Hearst the half interest for one hundred and eighty thousand.

Palmer repeated McLean's proposal to Hearst, and his prophecy of Hearst's reaction proved to be accurate, for the Californian answered: "Tell McLean I will give one hundred and eighty thousand dollars for the entire property."

When Palmer returned to McLean's residence he found the owner of the *Journal* closeted with United States Senator David B. Hill who retired immediately into another drawing-room while Palmer stated Hearst's offer. "One hundred and eighty thousand dollars!" gasped McLean. "Mr. Hearst means that he'll give me one hundred and eighty thousand for half the *Journal*, doesn't he?"

"I'm afraid not," answered Palmer. "Mr. Hearst will give you one hundred and eighty thousand dollars for the *Journal*."

McLean had many millions, and he enjoyed money as the musician does music. This discord of one hundred and eighty thousand dollars almost pained him to tears. One of his feet, swollen with gout and encased in thick compresses of flannel, was resting on a chair. Hearst's offer of one hundred and eighty thousand dollars gave his gouty foot an acute twinge.

In his hand McLean held one of the latest editions of that day's *Journal*. Anxiously his eye ran through its columns and estimated approximately the advertising, the lowest since he had bought the paper. To be sure it was the end of summer and the town was in the doldrums, but who could say that advertising would not keep on slumping until the merchants would almost wholly withdraw their patronage? Already McLean had learned from the business office that the circulation for the day was increasingly low. The meager advertising, the pitiful circulation, the shock of Hearst's offer, and above all, the gout, depressed McLean's morale to the vanishing point and made his discomfort unbearable. If only he could escape signing another check to cover the *Journal's* losses, he felt that his pain would be allayed and he could walk across the room without wincing.

McLean left Palmer in the front drawing-room for a few minutes while he hobbled through the folding doors to confer with his good friend and attorney, the Democratic United States Senator, David B. Hill, who was awaiting the outcome of the conference. Shortly afterwards McLean returned wearing a pained, reproachful expression. "Is that absolutely the best that Mr. Hearst can do?"

"It is," replied Palmer.

"All right, I'll accept the offer," mournfully said McLean, and the national career of William Randolph Hearst began.

This conversation occurred early in August, 1895. When Hearst heard the news from Palmer that he was owner of the New York *Journal* subject to the payment of the purchase price he was jubilant. Immediately he arranged to transfer the sum required. It was almost as great a day for Hearst as that day in 1887 when he saw his own name at the head of the *Examiner* editorial column.

Joyously Hearst went down to Park Row and walked around the triangular Printing House Square, looking up at his New York newspaper, the *Morning Journal*. Now that the paper had become his, the dingy sign and the low building at the corner of Spruce Street and Park Row seemed beautiful, even in the humid August sunshine. His eyes rested on the tall Syndicate Building opposite the Federal Building in Printing House Square. Splendid and impressive, twenty stories high, the tallest building the world had ever seen, it seemed almost to pierce the sky. Hearst looked over at the shining gilt dome of Pulitzer's *World* Building. Pulitzer called it his monument, and said that the *World* was his heart. Would that dome always gleam high in triumph? As Hearst walked around Printing House Square this City Hall Park seemed the most wonderful park in New York. The *Journal* was housed in the second and third stories of Greeley's *Tribune* Building. Hearst imagined Horace Greeley there, the boy who arrived by canal boat from western Pennsylvania with his fortune of ten dollars, and all his clothes in a bundle on his back. Across the street from the *World* was the *Sun,* the paper of Charles A. Dana, pupil of Greeley. James Gordon Bennett's *Herald* had moved uptown to Herald Square. Bennett followed the traditions of his father, who had done brilliant and daring things in journalism. The son lived on his yacht traveling from New York to Paris. He maintained his paper at three cents, and swayed the New York of the clubs, cotillions and Newport, in spite of the fact that the *Herald* had the most obscene "Personal" column ever known in decent journalism. In Printing House Square stood a figure of Benjamin Franklin, that great printer, journalist and American of more than a hundred years gone. Here in the City Hall the body of Franklin had lain in state.

In Printing House Square, Hearst read the political story of New York. He recalled that when the city had fifty-eight thousand inhabitants, here on the site of the *Tribune* Building in which his *Journal* was housed, stood the tavern of Abraham Martling, or "Brom" Martling as he was known in 1798, a sachem of Tammany Hall. In Martling's time this wigwam of Tammany was on the very outskirts of the city. Every night here gathered the Tammany braves to drink, smoke and swap yarns. Sachem "Brom" Martling built his tavern here, and at the north side in a one-story wooden shack, Tammany held its meetings after moving up from Borden's tavern in Broad Street. This wigwam of Tammany's was contemptuously styled by Hamilton and the Federalists, "The Pig Pen." What political plots were here hatched! Tammany voices still lingered in the air, although in 1818 Tammany moved over to Park Row and Frankfort Street, and later on far up to the new Tammany Hall in Fourteenth Street.

How curious and strange that after all these many years on this very spot now stood a tall slender young man, with a nonchalant manner, collegiate clothes, a bright-banded straw hat, and a habit during serious moments of taking a few absent-minded dance steps—a young man who would yet give Tammany battle. Only the very observant recognized a mind like crystal shining through his penetrating blue eyes, and that his voice, height and head were like those of Charlemagne.

At first Hearst did not make public that he had bought the *Journal,* but he paid for it October 7, 1895. Immediately he telegraphed Sam Chamberlain, Arthur McEwen, Charles Dryden, Homer Davenport and Winifred Black to come to New York. Davenport, the naïve Oregon genius, carried a carpet bag, and was greatly troubled because he had squandered twelve dollars for food on the journey. Laughingly Dryden remarked, "We had to blindfold Davvy and back him into the elevator."

With this skeleton organization from the *Examiner* Hearst took charge of the *Morning Journal.* Sam Chamberlain was managing editor. Not only did Chamberlain know New York, but he had much tact in handling men. His manners and his tailor were the best in Park Row. Editors and reporters admired his intelligence, understanding, scent for news and executive ability. In response to his considerate and friendly treatment they gave their best.

Chamberlain retained some of the *Journal* men, but he had considerable difficulty in assembling a staff to produce the kind of paper Hearst had in mind. The swift success of the San Francisco *Examiner* was well known to New York newspaper men, but Hearst was still regarded by many of the profession as a rich youth who, having made a great hubbub on the Pacific coast, was now ambitious to play with a New York newspaper. In order to obtain the best men, high salaries and long contracts were necessary. These contracts and salaries were the beginning of Hearst's unpopularity with publishers, and were probably responsible for personal attacks by competitors. Before other publishers were aware of his liberal opinions, they feared and in consequence hated him because he increased salaries. Hearst never hesitated to pay for talent, and after he came to New York to remain, the half-starved reporter with frayed collars and cuffs was changed into a decently clothed citizen. After Hearst announced his ownership of the *Morning Journal* a new scale of newspaper salaries was established.

Shortly after Hearst's advent in New York, before he officially took over the *Journal*, as a new and eligible bachelor from the West, he was entertained by many persons highly placed socially. At these dinners he was given adroit, indirect suggestions of policy for his new paper from the standpoint of fashion. The *World* was berated as a scandal sheet. This, that, and the other disgraceful article had been published by Pulitzer.

Hearst listened to what his new acquaintances said, and smiled his inscrutable smile. He did not say that he had made up his mind to have a paper as much as possible like the *World*, only he would out-*World* the *World* and out-Pulitzer Pulitzer.

Printing House Square and Park Row have not changed much since that summer in 1895, but the city itself has passed almost beyond recognition. In Printing House Square still exists the City Hall as it was when on stormy nights reporters plowed through snowdrifts six feet deep, and there still stands the Federal Building in which the downtown post-office is located. The *World* newspaper is buried, but the great glittering dome erected by Pulitzer as a monument shines on. The *Tribune* Building where the *Journal* was housed, with a few stories added, is still at the corner of Park Row and Spruce Street. The Syndicate Building of twenty-two stories, New York's skyscraper of 1895, to-day is not awe inspiring, it is almost a shack. When Hearst came the spires of Trinity Church always seemed to look down in reproach on the greed of Wall Street. Now Hamilton's tomb, the monument of the martyrs of the British prison-ships, and even the spires of

Trinity, are lost in a pocket in the shadows of towering, gray surrounding buildings.

When Hearst came in 1895, New York began at Twenty-third Street and ended at Forty-Second. Ladies who lived in the sixties considered it an all-day's journey to drive down to Fourteenth Street and shop. The Rialto was on the south side of Fourteenth, and only overadventurous damsels were said to promenade there unchaperoned.

At Thirtieth Street just off Sixth Avenue was the old half-world police station. Segregated vice was huddled into the area comprehended within that police precinct from Fourteenth Street to Forty-second, and from North River to Fifth Avenue. Protected by the police here gambling houses filled with every iniquity ran wide open and unafraid. Vice wantoned.

Fashionable hotels were the Brevoort for diplomats, and the Brunswick for millionaires. The Fifth Avenue Hotel was the meeting place for New York Republicans. Near by was the Hotel Bartholdi where prize-fight contracts were signed, and where pugilists and their managers foregathered. Above the Fifth Avenue Hotel was the Hoffman House run by Ed Stokes, the man who killed "Jubilee" Jim Fiske. Here were the headquarters of all good Democrats, and on election night Charley Mahoney, manager of the bar, was likely to have a million in bets tucked away in his safe. Delmonico's was at Twenty-sixth and Broadway running through to Fifth Avenue. Daly's Theater, Wallack's, Booth's, The Empire, The Casino, Weber & Fields, and virtually all other theaters in New York were scattered along Broadway to Forty-second Street. Shanley had opened a restaurant at Forty-second. Rector's at Forty-third and Forty-fourth streets had not come into existence.

Ward McAllister had coined the phrase "Four Hundred," and was the organizer of "elegant" cotillions where ladies and gentlemen shook hands high in the air. Young girls tried to look like the drawings of Charles Dana Gibson. Ladies sometimes wore pads on their hips to make their waists seem wasp-like. Their skirts were seven yards wide. Newport was the fashionable summer resort, and the remote Mrs. Astor was the leader of the great world. Commodore Vanderbilt was the richest man in town. Croker was political boss. Strong was Mayor.

On Broadway were cable-cars, and the Elevated on Second, Third, Sixth and Ninth Avenues took the New Yorker up-town and downtown aided by surface lines on other avenues and side streets. Four-wheelers and hansom cabs conveyed New Yorkers about town. "Hackers" were outlaws. They re-spected no legal rates. When people didn't use hacks, cabs, cable-cars or the Elevated, they bicycled. Some daring women wearing voluminous bloomers took to bicycling, as thirty-five years later their granddaughters would take to the air.

On November 8, 1895, the day following the State election, W. R. Hearst's name appeared for the first time on the edi-torial page of the *Morning Journal*. Charles M. Palmer became business manager and kept the old staff, but he looked for assistants in the advertising and mechanical departments.

In those days the fight for news supremacy in the New York newspaper offices was bitter and primitive. Reporters were al-ways at each other's throats. Men from the *World* frequently taunted the *Journal* reporters with "No one from the West lasts in New York. McLean got tired and quit. So will Hearst. You fellows better grease your shoes to walk home."

Over in the gilt dome of the New York *World* the far-sighted and shrewd publisher, S. S. Carvalho, was saying to the proprietor, "Mr. Pulitzer, this young man Hearst from Cali-fornia, I think is the first serious menace you have had since you came to New York."

"Menace!" stormed Pulitzer. "That kid! What can Hearst do? McLean was a business man. He gave it up. He knew the value of money. Hearst doesn't."

"That's precisely why Hearst is a danger," said Carvalho. "McLean knew the value of money. Hearst doesn't—that's his strength. That's why he won't quit. Don't let him get started. You should spend more money for promotion and publicity."

Success-dizzy and arrogant by nature, secure in his own supremacy, at the height of his power, Pulitzer would heed no counsel. He was surrounded by writers like Carvalho, Arthur Brisbane, Charles Edward Russell, Morrill Goddard, Farrelly, and artists like Richard Outcault and George Luks. His confidence was unshaken.

One day Hearst was introduced to Pulitzer. Had the Californian worn spectacles like Greeley, or a beard like Dana, Pulitzer might have been perturbed. Poor kid, with a straw hat banded with a blue ribbon and with self-effacing manners! Pulitzer patted him on the back. He was almost inclined to pity him.

Hearst took a bachelor apartment near the Hoffman House, joined the fashionable Union and Metropolitan clubs, and went to the theater every night. But fashion and clubs occupied a small part of his life. Each afternoon he appeared at the office, and asked the editors for the high spots of the news. Already dummy drafts of each page of the newspaper had been prepared by the editors. His invariable remark was, "Let's see the little papers."

Hearst studied the "little papers." He shuffled the stories, played down some, played up others, altered one feature, added another, selected the pictures to be used, decided where the stories should be placed, chose even the type and style of heads. Then the editors went down into the composing-room in the black bowels of the building to make up the paper.

When they were out of the way off came Hearst's coat, up went the shirt sleeves, and out came the blue pencil attacking the proof-sheets. Hearst became a shirt-sleeves' editor.

Just as the printer was locking up the pages Hearst would appear in the composing-room and mildly remark to one of the editors, "That's a fine picture on page three. I think it would be better on page one."

"It's edition time, Mr. Hearst," the editor would protest. "We must catch the mail train with this edition."

"The paper must be right. Nothing else matters," insisted Hearst.

Nothing else did matter. Every heading, picture and news article had to be placed precisely as he desired. Rumors of the way Hearst worked floated over to Pulitzer in the *World* dome. They were rather surprising, but the eminent Mr. Pulitzer buoyed himself up by repeating, "Hearst is only a kid. He'll bankrupt his mother, go broke and return to California."

Then suddenly the price of the *Morning Journal* dropped to one cent. Into the office of the *World* the news crashed like doom.

CHAPTER XIX

CONQUERING NEW YORK

THE new paper was the talk of New York. No daily published in the city had ever contained more than ten or twelve pages. New York read Hearst's *Morning Journal,* sixteen pages for one cent. It had a daily page of cable despatches from special correspondents darting all over the world.

A few weeks after Hearst was established in New York he discussed the *Journal* with Bradford Merrill, managing editor of the *World,* who was dining with him. "I don't see how it can pay," said Merrill.

"It must," answered Hearst. "Greeley made his *Tribune* pay. The first week he took in only ninety-two dollars. A newspaper that doesn't pay is either an eleemosynary tract or a subsidized organ of private interests. The more prosperous a newspaper is, if it promotes public welfare, the more power it has for good."

John T. Delane, the great editor of the London *Times,* was supercilious about news, but he concentrated on editorials. The first James Gordon Bennett almost ignored editorials, but drove hard after the news. Hearst insisted that both editorials and news were important. News presented facts, editorials awakened the conscience of the people.

Although Hearst had established a penny paper, Pulitzer still did not realize the seriousness of the California menace, not even when he saw epigrams coined by Hearst, in the streetcars, in the Elevated, on bill-boards, everywhere. One was "You can't get more than all the news. You can't pay less than one cent." Startling publicity feats, spectacular advertising and fireworks, as well as complete news service, unusual pictures and wit and humor that had built up the San Francisco

Examiner now focused the eyes of New York on the new paper, the *Journal*.

But Pulitzer showed no alarm until the *World's* circulation began to drop. Soon it tobogganed. Then in panic Pulitzer decided to reduce the price of the *World*. His explanation was, "I'd rather have power than profits." No longer did the *World* reporters taunt the *Journal* reporters with, "Better grease your shoes so you can walk back to San Francisco."

In truth, the *World's* profits each day lessened. Pulitzer began cutting the salaries of his staff and dismissing men. "By this time," said one of the staff to the writer, "the *World* men didn't care what landed on Pulitzer, so long as it was something large and heavy."

Hearst was spending money with dramatic effect, but Pulitzer economized. Occasionally Pulitzer perked up and hired a band for publicity. Hearst hired five bands. He did everything several times more spectacularly than did Pulitzer. Until Hearst came Pulitzer never sent men out of town on assignments. Now he despatched some to South Africa. So did the *Herald*. Bennett and Pulitzer tired of expense. Hearst spent more. He sent Julian Ralph to London and Charles Michelson to Cuba. Stephen Crane went to the Balkan war, then to Alaska and Venezuela. Hearst had several coffee wagons going about New York distributing coffee and sandwiches to the hungry and unemployed. If the weather was especially cold, sweaters were given away. When Hearst was called a waster, he replied, "If I save one life, that is enough." Hearst spent more and more, and Pulitzer spent less and less. In all departments of the *World* the order was, "Retrench!"

During the first few weeks the *Journal* circulation went from fifty to one hundred thousand, but Hearst did not rest. His eye was on the *World's* successful Sunday paper filled with startling novelties, racing ahead of the daily, gaining eight thousand a week. Its editor was Morrill Goddard. Hearst recognized a man with unique talent. Goddard knew how to interest every man, woman and child. He appealed to every strata of society. Hearst's Sunday editor would have liked to convince his employer that the *Journal's* Sunday paper was as interesting as the *World*. Hearst knew better.

Goddard came from Maine, a graduate of Dartmouth—1885. He had cut away from accepted news standards and published articles that made the hair of the respected Charles A. Dana of the *Sun* stand on end. After Goddard "scooped" all his rivals by trailing President Cleveland and his bride on their honeymoon at Senator Davis' country place in Maryland, he was discovered by Ballard Smith, and he became Sunday editor and the pet of Pulitzer. He had a genius for sensing what would interest New York, the newest fashionable divorce, the romance of a beautiful actress, or the birth of a baby chimpanzee. Goddard's startling fact stories were more romantic than romance.

Suddenly Hearst determined to depose his own Sunday editor and employ Goddard. This occurred when the *Sunday World* published the exclusive story of Stanford White's stag "Girl-in-the-Pie-Dinner," at which was served as dessert a huge pie carried on the shoulders of four men and placed upon the table. Out of the pie stepped nude a popular New York model. The *World* published a seven-column picture of the girl tripping out of the pie. The men attending the dinner were so well known that the story made a staggering sensation throughout America. The current French phrase of the moment to describe such a situation was *fin de siècle*, but this was *fin de globe!*

Hearst never considers a news beat annihilating. The news lasts only a day, but it is most important to employ the man responsible for the "beat." The writer or editor continues to stimulate circulation. Goddard was invited by Hearst to call on him at his apartment.

Morrill Goddard was fairly well satisfied with his position on the *World*. He was highly appreciated in the office into which as an unknown youth of nineteen from Dartmouth he had wriggled his way by the greatest self-denial, resourcefulness and persistence. But it always rankled when he heard people say that he succeeded with his Supplement because he was on the paper of the great Pulitzer. He longed for the adventure of leaving the *World* and demonstrating another success on the *Journal*. He wished to see whether he could develop the Sunday Supplement of a new paper in the making. Goddard's only fear was that Hearst would tire of his magnificent extravagance, as McLean had wearied of his paltry losses, and return to San Francisco. Should Hearst leave New York Goddard realized that he would find himself idle. When Goddard called on Hearst, the publisher asked how great an increase in salary he would expect.

"None," replied Goddard, "but if you go back to San Francisco I shall be left in the lurch. What security have I in case you decide to give up New York, as people say you are likely to do?"

Hearst smiled, fumbled in his waistcoat pocket, found a wrinkled piece of paper and tossed it over to Goddard with the remark, "Would that be sufficient security for your salary for two or three years?"

It was a Wells, Fargo draft for thirty-six thousand dollars. Goddard was amazed, but he was loyal to his assistants on the *World*. "I can't leave my staff—"

"I'd like to employ every one on your staff," answered Hearst.

And so Morrill Goddard and his entire staff, except the stenographer, went to the *Journal*. With the departure of Goddard and his staff for the *Journal* the last trace of Pulitzer's patronage of Hearst disappeared. When Hearst gave a large dinner at Delmonico's celebrating the fact that the *Journal* had passed the *World* in circulation, panic in Pulitzer's office became pandemonium.

Selection of Morrill Goddard by Hearst in 1896 was one of his wisest choices. Since that date Goddard has been the force behind Hearst's *American Weekly*. Each Sunday, thirty million people read what Goddard assembles and edits. He senses life's dramas. A mystery story never escapes him. He makes poetry of science. In his nands an archæological discovery has the beat and thrill of the cinema. More quotations are made by the *Literary Digest* from the *American Weekly* edited by Morrill Goddard than from any other publication. Goddard is one of the least conspicuous, but one of the ablest and most highly paid newspaper editors in the world. The *American Weekly* earns several millions a year.

Goddard's ability made itself felt on the *Journal's* Sunday paper, and his departure shook the foundation of the shining *World* tower. Pulitzer continued slashing salaries and dismissing men, but every day Hearst spent more and more. Carvalho, the publisher and business manager of the *World*, was already dissatisfied with Pulitzer because of what he considered unfair treatment accorded him in connection with employment on the St. Louis *Post-Despatch*. He pleaded with Pulitzer to spend. He told his employer that Hearst could think as no other editor in New York could think. Of supreme intelligence himself, Carvalho said to Pulitzer, "Hearst is one of the truly intelligent men in the United States. He knows where he is going, and he'll arrive."

Pulitzer had an unvarying reply, "He can't last. Even the Hearst fortune and the San Francisco *Examiner* can't keep him going much longer."

"He'll go a long time, and very far," answered Carvalho.

Pulitzer could not be shaken in his refusal to spend money, not even when he lost Managing Editor Farrelly of the *Evening World*. Once more Hearst reached out, and captured Rudolph Block, a star reporter, who later proved to be of great value as his art director for thirty-five years.

When Hearst had been in New York four months he decided that S. S. Carvalho, business manager and publisher of the *World*, was a man not only valuable to him, but most necessary to Pulitzer. So he sent for Carvalho. Charles Edward Russell told the writer that he believed Carvalho carried in his head more complete details of the publishing business than any one he ever knew. Everything in connection with the business and editorial departments of a newspaper had been done by Carvalho. He was a great reporter, a brilliant city editor, an extraordinary managing editor trained under the late Charles A. Dana. As business manager and publisher he was the Gibraltar defending the Pulitzer property. On April 1, 1896, he left the *World* and went to Hearst.

Carvalho understood New York, and with his powerful personality he gave solidity and momentum to the *Journal*. During the year after Carvalho became a part of the *Journal*, Charles Edward Russell was taken from the *World* and made city editor. Russell was one of the ablest city editors in New York. He has since been a candidate for President on the Socialist ticket, and has written many books, one of them being the life of Charlemagne.

About this same time in 1897, when Russell went from the *World* to the *Journal*, in another spasm of economy Pulitzer materially reduced Arthur Brisbane's salary. Pulitzer said, "It oughtn't to cost very much to get Socialist editorials written."

Brisbane replied, "It will cost a good deal to get them well written by a man who believes them."

Brisbane offered to work for Hearst for one hundred and fifty dollars a week, although he had received fifteen thousand a year when Pulitzer employed him. Gladly Hearst gave him a position on the *Journal*. Brisbane has a Voltairean mind. Humor, wit, genius in choosing subjects, microscopic perception, skill in condensation and writing and immense learning belong to Arthur Brisbane. His intellectual background was unusual. His father, Albert Brisbane, a capitalist of northern New York, was a follower of Fourier and also a member of the Brook Farm colony. Albert Brisbane paid the New York *Sun* one hundred and fifty dollars a day for publishing extracts from Fourier's *Economics*. Arthur Brisbane lived as a youth in France. Instinctively he was for the under-dog. He had done settlement work on the East Side. His were the first editorials ever read in the United States by great numbers of plain people. When he found the janitor and elevator man wrangling over his *Journal* articles he was delighted. Whenever he was in the Elevated he watched workmen read his editorials. If the article was not read to the end Brisbane felt that it was a failure.

Hearst has always been opposed to large type. Brisbane wished to have his editorials printed in such large type that they could be read across a street-car. He knew that "scare heads" were a short cut to circulation. The type in old files of the *Examiner* is conservative, and few double heads are shown. Hearst considers that large type defaces a newspaper. Brisbane invented what is called a "double-truck" picture, one covering two pages, when he wished to print a baby buffalo life size. Gleefully he said that no type in the printing office of the *Journal* was large enough for him, and so he had wooden type made seven inches high. He thought large type the show window of the newspaper. Some of his heads were seven columns wide. Brisbane has telegrams from Hearst declaring that he would rather not have circulation for his papers than see them defaced with large type.

Circulation grew. Brisbane did not have his salary increased, but he had an agreement with Hearst that he should receive a certain percentage of the money accruing from the circulation. Soon his income passed far beyond his salary of fifteen thousand of the *World* days.

After Goddard, Farrelly, Carvalho, Brisbane and Russell joined the staff of the *Journal* the morale of the *World* was broken, and there was despair under the shining dome. Eagerly men deserted to the new Hearst paper. In those days Hearst seldom left the *Journal* office until three or four in the morning. As he said to Bradford Merrill, the *Journal* had "got to go."

Hearst concentrated steadily on his art department. One of his first moves was to enter the color field on Sundays against

Puck and *Judge,* two small-sized comic color papers. In order to do this he needed a color-press. He told George Pancoast how one could be made. Pancoast drew the plans, and Hearst looked them over. Then Hearst, Pancoast and Jack Follansbee went to a circus in Madison Square Garden. Even while looking at animals in a circus Hearst was always working in his subconscious mind. Pancoast recalls that while they were in the circus, Hearst suddenly exclaimed, "George, you've got it!"

And Pancoast had the first color-press. With a color-press and Hearst's keen and unique sense of humor, the *Journal's* circulation soared. From the beginning Hearst fostered the best cartoonists and caricaturists. Hotly contested was the battle between Hearst and Pulitzer for the most popular comics. Dick Outcault, a clever artist, had been making for the *Sunday World* a series of half-page color comics called "Hogan's Alley," in which every day he pictured a little boy in a bright yellow shirt, and wearing an impish expression. Hearst liked this picture, and he made Outcault a liberal offer, that was accepted. Outcault went to the *Journal.* He felt that he had been underpaid by the *World,* and so he gladly changed employers.

Brisbane who had succeeded Goddard in charge of the *Sunday World* at once recognized how great an asset he had lost and induced Pulitzer to outbid Hearst. Back went Outcault with his imp to the *World* office. Then Hearst outbid Pulitzer, and Outcault and his imp transferred themselves again to the *Journal* office. By this time Outcault was getting more money than he had ever dreamed of. Legally the *World* owned the title "Hogan's Alley," and so the *Journal* called its series "McFadden's Row of Flats," but it had the same boy in the yellow shirt. To offset this Brisbane had George Luks continue the "Hogan's Alley" series, and put in each picture the boy in the yellow shirt. Before long Luks drew two boys in yellow shirts. The struggle for the "Yellow Kid," and the circulation that went with him, everywhere attracted attention.

Ervin Wardman was then editor of the New York *Press,* an unsuccessful journal established by the manufacturers to propagandize for tariff. Wardman attacked more fortunate newspapers. He wrote editorials ridiculing the see-saw contest for the best comics, and invented the term "yellow journalism."

After Rudolph Block assumed editorship of the comic section it was of unexampled brilliancy. Probably the most successful comic of those early days, and one that was the beginning of comics in the United States, was created by Hearst himself, the "Katzenjammer Kids." After he bought the *Journal* he brought forth his *Bilder Bücher* collected by him on his first trip to Europe as a ten year old. He showed them to Rudolph Dirks. From Hearst's collection Dirks developed the Katzenjammer Kids. Thousands bought the *Journal* for these new comics. When Pulitzer later employed Dirks after much litigation it was decided that the artist had no legal right to the name Katzenjammer Kids because he had not created the idea.

Hearst says that comic pages bring the largest immediate circulation. Early he assembled an unequaled staff of comic artists, Corey, Opper, Swinnerton, Tom Powers, Outcault, Dorgan (Tad), Briggs, McManus, and many others.

Frederick Burr Opper is living at New Rochelle, New York. He came from Madison Lake, Ohio, and has been a cartoonist for nearly sixty years. In 1899 he began working for Hearst. Already he had sold pictures to *Phunny Phellow, Wild Oats,* Frank Leslie's *Jolly Joker* and *Budget of Fun.* When Hearst bought *Puck,* Opper came to Hearst's Comic Sunday Supplement. Among his most famous cartoons was that of "Uncle Trusty," a gross, heavy character who was always oppressing a forlorn little man labeled the "Common People." During the McKinley campaign Hearst used Opper's cartoons against the administration. One of the most popular with the general public was "Willie and his Papa." "Happy Hooligan" and the "Mule Maud" had a wide appeal.

Closely allied with comics was color-printing. In the early

nineties Hearst met this problem. In 1893, R. Hoe and Company built a color-press for the New York *Recorder*, but Hearst did not consider the press practicable. As a result of his suggestions and insistence his engineer, George Pancoast, built a press which did fine printing. Many of the methods of plate-making that originated on the *Journal* are now used everywhere. Hearst volunteered to be responsible if the presses planned by him and his engineer were a failure. R. Hoe and Company equipped the new presses so that three colors were added to four black pages. All these devices were successful. In 1897, the Hoe Company, following a design made by George Pancoast, built a seven-unit press achieving the production of a four-page comic in four and three colors, and a twelve-page magazine with a three-color cover and back page. This press was later increased to ten units adding a fourth color to the magazine color, and eight more units in black.

In 1896, large web presses were driven by belts either from motors or line shafts. In the *Journal* press-rooms one position was found where a press could be located, but there was no room for belted drives. Hearst had scant respect for precedent. He told Pancoast to gear the motor directly to the press. The Bullock Teaser System of variable voltage control, was used. Hearst authorized the experiment necessary to perfect the new press. Crash! Twenty gears were stripped of their teeth.

The manufacturer warned Hearst against further experiment. "The slip of the belt is a necessary element of safety in transmission of power. You must bear the expense of all injury to the press."

Hearst went on. More gears were stripped, and more. At last the soundness of the principle of directly gearing motors to large presses was demonstrated. To-day all presses are equipped with a chain connection. From these inventions in color-presses George E. Pancoast derives a substantial income.

Hearst carefully studies all plans of new buildings to make sure that straight line production is assured. The main plant of the New York *Journal* and *American* is the best example of straight line production, but the Detroit *Times* and Los Angeles *Herald* plants are equally efficient. The New York plant runs twenty-four hours a day. Often six thousand plates are cast in the stereotyping department in one day. An average of eight hundred rolls of paper are consumed daily, and seven thousand pounds of ink are used. There are three twenty-four cylinder color-presses. They produce the color section for the Saturday *Journal* and *American Weekly* and *Puck Comic* for the Sunday *American*. The route of production of the daily is a perfect straight line from "copy" in the composing-room on the sixth floor to the tail-board of the delivery trucks. Stereotype plates leave the finishing machines, are automatically carried to presses by conveyors, and are later reversed, returning the plates to the casting furnaces.

Printed papers are carried from the presses to sixteen delivery heads on the floor above the press-room. Here the bundles of papers are made by machines. The tied bundles go automatically to chutes and are distributed across the delivery platform. Ten delivery trucks are within five feet of the chute outlet. In all Hearst's twenty-five newspaper buildings this same process is used. The main plants of the *Journal* and *American* are the largest in the world. Two remote plants in midtown and the Bronx enable the *Journal* to print simultaneously at these points. Papers can be on the street in seven minutes after news is received.

Hearst has rare typographical sense. Charles Edward Russell describes him working in the early days at the *Journal* office. With a blue pencil he pored over type books creating effective designs for the first and last pages of his paper. Palmer and Little named a new type, "The Hearst."

Hearst studied the *Journal* by placing it on the floor, moving it about with his feet, and looking at it from a distance in order to get a better perspective. He came to be called, "The man who edits a paper with his feet." If he didn't like an article, he would mark it "Punk." Sometimes he wrote praise with a blue pencil. Frequently he looked up a writer, commended him, and at times had a bonus sent by the business office.

One day Hearst saw the *Journal,* and he did not like its make-up. "Never shall a paper looking like that go out on the street with my name on it!"

"Mr. Hearst, it's on the presses," protested the flurried foreman.

"I don't care if it's on the wagon. Bring it back!"

To the horror of the circulation manager the paper was brought back, made over and the entire run lost.

Even during the depression in 1896, only three years after the great panic, the *Journal* passed from fifty thousand to two hundred thousand in circulation. Local and general news were dependable, but in appearance the paper was sensational. Lillian Russell, the most beautiful woman of her day, five feet, three inches tall, had reduced in weight from one hundred and sixty-five to one hundred and fifty-five pounds. She blushed when asked why she refused to wear tights. "Nature has been too generous," she coyly said. Bernhardt was interviewed about her dogs, lions and tigers. Shocking news! Women were beginning to smoke. Impossible to believe—they were wearing bloomers on Broadway. Robert Ingersoll, the infidel, was forbidden to speak in colleges. Charles Michelson's interview with Gomez on the recognition of Cuba by the Senate, February, 1896, was given a great display. Winifred Black, Dorothy Dix, and Ella Wheeler Wilcox supplied feminine sympathy and understanding. News writers gravitated toward long contracts and high salaries in the *Journal* office. They filled the narrow hallways. Charles Trevathan, who later wrote the first ragtime song for May Irwin, wailed, "No one but the cashier knows I'm on the paper."

Many ne'er-do-well, happy-go-lucky reporters were unable to keep up the pace for more than a few weeks. Drink made them lag behind. Alfred Henry Lewis, author of *Wolfville Folks,* remarked to Hearst, "For a man who doesn't drink you have suffered more from whisky than any one in the world."

Hearst laughed. When told that one of his Bohemian writers, during a festive evening, had thrown a beer mug through a large costly mirror in a saloon with the result that Hearst was liable for the bill, he laughed heartily and said, "Isn't that just like Jack?"

When Pulitzer realized that the *Journal* had a circulation of two hundred thousand, the groggy champion of Park Row staggered. The *World's* circulation was melting like snow before the sun. One day Pulitzer burst into the *World's* local room and frantically moaned to his city editor, "I have nothing but teetotalers. They never get news. My men are sober, dull commuters. Hearst has taken all my brilliant drinking men. For God's sake, get me at least one good drunkard."

CHAPTER XX

SUPPORTS BRYAN

PROBABLY 1896 was the most stirring and the most glamorous year of Hearst's life. Thirty-three years old, metropolitan success approaching, gambling with destiny—he lived a dozen existences. If the *Journal* failed, with it would go down the *Examiner,* and the Hearst fortune would be impaired. But armored with faith that was a shield against misfortune, Hearst went from venture to venture, just as George Hearst in his thirties went from mining camp to mining camp in California.

In the spring of 1896, Hearst experimented with a flying machine, soaring over Staten Island. He battled in Congress for cheaper freight rates for farmers. He demanded postal savings-banks. He had an eye on European powers in Brazil and Venezuela threatening the Monroe Doctrine. Susan B. Anthony was a commissioner for the *Examiner* and *Journal,* writing on suffrage. Hearst defended Oom Paul Kruger in South Africa. He fought for the San Pedro harbor for Los Angeles, instead of Santa Monica desired by Huntington. He sent James A. Creelman to Madrid to try to bring about the freedom of Cuba. Suddenly Charles Michelson, Hearst's correspondent, was incarcerated in Morro Castle. "Free Cuba!" Editorial after editorial appeared in the *Examiner* and *Journal.* "Cuba must be free!"

Deep as was Hearst's interest in public affairs, he allowed no detail of news to be neglected. In 1896, more detective work was done by reporters than by the police. *Journal* men solved the Guldensuppe murder mystery. In June of this year the legless, armless, headless body of a man was found floating in East River. Who was he? Why in the river? Murder! What was the motive? The city editor was like a bloodhound leading a pack. Get out! Every man in the local room! Find out who the corpse had been! Who killed the dead man! Why? A thousand dollars to the man identifying the torso!

The *Journal* staff went baying up and down Manhattan. Staffs of other papers followed, eager to seize any clue scented by the *Journal* men. An arm was picked up in East River. A leg! Another arm—another leg was found! Gradually the dead man was pieced together. Excitement in the city rose. Who would find the head? Whom would that missing face accuse? Even the headless body seemed to entreat the reporters to help find the guilty murderer. Thousands viewed the body. Children looked for fathers. Mothers for sons. Sweethearts for lovers. Wives for lost husbands.

Then a *Journal* reporter found a Long Island storekeeper, Mrs. Max Riger, who had sold part of the oil cloth in which the body was wrapped. The first clue. The *Journal* office was excited. On went the pack! Who was that headless man?

Little George Arnold, a general news man on the *Journal*, had been out of town for a few weeks. He came back and hurried to the morgue to see if he could identify the body.

No detail of that dead man on the slab escaped Arnold. He noticed everything, even that the hands of the man were curiously calloused. Arnold fancied that something about that body was familiar. Or did he imagine it?

Puzzled, he went to the Murray Hill Turkish Baths and asked for his rubber, Guldensuppe. "He hasn't reported in for several days," was the answer.

Arnold's mind flashed back to the corpse on the cold slab. He stared at the stranger masseur manipulating his body. The man's hands were curiously calloused like the hands of the dead man. Now Arnold recalled that Guldensuppe was built like that man at the Morgue. He could hardly wait to finish his bath. He hastened away, taking with him two Murray Hill Bath rubbers to identify, if possible, the dead man.

Had they ever seen the headless man before? This was

Arnold's first question. Perhaps. Was he Guldensuppe, the rubber who hadn't reported in? Yes, Guldensuppe was built the same. His hands were identical. Those were Guldensuppe's curiously twisted toes. Arnold rushed back to Park Row. In a few minutes the *Journal* was everywhere in the streets. On the tongue of New York was the name of the missing man, Guldensuppe. Little George Arnold waved his thousand dollars up and down Park Row. From that time the *Journal* had a "scoop" on each step leading to the crime.

"Don't let any other paper get a smell of it!" ordered the city editor. The Guldensuppe murder mystery remained in the general local room.

Why was the man killed? He had no money. Jealousy! Find the woman!

Mrs. Nack was found by the reporters. Her husband, Herman Nack, estranged from his wife, told the police she lived with a man named Guldensuppe, who had been missing several days. Mrs. Nack was questioned. She brazened through a denial.

Then a *Journal* man found a surrey in which Mrs. Nack had been seen riding to the ferry with a strange man. Again she was questioned. Yes, the strange man was a friend of hers, Martin Thorn. His real name was Torsewski. He was arrested. Mrs. Nack saved herself. She confessed that she and Thorn, her paramour, had killed Guldensuppe from jealousy. Guldensuppe had been lured to death by Mrs. Nack in a house Thorn had rented on Long Island. At last the missing head was dragged from the river. Guldensuppe's identification was complete. Thorn was electrocuted. Mrs. Nack served fifteen years in prison.

During the solution of this murder mystery the *Journal* reporters scored so many "beats" that they seemed uncanny, occult. Park Row talked of "Hearst luck." For years the phrase persisted. California and Nevada miners talked of "Hearst luck" while George Hearst piled up his fortune. Luck always did come roaring toward him, but it was aided by intelligence, concentration and energy. The solution of the Guldensuppe murder mystery was one of the many "beats" that skyrocketed the success of the *Journal*.

Then came Hearst's first great national campaign, the battle for silver currency. As early as 1895, "Coin" Harvey had explained in the San Francisco *Examiner* the relation between silver and prosperity. He pointed out that in 1893, before silver was demonetized, wheat sold in Chicago at one dollar and forty cents a bushel, cotton at eighteen cents a pound, and silver at one dollar and thirty-two cents an ounce. After demonetization of silver, wheat dropped to sixty cents a bushel, cotton to seven cents a pound, and silver to seventy cents an ounce. When silver was abundant, prosperity and fair prices followed. When silver rose and fell, farm products rose and fell.

Daniel Webster said that it was contrary to the letter and spirit of the United States to demonetize either gold or silver. "They are the money of the Constitution." Webster's opinion was supported in 1895 by a new champion of silver currency, who flashed before the public. He might have stepped out of Shakespearean drama, this handsome, dark, magnetic man not yet thirty-five, William Jennings Bryan, who played an important part in Hearst's life, and in the career of the *Journal*.

It is not often that a man leaps into national prominence by sheer force of eloquence, as did Bryan. Possessed of no skill in intrigue, and totally without power of patronage, simply by persuasive speech this champion of the lowly wrested the control of the Democratic Party in Nebraska from the Administration and landed in the fifty-second Congress. President Cleveland had enlisted Republican votes and was trying to repeal the Silver Purchase Clause in the Sherman Act. Soon after Bryan entered the House, young, provincial, unknown in national life, he made a three-hour speech for silver that commanded the attention of his colleagues, but he broke with the Democratic President. In spite of Bryan's oratory, Cleveland drove through his legislation. To the joy of both Democrats and Republicans the Nebraskan was defeated for Congress.

In 1895, ex-Congressman Bryan spoke at Metropolitan Hall in San Francisco. Hearst did not meet him, but he heard much of the orator's eloquence and power. The *Examiner* had an editorial on Bryan's speech. Davenport made a caricature of Bryan attending the trial of Durant, the Sunday School superintendent, who killed two girls in a Baptist church, ravished them and was later hanged. It was Davenport's first caricature of the future Democratic leader.

In San Francisco, Bryan declared war on Cleveland. It was clear that he had an eye on the Presidency. In turn the President placed every obstacle in the way of the Nebraskan's political advancement.

In July of 1896, when the Democratic Convention met in Chicago, Senator Stephen M. White of California was chairman. The keynote of the platform was, "Remonetize silver at sixteen to one." Battle began—hard-hitting, brick-throwing, ear-chewing Democratic battle. New York and the East, against the South and the West. Cleveland, Olney and Hill and the East would have won, had not Bryan appeared to speak for silver. The man seemed inspired, speaking, as he said, for a cause as holy as the cause of liberty, the cause of humanity. One shining, burning phrase still thrills through the years, "You shall not press down upon the brow of labor this crown of thorns; you shall not crucify mankind upon the cross of gold."

Even weary, bored, cynical reporters applauded. They had thought oratory as dead as Cicero, but here lived an orator. The convention of sixteen thousand went mad. Chicago went mad, California, Texas, Washington, Florida—all those crowds standing before bulletin boards devouring words of magic, were drunk on Bryan's eloquence. Everywhere the man in the street fell under the spell of Bryan's words and surrendered to the power of the new political hero from the Platte.

Appearing at a crisis in history, at a single bound William

Jennings Bryan became the foremost man of his party. For the first time by one speech a candidate overthrew party machinery and obtained the nomination for the Presidency. On the fifth ballot, William Jennings Bryan, the defeated Congressman from Nebraska, who entered the convention as a reporter, was named to head the Democratic ticket. Arthur Sewall of Maine, was nominated for the Vice-Presidency. On that July day Bryan could have been elected President.

Never were there such raw after-convention wounds as those resulting from Bryan's nomination. Wall Street, New York City, was stunned. An unknown, wild-eyed spellbinder from the Middle West was threatening political and economic sanity, on his way to the White House. Herr Most, the anarchist, could not have been worse. Already the red flag was waving in Washington, so said Cleveland conservatives. As for Republicans, John Hay called Bryan an anarchist.

To make matters more impossible Bryan was nominated by the People's and National Silver Parties. Where could the great Democratic leaders go politically? David B. Hill and Bourke Cockran found refuge in the arms of the Republican Party.

For the comfort of President Cleveland, who could not vote the Republican ticket, the "Gold Standard" Democrats nominated Palmer and Buckner, and repudiated the "sixteen to one" Chicago platform. The Democratic papers that had not come out for the Republicans McKinley and Hobart, declared for Palmer and Buckner—all except the New York *Journal*. What would the *Journal* do?

Hearst conferred with his editors and executives, Sam Chamberlain, Arthur McEwen, Alfred Henry Lewis and Business Manager Charles M. Palmer. Alfred Henry Lewis hated the "boy orator" from Washington days. Palmer especially opposed Bryan. By nature conservative he did not believe in increased purchase of silver by the Government. It would result in inflation. Merchants and advertisers would oppose it. The *Journal* could not afford to lose advertising. He thought that to support Bryan would destroy the *Journal*. There was only one thing ror the paper to do—remain silent, or support McKinley.

McEwen was for Bryan. Hearst said little. Absent-mindedly he tapped on the window pane while the editors argued. When McEwen advanced his arguments for supporting Bryan, Hearst's gray-blue eyes brightened.

After the conference was over Hearst quietly asked McEwen to write an editorial announcing that the *Journal* declared for Bryan and Sewall. During the campaign McEwen did some of his best work. His *Journal* editorials were telegraphed to the *Examiner*. It was discovered and published that in 1890 McKinley declared for free and unlimited coinage of silver. During the remainder of the campaign the *Journal* and *Examiner* had one or two daily editorials supporting Bryan and Sewall, and attacking McKinley and Mark Hanna.

Homer Davenport's genius soon flowered, and his first cartoon of Mark Hanna attracted as much attention as *Journal* editorials. He caricatured McKinley seated on the knee of Hanna, or being led by the gross boss dressed in loud clothes covered with dollar signs. It was generally believed that McKinley was annoyed by the Davenport caricatures, but Louis Lang said that McKinley showed his collection of Davenport's cartoons of himself and Hanna carefully preserved by him for his private amusement.

Sometimes the *Journal* editors did not think the cartoon worthy of Davenport, and in the conference it was rejected. The artist would leave the editorial council depressed. Hearst would sometimes throw his arms over Davenport's shoulder and say, "What's the matter, Davvy? Don't they treat you right? Bring your cartoons to me. I'll run them."

Hearst relates an incident that still diverts him in connection with his declaration for Bryan. When he purchased the New York *Journal* he was only dimly conscious that at the same time he acquired from Pulitzer a small daily German paper, *Das Morgen Journal*. The paper had an insignificant circulation, but when Hearst became aware of its existence he told the editor that the German paper should follow the lead of the *Journal*. *"Sehr gut!"* agreed the German editor. "We have already supported Herr Bryan since three days."

When the *Journal* declared for Bryan, Pulitzer cheered up. At last, Hearst had made a disastrous mistake. Now the San Francisco men would walk back home. Hearst's own staff agreed with Pulitzer. Editors' conferences were like funerals. They thought their contracts worthless. Deepest of all in gloom was Business Manager Charles M. Palmer. No other large paper in New York, or in the entire East supported Bryan. Hearst was called a traitor to his class. To think of a man born in the purple supporting Bryan. Advertising was withdrawn from the *Journal*. Sane business men would show this young demagogue from California that he couldn't foist a long-haired lunatic like Bryan on the nation and bring about ruinous inflation.

Hearst was only thirty-three, beating his way alone through a maelstrom of business disapproval, but in the storm he sought no safety. Business Manager Palmer reported losses of one hundred thousand a month, but Hearst did not alter his policy. To all departing advertisers his answer was, "I'm sorry, but your withdrawal from the *Journal* leaves that much more space for Mr. Bryan."

Day after day, week after week, Julian Hawthorne, Alfred Henry Lewis, Arthur McEwen and Henry George attacked Hanna, the trusts and Wall Street. McKinley, whose personal debts had been underwritten by Hanna and some of his friends, was called the "Syndicate-Owned Candidate." The business and articulate sentiment of the country was arrayed on the side of McKinley and Hanna and Prosperity.

Hearst's policy was, "We are unalterably opposed to the single gold standard which has locked fast the prosperity of an industrious people in the paralysis of hard times. . . . 'You cannot crucify mankind upon a cross of gold!' "

The Democratic Party had not enough money for postage stamps. In the *Journal* and *Examiner* Hearst offered to duplicate every dollar contributed to the Bryan campaign fund. He paid the expenses of many meetings and furnished money for organizing Democratic clubs, and also for their national convention at Indianapolis. The business office of the *Journal* despaired.

But into the circulation department came a deluge. The flood of circulation was almost beyond control. From New England, Pennsylvania, Baltimore and cities of New York State as far west as Buffalo, came orders from the big news-dealers for the *Journal.* Mail subscriptions poured in from all parts of the country. No other newspaper in any eastern city of size supported Bryan. Hearst's policy brought to the *Journal* all voters that believed in "sixteen to one." Never did a newspaper make such rapid growth.

The limited mechanical equipment of the *Journal* could not take care of the rising circulation. New presses could not be found to meet the hurried, urgent demands. Business Manager Palmer assembled parts of presses, and the *Journal* was temporarily equipped to meet the sudden overwhelming request for newspapers.

Even families were broken up and long friendships annihilated by hectic arguments about Bryan. It is not strange that the *Journal* became a business outcast. Hearst's losses were appalling, and yet he would not yield to fear. This steadfastness and courage established his popularity with the masses.

Winifred Black was sent by Hearst to travel through the United States with William Jennings Bryan and Mrs. Bryan. The candidate made six hundred speeches in twenty-seven states, always wearing a shiny, gray-black alpaca coat. On hot days he took off his collar and was in shirt sleeves. He became the prophet of the masses. Western universities received him with open arms, but Yale drove him off the platform. Mrs. Black tells of Bryan's stage fright in Chicago. Like a small boy going to his mother Bryan said to his wife, "I'm afraid of all those people, I can't speak to them." Mrs. Bryan took his hand and said, "William, talk to them just as if you were speaking from the stoop to our folks at home." He went out and from the hotel balcony addressed the thousands in the street, and never aroused greater enthusiasm.

As election day approached clergymen were implored to save the "honest dollar." Wavering journals were dragooned. Splendid daylight parades were staged. "A full dinner pail" was promised by McKinley and Hanna. Employed workmen were warned that if Bryan was elected they would lose their jobs. The unemployed were told that a vote for Bryan was a vote for continued hard times. Intelligence, organizing ability and the power of wealth were united for the "full dinner pail." Capital was organized on a splendid scale for both attack and defense.

In spite of the eloquence of the silver orator, William Jennings Bryan was defeated by a popular vote of five hundred thousand. On election day Hearst learned the result over the wires in San Francisco. Bryan slept in his Nebraska home through most of the afternoon. Two days later he sat down to write a telegram of congratulation to McKinley. During the writing of the telegram he paused twice to relate humorous anecdotes. When asked about his plans for the future Bryan answered, "The fight has just commenced."

Hearst requested Winifred Black to send for him anonymously a cartload of flowers to the William Jennings Bryans. After the election was over he published an editorial closing with the words, "Forget the rancors and excitements of politics as soon as possible—parting with no convictions, but remembering there is a time for all things—and settle down to business. The country needs a rest."

Pulitzer had hoped for an empty dinner pail for the *Journal*. On the contrary, the dinner pail of the *World* was emptying. Circulation dropped further. September showed that four hundred and seven thousand *Journals* were sold daily. Bewildered, Pulitzer wondered how people could continue to buy a paper that had stood for "sixteen to one." To add to Pulitzer's trouble the *Evening Journal* appeared on the streets in the afternoon for the first time, September 28, 1896.

One year from the day that the *Evening Journal* was founded the paper had a birthday party at Delmonico's and entertained many of the most prominent citizens of New York. Chauncey M. Depew declared that the success of the *Evening Journal* was the most remarkable phenomenon in the newspaper world seen by him during forty years in New York.

At last Pulitzer conceded that the young man from California was remarkable. Instead of walking back to San Francisco, Hearst had built up the *Evening Journal* until it had the largest circulation ever known in the English-speaking world, five hundred and ten thousand, one hundred and ninety-seven. The *Journal's* circulation has gone above, but has never dropped below that figure.

CHAPTER XXI

CUBA—EVANGELINA CISNEROS

AS soon as McKinley was elected Hearst wondered what the new President would do about Cuba. This same question was in the mind of most Americans when McKinley entered the White House, March 4, 1897. Cuba, the Pearl of the Antilles, that gorgeous crescent island of flowers and palms, said to be cursed with beauty, was called by Columbus, "The most beautiful land ever beheld by human eyes." It had been a refuge for slaves from Santo Domingo, brutally subjugated by Hernando Cortez, and a victim of pirate pillage and Spanish tyranny. For nearly a century Cuba had fought for her liberty, in 1823, 1826, 1830, 1848, 1850, 1851, and in the war from 1868 to 1875. Again Cuba was battling for liberty.

President Cleveland had behaved as if Cuba needed only rhetorical sympathy. Would President McKinley do more? America wondered, and so did Hearst. The *Sun* and the *World* were both mildly pro-Cuban. The *Herald* was pro-Spanish. Alone of all the papers in New York each day the *Journal* in large letters proclaimed, "Cuba must be free!"

The Cuban situation each hour grew more tense, but Hearst sent one of his staff, Grover Flint, to Cuba to present a handsome jeweled sword to General Maceo. Charles Michelson, one of the *Journal-Examiner* correspondents, was imprisoned in Morro Castle. Patriots were incarcerated in camps of *reconcentrados*. Revolutionists were shot down. Governor-General Weyler grew to deserve his nickname, "The Butcher."

Spain had established a censorship in Havana making it difficult to get news, and so Hearst decided to send to Cuba Richard Harding Davis, the most popular American novelist of his day, and Frederick Remington, the leading artist of the

New York magazine world. At that time there were many Spanish spies in New York who reported to Governor-General Weyler the movements of American sympathizers and betrayed their relations with Cuban revolutionaries. With Michelson incarcerated in Morro Castle, Davis and Remington considered the journey one of peril. They planned to embark late at night on a special steamer which was to sail from a remote wharf in order to avoid the espionage of Spanish spies.

In appearance Davis was like one of his own heroes of fiction reporting a South American revolution. During the Greek and Turkish war he had had some experience in the field. Davis appeared at the *Journal* office with a complete camp equipment consisting of two heavy sole-leather trunks, which, when placed a few feet apart and connected by wooden bars, made the foundation of his camp bed. He also had an elaborate saddle, bridle and saddle blanket of which any field commander might have been proud. Remington had never been on a battlefield, and he was distinctly nervous that night while he and Davis waited at the *Journal* office till they should set out for Cuba. Davis was dignified and remote, the silent military man of iron, while he sat in Sam Chamberlain's office several hours before boarding the steamer. Frequently Remington nervously sprang up and rushed out to an all-night refreshment stand in order to stimulate his courage for Cuba. His courage was so much overstimulated that by the time he and Davis were loaded into the closed hack awaiting them in the side street he didn't know or care whether they were going to Cuba or Coney Island.

Davis and Remington arrived safely in the insurgent camp without encountering any of "Butcher" Weyler's men and sent back from Cuba much interesting material. Hearst's large yacht, the *Vamoose,* was ordered by him to Havana to be used as a dispatch boat after it had its trial trip in New York Bay.

The *Vamoose* had its own story. While Hearst lived in San Francisco he owned a speed-boat, the *Aquila,* built by the Herreshoffs in 1891. It was about fifty feet long, the fastest speed-boat on the Pacific coast. Hearst often raced the Sausalito ferry with the *Aquila*. On one historic trip Mrs. Phebe Hearst took the *Aquila* down to Alviso, Santa Clara County, when she visited her parents, the Appersons. On this journey the bay was choppy and Mrs. Hearst was wet to the skin. So she decided that her son should have the largest boat that could be shipped by rail from New York. She ordered the *Vamoose,* one hundred and twenty-seven feet long. The cost of the boat was eighty thousand dollars, speed guaranteed at twenty-six miles an hour, or the sale invalidated.

Then a new problem arose, how to transport the *Vamoose* across the Isthmus of Panama. Tops of bridges were removed, and it was decided to take down the upper part of two small bridges for a day. A crib was built covering three cars of the Panama Railway Company. The *Vamoose* was about to go forward when the engineer of the road reported that Colonel Rives, president of the railway company, declined to accept the yacht as freight. Rives held to his refusal because there had appeared in the *Examiner* an unfavorable review of a sensational novel, *The Quick or the Dead,* written by his daughter, Amélie Rives. Colonel Rives was so fixed in his decision that the yacht was returned to New York. Later Hearst sold the *Vamoose* and fitted up the *Buccaneer,* a comfortable boat lacking in speed. This yacht was presented to the Government.

News was made every hour in Cuba, and the *Vamoose* was of service in conveying Key West reports uncensored. In February, Frederick Remington drew and sent from Cuba to the *Journal* a five-column picture showing a nude young woman, clothing scattered over the ground, surrounded by Spanish soldiers and officials who had been searching her. This was one of the indignities inflicted on women aboard American vessels in Havana by Spanish officials.

The picture and the article in the *Journal* caused Congressman Amos J. Cummings to introduce a resolution in the House of Representatives demanding any information that the Secretary of State might have concerning the incident. Later, Senators Frye, Daniels and Lodge spoke on avenging Spanish insults. Senator Allen denounced the selling of Cuban girls into slavery as revealed by the New York *Journal*. But barbarism continued to reign in Cuba. In spite of Hearst's daily editorial protest, and flaming speeches of Congressmen and Senators, the McKinley Administration took no action.

Bryan joined the staff of the Hearst papers. From the beginning of the "full dinner pail" McKinley Administration the *Journal* and *Examiner* criticized both the President and Hanna, the forceful boss who dominated the Administration. During the entire year these criticisms continued. Senator John Sherman of Ohio was conveniently elevated by McKinley to the position of Secretary of State in order to make way for Hanna as United States Senator. Governor Bushnell of Ohio appointed Hanna to the Senate to succeed Sherman.

When Hanna was later elected on January 11, 1898, the *Evening Journal* charged that he had obtained his election by bribery. From Cleveland, Ohio, came a report on April 4th, saying that the Senate Committee had found Senator Hanna guilty of bribery, and that the seat he occupied was purchased. Later the committee gave evidence revealing that Senator Hanna's seat had been bought. A four-column cartoon by Davenport picturing Hanna in stripes was printed on the day of the report.

But criticism of the President was suspended by Hearst when President McKinley came to New York as the guest of the city in April, 1897, to view the transfer of the body of ex-President U. S. Grant to his new tomb on Riverside Drive. Hearst ordered a grandstand constructed so that orphans and descendants of veterans who were in the Civil War with Grant might see the dedication. More than a million persons watched the parade. The first page of the *Journal* showed a flag in colors with Grant's face in the center, all occupying three-quarters of a page.

Hearst could never have achieved his predominance as an editor without widely varying interests. In May of 1897, he plunged whole-heartedly into looking after the families of twenty-four thousand tailors who had struck for higher wages. Many of the unemployed with their families and furniture were about to be ejected into the streets by landlords when their rent was paid by a fund provided by the *Evening Journal.* Tears came to tired eyes, and unuttered words of gratitude quivered on lips when reporters brought aid to the needy. In thousands of humble homes Hearst's name came to be spoken with blessing. Contractors appointed a committee to put an end to the *Journal's* relief work in order to force the destitute strikers into submission. Soon after the strike was settled the *Journal* launched a crusade to conserve the health of tenement children by giving them daily trips to the seashore.

Another effort to benefit the public was an investigation by the *Journal* of a promenade on Brooklyn Bridge, declared unsafe for pedestrians. The first of the *Journal's* many attempts in New York to protect the public at grade crossings was initiated in 1896, and the crusade went on during 1897. Five persons were seriously injured or killed because of criminal negligence on the part of officials of the Long Island Railroad Company. Common appliances for safety were demanded by the *Journal.* During this same year an article was published arraigning the D. S. Dent Company for swindling five thousand persons out of approximately five hundred thousand dollars.

In the summer and autumn of 1897, Hearst took part in his first campaign in New York City elections. He supported Robert A. Van Wyck for Mayor. When Van Wyck was elected he announced that credit was due to the *Evening Journal* for presenting the issues clearly, and in a manner that appealed to every Democratic voter. Van Wyck declared he would work for all reforms advocated by Hearst, such as cheaper gas, more schools, and the eight-hour law.

San Francisco was always the center of important news, and in the summer of 1897 excitement arose over the new Alaskan gold-fields. From the San Francisco *Examiner* Hearst sent to Alaska a large group of news writers who described the new Eldorado. Joaquin Miller, the poet of the Sierras, spent the winter in the gold-fields writing for him.

While Hearst was in London about this time he discovered what is technically called the "fudge," for insertion of the latest news on the front page. English publishers were using hand-set type in their "fudges." On his return Hearst put the problem to George E. Pancoast, his mechanical superintendent —how could a linotype be made to set a "fudge" and gain time? Pancoast designed the first beveled slug cast from a mold to the segment of the printing cylinders. These segments placed in a holder are the equivalent of the stereotype plate, and can be attached to the press in a few seconds. The first "fudge" in America was used to bulletin the Corbett-Fitzsimmons fight at Carson City in 1897. It enabled the *Journal* to place the details of this encounter on the streets fifteen minutes ahead of any of its competitors.

Since that time the "fudge" has been in daily use in Hearst's evening papers. As a result of this printing novelty the Harlem plant for years has distributed papers in the ball park before half the fans left giving the score of the game they had just seen. To-day most metropolitan evening papers employ this device.

During all these mechanical developments, social crusades and political campaigns there sounded in Hearst's ears the appeal of Cuba for help. Men, women and children, suffering and starving, were imprisoned in pest-ridden spots. Suddenly in August, 1897, there rose from the southern sea a face, a girl's face that seemed to symbolize Cuba—Evangelina Cisneros, eyes limpid and dark, features flawless, hair flowing, and a smile flashing over her vivid young countenance like the play of colors of a humming bird.

It was in August, 1897, when George Eugene Bryson, the Cuban correspondent, wrote of Evangelina Cisneros and Hearst read the girl's story. Evangelina was eighteen, born of one of the gentlest families in Cuba. For a year she had been incarcerated in the *Recojidas,* a Havana prison, not because of rebellion against Spain, but because she resisted the insulting advances of Colonel Berriz, a favorite aide of Captain-General (Butcher) Weyler. The Captain-General himself had ordered Evangelina's father torn away from the motherless girl and locked up in prison. The unfortunate man was condemned to death, but the sentence was later commuted to confinement for life in Ceuta, a Spanish island prison off Gibraltar. When he parted with his daughter he gave her a dagger and said, "Courage is king. Be brave, my beloved."

Then Evangelina was taken to the *Recojidas,* a great cage for abandoned women in Havana. Men came in from the streets, clutched the prison bars, looked at the women and made coarse jokes.

When Hearst read Bryson's article on the plight of this girl his indignation against her imprisonment rose, and he gave orders to the correspondent to "Rescue Evangelina Cisneros from the *Recojidas,* no matter what it costs."

As an aide to Bryson, James A. Creelman, energetic, resourceful, a man who never failed, was placed by Hearst in charge of arousing public sentiment in the United States for Evangelina's release. Response was immediate, and several hundred thousand names of women were signed to the petition to the Spanish government. The Queen Regent of Spain was cabled to intercede for clemency by Mrs. Jefferson Davis, Mrs. John A. Logan, Mrs. Julia Dent Grant, Mrs. Mark Hanna, Mrs. William C. Whitney and Mrs. Frances Hodgson Burnett. Mrs. Julia Ward Howe and heads of religious orders sent pleas and prayers to his Holiness Pope Leo XIII to request the Spanish government to abstain from military vengeance. Pope Leo recommended to Her Majesty special clemency for Evangelina. The wife of the American Ambassador at Madrid, Mrs. Hannis Taylor, presented appeals of American women. Daily the lovely face of Evangelina appeared in the *Journal* and *Examiner,* and soon there came to Hearst from every remote corner of the United States messages of thanks for his efforts to rescue the beautiful Cuban. Day by day mounted the rage in the United States against the Spanish government.

Evangelina herself knew nothing of what was going on in the outside world. For a year she had lived in prison thinking she would rather be dead and in her grave, with a cross at her head and a stone at her feet. Often she looked at her father's dagger and said, "Courage is king."

Evangelina was greatly surprised when the prison warden visited her cell and showed her a picture of herself in the New York *Journal*. "You have friends, señorita. They will weep when you stand up before the soldiers with a bandage over your eyes and hear the word, 'Shoot!' "

Evangelina was astonished. "How comes my picture in this far-away paper, the New York *Journal?* What do they know about me?"

No one knew. The girl said her beads devoutly. Then George Eugene Bryson, the *Journal* correspondent, came to see her. Now she knew she had the protection of all the saints.

"Señorita, the *Journal*, the paper I represent, is trying to have you released. Mr. Hearst has put his foot down, and when once he puts his foot down he never raises it."

"Mr. Hearst—a señor I never heard of."

"From now on you will hear of Mr. Hearst."

Even the jailer was more kindly to Evangelina when Mrs. Fitzhugh Lee, wife of the Consul-General, and her daughter called. Immediately the jailer transferred the girl to another part of the prison where she could take a bath, cook her own food, and have books to read. Evangelina began studying English in order to be able to talk with Bryson when he came. She saved all the New York *Journals* that he brought, cut out the pictures of her new far-away friends and pasted them on the walls of her cell. Surely the Holy Father would be able to obtain clemency for her.

Suddenly Evangelina's friend, Bryson, correspondent of the *Journal,* was banished from Cuba. The girl herself was placed incommunicado. Weyler, Captain-General of Cuba, was indignant because Hearst had interceded for Evangelina. Depuy de Lome, the Spanish Minister at Washington, supported Weyler. Colonel Berriz was an especial protégé of Weyler. His defense was that he had not attempted to assault the girl. Evangelina was visited by the Marquis of Cervera who asked her to withdraw her accusation against Berriz. Such reversal was her only hope of clemency. Evangelina told Cervera that she would die first in the *Recojidas*.

Then Evangelina's confinement became more rigorous. Hearst knew that "Butcher" Weyler was determined to send Evangelina to Ceuta or force her to retract her accusation. At this moment he asked Karl Decker, a gallant Virginian of the Washington office of the *Journal*, to go to Havana and carry on the struggle to release Evangelina. Decker did not speak Spanish, but he knew Cuba. He had spent three months with Gomez, head of the revolutionists. He had common sense, imagination, resolution and courage. On the 20th of August, 1897, he began work.

Decker quickly obtained the assistance of Consul-General Fitzhugh Lee who lent him his aides, Don Rockwell, one of the consular clerks, and William B. MacDonald. Rockwell spoke Spanish, and was "contact man" for Decker. Another able assistant was Paco Debesche, a Cuban. After having engaged these men Decker took up his residence at the Inglaterra Hotel in the heart of Havana. His office was near the American Consulate, and soon he was known as the *Journal* correspondent. Decker and his assistants agreed never to recognize each other. In the early morning hours they met in a little half-furnished room in the lower part of Havana and plotted Evangelina's escape.

The *Recojidas* was in the poorest part of Havana surrounded by a huddle of squalid huts. By two alleys only could the jail entrance be approached. The thick forbidding walls towered high, and no window was visible. Decker was baffled, but he kept on. After weeks of frustration he spoke with

Evangelina in the squalid jail courtyard, which steamed in the hot white glare of the August sun. The girl had as companions half a hundred negresses and women of the streets condemned to prison for violent crimes.

During this interview Decker smuggled a note to Evangelina asking if she had any suggestions to offer for her escape. In answer she sent the following message: "I'll go down by way of the roof with a rope descending in front of the building. I'll require opium or morphine to lull to sleep my companions. The best way to use opium is in sweets. I'll need acid to destroy the window bars. Three of you come and stand at the corners of the building in the street. A lighted cigar will be the signal for me to delay. A white handkerchief will indicate that I can swiftly descend. Write if you agree."

Evangelina sent a plan of the building. To Decker's surprise there was a window at the end of the second-story apartment which ran along the street at the side of the prison, but the window did not extend to the front of the building and was not visible. The flat roof upon which it opened was about twenty feet wide.

Fortune favored Decker. A house next door to the jail became vacant. Decker rented it, and sent a colored man to whitewash the building. The negro carried a ladder about twelve feet long and left it in the house—accidentally.

When Decker and his assistants took possession of the house they felt as if they were engaging in one of the romantic and heroic exploits in the days of the Cid. No morphine was sent by Decker to induce sleep in Evangelina's cell companions, but the resourceful girl pretended to the prison physician that she had an aching tooth. At first the doctor refused her laudanum. Moaning she walked up and down her cell and begged.

"Twenty drops of this kills," warned the physician as finally he granted her request. "Be careful, little one."

The women in the cells slept soundly because Evangelina dropped laudanum into the coffee, just enough to make them drowsy. The girl quietly wrapped a sheet around her so that if any women in the cell woke, she would appear to be in a night-dress.

About half-past one the neighborhood noises quieted, and Decker and his men threw the ladder diagonally across the right angle between the roof of their house and the flat roof of the prison. The short decrepit ladder was held in place at each end by a man. Suddenly a large piece of the weak prison cornice clattered down into the street. Out came the old warden, Don José. Quickly the ladder was withdrawn. Two men were left on the flat roof of the jail. The third was on the roof of the house to handle the drawbridge and guard the retreat. Candle in hand, Don José stared about in the soft Cuban night which was as bright as midday. Then he reëntered the *Recojidas*. "*Aler-r-rta!* All is well!" half sang the sentinel of the nearby barracks. Again Decker put the ladder in place and crept softly across the roof to the window indicated by Evangelina.

For two hours and a half she had stood there patiently watching the men at work, waiting. Decker put his hand through the bars and touched her. "Quiet! We'll soon get you out of here." Decker began sawing the window bar. It rattled.

There was a noise from the women in the cell. Evangelina shuddered, and whispered, "Go! Come back to-morrow night."

All next day Decker wondered whether the attempted escape had been discovered by the warden, but he felt protected by invisible spirits. He hid a pair of Stillson wrenches under the mattress in his room. In the street near the house waited an old carriage for Evangelina to drive away in. One of Decker's men chatted with Don José, the warden, and invited him to a drinking bout. When the neighbors retired for the night Decker and his assistants locked the windows and barred the shutters. They took off their shoes, and moving quickly placed the ladder on the roof. Decker saw tied to the bar of Evangelina's window the white handkerchief agreed upon as the signal. The mutilated bar had not been discovered.

"*Aler-r-r-ta!*" sounded through the tropic night.

In stocking-feet the rescuers quickly traveled to the window. There stood Evangelina, her hand thrust out for liberty, calling down upon Decker's head the benediction of all the saints.

"Quiet!" sternly commanded Decker. With a small wrench he gripped the bar below where the cut had been made the previous night. He seized the other part of the bar with a large wrench and swung all his weight forward upon the handle. The bar snapped with a clear ringing sound. Breathlessly he waited a few seconds. No alarm. Decker pulled the bar toward him, placed under it his shoulder, seized the crossbar above his head, drew himself up and bent it. With his wrench he twisted it into a V. Quickly grasping Evangelina about the waist he dragged her through the opening.

Evangelina was so happy that she made a little outcry. Decker covered her mouth with his hand. The girl fearlessly walked across the vibrating ladder as though on solid ground, arms outstretched to keep her balance. When she reached the roof one of the men caught her in his arms.

"*Mis zapatos!*" Evangelina cried as her feet touched the cold tiles of the room. "*Deme mis zapatos!*"

She was not given her shoes. The ladder was quickly drawn back upon the roof and there left. Within five minutes the girl was in the carriage with Carlos Carbonnel, one of Consul-General Fitzhugh Lee's staff. Carbonnel drove as fast as the horses could go through the narrow, twisting streets, into a deserted thoroughfare where lived his aunt who had promised to conceal the girl. Evangelina entered her refuge just as there sounded the sentinel's call from the barracks, "*Aler-r-r-ta!*" This occurred at three o'clock Thursday morning November 12, 1897.

The next day Decker saw that Evangelina received a suit of disguise for her departure, the blue serge uniform of a sailor. She trimmed her hair about her face, then plastered it down with a little pomade. Wearing a sailor suit she walked up and down the room practicing a man's stride. Her feet looked large in boy's shoes, and she tried to conceal them.

With her blue serge suit she wore a butterfly necktie and a large slouch hat. It all seemed like a dream to the girl. She had been in prison fifteen months.

At five o'clock on the third day after her escape Evangelina's rescuers came to escort her to the steamer.

"Take long steps," said Decker. "Don't recognize us, or look round. We'll be near until you are safe on the *Seguranca*. The steamer will take you to New York."

As Evangelina stepped into the street a swirl of wind caught her hat and tossed it across the thoroughfare. She quickly replaced it on her head and started jauntily down the street followed by Decker and his assistants at a little distance, all armed with concealed revolvers. The sidewalks were so narrow that when two people met one was obliged to step down into the roadway. Fortunately it was dinner hour in Havana, and pedestrians were hurrying to their meals.

At last Evangelina reached the dock. Few people were in sight. The girl stood puffing at her cigar trying to blur her outline in a great cloud of smoke. The *Seguranca* would start in an hour. The steamer setting out for liberty land lay far out in the harbor. A line of heavy smoke drifting back from her funnels showed she was ready to sail. In the *Regla* the lights were popping out in bright spots. Evangelina wondered if the launch would ever start.

Suddenly the little propeller of the launch gave a few tentative whirls, and the waiting passengers hurried aboard. An officer of the *Seguranca* looked at Evangelina's passport. It was for Juan Sola, age eighteen; by occupation, sailor. "*Bueno!*"

Once in her cabin Evangelina crawled under the lower berth and lay like dead. When she heard a step she wondered whether the police had come. She was only three days away from the *Recojidas*. What would happen if she were taken back?

Decker dared not go on board with Evangelina because his presence would have attracted the attention of the inspector. He and his men sat at marbletop tables in front of the Café

Lux overlooking the harbor, and from there watched the *Seguranca* steam triumphantly for New York. When she passed from sight, the *Seguranca* gave nine hoarse blasts signifying that all was well.

Decker and his men drank a silent, deep toast, and that night there was revelry in Havana. American songs rang through the streets. It was discovered that Evangelina had fled. Sixty arrests were made. Even the colored man who white-washed Decker's house was suspected and placed under arrest. So was the driver of the carriage.

Nearly paralyzed with anxiety and fear Evangelina lay in her hiding place for two hours. Then there was a heavy step in the room. Her breath did not come. She was being searched for. If she was taken out on deck, she made up her mind to jump overboard. Back to that jail she would not go.

A man struck a match. "Evangelina!" some one called. Silence. "Señorita Cisneros!" A friend. Evangelina crawled out from under the berth. "We're far from Havana. Come up on deck. See how you like liberty."

This was too much. How could she go on deck? She felt so weak that she remained in the stateroom and cried, and cried. Then she changed the sailor's clothes for the dress worn by her when she escaped from prison.

Finally Evangelina realized that she was safe under the Stars and Stripes. She went on deck. Passengers gathered round her. Ladies kissed her and told her she was brave and wonderful. Chairs, rugs, ices were brought. She was treated as if she was the greatest woman in the world. So bewildered was she that she didn't hear much said by the passengers. At night she pointed out to one of her friends what she thought was a star. "I've never seen a star so bright."

"Hatteras light!"

"The country of Washington! America!"

Evangelina kneeled down and thanked God that her new country was near.

Decker rapidly set down on paper all that had transpired

in bringing about Evangelina's release, and sent it by a purser to Key West. The New York *Journal* published Evangelina's story on Sunday morning, October 13th. The Spanish Ambassador, Depuy de Lome at Washington, was filled with indignation. He denounced Hearst and the *Journal,* but America was thrilled by the heroic rescue of the girl. In Havana, Decker was warned that he would be placed under arrest. He decided to take chances and conceal himself among the insurgents.

Hearst who was in Philadelphia, sent him a cable, "Good work. Return immediately."

Decker left for New York on the Spanish steamer *Panama* with a forged visé on his passport.

When the *Seguranca* passed up New York Bay, Evangelina was so excited that she could not look out on the water. She remained in her stateroom and wept. Why had this editor, a stranger, reached out to her from this great city of New York for more than a thousand miles and broken the bars of the *Recojidas?* In the crowd of smiling cheering people, Evangelina saw her first American friend, George Eugene Bryson, the *Journal* correspondent, who had been banished for trying to save her. She could not speak, but she took his hand and followed him into the launch. Women were hugging her and weeping. From the *Recojidas* to New York City with thousands of friends. In a blaze of welcome the bewildered girl drove up Broadway.

Hearst arranged for Evangelina to live at the Waldorf-Astoria chaperoned by Mrs. Sloane, since the widow of General Nelson H. Henry; Miss Anne O'Hagen, now Mrs. Bruning; and Miss Emma Kaufman, formerly of California, now Mrs. Shinn. Their recollection of Evangelina is clear. They describe her as riding hatless, wearing a simple cloth gown. Her nails were especially neat. She had manicured them with a common pin.

People stormed into Evangelina's rooms. Decker arrived from Cuba to escort her to her reception at Delmonico's. What a royal reception! Every one happy, every one making a speech. Even Evangelina made a stammering, half-crying speech in English. The crowd was too great for Delmonico's. It flowed over into Madison Square, one hundred and twenty thousand friends Hearst had made for Evangelina.

Decker accompanied her to Madison Square escorted by police, sailors and soldiers. The crowd cheered and welcomed her from captivity, honoring Decker, lauding her. Here was romance in flesh and blood. An eighteen year old girl in white. Her movements all grace and charm. Evangelina looked like the heroine of all time, the symbol of Cuba, the Pearl of the Antilles. One hundred and twenty thousand people sang Cuban songs and patriotic American airs. Fireworks filled the sky. If only Havana could hear New York shout! No longer was there any doubt that Cuba would be free.

When Evangelina met Hearst she kissed his hand. He arranged that she was to be presented to President McKinley. Never was a girl so happy. Joan of Arc had delivered France. At last Evangelina could do something for her country! Mrs. Sloane escorted her to Washington where she was placed in charge of Mrs. John A. Logan. Later she became the guest of Mrs. John W. Foster, widow of the Secretary of State of President Harrison.

On the way to the White House with Mrs. Logan, Evangelina tried to assemble a speech to utter when she would meet the President: "I come to speak to you, Mr. President, for the helpless women and children of Cuba...."

Mrs. Logan said, "You're trembling, child."

"Yes, madam," confessed Evangelina, "I tremble more than I did when I helped Mr. Decker break through the bars of *Recojidas;* or when I gave laudanum to my fellow prisoners; or when I crossed the ladder to safety; or when dressed in boy's clothes I went through the streets of Havana. I must speak for Cuba to the President."

Mrs. Logan and Evangelina stood in the White House reception-room, waiting. The door opened, an usher announced, "The President of the United States."

The prisoner of the *Recojidas* stood face to face with the President. Speech was forgotten by Evangelina. She had no need to utter words. When she looked into the face of President McKinley she knew that Cuba would be free.

Out of gratitude to America, and at the request of Hearst, Evangelina became a citizen of the United States. She lived in this country for a little more than a year when she married Carlos Carbonnel of Havana at the residence of Consul-General and Mrs. Fitzhugh Lee in Virginia. She now lives in Havana.

The wrongs of Evangelina Cisneros, her rescue, her beauty, the publicity given her life by Hearst, stirred the American people and quickened the war spirit in the United States. Americans realized that intervention was inevitable.

In Cuba the repercussion of Evangelina's rescue was felt. Placards were posted on billboards. *"Al agua con los Americanos!"* (To the water with the Americans). The Spaniards dared not attack Consul-General Fitzhugh Lee, but their hatred rumbled and roared. After Evangelina was rescued Hearst sent his yacht, the *Buccaneer*, carrying one gun, a one-pounder used for signaling, into Cuban waters. So great was the rage of the Spaniards against Hearst that the *Buccaneer* was seized.

CHAPTER XXII

SPANISH-AMERICAN WAR SCOOPS

DURING the first two years that Arthur Brisbane was on the *Journal* he found a new field for himself. Until this time he had written very few editorials. Now at Hearst's request he began the simple, instructive condensed editorials for which he has since become famous, and which made a new school of editorial writing in the United States. Brisbane's editorials, stimulating to millions whose minds had been neglected by editorial writers, vastly increased the circulation of the paper. He received a considerable percentage of the returns from new subscribers, and already he had an enormous income. Brisbane worked like a man on fire, resourceful, daring, tireless. His suggestions increased the advertising. He showed that he could make or unmake any play in New York, and he caused theatrical managers for the first time to realize the importance of extensive advertising. As one of Brisbane's reporters said to the writer, "A. B. is a hornet's nest of ideas. Talking with him an hour makes me feel as if I had been swirled around in Niagara Falls."

Brisbane always says, "You accomplish nothing, unless you burn much." The youth of his mind still burns. Hearst not only greatly appreciated Brisbane, but he engaged every able man or woman to be found in the United States. He said he would like to find a dozen more Brisbanes and pay them as large salaries. They would help him make a greater success. Every member of the *Journal's* staff was steamed up to the bursting point by Hearst himself. The *Journal's* circulation mounted.

In the editorial rooms Hearst and the staff had long daily conferences. Sometimes there were twelve or fourteen men at the table. Often Hearst sat silent, listening, while writers, editors, and artists debated suggestions for policy and news display. Frequently Hearst acted in opposition to the majority.

Charles Edward Russell says that after a large conference Hearst said quietly to the chief editors "Wouldn't five or six at the conference table do as well? Too many give me stage fright." At the smaller conferences Hearst talked with greater ease and freedom.

In 1898, the *Evening Journal* staff was everywhere. Coal barons were exposed as intimidating witnesses in a murder case in Luzerne County, Pennsylvania, when twenty miners were shot by Sheriff Martin and his deputies. Factory laws were shown as being violated in New York sweat-shops employing children. Joseph Leiter, the Armours and Eastmans were disclosed as raising the price of bread by speculating in wheat. An explosion in a Brooklyn school caused the *Journal* to investigate. A large number of the janitors were shown to be incompetent. The welfare and education of children had first place in Hearst's interest. As the result of neglect on the part of the Mayor twenty-five thousand school children were shown to be without seats. Hearst suggested that such buildings as Madison Square Garden and Grand Central Palace be used for schools. Finally the children were properly housed and seated. Hearst struggled for reforms in court practice, and in 1900, Justice Gaynor handed down an opinion abolishing the fees that had rendered it impossible for the poor to obtain justice in lower courts.

But no matter how many crusades Hearst engaged in during these days his absorbing interest was always in Cuba. The gallant, soldier-reporter, Karl Decker, was again in Cuba fighting with the insurgents. The press of the United States was sympathetic with Cuba, but no publication was so pro-Cuban as the Hearst papers. Hearst was the flaming crusader for the Pearl of the Antilles. He challenged Bourbon tyranny. He determined to drive Spain from this hemisphere. From the wide publicity given by him to his purposes and ideals, perhaps

more than from any other cause came the Spanish War. Without Hearst Cuba might still be under the heel of Spain. He
speaks of the conflict that arose as "our pet war."

"Free Cuba!" wrote Hearst daily, but slaughter of Cubans
continued. Women were ravished, children starved and patriots
were shot on the firing line. Only one hundred miles away
from this great land of freedom such deeds were done. To
the Administration at Washington Cuba was no affair of
ours.

In vain Evangelina Cisneros traveled through the United
States pleading for liberty, for her suffering country in memory
of brave patriots who for a century had offered up their lives,
and pleading in the name of her imprisoned father, and in
the name of the crucified One. This mighty Government had
no aid for struggling Cuba.

Hearst sent a commission to investigate conditions. In
March, one of the *Evening Journal* commissioners, Senator
Thurston of Nebraska, addressed the Senate and thronged
galleries. He arraigned the "money changers who cowardly
cried for peace. I do not read my duty on the ticker. I do
not accept my lessons in patriotism from Wall Street. I depre-
cate war, but the time has come when muskets ought to go
with food."

Temporarily depressed by the inactivity of the Government, Hearst said he would give up fighting for Cuba, but the
cause of liberty drove him forward.

Then the Spanish Minister Señor Dupuy de Lome wrote a
letter characterizing President McKinley as a "low politician
catering to the rabble." A facsimile of the letter came to the
office of the *Journal*. Through Minister Woodford, President
McKinley requested that Spain withdraw her Minister. By
cable he demanded that de Lome resign. Vice-President Hobart,
Senator Lodge and other Republicans conferred with the
President and told him de Lome must not be permitted to
resign, he must be dismissed. The President made the demand
of Spain. On the following day Spain began to prepare for war.

Havana was like a volcano. It was said that Cuban patriots planned to dynamite Havana in order to wipe out the last vestige of Spanish power. What would happen?

On January 25th, the Battleship *Maine* arrived in Havana harbor. The *Maine* was the pride of the navy. During the night of the 15th of February, 1898, a sound like thunder shook Havana, shook Washington and the world. The *Maine* was blown up. Two hundred and sixty-eight American lives were lost.

How did the explosion of the *Maine* come about? Captain W. T. Sampson who was in charge of the Atlantic fleet was President of the American Board of Inquiry. After an extended examination of the subject on March 21st, he reported that the walls of the *Maine's* magazine were bent inward. This evidence indicated that the *Maine* was destroyed by a mine. Was it an accident? Was it the work of Cubans, who by this explosion hoped to force the United States to declare war on Spain? Was it the act of a half-mad Spaniard who hated and feared the United States? No one will ever know.

Not since the firing on Fort Sumter had there been such rage as that caused by the explosion of the *Maine*. No longer should mercy be shown a nation that tortured women and children and sent to eternity American soldiers defenseless in sleep. From North, South, East and West came the cry, "Drive Spain from the continent!" "Free Cuba!" "War!" President McKinley rose from his bed and summoned his advisers.

Hearst ordered the first page of his papers printed in color and festooned with flags. On the day after the explosion of the *Maine,* he offered a fifty thousand dollar reward for the detection of the perpetrator of the crime. He gave a thousand dollars toward the fund to erect a shaft in honor of the dead sailors. Throughout the land boomed, "Remember the *Maine!*"

In Chinese waters, Dewey's fleet assembled at Hongkong to stand in readiness. The North Atlantic squadron was sent from Hampton Roads into the waters of Florida for maneuvers. Captain Sampson, senior officer of the North Atlantic

Squadron, was appointed Commander-in-Chief with rank of Acting Admiral. The flying squadron under Commodore W. S. Schley was stationed at Hampton Roads. Large supplies of ammunition were ordered. On March 9th, Congress voted fifty million dollars for national defense.

It was said that Senators Elkins and Hanna opposed war, and that the President was for peace. Hearst led the national press storming at the Administration to free Cuba. Finally in a lukewarm message McKinley asked Congress to authorize intervention. He signed the resolution of Congress declaring that relinquishment of authority by Spain in Cuba was the object of American action.

Hearst wrote an editorial stating that "McKinley, the man of diplomacy, was a cinder in the eye of the American people. But McKinley, the man of action, begins well. He has signed the war resolution of Congress and sent his ultimatum to Spain."

America challenged. Spain was given forty-eight hours' grace. On the 20th of April, Congress passed a resolution demanding the withdrawal of Spain from Cuba. Noon, April 23rd, was set as the latest day for reply. Two days later Havana was blockaded.

Before the resolution of Congress could be delivered to the American Minister at Madrid, the Spanish government sent Minister Woodford his passport. On April 24th, the Spanish government declared war. One day later Congress announced that a state of war had existed for four days.

From the *Journal* and *Examiner* offices rockets shot skyward, flashing through the night the news that war had begun.

On April 25, 1898, the first shot of war was fired by Spain. It struck the *Evening Journal* dispatch boat close to Morro Castle and fell into the sea. The crew of the dispatch boat jeered at the Spaniards. Recently Hearst purchased several mortars from Morro Castle bearing the arms of Ferdinand and Isabella and placed them on one of the terraces at San Simeon.

Hearst's anxiety, and the anxiety of a nation were for Commodore Dewey in the Pacific. On April 26th, the order was sent from Washington: "Dewey, Asiatic squadron, commence operations at once, particularly against Spanish fleet. You must capture or destroy them. McKINLEY."

Hearst offered a reward of one thousand dollars for the best new idea for carrying on the war. It was feared that the Spanish fleet would dash through the Suez Canal and attack Dewey. In his desire to aid, Hearst chartered a coaling vessel, ordered the Captain to fly English colors, and sent it to the Suez Canal. The officer was told by Hearst that should the Spanish fleet try to go through the Canal to attack Dewey, a hole in the ship should be opened and the vessel sunk in the canal to delay the Spaniards.

When war was declared Dewey was on board the *Olympia,* his flagship, in the bay of Hongkong. Asiatic and British ports were closed to him. He steamed out of the bay to conquer or die. Fearing counter-orders Dewey cut the cable connecting with the United States. For days nothing was heard of him.

In the United States there was a long anxious Sunday of waiting. Prayers were offered up for Dewey somewhere off the coast of China. Rumors of victory came. Rumors of defeat persisted.

No one knew the truth until suddenly there was brought into the *Journal* office a message on a crumpled bit of paper and given to City Editor Charles Edward Russell. It was from London saying, "The Exchange Telegraph Company reports from Hongkong persistent rumors that something important has happened in Manila." This message was published as a "flash."

Then came the special cable printed by the New York *Journal* more than an hour ahead of any other paper:

Washington, May 7. Following is first official report received from Commander Dewey at the Navy Department: "Manila, May 1, 1898—Squadron arrived at Manila at daybreak this morning and immediately engaged the enemy and disabled the following vessels; cruisers *Isla de Cuba, Reina Cristina, Castilla, Don Antonio de Ulloa, Isla de Luzon, Velasco;* small gunboats, *El Cano, General Lezo, Marques del Duero;* armed transport *Isla Mindano,* and the water battery at Cavite. American squadron is uninjured, only a few men were slightly wounded. The only means of telegraphing is through the American Consul at Hongkong. I shall communicate with him.

"DEWEY"

Later reports showed that when Dewey sighted the Spanish fleet on his own flagship the *Olympia* he led toward them followed by the *Baltimore, Raleigh, Petrel, Concord* and *Boston,* at four hundred yard intervals. Within five thousand yards of the fleet he ported helm. At 5:40 in the morning Dewey opened fire. He stood westward along the Spanish line, using his port battery turned to starboard. Then he stood back, gradually decreasing his distance to two thousand yards. At seven o'clock the Spanish flagship tried to come out and fight at short range, but she was driven back. It was the last death struggle of the Spanish squadron.

At 7:30 Dewey withdrew, gave his men breakfast and consulted with his commanding officers. Suddenly two Spanish ships burst into flame. Dewey knew that the battle was over. Out of seventeen hundred and forty-eight Americans in action only seven were wounded.

Dewey's ship rescued the survivors of the Spanish fleet. The slaughter had been great. Out of the total of eighteen hundred and seventy-five, one hundred and sixty-seven were killed and two hundred and fourteen wounded. Dewey raised the flag over Cavite, paroled its garrison and awaited the arrival of a land force to capture Manila.

When the *Journal* printed the first report of the battle at two o'clock Sunday, May 7th, one million, four hundred and eight thousand, two hundred papers were sold. Six days later Hearst printed the first authentic account of the battle, and the circulation jumped to one million, four hundred and sixty-eight thousand, seven hundred and sixty-nine, at that time the largest circulation known in the history of the world. On this same day the *Evening Journal* printed one hundred and forty-six more columns of advertising than its nearest contemporary.

CHAPTER XXIII

BATTLE-FIELDS

THE great struggle of the Spanish-American War centered about the island of Cuba and in the operations near Key West. During the month of March, Admiral Cervera assembled the Spanish squadron at the Cape Verde Islands, and on April 24th, he left for Porto Rico.

Hearst perfected a system of communication with the fleet and army in Cuba by establishing daily connection by dispatch boats with Kingston, Jamaica, the nearest cable station. Every night these dispatch boats crossed the Caribbean Sea to Kingston or to Port Antonio. The copy was taken across the island by rail, or sent by carrier pigeons. "Scoop" after "scoop" was achieved by the *Journal*. At one time Hearst had under charter six steam vessels, a Brazilian cattle-boat, a Red Cross boat, a yacht, and an ocean-going tug. He became so preëminent in gathering news that rival journalists hired queues of boys to stand in front of *Journal* bulletin boards to obtain the earliest news and rush it to their offices.

Arthur McEwen determined to lay a trap for pilfering competitors, and so he concocted a hoax. A news item was fabricated by him about "Colonel Reflipe W. Thenuz, an Austrian officer who died fighting gallantly."

The *Evening World* swallowed the hoax. In the next edition the *Journal* blared the story that the *Evening World* had been caught as a news thief. "Reflipe W. Thenuz," were the words that proved the *World's* guilt. Rearranged the letters in the name of the "Austrian officer" spelled "We pilfer the news." This story became historic in Park Row, and is still recounted.

In those stirring, rushing war days the public greedily devoured the news, and extra after extra was tossed out into the streets. Not since the Civil War had there been so much excitement. Bryan volunteered with a silver regiment from Nebraska. Hearst thought of a cowboy regiment, but he was preceded in this plan by Colonel Leonard Wood and Lieutenant-Colonel Theodore Roosevelt with their Rough Riders. At his own expense Hearst equipped a regiment of cavalry.

On the second of June, 1898, the *Journal* was the first newspaper in the world to publish the news of Admiral Schley's bombardment of Santiago. The "scoop" was brought by dispatch boat. When the United States learned that Schley on the great battleship *Oregon* had made the journey of sixteen thousand miles from the Pacific, had turned back Admiral Cervera's Spanish squadron on the point of leaving Santiago, and had attacked the battery of the city at long range, the entire country was ecstatic with patriotism.

Twenty-four hours later on June 3rd, appeared a new hero, Richard P. Hobson, a naval constructor. With a crew of seven men Hobson entered Santiago harbor, and sank the collier *Merrimac* at the channel entrance hoping to block the egress of Cervera's squadron. The collier sank in the broad part of the channel, and the intrepid adventure was in vain. Hobson and his men were captured by Cervera, but the nation seeing only the young valor of the exploit cheered from the Atlantic to the Pacific. After Santiago was captured Cervera exchanged Hobson and his men for Spanish prisoners.

Richard Harding Davis, John Barrett, Honoré Laine, Stephen Crane and many others sent exciting news from Cuba. Hearst himself could not keep away from the war. He obtained a commission of Ensign, chartered the *Silvia*, a large tramp steamer, and left for the front, taking with him the war correspondent, James A. Creelman. Edward Marshall, a brilliant descriptive writer, and Jack Follansbee, Hearst's closest friend, were also on board. Then there was J. C. Hemmant, a well-known photographer with vast field experience, who carried the first motion-picture apparatus into a war zone. The *Silvia* also had a complete newspaper plant with men to get out a daily paper covering events in the army, fleet and camp among the soldiers and sailors.

Hearst reached Siboney just as General Shafter was landing his forces to attack Santiago. He made his headquarters in a group of shacks occupied by correspondents, and occasionally made a trip to Jamaica on the *Silvia*.

One of the first things Hearst did after landing was to obtain the flag of the *Merrimac*, the collier which had been sunk by Hobson, and send it to hero Dewey at Manila. Then he interviewed Captain Sampson, General Shafter and General Calixto Garcia, the commander of the Cuban revolution. For the first time, "W. R. Hearst" appeared as a writer. He signed his name to articles.

Shafter was described by Hearst as a "sort of human fortress in blue coat and flannel shirt." Garcia saluted the editor with tears streaming down his bronzed cheeks. There had been doubt as to whether Garcia would accept the direction of Shafter, but Hearst was pleased when he saw Garcia take Shafter's hand and heard him say, "I thank you and your soldiers for coming down here to help me fight the enemies of my country. We will serve with you and take orders without question, but do not surrender the Philippines to Spain. . . . The Spaniards will fight with obstinacy, like bulls, merely because they have horns."

Then the venerable Garcia, in spotless white said to Hearst, "I present to you the flag of the eastern department of the Republic of Cuba in commemoration of the services of your paper for liberty. The colors of the flag are faded, and it is pierced with bullet holes, but brave men have died under it. This flag is the best thing the Cuban Republic can offer its best friend."

Hearst sent the flag of Cuba to the *Evening Journal* office. Then he described what he saw:

From the top of the ridge where I write I see the monstrous form of Sampson's fleet lying in semi-circle in front of the entrance of Santiago harbor, while here at our feet masses of

American soldiers pour from the beach into the scorching valley. Vultures wheel lazily above the thorny, poisonous jungles. They have already fed on corpses of slain Spaniards. Santiago and the flower of the Spanish fleet are ours, although hundreds of men may have to die before we take possession of them.

When the Spanish-American War was declared the total military forces of the United States consisted of twenty-seven thousand, eight hundred and twenty-two regulars and one hundred and fourteen thousand, six hundred and two militia. General Shafter personally led a large part of the American army.

In his letters to the *Journal* and the *Examiner* Hearst asked for the confidence of the people:

General Shafter and his officers have accomplished almost a miracle in landing sixteen thousand soldiers with food, arms, ammunition and equipment in small boats through a rough surf on the steep dangerous beach, between ugly reefs in almost killing heat.... The work was all done and well done in four days.... The spirit of the army is high.

Although Hearst rode from camp to camp interviewing commanders and inspecting battle-fields, and he also visited the fleet, he found time to bring out the *Examiner-Journal*, the first American paper on Cuban soil. It was published for the army and navy. Gaily Hearst wrote that he did not expect it to pay.

General Calixto Garcia congratulated the infant paper, and even President McKinley felicitated the youngest journal as an "unique exemplification of modern journalism."

After Shafter landed in the advance toward Santiago it was found necessary to attack two positions held by the enemy. Lieutenant-Colonel Theodore Roosevelt with his Rough Riders commanded one charge. Yelling like a Sioux he led his regiment. Suddenly his horse hesitated, staggered and fell dead. Roosevelt twisted out of the saddle, landed on his feet, and waving his sword cheered his troops onward. Over the crest of the hill and into the trenches of the enemy he rushed, and thus was born a Presidential boom.

In this intrepid charge Edward Marshall, special correspondent of the *Journal*, was shot twice in the spine. Stephen Crane the novelist, George Coffin the artist, H. G. McNichol, and two barefoot Negro sailors from the dispatch boat *Kanapaha* brought Marshall to safety over a five and a half mile climb to the field hospital about one hundred yards in the rear of the battle-field.

At first Marshall's condition was thought hopeless, but late that night under a mango tree that served as a roof for the hospital, Dr. William S. Gorgas, later of Panama fame, performed by candle-light a desperate operation. Marshall's left leg was amputated. He recovered and led an active life as writer and editor. He survived three train wrecks, a lake steamer wreck, and two hotel fires. In 1916, when a torpedo cut in two and sank the British channel steamer *Sussex*, Marshall was aboard. Unable to swim he clung to wreckage for hours until he was picked up. He lived until 1933.

On July 4, 1898, the *Evening Journal* and *Examiner* published a full-page article of the battle of El Caney written by Hearst:

With the army in front of Santiago, July 1, midnight, via Kingston, Jamaica—To-night as I write, ambulance trains are bringing wounded soldiers from the fierce battle around the little village of El Caney.

Siboney, the base of the army, is a hospital, and nothing more. There is no saying when the slaughter will cease. Tents are crowded with wounded, and hard worked surgeons are busy with medical work. There is an odor of antiseptics, and ambulances clatter through one narrow street.

Under the fierce firing of far heavier artillery than it was supposed the Spanish had, the American infantry and dismounted cavalry have done their work and done it nobly.

I have been at the artillery positions all day to see what our guns could do. There is no question of the skill and courage of

American gunmen. Their work is as near perfect as gunnery gets to be, but there was no artillery to speak of. The War Department furnished the necessary heavy guns, but they remained in the rear because of the difficulty of transportation from the coast.

Hearst wrote of an early ride on horseback with Honoré Laine, a Colonel in the Cuban army, who was serving as the *Journal's* correspondent. They passed over eight miles of difficult country, dodging bullets, making for a tile-roofed house where they expected to take luncheon.

We found that a shrapnel ball had passed clean through one of our cans of pressed beef which our pack mule was carrying.

We turned to the right toward our battery on the ridge. When we were half way to the battery, the second shell which the Spaniards fired burst over the American battery not ten feet over the heads of our men. Six of our fellows were killed and sixteen wounded. The men in the battery wavered for a moment, then rallied and returned to their guns, and the firing went on.

We passed to the right again where General Shafter's war balloon was ascending. Six shells landed in this vicinity, and then our battery ceased firing. The smoke clouds from our guns were forming too plain a target for the Spaniards. There was no trace to be seen of the enemy's battery because of their use of smokeless powder.

Off to the far right of our line of formation Colonel Capron's artillery which had come through from Daiquiri without rest, could be heard banging away at El Caney. We started with a view of going where we could observe military operations, so we directed our course thither.

We found Colonel Capron blazing away with four guns where he should have had a dozen He had begun shelling El Caney at four o'clock in the morning. It was now noon, and he was still firing. He was aiming to reduce the large stone fort which stood on the hill above the town and commanded it.

Colonel O'Connell had laid a wager that the first shot of some one of the four guns would hit the fort, and he won his bet.

Since that time dozens of shells have struck the fort, but it is not yet reduced. It became much weakened, however.

Through glasses, our infantry could be seen advancing toward the fort. As the cannon at our side would bang and the shell would swish through the air with its querulous note, we would watch its explosion and then turn our attention to the little black specks of infantry dodging in and out between the groups of trees. Now they would disappear wholly from sight in the brush, and again would be seen hurrying along the open spaces, over the grass-covered slopes or across plowed fields. The infantry firing was ceaseless, our men popping away continuously as a string of firecrackers would pop.

The Spaniards fired in volleys whenever our men came in sight in the open spaces. Many times we heard this volley fire and saw numbers of our brave fellows pitch forward and lie still on the turf while the others hurried on to the next protecting clump of trees. For hours the Spaniards had poured their fire from slits in the stone fort, also from their deep trenches and from the windows of the town. For hours our men answered back from trees and brush and gullies. For hours cannon at our side banged and shells screamed through the air and fell upon the fort and town.

And always our infantry advanced, drawing nearer and closing up on the village, till at last they formed under the mangrove tree at the foot of the hill on which the stone fort stood. With a rush they swept up the slope and the stone fort was ours.

You should have heard the yell that went up from the knoll on which our battery stood. Gunners, drivers, Cubans, correspondents, swung their hats and gave a mighty cheer. Immediately our battery stopped firing for fear we would hurt our own men, and dashing down into the valley hurried across to take up a position near the infantry which was now firing on El Caney from the blockhouse and entering the streets of the town.

The artillery had not sent a dozen shots from its new position before the musketry firing ceased and the Spanish broke into small bunches and fled from El Caney in the direction of Santiago.

Laine and I hurried up to the stone fort and found that James Creelman, the *Journal* correspondent with the infantry column, had been seriously wounded and was lying in the Twelfth Infantry Hospital. Our men were still firing an occasional shot.

From the blockhouse and isolated trenches from which the Spaniards could not safely retreat, flags of truce were waved. Guns and side-arms were being taken away from such Spaniards as had outlived the pitiless fire, and their dead were being dumped without ceremony into the trenches after Spanish fashion.

When I left the fort to hunt for Creelman I found him bloody and bandaged, lying on his back on a blanket on the ground, but shown all care that a kindly skillful surgeon could give him. He was pretty well dazed and said, "I'm afraid I can't write much of a story. If you will write it for me I will describe it the best I can."

Creelman's story was taken down by Hearst. The correspondent had been struck by a bullet from the Spanish trenches just as he seized the Spanish flag and waved it before the American troops. Creelman received the surrender of the Spanish commander. He was transported to the *Silvia* to be treated for his ugly shoulder wound made by a dum-dum bullet. He was ill for weeks, but he lived to see the World War. He died in Berlin February 12, 1918.

Hearst forwarded by mail to the *Journal* the Spanish flag captured from the enemy's fort. El Caney was defended by Brigadier-General de Rey, who died fighting after losing four-fifths of his men in action. The American losses exceeded even those of the Spanish.

Hemmant, the photographer on the *Silvia*, kept up a lament that he was not getting any real action pictures. The Spanish fleet was believed to be securely bottled up in the Santiago harbor. Hearst thought that in lieu of action it would be best to be with the American fleet on the Fourth of July. The national salute would be fired by battleships, and that would be a fair imitation of war. Hearst gave orders to the captain of the *Silvia* to steam toward the American fleet for the national holiday.

Admiral Sampson also believed that Cervera's Spanish Armada would not leave Santiago, and early on the morning of July 3rd, he went to confer with General Shafter at Siboney with regard to combined operations at the harbor entrance. At 9:31 when he had gone about five miles, the *Maria Teresa* came out of the bay of Santiago. Admiral Schley took command and stood in toward the Spanish ships with the *Indiana, Oregon, Iowa* and *Texas,* the armored cruiser *Brooklyn,* and the yacht *Dixon.* The Americans began heavy firing. Cervera's flagship, the *Maria Teresa,* and the *Vizcaya,* the *Colon* and *Oquendo,* answered. Far beyond the American ships went the Spanish projectiles. The *Maria Teresa* and the *Oquendo* took fire. The *Vizcaya* and *Colon* tried to escape. After them went the *Brooklyn, Texas* and *Oregon*—the *Oregon* opening her thirteen-inch guns. Down came the Spanish colors. The great steel and iron creatures were beached. The *Vizcaya* burned on the shore. Admiral Cervera was taken prisoner. Captain Villamil, commanding the torpedo flotilla, went down with his ship. The entire Spanish fleet was destroyed.

The gallant conduct of Lieutenant-Commander Philip Wainwright at the battle of Santiago will long be remembered. When his ship sank the *Pluton* in deep water and compelled the *Furor* to run ashore, the American crew cheered. "Don't cheer, boys," said Wainwright, "the poor devils are dying." Immediately he began rescuing the vanquished foe.

Before going into the fight Admiral Cervera had cabled his government that he wished to destroy his vessels. For political and dynastic reasons Madrid ordered him to make a sortie at any cost. Five hundred Spaniards were killed or wounded. The survivors, except a few, who escaped to Santiago, were made prisoners. On the American side only one man was killed and ten were wounded.

At daybreak on the Fourth of July Hearst's yacht, the *Silvia,* approached Cuba and the editor learned what had occurred. After the burning *Vizcaya* steamed the *Silvia* at full speed. With a correspondent and a cameraman Hearst boarded her. The decks were so hot that he had to walk on his heels. Everything combustible was charred and smoldering. When Hearst described the scene on July 5th, for the *Journal,* he pictured the wrecked leviathans of the Spanish navy, as "Lying with their heads in the sand as if to hide from themselves the sight of their own destruction and humiliation."

The *Suwanee* came up and sent the famous Lieutenant Blue ashore in a boat to look for survivors of the Spanish crew and take them prisoners. Although the *Silvia* had neither life-boats nor life-preservers Hearst followed the *Suwanee* through the strong running surf along the rocky beach. He saw a breaker hurl Lieutenant Blue overboard into the white froth of the sea.

It was too late to turn back. The *Silvia* was in the breakers. Huge waves rose under and over the boat and thrust it onto the shore. When the first scrape of gravel sounded under the keel, Hearst and all the others jumped out and dragged the boat upon the beach. Lieutenant Blue was safely hauled to shore by his crew.

Hearst next had headed the *Silvia* for the *Infanta Maria Teresa* which had been first of all the Spanish ships to give up the flag. The editor was seeking Spanish prisoners. The *Infanta Maria Teresa*, lying on the beach to the east, was not in such bad condition as the *Oquendo*. Still smoldering, the flagship seemed to protest against destruction, for occasionally her cartridges popped as if in feeble endeavor to wage battle.

Hearst scanned the shore for Spaniards. Finally he saw a score of figures huddled together in a cove of the beach. He shouted to them, and some of the reporters made demonstrations with firearms. "The poor cowed fellows," wrote Hearst to the *Journal*, "with great alacrity waved a white handkerchief or shirt in token of surrender."

Hearst jumped overboard and swam ashore to tell the Spaniards that he would take them on his boat to the Admiral. The Spaniards appeared grateful, for they dreaded the Cubans far more than the Americans. The ship's launch was sent for. Hearst and the two photographers stood guard over the Spaniards. Vultures were feeding on corpses. Before taking the Spaniards aboard his yacht Hearst compelled them to bury their dead. On board the *Silvia,* he gave his prisoners food and clothing.

From the twenty-nine wounded men, who had been in the heat of the fight, he learned how the Spanish crews deserted their guns under the deadly American fire and had been shot down by their own officers. As the battle grew more desperate fine wines and liquors of the officers' mess were given to the crews so that with drunken courage the men would carry on the hopeless fight. At last the officers gave themselves up and deliberately scuttled their ships on the shore.

Hearst transported the prisoners on the *Silvia* to Admiral Sampson who thanked him courteously and asked him to deliver the prisoners on board the *St. Louis.* Hearst complied, and received a receipt from the marine officer in charge. This receipt was forwarded to the *Journal.* At last Hemmant, the photographer, was happy. He had pictures of Spanish prisoners kissing the American flag and cheering the victors.

On board the *St. Louis,* Hearst found Admiral Cervera, a fine imposing figure in full dress uniform with gold braid and several decorations on his breast. Hearst smiles as he recalls that the effect of the Admiral's dazzling uniform and proud, courtly dignity was somewhat impaired by the fact that his trousers were damp from wading ashore when he es-caped from his burning ship.

After delivering the prisoners Hearst visited the wreck of the *Vizcaya* while the photographer took pictures. Only a few months before, the giant battleship had anchored in New York Bay and awed the great city. Now seated on one of the dismounted guns on the *Vizcaya,* Hearst wrote an article describing the wrecked battleships.

The Spanish fleet was destroyed, but there still floated over Santiago the red and yellow of Castile. An order had been sent by General Shafter to the Spanish commander to surrender. The alternative was bombardment of the city on the Fourth of July. With proud defiance the red and yellow still waved. Admiral Sampson fired a number of shots into the city at long range. The threat of Shafter and the bursting shells caused an exodus of civilians toward El Caney. The city still held out.

Soon a new enemy appeared among the American forces. Deadly tropical malaria raged. Yellow fever was feared. Soldiers were lying in trenches wet to the skin. From Cuba, Hearst wrote several articles and sent them by special dispatch boat. He urged the President to cease all discussion, order an immediate attack, and get the soldiers out of the fever-stricken trenches. "Take Santiago in a day!"

On the 12th of July, General Nelson A. Miles, Commander-in-Chief, arrived with reinforcements. For reasons of health these men were detained on board ship, but their numbers were a threat to the Spanish. There was little more fighting. On the 17th of July, 1898, the imperial red and gold of Spain sadly floated down forever, and the Stars and Stripes were unfurled over the Pearl of the Antilles.

Four years later Hearst was deeply touched; Cuba's flag was raised over the new Republic. From President Tomas Estrada Palma, first President of Cuba, came the cable message to Hearst: "I do not believe that we could have secured our independence without the aid which you rendered."

Siboney, El Caney and Santiago, the crescent-shaped be-flowered island itself, held Hearst's memory. Youth had dreamed true.

CHAPTER XXIV

GAS-TRUST CRUSADE

AFTER Hearst returned from Cuba, more than ever he became a crusader. He plunged into work in New York. He belonged to fashionable clubs, but he seldom entered them. He loved his newspapers. As he has often said, building up a newspaper was never work, it was play. His playmates were those who helped to create his newspapers. His game was Park Row. The field of his game was the United States.

Hearst's favorite recreations were the theater and window-shopping. Fifth Avenue saw him loitering before shop windows, his eyes always seeking rare art objects. He attended almost every auction of consequence, or sent a representative with a list of objects interesting him and the price he was willing to pay. With the years his fever for collecting burned higher. Textiles, ceramics, armor, plate, sculpture, paintings, tapestries, everything unusual, beautiful, rare and difficult to obtain enthralled him. Often he consulted with Brisbane and other editors while in auction rooms, suggesting articles between bids.

When first he arrived in New York, Hearst lived at the Hoffman House. Then he took the third floor in the Worth House across Twenty-fifth Street owned by the Hoffman Company. He could not procure a lease, as the hotel people had the place listed for sale, but he ripped out the interior and had it wholly rebuilt. He put in beamed ceilings, tiled floors, rare mantels, and furnished the rooms with antique furniture and tapestries. Just before the apartment was finished he went to Europe. While he was abroad the building was sold and razed.

Many of the fittings were saved and installed in the residence at Lexington Avenue and Twenty-eighth Street which

Hearst called the "shanty." Here he lived several years. George Thompson, his butler, made a happy home for his employer, Arthur Brisbane and Jack Follansbee. George had been a waiter at the Hoffman House and he remained with Hearst for more than thirty years, when he died. George had initiative and executive ability. He always knew precisely what should be done. He became as much a part of the house as the furniture. For a long period he was pensioned, but at the end his greatest joy was to be summoned by Hearst to serve wine at a large dinner. George had English frankness in his comments, and Hearst enjoyed listening to his opinions. He spoke of the Madonnas that Hearst was collecting as the "McDonoughs." Hearst liked joyous clothing. He had hundreds of neckties, many in bright colors. Once he purchased some new scarfs.

"What do you think of them, George?" asked Hearst.

"Well, Mr. Hearst, I don't know as they are any worse than the others," was the reply that greatly diverted the editor.

For rapidity and suddenness of growth in two and a half years no newspaper ever equaled the *Evening Journal.* Arthur Brisbane's percentage on the increase in circulation was so great that Hearst's profits were comparatively small. The publisher decided to abandon the percentage arrangement and fix definitely Brisbane's salary. From receiving one hundred and fifty dollars a week Brisbane rose to having the largest salary ever paid an editor—a quarter of a million dollars a year.

In order to check the growth of the *Evening Journal's* circulation, Hearst increased the price of the paper from one to two cents, but there was no material drop. On April 1, 1918, the normal circulation was seven hundred and thirty-one thousand and forty-seven.

From the art department came much of the *Journal's* success. There was an artist, de Lippman, who made huge doubletruck line drawings across two inside pages showing trials, horse shows, conventions in Madison Square Garden, and all large spectacles. On October 3, 1898, Hearst printed the first half-tone picture to appear in a New York daily, a photograph of Caroline Miskell Hoyt, wife of the dramatist Charles Hoyt, and called by her husband the most beautiful woman in the United States. The half-tone of Mrs. Hoyt was accomplished by inserting a zinc etching in the stereotype plate, but it slowed up stereotyping, and did not permit making over during the day the page that carried the half-tone.

Hearst's knowledge of photography enabled him to direct experiments in molding and casting plates from zinc half-tones assembled in the form. The most suitable half-tone screens were selected, proper depth was obtained in the etching, and the moisture contents of the "mats" was accurately determined to get full depth in the mold. When these steps were perfected for the first time it was possible to print photographic reproductions of news events at news speed.

Years later wet "mats" were superseded by dry "mats," but the methods originated in the *Journal* are in use in all newspaper plants to-day. After the first successful half-tone only a few artists were kept for decorative work. Camera men replaced artists. For years every reporter carried a camera. Photographs became as important a part of the paper as the news, and there was never-ending rivalry to see which newspaper could obtain them exclusively.

In 1896, the first color section ever printed in a daily newspaper astonished New York. The picture was drawn by Archie Gunn. A three-color process was used outlined in black. Later in the year, *McFadden's Row of Flats* written by E. W. Townsend, author of *Chimmie Fadden* and illustrated by R. F. Outcault, attracted attention. It was in two colors with a black outline. The special supplement honoring the Grant monument and printed in three colors in 1897, astounded New York, as did the Christmas supplement the same year, when the Sistine Madonna appeared in three colors. During that same year the first combination of colors and half-tones was used in a newspaper. A page of the *Journal* was devoted to scenes from Frank Daniels' new play, *The Idol's Eye*. One of the most popular pictures was "The Pickaninny's Christmas Dream" by Kemble in December of 1897. In this same year Frederick Remington's Cuban sketches showing buzzards devouring the dead added a serious note to the supplements.

In 1898, appeared the first double-page picture in color ever printed on a newspaper press. It was the "North Atlantic Squadron on Her Way," by Carlton T. Chapman, and it marked a new era in newspaper illustrations. This same year Hearst printed the first cook-book in colors, and the first dress pattern was given away by a newspaper. In 1900, came the first full comic section printed by a newspaper. This appeared on August 19th, in three colors. On St. Patrick's Day the harp and shamrock were printed in green.

In one day more than one million, two hundred thousand papers came from the presses. Four or five large presses were needed to obtain a color. Hearst noticed the slightest change in hue. No matter how large the presses were the Hoe Company could not make machinery large enough. Hoe would not guarantee the presses, but they worked well. With pride Hearst looked at the huge whirring machines and said, "No one can short-circuit that plant."

With two large papers, the *Journal* and the *Examiner,* at his command, Hearst began profoundly to alter the life of America. Arthur Brisbane calls him one of America's five great men: Washington, who founded the Republic; Lincoln, who saved it; Edison, who gave it light; Henry Ford, who taught it to move; and Hearst, who freed the masses from mental inertia and taught them to think. Workers who hitherto had avoided print as an insoluble puzzle, now began to read Hearst editorials.

At this time in New York illegal combinations of capital were running amuck, unrestrained by public authority, using their power to maintain artificial price levels. Powerful industrial units were secretly obtaining rebates from railroads.

Their rivals could not compete. Brazenly elections were stolen and bought. The people were powerless but resigned.

Then came Hearst, champion in the courts of the inarticulate masses against franchise grabbers, corrupt public officials, ballot-box stuffers, bosses and trusts enthroned. To-day at seventy-two years of age his eyes still flash gray steel when he listens to a recital of injustice. At that time fresh from Cuba, corrupt New York became another Cuban battle-field. He helped the Brooklyn trolley employees get their hours of work reduced from twenty to ten. He closed obscene penny-in-the-slot machines. He revealed that many school buildings on Manhattan were so faultily constructed as to imperil the lives of one hundred and thirty-two thousand school children.

In saving the forty miles of streets which the Board of Aldermen had voted to the Nassau Railroad Company of which Thomas L. Johnson was president, Hearst dramatically came in contact with the railroad magnate, later to become a reformer, the Mayor of Cleveland, and the inspiring leader of the liberal movement in the Middle West. Johnson had lost a franchise worth ten million dollars, but he had the fair-mindedness to write Hearst:

You may be surprised to hear, far from denouncing the *Journal* I believe you have acted in the interests of the people. I am a railroad man, it is true, but this is not a railroad question. . . . The stand you have taken in sustaining an injunction is a great stand. I believe that the people will appreciate your efforts in their behalf. As a business man I must say that I think newspapers are often inclined to meddle too much in business questions, but I say that you deserve credit in obtaining this injunction.

THOMAS L. JOHNSON

Light, fuel, heat and power for New York City were also Hearst's crusade. In December, 1896, he discovered that the Standard, Mutual, Equitable and East River Gas Companies had agreed to divide the city at the expense of the public. Stealthily this corporation, the Consumer's Fuel, Gas, Heat and Power Company had put through the Board of Estimate and Apportionment, the city's franchise-granting body, a measure permitting it to lay fuel-gas mains under every street and public place in New York City. It was a privilege worth tens of millions, but no compensation was to be given the city. Hearst found it out. He had a reformer's zeal, optimism, determination and faith.

Late one night he awakened Clarence J. Shearn, counsel for the *Evening Journal*: "Something must be done," he said. "What can we do?"

Shearn thought hard. It was too late to prevent granting the franchise. That had been done. He thought of the New York State taxpayer's act. Shearn knew this measure authorized a suit in the name of any taxpayer against a public official to prevent waste of public funds or an illegal public action. Hearst must prevent the Mayor from signing the franchise.

Under the New York State taxpayer's act, Hearst and Shearn brought suit. Judge Roger Q. Pryor enjoined the Mayor from signing the franchise.

Sensation startled and stirred New York. Would Hearst be able to block the Gas Trust and the Mayor? The franchise was not signed by His Honor.

Hearst's battle with the trust moved to Albany. Gas bills had become as high as rent. Senator Cantor introduced a bill to lower the price of gas in New York City. The Gas Trust representative defied the legislature. He failed to appear for the joint hearing on the Cantor Dollar Gas Bill. The Assembly committee also refused to appear. No dollar gas at this session.

Then entered Boss Richard Croker of Tammany. He had seven senses in connection with public events. Keenly conscious that the *Journal* had the largest circulation of any paper in New York, Croker declared that he would reduce gas to ninety cents a thousand.

Then on April 6, 1899, Hearst outlined a plan in the *Evening Journal* for the construction of a municipal gas plant in and for New York City. All Borough Presidents endorsed the project. Then Croker himself declared he would reduce the gas bill of every citizen one-third and put five million dollars in the city treasury. He demanded a municipal gas plant. Mayor Van Wyck declared that New York City should own its gas plant.

On May 9, 1899, all gas companies in Manhattan slashed their rates to sixty-five cents. The Amsterdam Light and Gas Company dropped to fifty cents.

Hearst had won his long battle, but conditions were too perfect. One year later the *Evening Journal* announced that a Gas Trust had been formed and it had the city by the throat. The Consolidated Gas Company had gobbled up the Amsterdam Gas Company. Russell Sage's Standard Gas Company would soon make a mouthful of the Union Gas Company of Brooklyn. Then the Trust or Consolidated Gas Company blithely skyrocketed gas from fifty cents to one dollar and five cents, the legal limit.

Just as Hearst was having Carey T. Hutchinson, a well-known civil and electrical engineer, draw plans for a municipal gas plant, New York learned that John T. Oakley, commissioner of water supply, gas and electricity, had signed secret lighting contracts that made the new Gas Trust a virtual gift of nine millions.

Hearst resorted to law. Supreme Justice Marrau of the Supreme Court, enjoined Mayor McClellan and other city officials from paying one million, two hundred and fifty thousand to the Gas Trust. At the same time Attorney-General Cunnenn at the request of Clarence J. Shearn, Hearst's attorney, hauled the Gas Trust before the court.

Hearst procured an injunction restraining Mayor McClellan from paying back charges of a million, two hundred thousand dollars. In January, 1905, he filed complaints against all the gas companies on behalf of the consumers. For weeks these cases were tried before the Gas Commission. Hearst was represented by Clarence J. Shearn and William A. DeFord, assisted by Professor Edward W. Bemis, an expert from Cleveland, Ohio. These hearings resulted in recommendations by the Gas Commission for eighty-cent gas.

All these activities on the part of Hearst were the background of the formation of the Municipal Ownership League on December 22, 1904. This organization first appeared in Albany with William Randolph Hearst as chairman. Other members of the committee were, Senator John Ford, Judge Samuel Seabury, Thomas Gileran, C. Augustus Haviland, Melville G. Pallister, Dr. John H. Burns, Dr. John H. Birdner, Judge John Palmieri, Carl Hauser, and Clarence J. Shearn.

This committee laid before the Governor facts concerning the city's lighting contract. They asked for legislative investigation. They also asked for the construction of gas plants. They requested that the city take over the trust-owned plants at their actual value by condemnation proceedings. Governor Higgins took the matter under consideration.

One year later Hearst presented to the legislature a petition signed by one hundred and fifty thousand citizens of Greater New York demanding an investigation of the gas monopoly. The petition was granted, and the Stevens Legislative Investigating Committee was appointed.

The Gas Trust thought this was "just another committee." It was far more. It was the beginning of the career of Charles Evans Hughes. He became chief counsel of the Insurance Investigating Committee. The gas and insurance investigations established his reputation and made him available as a candidate for Governor.

Hughes brought out that the Consolidated Gas Company owned outright every gas and lighting company in Greater New York and a number of concerns outside. The corporation could press a button and darken New York City. With its own statement as a basis of calculation, the Gas Trust was making a profit on the sale of gas of 17 per cent on the cost of the plant and the mains of the company. This was in addition to the side profit of nearly nine millions on a twenty-one million dollar stock issue—a 40 per cent profit in all. Hughes also brought out that the New York Contracting and Trucking Company of which John J. Murphy, brother of Charles F. Murphy of Tammany Hall, was president, had a fifteen million contract to build a plant for the Consolidated Gas Company in Astoria, Long Island. Why?

Hughes subpoenaed Charles F. Murphy. He also summoned Mayor McClellan, Comptroller Grout and Commissioner Oakley.

The Stevens Committee reported in favor of eighty-cent gas. A recommendation was made for a State Commission of Gas and Electricity. The legislature created the commission, but eighty-cent gas was defeated by McCarren in the Senate.

Clarence J. Shearn conducted a long hearing before the State Gas Commission and on February 23, 1906, this gas rate was ordered into effect. A few months later the legislature passed the Eighty-Cent Gas Law. Federal Judge Lacombe immediately issued an injunction restraining the enforcement of the act.

On May 24, 1906, Hearst replied by having Clarence J. Shearn bring a test case against the Consolidated Gas Company, which was restrained from cutting off the gas of a consumer willing to pay eighty cents. In the highest court in the State eighty-cent gas was upheld.

More than one thousand injunctions were issued, and more than two thousand separate writs of mandamus compelling the company to supply gas at the legal rate. When consumers were unable to furnish a bond it was provided by Hearst. For more than two years he maintained a bureau in Shearn's office with a large staff to look after details.

On June 15, 1906, the Gas Trust received two blows. The court enjoined the trust from cutting off the supply of gas if the consumer refused to pay more than the eighty-cent rate. It was also fined for cutting off the gas supply. The trust answered, "We will make each individual go into court and obtain an injunction."

In January, 1909, the Supreme Court sustained the Eighty-Cent Gas Law. Immediately Hearst created another department of the gas bureau and aided twenty thousand consumers to recover their rebates. This bureau was maintained for years. Ten million, two hundred and sixty-seven thousand, two hundred and eighty-one dollars were refunded to the people by the gas company. This did not include the sums paid to thousands, who, owing to Hearst's injunction and mandamus proceedings, benefited by the eighty-cent rate. Nor did it include Brooklyn where gas companies recognized the validity of and accepted the Eighty-Cent Gas Law. Among the many crusades carried on by Hearst in New York City this one against the Gas Trust has always been gratefully remembered by plain people.

During Hearst's conflict with the Gas Trust, Lincoln Steffens was muck-raking, with incomparable skill, bosses and corporations. He thought he would like to reveal the real Hearst behind the scenes, instead of the Hearst appearing in his newspapers. Steffens knew Arthur Brisbane well, and he asked Brisbane to show him some of the private orders given by the publisher.

"Of course," said Brisbane. "Take them all."

After reading the confidential editorial directions given by Hearst to Brisbane, Steffens returned the orders with "There is no news in these instructions. They are so flattering to Hearst that if I published them, the public would say I wanted to get a job on his papers."

CHAPTER XXV

RAMAPO WATER COMPANY CAMPAIGN

PHEBE HEARST'S diary reveals that when Hearst was only ten years old his mother urged him to perfect his letters written to his father from Europe. His early letters show surprising maturity of style. Nevertheless, during the first ten years of his career as an editor he was diffident about writing. From Cuba he wrote articles to which he first signed his name. Editorials he avoided, but he made notes on backs of envelops, scraps of paper, sometimes using a blue pencil. He seldom sat at a desk. He wrote in bed, at the breakfast table, or during dinner when bored by a threadbare story. Sometimes while walking in the street Hearst asks his secretary, Joseph Willicombe, to jot down shorthand notes on his cuff. Articles he frequently writes late at night, when as he has stated, "a stray thought is likely to come swirling out of the darkness like a bat and light on you."

Arthur McEwen and Arthur Brisbane were Hearst's two favorite writers in the early New York days. After he outlined suggestions he asked Brisbane, McEwen or Charles Edward Russell to elaborate them into editorials. His notes were clear, vigorous and frequently humorous. Hearst says that Brisbane stirred him to write by saying, "You don't need any one to write editorials. Anybody can write. People forget to write simply enough." Finally Hearst wrote editorials and enjoyed the work. Now he says, "Anybody can write who can think."

In 1899, Hearst was delighted when his San Francisco *Examiner* published a great human poem, *The Man with the Hoe*. Overnight Sunday Editor Bailey Millard made its author, Edwin Markham, famous. From his understanding, eloquent, majestic lines, directly and indirectly Markham has earned a quarter of a million dollars. For several years he was literary editor of the Hearst papers.

Many of Hearst's editorial activities in 1899 touched upon women. His campaign for the abolition of capital punishment began on March 20th, when he protested in the *Evening Journal* against the execution of women for murder. Martha J. Place was condemned to death for killing her step-daughter Ida. Hearst opposed another death in the name of the law. Triumphant from bloody battle-fields of Cuba, Governor Theodore Roosevelt would not spare the life of Martha J. Place. After the woman had been executed the Governor said, "I hope I will not have to do it again."

At Passaic, New Jersey, factory girls were working from seven in the morning until eleven at night, with only fifteen minutes for dinner and fifteen minutes for supper. They appealed to Hearst for aid. In his papers he campaigned for, and had enforced, a ten-hour day as provided by law. In the Industrial State School for Girls at Trenton, New Jersey, it was revealed by the *Journal* that inmates were placed in straitjackets for punishment. The superintendent lashed the inmates, locked them in dark dungeons, and with her hand or strap beat the children. She caused the death of one girl. Governor Foster M. Voorhees was horrified. He investigated and bettered conditions. Children have always greatly concerned Hearst, and in 1899 he brought about the purchase of sterilized milk bottles for the poorer sections of Brooklyn.

At this same time Hearst addressed an editorial to President McKinley from San Francisco. He said that volunteers of the Oregon regiment, who had just returned from the Philippines, were without heavy clothing in their camp at the Presidio. Winds and fog threatened the men from the tropics with pneumonia. He wrote: "There are stores with overcoats in the Quartermaster's warehouse, but army regulations do not permit their issuance to the men. Is it not possible for Your Excellency to set aside the regulations and order the Quartermaster to issue the coats which are necessary for the health and lives of the men?"

President McKinley cut the bonds of red tape and ordered the Quartermaster to supply blankets, overcoats and uniforms to the volunteers.

In 1899, Hearst began another crusade in New York. It was against the fantastic Ramapo Water Company, a paper corporation without water. It did not even own Ramapo Lake, the source of the proposed supply. The company had only maps, and yet, it had a contract with Mayor Grant's administration empowering it to place pipes under every thoroughfare. One more vote and the company would have fastened itself on New York City for forty years at a cost of five millions a year. With the *Journal* Hearst stepped in and prevented the two hundred million dollar looting.

The water supply had always caused anxiety to New York City. In 1829, the city had its own reservoir on Thirteenth Street. De Witt Clinton suggested Croton River as a source of supply. New reservoirs were ever being recommended to the swiftly growing city. The Ramapo water project was adroitly presented. Levi P. Morton, who as Governor had signed the bill, was a stockholder in the concern. Respectable as the Morton connection appeared, it did not deceive Hearst.

In order that a stockholders' suit might be brought, Hearst purchased shares in the Ramapo Company. Then he engaged attorneys Einstein and Townsend to serve Silas P. Dutcher, president of the Ramapo Water Company, with an action compelling him to show cause before the Attorney-General why his company's charter should not be annulled. For five years the company had failed to file an annual report with the Secretary of State as required by law. Hearst's attorneys contended that the company had forfeited its contracts. Hearst formed a powerful Vigilance Committee headed by former Secretary of the Navy William C. Whitney and Abram S. Hewitt, former Congressman and Mayor of New York City.

After Hearst made an exposé of the company he began action in the Supreme Court to dissolve the Ramapo Water Company. The company's secretary vanished. With him the books of the concern dissolved into air. Mass meetings were held. From the report of Comptroller Bird S. Coler it was shown that not only was the water supply not needed, but the company was incapable of fulfilling its contract.

At his own expense Hearst engaged former Senator David B. Hill to go to Albany and make a speech for the anti-Ramapo Bill introduced in the Legislature by Senator Fellows. The measure was passed by the Senate and signed by the Governor. It prohibited commissioners of water supply from making any contracts for water except "with the assent of the Board of Public Approval and the approval of the Board of Estimate and Apportionment, together with the separate written consent of both the Mayor and Comptroller of the City of New York." The anti-Ramapo Bill was vetoed by Mayor Robert Van Wyck on the ground that it was unnecessary. The Mayor had been elected largely by the support of Hearst.

The editor continued with the battle. He caused Senator Slater to introduce in the Senate a bill repealing the Ramapo Act; it was passed. New York had the right to own its own water supply. Hearst rejoiced that he had protected the city's right to municipal ownership.

Peace had not long been declared after the Spanish-American War when revelations of military corruption were made. In the *Evening Journal* Hearst charged that embalmed beef had been fed to American soldiers. So much indignation was aroused that the Government ordered an investigation. The Nation shook with indignation.

Before the investigating committee that convened at Washington March 25, 1899, General Nelson A. Miles revealed that the army contract with Swift and Company called for beef that would keep seventy-two hours after arrival for delivery to the troops, but it had been necessary to condemn one hundred and ninety thousand pounds of beef in Porto Rico as unfit for consumption.

Governor Theodore Roosevelt told the court that when his men in Cuba tried to eat the beef:

I could have eaten my hat stewed with onions and potatoes just as well. . . . I ordered the entire lot thrown overboard. . . . As for the sick and wounded, they suffered so much in the hospitals from lack of attention when sent to the rear, that we found it best to keep them at the front and give them such care as our doctors could. We used everything we could find in the way of food in preference to "embalmed beef"—captured Spanish cavalry horses, ponies bought from Cubans, abandoned mules which had been shot. Our men took them in, skinned and cured them. By these means and the exertion of officers we were able from time to time to get supplies of beans, sugar, tomatoes and sometimes oatmeal.

Governor Roosevelt's testimony created a sensation. The sensation spread when it was shown that after a conference with the representative of Swift and Company, William A. de Caindry, chief clerk in the office of the Commissary General, altered the original contract.

Much against the wishes of Secretary of War Alger the Senate War Investigating Committee turned their attention to General Charles P. Egan, Commissary-General of Subsistence. General Egan said that Hearst and all other editors bringing charges against his department should be indicted for high treason for giving comfort and aid to the public enemy for the sole purpose of gain.

"Were I a man of wealth," declared the wronged Egan, "I would put journalistic knaves and purloiners of government secrets behind the bars where they belong."

Immediately Hearst placed a certified check of five thousand dollars in the Wells, Fargo Bank in New York City to enable General Egan to prosecute him for high treason. The General did not prosecute. He was dismissed from the army.

As the result of the "embalmed beef" investigation, the country became beef-conscious. In September of the same year Hearst revealed that the Beef Trust was forcing the retailer to the wall. There was no scarcity of cattle, but all meat was advanced from two to four cents. Meat Trust stock rose to be worth six hundred millions. From London came the news that a Beef Trust was being formed to control the world's market.

In 1901, Vice-President Roosevelt became President. Hearst engaged Ella Reeves Bloor to investigate New York slaughter-houses. Her revelations in the *Journal* were as astounding as they had been when she investigated the Chicago packing-houses. Because of his personal experience with "embalmed beef" President Roosevelt became interested.

Judge Grosscup of Chicago, in 1902, granted a preliminary injunction against meat packers alleged to have combined illegally to restrain trade. Sensational evidence was placed before James A. Garfield, head of the Bureau of Corporations. In 1905, Hearst's Chicago investigators gathered evidence which convinced Attorney-General Knox before he retired from office that the packers had violated the law. The public demanded action by the courts against the Beef Trust.

More than three hundred witnesses were subpoenaed to appear before the Grand Jury of the United States Northern District of Illinois. Two months later four corporations and twenty men were indicted. Among them were Ogden Armour, Charles Armour, Louis Swift, Edward C. Swift, Edward Tilden, Libby-McNeill and Libby, Edward Cudahy, vice-president of the Cudahy Packing Company, R. N. Morris and Edward Morris of Nelson, Morris and Company. The penalty was imprisonment for from one to three years, and payment of a fine of five thousand dollars. One year later Judge J. Otis Humphrey of the Chicago Federal Court declared that the millionaire meat packers and their employees under indictment for conspiracy were immune from prosecution. The court declared them guilty as a corporation, but not as individuals.

So ended the meat investigation, but Hearst was not cast down. At the head of his editorial column in large letters was announced his policy: DESTRUCTION OF THE CRIMINAL TRUSTS.

CHAPTER XXVI

ESTABLISHES CHICAGO *AMERICAN*

FROM the beginning William Randolph Hearst knew that he would have a newspaper in Chicago. In 1900, Senator Jones, Chairman of the National Democratic Committee, told him that in order for Bryan to win if re-nominated for the Presidency, the Democrats would need a newspaper in the Middle West. This statement was the immediate cause of Hearst's decision at brief notice to establish the Chicago *American*. Bryan must win. He would be nominated at the Democratic Convention meeting at St. Louis in a month. Hearst asked S. S. Carvalho, publisher of the *Journal*, to go to Chicago to establish the *American*. It must apppear in thirty days, on the Fourth of July.

Carvalho was the Hearst organization wizard. Shrewd, experienced, he never miscalculated, never misdirected his energies, but always drove toward his objective. When Carvalho set out from New York for Chicago Hearst had no further anxiety.

Carvalho enjoyed working for Hearst. Their minds met as equals. He recognized Hearst as another genius like himself. To-day he says with a smile, "Mr. Hearst always forgets my mistakes and remembers my successes. He will forgive anything, except not trying."

In Chicago Carvalho tried. Much of the plant equipment had to be brought from New York. Express cars were not to be obtained. Linotype machines were transported in Pullmans, the first and perhaps the only instance of a Pullman carrying machinery.

Carvalho decided not to establish the *American* in Newspaper Row. He rented an old building over the popular Steuben County Wine Company in West Madison Street, between

Fifth Avenue and Franklin Street. When Hearst entered Fifth Avenue it was deserted after dark. Soon, eight hundred men were working there day and night in three shifts. Dingy West Madison Street was brightened by the *American's* lights and it became a prosperous thoroughfare.

On schedule time the Chicago *American* was established July 4, 1900. William Jennings Bryan himself flashed the message, "Start the presses." Only five years earlier Hearst had entered Park Row, New York.

The first issue of the *American* bore the following message:

Lincoln, Nebraska

W. R. Hearst,　　　　　　　　　　　　　　　　July 4, 1900
　　Chicago "American,"
　　Chicago, Illinois.

DEAR MR. HEARST:

Chicago, Illinois, and the States of the upper Mississippi Valley are to be congratulated upon the establishment of the *American,* a name admirably suited to a paper which will represent an American policy for the American people on all questions domestic and foreign.

The fact that your paper was established not merely to make money, but because of your desire to aid the Democratic Party in the fight in the Central States, and because of the expressed desire of the Democratic leaders that you should duplicate in Chicago this year the splendid work done by the *Journal* and the *Examiner* in 1896, ought to commend the paper to the friends of democracy, and I am confident that a large circulation awaits the Chicago *American.*

Yours truly,

WILLIAM JENNINGS BRYAN

Arthur Brisbane, "A. B.," as he is called in the Hearst organization, edited the first edition of the *American* and remained in Chicago to put the paper on its feet. A large edition was circulated in the Democratic Convention Hall in St. Louis on July 4, 1900. On the next day, July 5th, Bryan was nominated by the convention for the Presidency.

Already Hearst had become president of a national association of several thousand Democratic clubs formed early in
the year. He made his début as a public speaker before this
organization and cured himself of stage fright. At the national
convention of the Associated Democratic Clubs in Indianapolis, Augustus Thomas, the playwright, announced that
for every dollar contributed by the clubs Hearst would give
another dollar to help elect Bryan. Hearst published large free
editions to increase the Bryan vote in the Middle West. He
could not imagine that the people would vote to continue the
McKinley Administration, dominated by the trusts and their
friend, Mark Hanna.

Despite Davenport's masterly cartoons, despite the able editorials of Hearst, Brisbane and McEwen, and despite the large
sums poured by Hearst into the campaign, the President was
reëlected, but by a diminished majority. With him was returned a Republican Congress. It was evident that Bryan was
regarded by the great middle class as unsound. The people
preferred McKinley's "full dinner pail."

But Hearst had much to do. Chicago was still to be conquered. When he entered Chicago, and Carvalho began sending for men from his office in the Security Building, he followed a trail strewn with failures. The Scripps-Booth invasion
had occurred in 1896. This capable organization had swallowed the *Mail* and *Express* and was looking for a purchaser
for their *Journal*. They were to go back to Michigan in 1904.
The Harrisons had failed to establish the *Times*. John R.
Walsh was losing money on the *Chronicle*. Yerkes' wealth
could not make the *Inter-Ocean* succeed. Joseph Dunlap had
abandoned the ill-fated *Despatch*. Kohlsaat was on the verge
of failure with the *Times-Herald*. Victor Lawson was concentrating on his afternoon paper, *The News*.

To the Chicago pressmen who gathered at King's Restaurant, Hearst looked like certain failure. Of course he had the
glamour of his success on the Golden Gate and in New York.
But could he succeed where so many able men had failed?

"He cannot," said the newsmen. Their verdict was, "You can't brass band Chicago!"

Charles Edward Russell became publisher of the Chicago *American,* and soon the pressmen changed their minds. When Hearst arrived, Chicago reporters were frequently being paid only fifteen dollars a week. Even star reporters received no more than thirty or thirty-five dollars. Hearst offered good reporters fifty dollars. Salaries went up in every department of the Chicago papers. The *American* comics, editorials and manner of presenting the news caused a vast army of untrained and unlettered people to read a newspaper for the first time. Principles of woman suffrage, direct vote for United States Senators, graduated income tax, municipal ownership and operation of traction companies, the initiative and referendum, workmen's compensation, a good living wage, honesty and efficiency in public service, improvement of schools, advocated by the *American,* gave the plain people vision of a new future for themselves and their children. With the creation of the *American* at last they had voice.

Hearst spent considerable time in his newest office. Chicago is a city of action, and Hearst is a man of action. He plunged into the whirling life of Chicago. As in San Francisco and New York he became the friend of labor and repeatedly came to the aid of labor unions. He helped settle the lock-out of Building Trades. He aided the teamsters and butchers in organizing unions.

The first crusade of the Chicago *Evening American* was made when the paper was only two months old. Brisbane, as editor of the *American,* discovered and submitted evidence to the Mayor that the packers were stealing water from the city for their huge industry by tapping water mains. The editor was called on by the Superintendent of Water to assist in running down the thieves. Brisbane assigned reporters to help the city officials. They furnished proof that the city mains had been tapped, and four of the packers' agents were indicted by the Grand Jury on evidence supplied by the *American.* Soon the superintendent of one of the stock-yard firms confessed that he had stolen the water, and the company paid the city six thousand dollars for the amount purloined. Other packers sent checks in payment for the water they had stolen.

One of Hearst's most far-reaching campaigns was for the five-cent fare throughout Chicago. In 1900, there were several surface carlines and four Elevated roads. The companies would not issue transfers, and it was necessary to pay two or three fares to travel from one side of the city to the other. Hearst crusaded against the traction interests in order to bring about the one fare all over the city.

In 1900, he exposed a deal between the Chicago General Railway and the Chicago City Railway to consolidate in order to perpetuate franchises about to expire. The *American* opposed the new franchise, but favored permitting the cars to be run on the license plan which would give the city full control. The Chicago Federation of Labor, the Chicago Teachers Federation and other bodies backed up this stand. The Municipal Ownership League filed with the Election Commissioners a petition gathered through the *American* containing nearly one hundred and fifty thousand names and asking that the question of Municipal Ownership be submitted to the people.

With the transfer fight the Municipal Ownership campaign went on. Hearst opened a Traction Complaint Bureau. So numerous were the complaints that within three days the Council ordered the service bettered on the West Side. Antiquated trailers were taken off cars, and the Chicago City Railway Company bought new cars and installed them in its service.

In 1902, a number of lawyers, politicians and traction employees were indicted by the Grand Jury for bribing juries in cases of traction officials. The accused men were found guilty and some threw themselves on the mercy of the court. Soon the Chicago Union Traction Company began to issue transfers.

Hearst did not rest with this victory. Immediately his attorney began litigation to compel the companies to issue transfers on each other's lines. This campaign resulted in the passage in 1905 of an ordinance compelling a universal transfer-giving on all lines.

In the Illinois Legislature Hearst supported the Mueller Municipal Ownership Bill which was passed in 1903. Two years later Edward F. Dunne was elected Mayor on the Municipal Ownership platform. Two to one the people voted against franchise extension. Hearst carried on the battle against the service of the surface cars, and in October, 1913, consolidation of the surface cars was brought about. Elevated lines were installed, and city transportation was given to every section.

One of the reasons for Hearst's varied and many achievements is that he is never content to sit down and admire himself for the victory of to-day. He always thinks about to-morrow. During all these campaigns Hearst hammered away in his papers for Municipal Ownership of the Chicago subways.

When Hearst first went to Chicago he swung hard at the perfectly organized Vice Trust. Chief of Police Joseph Kipley fled from the city to New Orleans. On his return he was ousted by Mayor Carter Harrison. The Grand Jury indicted seventeen heads of the Vice Trust, and for the first time the saloons were closed at midnight. Saloon licenses were increased in cost from five hundred to a thousand dollars. Police officers and patrolmen were dismissed. Hearst felt that women would protect women, and he waged a fight for the appointment of policewomen to protect girls from procurers.

Not only did Hearst battle for unfortunate women and the poor, but he struggled to compel the rich to pay their share of government expenses. Clarence Darrow and former Governor John C. Altgeld were employed by Hearst in his fight against tax dodgers. Millionaires, railroad companies and the largest business corporations were dodging their taxes. From year to year the campaign was carried on, and hundreds of millions of dollars were added to the assessment roll.

In the second year after Hearst's arrival in Chicago he plunged into a gas fight which lasted ten years. Mass meetings were held. The *American* editors were taken into court and ordered to jail. The case was carried to the United States Supreme Court which held that the city'had the right to fix the price of gas. In 1911, the Council passed a seventy-cent gas ordinance. Six months later the courts established the compromise rate of eighty cents.

The people responded to Hearst's crusades. They gave him added courage in May of 1902 to found the Chicago *Examiner.* Later the paper was merged with the *Herald.* Now Hearst had another arm for crusading. The *American* and *Herald and Examiner* fought a plan to close the kindergartens. Hearst championed the cause of Ella Flagg Young, one of America's leading educators who resigned from the school board because her work as superintendent was frustrated. The publisher called on Mayor Carter Harrison to aid Mrs. Young. The Mayor ousted five of the trustees, and the educator was re-elected Superintendent.

Hearst not only protested against old school employees being removed, but he won a campaign for a longer term for school teachers. From his interest in the welfare of teachers he discovered that daily fifteen thousand children went hungry to school. Hearst called on the women's clubs and churches to give the children penny lunches during the World War, and no more children were hungry in school.

In the midst of Hearst's crusades came news of the destruction of Galveston, Texas, and the loss of three thousand lives. Several neighboring towns were also wiped out. Each wave of the gulf bore a body, every ruin concealed a corpse. Famine threatened survivors.

With his own name Hearst headed a subscription list, and all his papers published appeals for help. People were urged to send food and clothing to Galveston. Information bureaus were opened in New York, Chicago and San Francisco. From each city speeded a relief train. First to arrive at Galveston with aid were the Hearst trains, hauled free by the Santa Fé. At the Waldorf-Astoria, in New York, the *Journal* and *Ameri-*

can held a Galveston Orphans' Bazaar. Fifty thousand dollars were obtained. Governor Sayers of Texas, thanked Hearst for having raised a relief fund of one million dollars. Miss Clara Barton of the American Red Cross called it "noble work on a large scale."

About this time Hearst began sending to the publishers of his five newspapers the same suggestions. This communication was received by his editors:

Crusades against public evils must be conducted. But I want to eliminate entirely all other attacks and unduly severe criticism.

Constructive, helpful editorials are not only much more interesting, but much more valuable—especially when they are based on accurate information.

Make your departments complete and reliable so that the reader will know that he can find a thing in your paper and that he can find it right.

Make a paper for the NICEST KIND OF PEOPLE—for the great middle class. Don't print a lot of dull stuff that they are supposed to like, and don't.

Omit things that will offend nice people. Avoid slang and a low tone.

Be fair and impartial. Make a paper for all the people and give unbiased news of all creeds and parties.

News and editorial character are built on reliability of statement. We cannot hope to build advertising on any other basis.

No man who misrepresents facts must be allowed on our newspapers. Honesty is a form of common sense.

Our newspapers must sell advertising only by their printed rate card. If your rate card is wrong, change it. If it is right, live up to every letter of it. There should be no double standard of morality involving buyer and seller of advertising. Men who make gentlemen's agreements are not wanted. Do not accept any advertising which is detrimental to the public welfare.

Our readers trust us. We would not deceive them in our news or editorial columns. We must not allow others to deceive them in our advertising columns.

CHAPTER XXVII

DEFEATS ICE TRUST

O N the hottest day in the summer of 1900, New York lay sweltering in the sun. Babies were dying of heat on the East Side. Suddenly the Ice Trust doubled the price of ice. No more small pieces were sold to retailers, nothing for five cents. Ten-cent pieces of ice were the cheapest to be had by the poor. This was what high finance called a perfect trust.

Then Hearst opened another battle. The editor made up his mind to compel the trust to sell ice at the old rate. The trust was really Charles W. Morse, who later served a term in Atlanta prison for falsifying the books of the National Bank of America.

In 1900, Morse had consolidated competing concerns selling ice; the New York, Knickerbocker, Consumers', Montauk, Standard, Continental, Hygeia, Crystal Lake, Union, Yonkers, City, Ridgewood Companies, and many others. They formed the American Ice Company with a capital of sixty million dollars. They owned the northern ice-fields and limited the supply brought into the city. They had a virtual monopoly of the docks in New York and independent ice could not be landed.

Through his attorneys Einstein and Townsend, Hearst notified the Attorney-General that he made application for the dissolution of the American Ice Company. He asserted that Charles W. Morse was jeopardizing the health and life of the community. Hearst himself had been largely instrumental in having the Donnelly anti-Trust Act made a law. In his petition he pointed out that the laws of New York prohibited combinations to create monopoly or restraint of trade in a necessity of life.

To Charles W. Morse, president of the Ice Trust, Hearst's

suit seemed naïve. His comment on the action was: "This company is in business to make money for stockholders. The American Ice Company is not a philanthropic institution."

Manifestly it was not touched by philanthropy. Hearst soon revealed that Mayor Van Wyck and his brother, Augustus Van Wyck, each had four hundred thousand dollars' worth of stock in the Ice Trust. In addition, one million, five hundred thousand dollars' worth of stock was divided among J. Sargeant Cram, president of the Dock Board, Commissioner Murphy, Tammany leader Carroll, and Judges McMahon and Newberger.

When these disclosures were made by Hearst, indignation meetings were held. The *World* started an investigation. The *Tribune* declared that the trust should be compelled to reduce the price of ice or go out of business.

The trust engaged two lawyers to defeat Hearst's activities. The Board of Aldermen was so demoralized by Hearst's suit that they could not meet. The Municipal Council appointed a committee to inquire into Hearst's charges that certain public officials were holding stock in the American Ice Company, a trust which had raised the price of ice 100 per cent, causing great stress and suffering among the poor.

Mayor Van Wyck and Morse were quickly forced into the hearing instigated by Hearst in the Jefferson Market Police Court. Before proceedings began DeLancey Nicoll, the Ice Trust lawyer, came to Shearn and said, "We throw up our hands. Drop these police-court proceedings, and we will reduce the price of ice from sixty to forty cents a hundred."

Ice sold at forty cents a hundred. The police court case was postponed until it could be seen whether the attempted policy of extortion had been abandoned. Tenement-house district wagons again sold five-cent pieces of ice. Organized charities were told that the Ice Trust would deliver ice in five-cent chunks.

Hearst had great satisfaction in these concessions, but in his newspapers he declared, "Prison stripes await any city official conspiring to extort money from the people by suppressing competition and increasing the price of ice."

Attorney-General Davies granted Hearst's petition to have the certificate annulled under which the Ice Trust could do business in New York.

"I am satisfied," said the Attorney-General, "that the American Ice Company is an unlawful combination conducting its business and restraining trade in violation of the law. . . . It is my duty to commence proceedings against the American Ice Company to prohibit its doing business in this State."

Conspicuously in the *Evening Journal* Hearst printed the following appeal to the District Attorney: "To Asa Bird Gardiner: Indict the Ice Trust, please! Indict the Mayor and other city officials who have betrayed their public trust. Don't wait for Roosevelt and a special Republican Grand Jury to do this for you!"

Hearst published the names of unrevealed stockholders in the Ice Trust: Richard Croker and family, stock valued at one hundred and twelve thousand dollars; Hugh A. Grant, former Mayor, one hundred thousand dollars; Charles F. Murphy of Tammany, forty thousand dollars.

Charles W. Morse, president of the American Ice Company, together with the directors of the company, were held by Magistrate Zeller sitting in the Jefferson Market Police Court, at one thousand dollars' bail. Panic shook Mayor Van Wyck, who was in the court room. He engaged an attorney to defend himself, but he was shielded by the trust officers when they were examined.

Now Hearst began two separate legal actions. One was a civil suit to annul the certificate allowing the trust to do business in the State. The other was criminal, to indict and convict officers of the trust. If found guilty they would be fined and imprisoned. He had issued a writ compelling the trust to make public the list of stockholders. Names of city officials were revealed who had aided the monopoly in robbing the people of New York.

By this time Clarence J. Shearn of the Einstein and Townsend office, later Justice of the Supreme Court of New York, devoted his entire attention to Hearst's legal crusades. Shearn formally demanded that he be permitted to inspect the trust books. Justice Chase ordered the books and papers of the American Ice Company produced.

Charles W. Morse refused to obey the order. Justice Chase cited Morse to appear to show cause why he should not be sent to jail for contempt of court. Mayor Van Wyck took the stand and made a desperate effort to save his friends, called by Hearst the "ice bandits." He obtained a week's respite.

Finally Morse decided to appear before the Referee and explain how Mayor Van Wyck came to have so much stock in the Ice Trust. It was revealed that certain bills were drawn up by Corporation Counsel Whalen embarrassing to the ice company. At the suggestion of the Mayor himself they were passed. Then, without giving a reason the Mayor vetoed the bills. Later these bills were sent to Albany. Why did Mayor Van Wyck himself suggest bills embarrassing the trust? Then why did he veto them? To force the trust to give him stock? Hearst disclosed that the Mayor paid for the stock with promissory notes unsecured.

Shearn asked Governor Theodore Roosevelt to enforce the law which could impeach the Mayor. As a possessor of Ice Trust stock the Mayor had conspired to raise the price of ice, injuring the welfare of the city.

"The law is plain," declared Hearst in the *Journal*. "Van Wyck has forfeited the right to act as Mayor. Steps to remove him under the law should be taken to-day."

The New York *Times* in an editorial praised the public service of the *Journal* and declared that Hearst had earned public gratitude. On June 4, 1900, the comptroller annulled all city contracts with the American Ice Company because city officials had stock in the trust.

About this time the Democratic State Convention assembled, and the name of Mayor Van Wyck was mentioned.

"Put him on the ice," howled the Democrats.

Governor Theodore Roosevelt was deeply interested in Hearst's disclosures, and he said, "As soon as Attorney-General Davies has had time to prepare thoroughly his case against the Ice Trust his suit will be pressed vigorously.... No man, Democrat or Republican, Judge or janitor, shall escape punishment." Sternly the Governor added, "The higher his official position and the greater his means, just so much more necessary is it to have him punished if he did wrong." Governor Roosevelt's statement was followed by the announcement of Morse that he would lower the price of ice.

After Van Wyck had been found out he was criticized even by Tammany. It was reported that the Mayor was going to resign. Hearst published a long petition of *Journal* subscribers, who requested Governor Roosevelt to investigate the charges against Mayor Van Wyck, to try the Mayor and take action necessary to remove him from office.

Officers of the trust fought back. They sent their counsel to Albany to try to nullify the statute under which the Referee acted in the proceedings for the people begun by the *Journal*.

Even Boss Croker turned on Mayor Van Wyck and Dock Commissioner Cram, and put them on the rack. Immediately afterwards he conferred with District Attorney Gardiner.

On the other hand, Governor Theodore Roosevelt delayed his investigation of the Ice Trust. He read petitions of New York citizens obtained through the *Journal*, but he announced that he had been requested by Mayor Van Wyck's counsel to suspend judgment.

Frankly the Mayor admitted that he had borrowed two hundred and fifty thousand dollars from Charles W. Morse, president of the Ice Trust, but he declared it was his right. He left the city promising to return in September.

Governor Roosevelt made a characteristic fighting speech about the Ice Trust. He declared that he, Attorney-General Davies and Secretary Young, would spend an entire night in looking over the evidence.

The next day the Governor said he would not reach a decision for some time. Two months later he announced that he would appoint a commission to receive testimony, shortly. As to the quarter million dollars which Mayor Van Wyck admitted on the stand that he had borrowed from Charles W. Morse, Governor Roosevelt said, "The charges against the Mayor are much more serious than I anticipated. Of course, the Mayor's answer may explain them. If it does not, I shall appoint a commission to investigate before I leave for the West."

Governor Roosevelt did not appoint the commission. Something far more important, to him, happened. He went West to confer with Senator Mark Hanna, chairman of the McKinley campaign committee. Roosevelt was nominated as the running mate of President McKinley whom he had often called a "chocolate éclair." Silence so deep as to be almost audible reigned at Albany about the Ice Trust.

This attitude of Roosevelt later was clarified by a telegram revealed as sent on September 25th, by B. B. Odell, Republican candidate for Governor, to the new candidate for Vice-President, at Cripple Creek, Colorado: "Wire Attorney-General Davies to be sure and not give out to the reporters the Van Wyck answer at this time. It must be held up until election is over. This will imperil chances, and get us into a serious wrangle. I have also wired Davies. B. B. ODELL."

No Republican chances were imperiled. There was no wrangle. Odell was elected Governor. Roosevelt was elected Vice-President. When questioned at his home in Newburgh about the telegram, Odell said, "Really, I am too ill to say anything." Vice-President-elect Roosevelt was interviewed at his Oyster Bay home. Snapping his teeth together he said, "I have nothing to say."

Vice-President-elect Theodore Roosevelt made his exit from the Ice Trust case by a public defense of Mayor Van Wyck:

A year before the *Journal* began its suit Mayor Van Wyck had bought from Charles W. Morse five thousand shares of stock of the American Ice Company. The Mayor paid for them with a check of fifty thousand dollars that he borrowed from Morse. For the balance he gave three promissory notes. At the time he did not know that the ice company had a contract to supply the city with ice. When he found it out he sold his stock. The Mayor denied all charges against him of aiding monopoly, preventing and restricting competition in the price of ice or permitting the American Ice Company to monopolize all available docks. He said that he had never heard of any violation of the law by the American Ice Company until the Attorney-General began proceedings against the company and its officers under the anti-Monopoly Statute.

Criminal proceedings were dismissed by the Grand Jury. Mayor Van Wyck decided to live in Paris. Attorney-General Davies obtained leave to carry the case to the Court of Appeals to annul the Ice Trust's charter. In 1902, Charles W. Morse retired from the directorate of the Ice Trust. One year later the company reported a deficit.

Hearst did not give up the struggle. In 1908, Attorney-General Jackson prosecuted the American Ice Company for violating the law. District Attorney Jerome defended the trust by asserting that it was not a trust and, therefore, the efforts of the Attorney-General were useless.

The Attorney-General answered, "I will keep moving against the Ice Trust until an end is put to the violation of the anti-Monopoly Law. If that law does not apply, I shall ask the Legislature to give us one that will."

Charges were filed against District Attorney Jerome for crushing independent ice dealers and for giving the American Ice Company the entire field. The Ice Trust escaped unscathed, and Jerome switched the investigation to four or five independent dealers who had furnished the only opposition to the trust.

There was a third effort to investigate the Ice Trust at the instance of Supreme Court Justice Goff, who instructed a special District Attorney to be sworn in. District Attorney Jerome declined to take action.

In October of the following year another investigation of the American Ice Company was begun at Buffalo before Justice Wheeler. The jury found the company guilty on two counts of violation of the Donnelly anti-Monopoly Law. Justice Wheeler imposed the maximum penalty of five thousand dollars.

On November 5, 1908, Charles W. Morse was found guilty of falsifying the books of the National Bank of North America and sentenced to fifteen years in Atlanta.

During these years of litigation Clarence J. Shearn, Hearst's counsel, was frequently awakened by his client at night for consultation concerning the legal struggles in which they were engaged. Judge Shearn says that he often wondered why Hearst gave so much time, peace of mind, and money to intense activity that brought him conflict, enemies, frequent defeats, or at best half-victories. One day Hearst explained his course of action to Shearn: "While I was in college I saw about me two classes struggling. On one side were capitalists to whom I supposed I naturally belonged. On the other side were masses of inarticulate people. Big business was always represented by clever and able lawyers. The other side was virtually unrepresented. I made up my mind to try to help the weaker side. I never changed. I shall keep right on."

CHAPTER XXVIII

McKINLEY'S DEATH

HEARST'S newspaper offices were electric with activity. Lost children were found. Thousands of sick mothers and children were given free outings at the ocean and beaches. In New York Hearst battled to retain hand-organ music grinders in the streets that the youngsters might dance. Boys were sent to the National Convention to see President McKinley nominated. The publisher got up a race between schoolboys of New York, Chicago and San Francisco to see which could outdo Jules Verne in going round the world. With twenty-two trucks he distributed four hundred thousand Christmas gifts in the New York tenement districts. He placed automobiles at the disposal of overcrowded city hospitals when the ambulance service was crippled because of heat. He campaigned for city baths. He started a movement for building bicycle paths on Brooklyn bridge. He established a bureau for justice and aid for strangers in Park Row. He sent popular bicycle riders on a tour from Nice to Naples. He crusaded for rapid transit for the city. He devised laws making buildings fireproof. He established a school of instruction for the general public in fire fighting. He opposed a system of privately owned chairs in Central Park. He insisted on a law compelling automobiles to be properly identified and licensed. He fought for increased pay for letter-carriers. He advocated an eight-hour day for policemen. He sided with Dana's striking printers, who had been locked out. He laid bare Boss Platt's methods in securing commissions for contracts. He exposed the failure of the Seventh National Bank.

In Chicago both the *American* and the *Herald and Examiner* had great influence. With his campaign in these papers Hearst enabled the city to own its own street railway. He always had in mind plain people like policemen, firemen and letter-carriers. Humble folk realized that they had a friend and advocate, and the circulation of Hearst's papers soared.

In 1902, there was more relief work. Thousands were made homeless by a devastating fire in Trenton, New Jersey. Hearst hired a special train of ten cars, kept it lighted and heated throughout the day to serve as a relief station for thousands to whom food, clothing and tents were distributed. When the top of Mount Pelée on the Island of Martinique was blown off, within three minutes the city of St. Pierre and adjacent villages were destroyed. No sooner did the news reach the United States, than Hearst had huge quantities of supplies of every description transported on steamers to the sufferers.

Hearst had always had the tendency to alter things—rooms, houses, buildings, yachts, newspapers. Wherever he appeared there was change, action. His interest in novelty never flagged, and he could manage five great newspapers as well as one— letters, telephones, and telegraph wires all aided. His interest might be local, but he was always acutely concerned with international events. Enthusiastically he wrote of the Czar's offer to disarm: "The peace conference that opened yesterday may be a failure—very likely it may be—but it will lead to other things that are not failures. It will always stand in history as the first concerted effort of the world's statesmanship to relieve the human race of the curse of war."

At the same time he urged a large navy; it was a power for peace. He published a letter written to him in 1900 by Admiral George Dewey: " 'In modern war who commands the sea wins.' This closing sentence of your editorial on Sunday last on *Command of the Oceans* expresses the truth so well demonstrated by the results of the naval battle of Manila and Santiago as to need little or no comment. But it is not in war alone that sea supremacy is of vital importance, and I would make the sentence read: 'In modern peace, who controls the sea wins!' "

Hearst still advocates a large navy, but in addition to command of the ocean he now urges command of the air.

No matter how many new campaigns held Hearst's attention, from the early days on the *Examiner* his mind turned to the possibility of a canal across the Isthmus of Panama. French capitalists under de Lesseps, cousin of the Empress Eugénie and hero of Suez, had attempted the undertaking, but had met with disaster. Hearst said it was folly to build a canal without locks as de Lesseps had attempted, and he declared for a waterway across Nicaragua. Hearst was delighted when the canal bill passed the Senate in 1895, and he urged driving it through the House immediately. Responding to big corporations who opposed the canal, Speaker Reed, in 1899, bulked his granite figure against the measure. Behind him were massed the Republican leaders. In 1900, Senator Morgan revealed the complications of the opposition: "Much money is being used to delay action in the Senate. . . . A great transcontinental railway is fighting the canal, and is using every means to defeat it."

By this time all of the Hearst press insisted with emphasis, "Dig and fortify the canal." One of the reasons why Hearst opposed McKinley in 1900 was because he realized that the fund collected to elect McKinley and defeat the Nicaragua canal would cost taxpayers in high freight rates many millions of dollars. In the summer of 1900, Collis P. Huntington, who dominated the Southern Pacific Railroad, died suddenly of apoplexy in the Adirondack mountains. Huntington was the most powerful opponent of any canal. Hearst in all his papers battled with renewed intensity for a waterway joining the two oceans.

In the midst of Hearst's most intense activities he frequently took unexpected journeys. Like his mother, Phebe Hearst, the publisher was strangely lured by Egypt with its mystery and its ancient silent pyramids. In the spring of 1901, Hearst was traveling up the Nile when his eye caught a paragraph in an English newspaper a fortnight old: "The Hay-Pauncefote

Treaty has been signed and ratified by the British Cabinet. All that remains is the ratification of the United States Senate. The United States and Great Britain are agreed that the proposed Nicaragua canal shall not be fortified."

Hearst forgot Egypt, its pyramids and its mystery. Again his mind was in roaring America. On the back of an envelop he scribbled a note, then sent a native messenger riding at high speed to the nearest cable office seventy miles distant. The following day the New York *Journal* received this message: "Better no canal than an unfortified canal. I would rather see every spade and shovel withdrawn from the canal than to see it built without the right to fortify it in the interests of our country. Fight ratification of the canal treaty with England."

James A. Creelman was sent as commissioner of the Hearst papers to oppose the treaty, but he cabled from Washington, "Fight hopeless. Treaty is as good as passed."

"If the treaty is passed," answered Hearst, "it should be abrogated. Fight!"

Theodore Roosevelt was Governor of New York at the time, but as Vice-President-elect he was very close to the McKinley Administration. One of his devoted friends was Secretary of State John Hay who had largely formulated the treaty. Roosevelt was usually hostile to Hearst, fearing that as a great controlling power of the opposing party, the publisher might become President. But on this occasion Roosevelt took a stand against the McKinley Administration and he wrote the Secretary of State, "You have been the greatest Secretary of State I have seen in my time. . . . But at this time I cannot, try as I may, see that you are right. Understand me, when the treaty is adopted, as I suppose it will be, I shall put the best possible face on it, and shall back the Administration as heartily as ever; but oh, how I wish you and the President would drop the treaty and push through a bill to build and fortify our canal."

Against the politicians and the Administration press Hearst led the forces opposing the treaty. The Senate dared not ratify the original draft of the treaty. The Hay-Pauncefote Treaty was modified according to Hearst's suggestions.

When the Senate Committee on Foreign Relations adopted the Hearst viewpoint, Secretary Hay, bitterly disappointed, sent a letter of resignation to President McKinley saying, "I can't help feeling that the newspaper attacks upon the State Department which have so strongly influenced the Senate, may be an injury to you if I remain in the Cabinet."

President McKinley had warm friendship, as well as much admiration, for his able, cultured Secretary of State. He refused to accept his resignation. The treaty as prepared was abandoned. After the ratification of the modified Hay-Pauncefote Treaty, the United States acquired the property through which the canal passes, and the Canal Zone now is as much a possession of the United States as the Capitol at Washington.

After Congress adjourned in 1901, President McKinley and several of his Cabinet made a leisurely journey through the South on the way to San Francisco to witness the launching of the battleship *Ohio*. In the southern States they were cordially received, and all traces of ill-will resulting from the Civil War seemed to have vanished. On his way back to Washington the President stopped for a month at Canton, Ohio, where he had lived for years before he became the Chief Executive of the United States. From Canton, McKinley went to Buffalo to make an address at the Pan-American Exposition on the sixth of September, 1901. In one of the public buildings of the Exposition there was held a great reception.

A young man with a pale fanatical face stepped out of the crowd. The President bent on him a kindly smile, held out his hand in genial greeting. The youth carried a handkerchief over his right hand. There was a thunderous crash. The President felt two tearing, benumbing blows, one in his stomach and one in his abdomen.

"Who are you?" cried the crowd to the assailant.

"Leon Czolgosz," answered the young man. "I am an anarchist. I am sorry I didn't kill him."

The President realized that two bullets had been buried in his body, but when he saw the ferocious crowd savagely leaping upon the youth who had done him this mortal injury he said, "Don't let them hurt him." Protected by the police from the infuriated mob Czolgosz was hurried away to jail, and President McKinley was carried to the Milburn residence in Buffalo.

When the telegraph wires ticked out the news of the Buffalo tragedy Hearst was in the office of the Chicago *American*. At that time Charles Edward Russell was publisher of the *American*. Just as the black-typed extras were being prepared telling of the attack on the President's life Russell recalls meeting Hearst in the composing-room.

Excitement was intense, and yet Hearst seemed unperturbed. But he recalled his years of opposition to and his criticism of McKinley and Hanna for their alliance with the trusts. He realized the savagery of public indignation flaming through the nation. "Things are going to be very bad," Hearst said to Russell.

In truth, things were bad for all critics of the McKinley Administration. An anarchist had attacked the President. Ferocious outcries came against all anarchists. Herr Most was arrested, and so was Emma Goldman. Hearst was called "teacher of anarchists."

All the newspapers whose prosperity had been lessened by Hearst, whose comfortable routines had been disturbed, all the corporations that had been thwarted by him, all their servants, all those who feared him, all those who envied him, spat forth bitter epithets of hatred.

Hearst newspapers were thrown out of clubs, hurled from news-stands into gutters. In Chicago a gun always lay on Hearst's desk. So many threats were made against his life, that when boxes of purported gifts arrived, Hearst had them burned for fear of bombs. One day he said to Andrew M. Lawrence, one of his executives, "They can't hang me." They couldn't hang Hearst, but they blamed him personally for his criticism of the trust-ridden McKinley Administration.

For a week the President seemed to be on the way to recovery. Then the kindly man turned over in his bed and said to his nurse, "Please let me see the trees. They are so beautiful." President McKinley realized that he was looking at the trees for the last time.

His eyes were lifted to his friends surrounding his bed. "Good-by, all," he said, "it is God's will. God's will be done."

President McKinley's funeral train moved out from Buffalo to tranquil Canton, Ohio, and the people mourned for the simple, plain American. President McKinley will be best remembered for his geniality and for having given thirty years' devotion to an invalid wife. In his aspirations he was like the average American. It was pleasant for the everyday man to visualize himself in a happy home, a village politician, being elected legislator, Representative, Governor and finally President. McKinley's irreproachable private life, his suavity, his church affiliations, his tragic ending, made people forget that his administration had been abject before great aggregations of capital, that during his time the trusts had been enthroned, and business ethics had been lowered to a marked degree.

In the tragic moment of national bereavement Americans shed salty, bitter tears of rage that the President was dead. No anarchist should be spared, no enemy of McKinley. Representatives of competing papers arrived in Buffalo to try to induce Czolgosz to confess that he was stirred to hatred of the dead President by reading the Hearst papers.

The assassin's only answer was, "I never saw a Hearst paper. I am sick. Why did I do this? I wish I hadn't. I was crazy. I can't breathe in this cell. I am sorry for the President. I think about him every night. If only he hadn't died. I wanted to do something heroic. I couldn't help it. I had to do it. I couldn't bear to see people bowing before a great leader, a servant of capital like McKinley."

The police could not believe that Czolgosz had been alone in his crime. They gave him what one super-patriotic writer of that time called the "splendid cruelties of the third degree."

For days Czolgosz was brought before the police. He was not allowed to sleep. The officers declared that they would torture him into confession or drive him mad. Day after day white and weakened by torture the prisoner staggered back to his cell. "The splendid cruelties of the third degree" brought no confession from Czolgosz except the words, "I am an anarchist."

Investigation revealed that Czolgosz, a taciturn youth of Polish parents, became melancholy because he had not succeeded. Many thought him weak. Others said he was lazy. For days at a time he would not eat, nor would he speak to his family. He wandered away to the woods, read and cooked for himself. He became an impassioned devotee of direct action and violence.

One golden Indian-summer day in October Czolgosz was taken to Auburn prison and strapped in a chair wired with death-dealing voltage. There was a flash of light, a sizzle of burning flesh, and Leon Czolgosz passed the line dividing the finite and the infinite.

Meanwhile, Hearst was as unpopular as a multi-millionaire can be who owns five successful newspapers. Over him broke a storm as violent as the Galveston flood. Rival papers reproduced Davenport's and Opper's cartoons of McKinley and the trusts. They flared Bierce's bitter verse. Hearst's papers were boycotted and burned. The *Sun* led the New York attack. The *Sun* had not forgotten that Hearst supported their printers at the time they were locked out.

Hearst did not attempt to shift the blame to others. He bore the battle-brunt.

In an editorial he replied that in both of Bryan's campaigns the *Sun* had indulged in frantic vituperation. In the cases of Grant and Garfield vituperation had been carried beyond the grave. The *Sun* had assailed General Grant as a "boodler," called President Hayes a "fraud," and said that Garfield was corrupted by bribes. The *Evening Post* had supported the attacks of the *Sun*. Hearst pointed out that the *Post*

had spoken of McKinley as a "liar, a renegade, a traitor."
The *Post* had accused President Cleveland of keeping his unfortunate illegitimate child in a Buffalo Alms House, although
he himself was well-to-do. The *Sun* had declared Cleveland
should be rejected by such a majority, that he would never
dare aspire even to the office of hangman.

Hearst published a page editorial in each of his newspapers
in reply to his assailants:

The murdered President is buried, and the world, out of necessity, turns from the past to the future, taking up the concerns
of life. . . . From coast to coast this newspaper has been attacked
and is being attacked with savage ferocity by the incompetent,
the failures of journalism, by the kept organs of plutocracy
heading the mob. . . .

Hearst asked why the Hearst papers were hated and howled
at by newspapers like the New York *Sun*.

Primarily because they stand for the democratic idea, because
they have stood, and still stand for the rights of the common man
as against the privileges of the larcenous man—for the man who
makes things as against the man who takes things. . . .

Who hate the Hearst papers? Those whom they fought, and
those who have been hurt in the newspaper business by a success
which is a rebuke to incapacity and inferiority, and a provocation
to envy and jealousy.

Who are they against whom the Hearst papers have fought?
Chiefly the predatory rich and crafty, and those who pile up
monstrous fortunes by pillaging the people inside and outside
the law. . . .

The Hearst papers are American papers for Americans. They
are conservative papers, for the truest conservatism is that radicalism which would uproot revolution-breeding abuses. . . .

One of the Hearst papers' offenses is that they have fought
for the people, and against privilege and class pride and class
greed and class stupidity and class heartlessness with more daring weapons, with more force and talent and enthusiasm than any

other newspapers in the country. All the enemies of the people, of the democratic people conscious and unconscious—all who reap where others have sown, all the rascals and their organs, and many fools caught by the malignant uproar, are yelling at the *Journal*.

LET THEM YELL.

Note the thrift of the parasitic press. . . . It would draw profit from the terrible deed of the wretch who shot down the President. . . . They are endeavoring to make merchandise for themselves of the blood of the murdered President by transmuting the public grief and horror into enmity against these newspapers. . . .

Shall we halt in advocacy of democratic principles? . . . Shall we cease to fight for the common man as against the privileged man, with pen and brain and artist's pencil and all the legitimate weapons known to the literary soldier and warrior of art?

Hardly. . . .

The Hearst papers are American newspapers, democratic news-papers, and as such they rely, as Lincoln relied, on the plain people. They will continue to promote the democratic idea . . . to do their chosen work for the enlightenment, for the uplifting of the masses, for the advancement of the Republic.

The people understand the Hearst papers . . . and for the people the Hearst papers are published.

After the storm subsided the *Journal* still had the largest paid circulation of any newspaper in the world. During the month of September, 1901, the paper showed a gain of one hundred thousand over the preceding year. It also carried more display advertising for September than any other New York paper. In August it gained three hundred and sixty columns daily, and in September three hundred and twenty-six columns. The *World* showed a loss.

CHAPTER XXIX

BREAKS COAL TRUST

"DIG the Panama Canal," wrote President McKinley to Congress in his last message.

Hearst now addressed an editorial to the new President: "Mr. Roosevelt, dig the Panama Canal, any canal, rather than no canal. The Panama route, if that is the only route to be had—that is the position of the American people."

Hearst favored the Nicaragua route because the air was less impure, and digging the canal would not take too heavy a toll of human life. Already two Federal commissions had recommended the Nicaragua route, but in 1902, Congress approved the purchase of the French Panama claim at a figure not above forty million dollars. Unless a canal strip could be bought from the Republic of Colombia the Nicaragua route would be chosen. American speculators had purchased the French concession from Colombia authorizing them to build a waterway through Panama. Unless some action was taken their rights would expire in 1904. American promoters swarmed in Washington.

President Roosevelt made a treaty with Bogotá, the capital of Colombia. The desired zone was granted to the United States for the promise of ten million dollars and an annual rental.

Then suddenly the Colombia Senate demanded a large increase in cash. They failed to obtain it, and rejected the treaty. President Roosevelt was blocked, but not for long.

The steps leading to acquiring territory for digging the Panama Canal sound more like the cinema than statecraft. Dr. Manuel Guerrero, a Panama revolutionist, and Monsieur Philippe Bunau-Varilla, a French soldier of fortune, came to

243

Washington to acquire funds for staging a Panama revolution, a safe revolution chaperoned by the United States. Bunau-Varilla saw Roosevelt in the White House and Secretary Hay in the State department. At once he sent word to his Panama friends that American war vessels would protect them in an uprising against Colombia.

The war vessels arrived. Revolution broke. American troops landed. The only casualty was a Chinaman accidentally killed. On November 3, 1903, the independence of Panama was proclaimed. Hearst urged President Roosevelt to open negotiations with Nicaragua and Costa Rica and gain permission to dig the canal through those countries. This plan was opposed by Senator Hanna and the railroad lobby.

The President recognized the paper government of the new Republic of Panama. Then he took the territory from Colombia, a country with which we were at peace.

Hearst called Roosevelt's conduct "rough riding to dishonor."

The President explained his act: "If I had followed traditional conservative methods, I would have submitted a dignified state paper of probably two hundred pages to Congress, and the debate would have been going on yet. I took the canal zone, and let Congress debate."

In spite of his opposition to the nefarious methods by which the canal zone was acquired, Hearst rejoiced that the project for which he had fought fifteen years was about to be realized. He could visualize ocean liners steaming across the Isthmus of Panama which as a lad he had crossed on one of his journeys to New York, suffering from a fever that almost cost him his life.

Ranking with Hearst's interest in the digging of the Panama Canal was his battle with a new trust that controlled anthracite coal. In 1901, the United States became billion-dollar-minded. The trusts were ever more menacing. Andrew Carnegie had received twenty-five millions in cash as part of the price of his Pennsylvania mills which were taken over by the brand new billion dollar Steel Trust backed by J. P. Morgan, of which Charles M. Schwab was president. The Coal Trust was especially exasperating. It was a demon inhabiting every one's coal scuttle, but it had not been possible to control the Coal Trust by law, or even legally defeat its existence. To these tasks Hearst set himself.

In the government inquiry held by a sub-committee of the Industrial Commission in February of 1901, in the rooms of the New York Chamber of Commerce, it was revealed that 90 per cent of the hard-coal mines were controlled by the railroads. High freight rates were used as a club to force the anthracite coal owners into a trust.

In July of 1901, the coal combine increased the price of coal seventy-five cents a ton. In order to produce thirty-four millions extra profits for the coal barons, every man, woman and child in New York City was to be taxed three dollars.

Hearst made up his mind to "smash the Coal Trust." He had Briggs, Opper and Davenport prepare a series of cartoons. On September 10, 1902, he sent his attorney, Clarence J. Shearn, to Albany to petition Attorney-General Davies to begin proceedings against the trust. The Attorney-General granted Shearn's petition to proceed to dissolve the Coal Trust. The petition presented evidence that a combination existed between the coal operators and the railroads. Before the month was over the price of coal was increased from twenty to twenty-two dollars a ton.

Then a strike broke out in the coal-fields. Hearst urged that a mediation committee be formed to call on Pierpont Morgan and beg him to use his influence with the president of the coal mining region railroads to listen to the miners. Hearst was certain that the strikers would be glad to return to work. John Mitchell, president of the United Mine Workers of America, announced that he would meet any committee to settle the strike. Hearst organized a large mass meeting in Madison Square Garden. Samuel Gompers, president of the

American Federation of Labor, and John Mitchell made addresses.

President Roosevelt besought the Coal Trust and miners to end the strike for the welfare of the public. The miners offered to leave everything in dispute to a board of arbitration appointed by the President, and return to work immediately. George F. Baer, president of the Coal Trust, refused to arbitrate and demanded more troops in the coal-fields.

Hearst had hoped that President Roosevelt's message to Congress on December 3, 1902, would aid the battle, but Roosevelt's comments on the trust were discouragingly qualified, "The Captains of Industry who have driven our railroad systems across the continent, developed our commerce and manufactures have, on the whole, done great good to our people. It would be most unwise to cramp or fetter the youthful strength of our nation. . . . Corporations engaged in interstate commerce should be regulated, if they are found to harm public interest."

Hearst was depressed with President Roosevelt's apathy, but at his own expense he sent costly investigators into Pennsylvania. They unearthed the Temple Iron Company which was the Coal Trust. This corporation started with capital stock of two hundred and forty thousand dollars and never mined a ton of coal. Its purpose was to increase its stock to two hundred and fifty thousand dollars with bonds of fifteen millions for suppressing competition in the transportation of coal. Clearly the Coal Trust was in combination with the railroads.

Hearst's counsel assembled the evidence and presented it to Attorney-General Philander C. Knox petitioning him to dissolve the Coal Trust under the Federal law. On the same day Hearst sent President Roosevelt a copy of the petition. He stated that the proceedings had been instituted pursuant to the provision of the Federal anti-Monopoly Law. The Reading Company, the Philadelphia Coal and Reading Iron Company, and the Central Railroad Company of New Jersey, were named as offenders. Hearst urged immediate action because of the gravity of the existing situation:

Any effective blow struck at the combination between the coal operators would tend to end the existing strike. . . . I am in possession of documentary evidence establishing an illegal combination to monopolize the coal trade among the several states. . . . I propose to show over the hands and seals of the corporations mentioned that an actual concert and combination control the country's anthracite coal supply. Owing to the exigency of the situation, and because I am in possession of this indubitable evidence, I request that an opportunity be afforded my counsel to present the case to the Attorney-General.

Respectfully,
WILLIAM RANDOLPH HEARST

On the same day Attorney-General Knox notified the President that he could find no evidence that a trust as a trust existed so that it could be brought under the anti-Trust Law. But at the same time he asked United States Attorney Henry L. Burnett for the Southern District of New York, to take evidence. Burnett collected evidence and reported it to Attorney-General Knox, but it slept unawakened in a pigeonhole.

In an editorial Hearst pointed out that Knox had been on the pay-roll of trusts and that it was futile to expect him to prosecute the very trusts whose influence had made him Attorney-General.

On the floor of Congress, John Sharp Williams and Senator Jones of Arkansas, asked Attorney-General Knox what evidence had been taken against the coal and railroad companies, but they received no answer, although people were hungry and starving in the coal-fields. Hearst himself sent several carloads of coal to Chicago to be distributed free among the poor. In New York he sold coal at five dollars a ton, the wholesale cost, in the tenement district.

While Hearst was endeavoring to induce the Department of Justice to prosecute the Coal Trust under the Sherman anti-

Trust Act, the Republican Congress came to the rescue of the trust and passed the Elkins Bill which repealed the penalty of imprisonment. By signing the Elkins Bill, President Roosevelt in advance pardoned the conspirators.

Then Hearst introduced a bill in Congress restoring the penalty of imprisonment for infraction of the Interstate Commerce Act. At last he succeeded in setting in motion the machinery of the Interstate Commerce Commission. That body immediately subpoenaed witnesses. On the stand, President Baer of the Coal Trust accused Hearst of the misdemeanor of raising wages and shortening the hours of labor. Baer refused to produce his books and papers, and declared that the editor was trying to make out that the businessmen of this country were a "gang of conspirators trying to evade the law."

Hearst's answer was that the persons composing the Coal Trust were not businessmen, but law-breaking monopolists, enemies of business. The miners' strike caused by the monopolization of coal had disturbed business for months, in fact, had almost brought about its paralysis.

Because Hearst attacked the Coal Trust he was called a demagogue and Socialist. While testifying before the committee investigating the Coal Trust he said: "As a businessman myself, dependent upon the prosperity of the community for the success of my various enterprises, I have a personal interest in the suppression of the sort of piracy the Coal Trust typifies. It is not, however, as a businessman that I am chiefly moved to exert myself. These conspiracies against the common welfare do worse than rob the public. They corrupt politics."

President Baer and his associates of the Coal Trust refused to answer questions put by the Interstate Commerce Commission. Proceedings were brought before Judge Lacombe to punish Baer for contempt of court. The refusal of the Coal Trust to produce its books before the Commission was sustained by the Circuit Court. This decision was reversed in the United States Supreme Court. Books brought before the Interstate Commerce Commission revealed that dealers were ordered black-listed for underselling. They showed that in order to kill competition of an independent road, the Reading, Lehigh, Delaware, Lackawanna and Western, Jersey Central, Susquehanna, and Geary combined and bought the Temple Iron Company's charter. Thus was disclosed how six railroads were able harmoniously to fix rates months in advance.

For his revelations about the Coal Trust, legislatures passed votes of thanks and sent them to Hearst. Even the conservative Springfield *Republican* declared he was performing a service that should have been performed by the Government.

Hearst addressed a half-page signed editorial to the President: "You, President Roosevelt, can end the coal famine. . . ."

The President decided to press criminal action against the Coal Trust. Morgan and Baer hurried to Washington, now ready to arbitrate the strike. The arbitration commission appointed by President Roosevelt decided that the striking workers had a right to demand higher wages and shorter hours. The strike was settled March 24, 1903.

After nine years of battle Hearst had the satisfaction of seeing the United States.Circuit Court declare the Temple Iron Company, or the Coal Trust, to be a combination doing business in violation of the anti-Trust Law. The court issued an injunction restraining the Temple Iron Company from doing business.

The revelations made by Hearst before the Interstate Commerce Commission, and the decision of the United States Circuit Court, aroused public sentiment to such a degree that the authority and power of the Interstate Commerce Commission were strengthened.

As a result, Hearst won another victory—the Interstate Commerce Court was established.

CHAPTER XXX

ELECTION TO CONGRESS AND
MARRIAGE

FOR fifteen years William Randolph Hearst had battled in his newspapers with great aggregations of wealth. Now he believed that if he were one of the lawmakers of the land he would be able to control the "criminal trusts."

Arthur Brisbane was about to be nominated as Congressman from the Eleventh District of New York City, but Brisbane and his friends thought that Hearst would be more effective in Washington. At the last minute, a change in nominees was made. Hearst was offered the Democratic nomination in the Eleventh District, for many years represented by Amos J. Cummings. On October 6, 1903, he accepted the nomination.

Never was such a campaign for Congress seen in New York as that made by Hearst. His retiring manner disappeared. He became a forthright speaker, especially quick in answering hecklers. Where the average candidate made four speeches a day, Hearst made ten or fifteen. So vast had become his enterprises, so numerous and generous were his activities, that in New York City people hung on rafters merely to look at him.

The campaign closed with a huge meeting in Madison Square Garden. At six-thirty the vast building opened. Sixty thousand people were waiting to enter. In ten minutes the building was filled. Thousands from the marching Democratic clubs swelled the vast concourse, and a large crowd flowed over into the open square. Here the people who could not enter the building watched the reproduction in electric lights of Opper's and Davenport's powerful cartoons of the trusts. Fountains of electric fire flowed in the square. Big balloons sailed toward the stars and burst in a gorgeous blaze. Multi-colored vivid lights, thousands of rockets shooting heavenward and bursting, tons of red fire lighting from the heights the Garden—all these made the streets bright as day. Fifty thousand shots were fired like rapid-fire artillery in a grand salute. Eight hundred and fifty policemen were required to keep the crowd in order.

Inside of the building spoke David B. Hill, former New York Governor and United States Senator, former Governor James H. Budd of California and Adlai Stevenson, Vice-President with Grover Cleveland.

Hearst spoke for only ten minutes. He said that the Republicans had done little for man, but much for money. Hearst wished to legislate for man. He said he did not hold the old-fashioned belief that every Republican was a rascal and every Democrat a saint, but the Republican Party as a political institution was so greatly indebted to the trusts, and under so many obligations to them, that Republicans would not legislate against trusts, nor would they enforce existing laws against great aggregations of wealth.

Hearst was elected by fifteen thousand votes, the largest plurality of any district in New York, and the largest ever known in the Eleventh District. No Congressman-elect ever entered the National Capitol with a more consecrated determination to benefit the common man than did William Randolph Hearst. When he took the oath of office he was forty. His festive collegiate clothing had been cast aside. He had grown somewhat stouter than when he arrived in New York, and he wore the frock coat and the broad brimmed soft black hat of the usual Congressman of the period.

Congressman Hearst took a house in Lafayette Square belonging to Admiral Ludlowsen, and shortly before vacated by Senator Root. In Congress Hearst early met and became a friend of Champ Clark, a representative from Bowling Green, Pike County, Missouri. Clark's district was near that in which Senator George Hearst and Phebe Apperson Hearst were born. Some relations of the Hearsts were named Clark, and Champ

Clark with his warm welcoming manner to the new Congressman seemed almost like a kinsman. The friendship between Clark and Hearst always endured.

Champ Clark was well on his way to be Speaker of the House of Representatives. He knew all the mazes of Washington, and he opened to William Randolph Hearst his experience, discussing with him his work, preparation of bills and the affiliations of members of Congress.

Hearst was too active, too overflowing with vitality to give all his time to the monotonous routine of the House of Representatives. His brain was ever awhirl with fresh projects. Listening to long speeches irked the impetuous Congressman. He had not the patience that made his father, Senator George Hearst, popular by listening to every speech made in the United States Senate while he served. Perhaps the difference lay in the fact that William Randolph Hearst entered Congress at forty and George Hearst was in his late sixties before he was seated in the Senate.

William Randolph Hearst prepared many bills to be introduced in the House, but he could not be kept fettered to his desk. As often as possible he escaped to the outside world. Unexpectedly he visited his newspaper offices. He yachted in the Atlantic. He dashed across the continent to San Simeon, his father's favorite ranch on San Simeon Bay in San Luis Obispo County, California. Here in an old-fashioned white ranch-house at the base of an enchanted hill he vacationed with friends. He had come here often with his father. Now he rode over these hills and planned to erect a house on the summit of one where he had camped as a boy.

Frequently Hearst went to Pleasanton, California, to visit his mother in her luxurious, hospitable Hacienda del Pozo de la Verona. He supervised alterations in the Hacienda, consulting with the young architect, Julia Morgan, a small unassuming genius, the first woman to be graduated from the Beaux Arts, Paris. Miss Morgan had just taken her Beaux Arts degree and was a friend of Hearst's mother and cousins. This meeting was

WILLIAM RANDOLPH HEARST AS REPRESENTATIVE IN CONGRESS

the foundation of a significant connection in Hearst's life, because later Julia Morgan was to be the architect of his Spanish Casa Grande and guest houses crowning the Enchanted Hill at San Simeon.

During one of these visits to his mother, Mrs. Hearst suggested that her son present to the University of California a Greek theater. Already Mrs. Hearst 'herself had endowed the university with immense sums for scholarships and buildings and archæological expeditions. To the Faculty and students she was a fairy godmother. While supervising construction of her buildings she had a residence in Berkeley where she entertained students and the Faculty, and renewed her own youth in aspirations of the youth of California.

With pleasure William Randolph Hearst granted his mother's request, and in 1903 he went to California to be present at the dedication of the Greek Theater.

At that time the nearest approach to an outdoor theater was to be found at Nîmes in the South of France, but this was almost a ruin. At Oxford, England, was a small outdoor theater. The Berkeley theater is semi-circular in form and two hundred and fifty feet in diameter. It is beautifully placed on a tree-covered hillside of the Berkeley campus. *Birds,* a comedy by Aristophanes, was the first production on its stage.

On the day of dedication of the theater Hearst, in his speech, gave credit to Benjamin Ide Wheeler for selecting the site. He thanked John Galen Howard, the architect, for designing and constructing the theater. He said that his mother was responsible for his interest in the project, and for that he thanked her most heartily:

As for me, I feel very much like a small boy who belonged to the baseball team. Somebody asked him, "Sonny, what position do you play on the nine?" The small boy answered, "I don't play any position, I just belong." I feel as though I just belonged. I am very happy to belong. I am proud to be associated in some way with this great university. I believe this university will eventually be the greatest in the world, because it is thoroughly American, and it is thoroughly Californian. No institution can possess both of these qualities and fail to reach the top.

Hearst spoke in opposition to the endowed university. He declared that a university should be dependent on the State, only, in order to be independent. When Hearst finished his speech he was cheered and congratulated, not only for himself as the donor of the handsome Greek Theater, but as the son of his mother.

During this same year Hearst's life became greatly enriched. On April 30, 1903, he married Miss Millicent Willson, daughter of Mr. and Mrs. George A. Willson of New York City. Bishop Henry Codman Potter, who was a friend of Mrs. Phebe Hearst, performed the ceremony at Grace Church, New York City. Mrs. Hearst was not well at the time, but she sent the bride a magnificent brooch.

The editor wrote his mother an exuberant description of the wedding: "It was cheerful, and not to be mistaken for a funeral."

Early in the morning reporters began to call for news. Hearst and his old friend, Orrin Peck, the portrait painter of San Francisco and Munich, dressed early, and waited in their frock coats at the Holland House. They were at the church before eleven. There were thirty guests. The chancel was beautiful with bright roses and apple blossoms. When Hearst and Orrin Peck stepped out to the altar the bride appeared with her father. The Bishop looked grand and solemn, but he was in his usual wedding humor after the ceremony.

Oscar's best wedding breakfast at the Waldorf was spread in the Astor dining room, but there were so many gifts, reporters and photographers, that the bride and groom had only time for bouillon and ice-cream before they took the three o'clock steamer for Europe, while their friends pelted them with rice.

The writer of these pages met them both for the first time that day aboard the steamer, *Kaiser Wilhelm II*, and there was never a happier pair than the William Randolph Hearsts when they set out for Europe on April 30, 1903.

The editor took his bride to his favorite shrines of beauty, and again saw them with fresh enthusiasm in the pleasure of tall, beautiful, dark-eyed Millicent Willson Hearst.

The Hearsts toured Europe. The publisher delighted in his swift new motor-car, and the independence of action that it gave him. He learned to drive. Intoxicated by the speed and power of the car, he seemed to have in his arms the strength and in his feet the swiftness of the automobile. He wished to go faster and faster. He longed to fly. By the time he reached London, Hearst realized that it would soon be the ambition of every one to own an automobile, and that the manufacture of these machines would be the beginning of a great industry.

In London there was a new magazine called *The Car*. Directly it came to Hearst's attention, the publisher decided to establish a magazine of the same character in New York. He bought several copies of *The Car* and mailed them to Carvalho. By cable he told Carvalho that he would like to have a magazine devoted to automobiles, and he requested him to look over *The Car*. Carvalho established *Motor*.

Hearst's editors advised him not to venture into the magazine world. There was a great difference, they told him, between creating a successful magazine and a successful newspaper. Hearst ignored pessimistic advice. He was headed for the magazine world.

After *Motor* had been established for a month, Hearst sent for George d'Utassy, who was circulation manager of one of his Chicago papers, and asked him to take charge of the infant magazine, *Motor*.

"You know I'm a newspaper man," said Hearst, "and the men on my papers tell me I should stick to newspapers. But I think that the difference between newspapers and magazines is difference in details, not in essentials. Let's show the men downtown that they are wrong. Don't bother them. If you need help, come to me direct."

Hearst gave d'Utassy a check for ten thousand dollars. "That ten thousand," said d'Utassy recently, "was the only cash put into the magazines during the years I was connected with them. I mean that literally. By using credit with printers and paper makers, and by giving bonds and redeeming them out of the profits when other magazines were bought, the Hearst magazine system was built up. With the issue of January, 1904, *Motor* began to make money. Victor Lougheed, technical editor, made the valuable suggestion of compiling the detailed specifications of all cars in the New York Motor Show. This feature of *Motor* has been continued, and for years the magazine sold the Show Number at a dollar."

Motor is the pioneer of the thirteen Hearst magazines. It covers every department of the automobile industry. This includes manufacturing and sales, jobbers, car distributors, car dealers, service stations and mechanics. Men of national prominence are its editors, and the same attention is devoted to interesting readers as in a general magazine. The Hearst magazines rank first in circulation and income of any magazines under individual ownership in the world.

Two years after Hearst ordered *Motor* established he formed the International Magazine Company and *Cosmopolitan* was purchased. In 1886, Schlicht & Field of Rochester, New York, had founded *Cosmopolitan*. In 1889, it was purchased by John Brisben Walker who lifted its circulation from twenty to one hundred thousand. Through Arthur Brisbane, Walker offered to sell the *Cosmopolitan* to Hearst. D'Utassy was asked to study the *Cosmopolitan* and make a report. He found that the *Cosmopolitan* had been the leader in the general magazine field, and that Walker, who had become a pioneer manufacturer of steam automobiles, had so neglected and starved *Cosmopolitan* that it was at the bottom of the list. D'Utassy reported that with proper management it could again be successful. He told Hearst that Walker wanted four hundred thousand for the magazine, but he was apparently being pressed by creditors, and if Hearst waited Walker would sell the property cheaper.

Hearst's reply was what d'Utassy calls a "financial lesson." "Perhaps you are right, but price is only one consideration. If I don't buy now, Walker may find another purchaser, or Walker may make money in his automobile business and not want to sell. Or the magazine may continue to deteriorate and not be worth anything. You say we can make money with it. I assume you mean 'real money!' If you don't, I don't want to buy at any price. If you do, buy now instead of waiting, and start to make money."

D'Utassy bought the magazine for Hearst for four hundred thousand dollars. It was paid for in bonds redeemable at the rate of 20 per cent a year. The profits more than redeemed the bonds. In less than three years it had more than a million circulation, and more advertising than its two closest competitors combined. D'Utassy explains why *Cosmopolitan* succeeded so quickly: "Sounds easily done, doesn't it? Each month the Chief took a copy, and in his loose running handwriting made comments on the margins of the pages. These comments always showed us where and how we could improve the next issue. I wish I had saved these marked copies. They could have been published as 'a guide to successful editing,' and would perhaps have saved many of our competitors from going on the rocks."

D'Utassy recalls one revealing incident of how Hearst edited the *Cosmopolitan.* It was connected with the publication of a series on *The Treason of the Senate,* by David Graham Phillips. Hearst was in Washington. D'Utassy sent him a form containing the first article by Phillips.

At two o'clock in the morning d'Utassy received a telegram from Hearst in which he said:

Violence is not force. Windy vituperation is not convincing. I had intended an exposé. We have merely an attack. The facts, the proofs, the documentary evidence are an important thing, and the article is deficient in them. For instance, there is one thing mentioned in the article which should be elaborated. The Albany capital is a great scandal. It is now falling to pieces.

The papers of the country are full of paragraphs jeering at the appropriate rottenness at the capital at Albany. It appears that Depew was a member of the building committee. We should have a picture and some quotations from reports, etc., showing the immense rottenness of the building and of the building board. We want more definite facts throughout. Supply them where you can. Then run the article if you want, and we will try to get the others later.   HEARST.

Hearst marked Phillips's article, and certain passages indicated by him were to be rewritten. Shortly after the telegram arrived there came a telephone call to d'Utassy. Was it too late to change? How many had been printed?

"About three hundred," replied d'Utassy, "but by running the presses day and night you can get the magazine out on time."

Three hours later d'Utassy received over the wire the last portion of David Graham Phillips's article rewritten by Hearst.

In relating the incident d'Utassy said, "David Graham agreed with me that it was 100 per cent better than his. He said that if he could write as well, he would double his price."

Another incident in connection with editing the *Cosmopolitan* is related by d'Utassy:

I told Mr. Hearst one day that he had been running the *Get-Rich-Quick Wallingford* stories for three years, and that at the shop it was thought that the public was getting tired of them. He answered by telling me about Outcault's "Buster Brown." He told his Sunday editors to try to get "Buster" away from the Sunday *Herald*. The Sunday editor reported that "Buster Brown" had been running three years in the *Herald,* and the contracts had three more years to run. Anyhow, the people were tired of "Buster Brown." Mr. Hearst insisted that a contract be made with Outcault commencing at the end of the three remaining years of the *Herald* contract. "And," Mr. Hearst said, "we finally got 'Buster Brown,' and it added a hundred thousand circulation to my Sunday paper. My opinion is that when editors begin to get tired of a feature, the public is just beginning to like it." That talk gave us our successful formula, "Find out what your readers want and give it to them. And give it to them regularly!"

An amusing incident in connection with engaging an artist for the *Cosmopolitan* covers is related by d'Utassy. Several artists were tried. The editors came to the conclusion that the designs of the late Harrison Fisher were the best, and a long contract was made with him. When the first Fisher cover appeared Hearst was in California. He sent d'Utassy a telegram saying he liked the cover, but he saw that the *Saturday Evening Post* also had Fisher covers and that Scribner published his books. He asked d'Utassy to find out how much Fisher would charge for an exclusive contract, limiting his work to *Cosmopolitan* covers.

"I saw Mr. Fisher," said d'Utassy. "He named a price—a big one. I wired Mr. Hearst. He answered by wire: 'Don't hire Fisher, but ask him to give me a job.' That was more than twenty years ago, Fisher did *Cosmopolitan* covers until his death."

Hearst always imagined the *Cosmopolitan* as a great national magazine. He instructed the editors to print, "not only that which is best, but that which is universally recognized as best." He advised them to buy, "not only the best in art and literature, but to buy it exclusively," so that the best would be found in Hearst periodicals, and nowhere else. *Cosmopolitan* with a circulation of one million, five hundred thousand has the largest news-stand circulation of any twenty-five cent magazine in America. Among the writers whose work has appeared in *Cosmopolitan* are George Bernard Shaw, Winston Churchill, Albert Einstein, Rudyard Kipling, Ida M. Tarbell, Raymond Moley, André Maurois, Stewart Chase, Emil Ludwig, the Grand Duchess Marie, John Galsworthy, Hendrik Van Loon, Pearl S. Buck, Edna Ferber, Fannie Hurst, Kathleen Norris, Sir Philip Gibbs, Ernest Hemingway, Rupert Hughes, Nina Wilcox Putnam, Vicki Baum, H. G. Wells, Franklin D. Roosevelt, Calvin Coolidge and Mussolini.

In 1907, Hearst acquired *Motor Boating,* a virtually defunct magazine purchased merely for the name. As usual he selected an able editor, Charles F. Chapman, who is still editor. *Motor Boating* is the magazine of yachtsmen and owners of motorboats. It has had a steady dependable growth and success.

CHAPTER XXXI

CONGRESSIONAL CAREER

WHEN the William Randolph Hearsts returned from Europe they went to the Hacienda at Pleasanton, California, to be welcomed by Phebe Hearst. The mother of the publisher had always wished for a daughter, and it was her pleasure to present Millicent Hearst to her large circle of friends and relations.

In 1904, Hearst's life became complete. On April 10th, in New York City, occurred an important event, the birth of his first child, a son named George for the Senator. There probably never was a boy with so many toys as Master George Hearst. On the preceding Christmas Eve, William Randolph Hearst had played Santa Claus for Mrs. Hearst's young cousins, the Murrays. Now Baby George Hearst with his smiling, wondering blue eyes, joined the group of children. They were delighted by the visit of the white-bearded, red-coated, merry-voiced old gentleman, who came down the chimney in the Hearst house laughing and ringing his sleigh bells.

Directly George was born Mrs. Phebe Hearst fitted up a room at the Hacienda adjoining her own, and she wrote that her grandson should be brought immediately to visit her. George Hearst and the four brothers who followed, together with their nurses, governesses, and tutors, passed happy summers with their grandmother at La Hacienda del Pozo de la Verona, and at Wyntoon, Mrs. Hearst's magnificent German castle on McCloud River, not far from Mount Shasta where the last Indian war in California was fought.

In 1904, Hearst moved forward rapidly. In New York it was necessary to find larger quarters for the growing *Evening Journal* and the *American*, which for two years had been the name of his morning edition of the *Journal*. The papers were moved to the Rhinelander Building at 238 William Street. In Boston, Hearst's Boston *American* was established, and in this same year the Los Angeles *Examiner* came into existence.

In all the cities in which Hearst acquired newspapers, he made local campaigns. From the beginning the Los Angeles *Examiner* advocated a free harbor for the city, the building of a dry-dock and a naval base at San Pedro. The dry-dock has been built. The United States Government fortified the harbor and made it a naval station and submarine base. The spring of 1904 saw a six and a half million dollar municipal power bond issue passed in Los Angeles, assuring the city of a municipally owned electric system, one of Hearst's cherished plans. Another project was an aqueduct for the Owens River, which, in 1905, was passed by the City Council. This measure assured a water supply for a million people and irrigation for thousands of acres.

The Los Angeles *Examiner* made a crusade to close the squalid underworld dives largely owned by an extremely rich woman. She was so touched by the *Examiner* crusade that she sold the dive buildings and joined the crusaders.

In Congress, one of the first measures taken up by Hearst was the popular election of United States Senators. He introduced a bill to amend the Constitution so as to provide for the election of United States Senators by direct vote.

After he was appointed to the Labor Committee in the House of Representatives he sponsored a bill to establish the eight-hour day for mechanics and workmen employed on contracts for the national government. The measure met with violent opposition, but was eventually enacted into a law.

In 1905 and 1906, Hearst introduced a new bill to have the Federal Government give each State a sum equal to that appropriated by the State for building good roads. He fostered a bill compelling each department of the Federal Government to detail to Congress estimates for appropriations. He introduced a measure aimed at the Standard Oil Company prohibiting commerce between the States in any product of the soil, if it could be shown to be the result of a monopoly established by restraint of competition, supply, transportation or price. If this bill had been passed and enforced, it would have left no loophole of escape for transgressions of law, by Standard Oil. In another measure proposed by Hearst he tried to have pipe lines made common carriers by placing them under the supervision of the Interstate Commerce Commission, and subjected to the same legal control as carriers that govern railroads. Hearst engaged Ida M. Tarbell, biographer of John D. Rockefeller, to write a series of articles for the New York *American* interpreting the publisher's measures before Congress.

Hearst introduced a bill to compel prosecuting officers to take legal measures against criminal trust officials. A bill presented by him was to amend the Sherman anti-Trust Law so that trusts could be prosecuted more easily.

Far-reaching were the consequences of the bill sponsored by Congressman Hearst in 1905 to increase the power and jurisdiction of the Interstate Commerce Commission. The railroads aggressively fought this proposed law.

President Theodore Roosevelt immediately realized the importance of Hearst's bill and had it incorporated into Administration legislation. The Republicans cut the bill in two at the end of the fifth section. Esch of Wisconsin, in the Senate, introduced the first five sections as his own bill. In the House, Townsend of Michigan, presented the remaining•eight sections as his bill. The Esch-Townsend bill was enacted into a law and signed by President Roosevelt.

While in Congress Hearst sponsored a bill authorizing the President to purchase a complete system of electric telegraph lines giving communication with all parts of the United States and foreign lands.

Another bill introduced by the Congressman, and which was easily made into a law, increased the salaries of the Chief

Justice and Associate Justices of the United States Supreme Court.

To-day the United States would be at a loss to know how to get on without the Parcel-Post System, but when Hearst proposed the measure there was outcry against a "dangerous novelty." The "dangerous novelty" presented by Congressman Hearst ultimately became a law. For years it has been in successful operation, an enormous aid to business, and a convenience, especially to the poor.

Congressman Hearst presented many bills, and yet he did not feel that he needed to be always at his desk in Congress. His newspapers fought his battles, but during his two terms he was ever watchful of Congressional activities. While Hearst was in Congress he began in New York one of his most popular crusades—the abolition of Death Avenue. This street was New York's crying shame. Through the city the New York Central Railroad ran a steam train with the record of having killed more people than any other train in the world. Without pity or heed it went through city thoroughfares. Most of the street crossings were unguarded. Children were mangled on their way to school. Hearst had a son of his own. These unprotected little boys and girls were from homes so humble that their parents had no means of protecting them. In 1905, another child was killed. Canal, Christopher, Twenty-third, and Forty-second Streets, where the steam trains ran, all called to Hearst. The crusade was on.

That this campaign was to be fiercely fought, Hearst well knew. The New York Central had an annual income of eighteen million dollars from Death Avenue. The sum was almost impregnable, but Hearst believed that he could win through the Legislature and the courts. Chauncey M. Depew, chairman of the executive committee of the New York Central, was ordered to appear before Justice Dowling to be examined by Robert L. Stanton.

Since 1846, the New York Central had owned its franchise which expired in 1896. The company claimed to operate under a special charter that would live forever. Hearst questioned the immortality of the New York Central. The company threatened that if its tracks were removed from Death Avenue, its freight traffic would be diverted to Boston.

Then Assemblyman Hoey of Manhattan, introduced a bill in the Legislature. The result was a compromise, but a victory for the West Side. The new route should be decided by local authorities. Steam should be discontinued as motor power. Along Riverside Drive tracks should be covered. Cost of all changes was to be borne by the company. Cost of approaches was to be borne by the city. No Elevated structures were to be allowed on Tenth and Eleventh Avenues. The question of franchise was to be determined by the courts. The New York Central agreed that at and near West Fifty-ninth Street, and to the South, the tracks should be carried over West Fifty-ninth Street and other thoroughfares and parks, by viaducts at a proper height above the street level. Suitable subway structures should be provided under West Fifty-ninth Street, avenues, streets, and public wharfs. The company was to construct these viaducts and subways. The Hoey Bill was killed in the Senate.

In 1911, Clarence Shearn drew up the McManus-Boylan Bill. It asked for the revocation of the right of the New York Central and Hudson River Railroad to maintain and operate a steam railroad in the streets of New York. The *Journal* printed a petition for its readers to sign in order to get rid of the tracks on Death Avenue.

Then the railroad tried to rush through the Gaynor-Tompkins Bill. This gave the company everything—city streets, public parks and water-front on the West Side of Manhattan from Sixtieth Street to Spuyten Duyvil. The bill contained no penalty if the company did not remove its tracks.

The New York Central was desperate. Mayor Gaynor was pressed into service. So were attorneys from the office of the corporation counsel, Senator McClellan and Assemblyman James A. Walker, later Mayor of New York. Boss Murphy of

Tammany Hall aided, and so did all his lobbyists and legislators. Murphy visualized fat contracts for sixty million dollars' worth of work to be distributed in Manhattan.

At last Death Avenue was doomed, but it cost the city the entire water-front from Sixtieth Street north to Spuyten Duyvil. Senator J. Griswold Webb introduced a measure in the Legislature that was approved by the City, State and transit authorities containing plans for the track removal.

Less than twenty-four hours before his sudden death, Ira A. Place, senior vice-president of the New York Central, withdrew all objections to the city's plan. The Transit Commission ordered the railroad to abolish ninety-three grade crossings along Eleventh and Twelfth Avenues. Tracks on Canal Street were also to be removed. From Canal Street to West Thirtieth Street the tracks were to be elevated. From Thirtieth to Seventy-second Streets tracks were to be in an open ditch. From Seventy-second Street north the tracks were allowed to remain.

In 1929, came plans for the elimination of the grade of the New York Central along the West Side, and the beautification of the water-front. At noon on the last day of 1929, Mayor Walker drew the rusty spike from the New York Central tracks at Sixtieth Street and Eleventh Avenue. With the old year Death Avenue died. It was the beginning of the end of surface railroad tracks on the western rim of Manhattan Island. And so ended the twenty-four year struggle by Hearst for the elimination of Death Avenue.

CHAPTER XXXII

PRESIDENTIAL CAMPAIGN

AMERICAN youths are told in school that it is possible for them to be President of the United States. Every normal American boy at some time hopes to live in the White House. William Randolph Hearst's father had been a United States Senator. The editor often thought of the laws that he would advocate if he were President. Now came what seemed an opportunity.

Theodore Roosevelt had been nominated by the Republicans in Chicago. A young dynamic Democrat was necessary to defeat him. Leaders of the Democratic Party thought that Hearst would most effectively compete with the hero of San Juan Hill. It gave him pleasure that the movement started in California, his native State. When William Randolph Hearst was forty-one he allowed his name to be presented at the Democratic Convention which met at St. Louis in July, 1904.

William Jennings Bryan nominated Cockrell of Missouri. Judge Alton Brooks Parker was brought forward. Then D. M. Delmas, a Californian, and one of the great orators of the West, rose and said: "For the first time in history California presents as a candidate for the great office of Chief Executive of the Republic, one born and reared on her soil, William Randolph Hearst."

Delmas spoke of Hearst's fidelity to the nominees of the Democratic Party. He recounted his candidate's many acts of benefaction, his democratic impulses, hospitals established by him, universities aided, private distress relieved, the needy fed and sheltered during long bitter winters in New York. Delmas said that the great question of the day was neither tariff nor tariff revision, nor the money standard, nor regulation of currency, nor control of banks, nor expansion, nor imperialism, important as they were:

The question which confronts the American people to-day, which has confronted them with ever-growing insistence since the Civil War, is whether this Government shall be carried on for the benefit of the people, or whether it shall be manipulated for the benefit of the privileged class.

Delmas said that the words of Hearst spoken when he accepted his nomination for Congress might have been uttered by Jefferson:

I have devoted all my energies and abilities, whatever they may be, to the cause of the plain people, and I shall continue to do so.

The speaker closed with a magnificent peroration, and then presented his candidate:

The unconquered antagonist of all schemes by which man, trampling right and justice underfoot, builds his fortune upon oppression and wrong, the foremost living advocate of the equality of man ... the champion of the rights of toil, the foe of privilege and monopoly, the friend of all who labor and are heavy laden. . . . William Randolph Hearst.

Clarence Darrow of Chicago who seconded Hearst's nomination said he was instructed by almost the unanimous voice of the Democrats of Illinois:

Even at this late hour it would be well to remember that the whole Democratic Party is not inside these convention walls, much less in the seats of delegates assembled here. . . . It is not made up alone of pawnshops in the narrow, crooked lane which men call Wall Street—shops where human souls are placed in pawn for gold. The United States is the countless millions who do their work and live their lives and earn their bread without the aid of schemes or tricks. . . .

To restore the rule of the people, to insure their welfare, their happiness, their prosperity; to make and keep our land a republic of law, and that law the people's will; to win allegiance to its institutions from other peoples and extend its power, not at the cannon's mouth, but by the agreement of its principles and policies with the noblest ambitions of mankind, is the mission of the Democratic Party....

It may be that the hour of reason and judgment has passed by, that this Democratic Convention will be unmindful of the call of the humble and the weak; but some time when the fever of commercialism has run its course, when humanity and justice shall once more control the minds of men, this great party will come back from the golden idols and tempting flesh pots, and once more battle for the rights of man.

After Bryan had placed in nomination Cockrell of Missouri he said:

If it is the choice or wish of this Convention that the standard shall be placed in the hands of the gentleman presented by California, the man who though he has money, pleads the cause of the poor; the man who is best beloved, I can safely say, among laboring men, of all the candidates proposed; the man who more than any other represents peace, make Hearst the candidate of this Convention, and Nebraska will be with you.

Hearst received two hundred votes, twenty from California. Not enough to nominate, but he was happy because the Democratic platform adopted many of the policies of the Hearst papers: civil service reform, the merchant marine, the protection of labor, election of Senators by direct vote of the people, the Isthmian Canal, the arraignment of the trusts.

Judge Alton Brooks Parker received six hundred and fifty-eight votes, and on July 9th, was chosen by the Democratic Party as its Presidential candidate. Henry G. Davis was nominated for Vice-President.

In the Republican landslide Roosevelt and Fairbanks were elected. Representative Hearst's candidacy for Congress held the entire West Side of Manhattan and saved it from the Republicans. Hearst had the plurality of eleven thousand, three hundred and ninety-seven. He said he would support whomever was nominated, and he campaigned for the Democratic ticket. Judge Parker has been almost obliterated from the national consciousness, and even from the memory of Tammany Hall. One of the older members recently recalled him dimly as, "That queer old guy who went to bed every night of the campaign at eleven o'clock."

While he was in Congress Hearst did not make many speeches, but through his seven papers he spoke in a masterful way to millions. These papers were: the New York *Journal*, the New York *American*, the Chicago *American*, the Chicago *Herald and Examiner*, the Boston *American*, the Los Angeles *Examiner* and the San Francisco *Examiner*. The platform of the Hearst papers was:

PUBLIC OWNERSHIP OF PUBLIC FRANCHISE
DESTRUCTION OF CRIMINAL TRUSTS
NO PROTECTION FOR MONOPOLIES OR TRUSTS
GRADUATED INCOME TAX
ELECTION OF SENATORS BY THE PEOPLE
NATIONAL, STATE AND MUNICIPAL IMPROVEMENT IN THE PUBLIC SCHOOL SYSTEM

On January 19, 1905, the Chicago *Tribune* published an interview with Hearst concerning his candidacy for the Presidency: "How would the average conservative citizen look upon your nomination for the Presidency?" Mr. Hearst replied:

That depends upon what you mean by conservative. For myself I should define conservatism as the preservation of those qualities, of rights and principles of proved value to the American people.

I think the fundamental American ideas which have developed this country making its natural wealth and greatness, while fostering the individual happiness and prosperity of its citizens, should be conserved.

I am conservative in the sense that I believe in the spirit and in the letter of the United States Constitution, the Declaration of Independence, and in the character and purposes of such men as Washington, Jefferson, Jackson and Lincoln.

He was in conflict with so-called conservatives that exploited the people for their own profit:

They are reactionary—not conservative. I do not consider the Steel Trust conservative, for instance.

I do not call conservative that system which diverts people's savings from such really conservative investments as the savings banks and the legitimate business enterprises of the country into the pockets of speculators and spenders.

I think those friendly to the Shipyard Trust, or planning Shipyard Trusts in the future, would look upon me as a dangerous person. I hope so, at least. I know I have not consciously sought their approval.

I am not opposed to legitimate organizations, for the great work of the nation must be conducted along the lines of extensive combination enterprises.

Our nation itself is a governmental combination, gaining strength and efficiency by uniting many states into one grand union for the benefit and protection of all. . . . Safeguarding with especial care the interests of the weak. . . .

"On what issues, Mr. Hearst," asked the reporter, "do you think the next Democratic campaign will be fought out?" Mr. Hearst replied: "The trust issues. . . . The trusts must be kept within the law. If there are no laws strong enough to protect the people, then such laws must be made. . . ."

"What is your attitude in regard to the tariff, Mr. Hearst?":

To-day we see industries that have developed under a tariff system absolutely indifferent to public welfare. These monopolistic industries, utterly devoid of any patriotic interest in the nation's welfare, use the tariff to put home consumers at a disadvantage compared with foreigners. The Steel Trust, for instance, sells for $22.00 per ton in Canada the steel for which it charges $28.00 at home.

When it becomes obvious that an enterprise fostered by the

tariff is a menace instead of a benefit to the country, it should be deprived of all tariff protection or benefit.

Hearst was asked about labor unions and he answered:

The distribution of wealth is just as important as its creation.... The labor union in enforcing a high scale of wages, brings about the distribution of wealth throughout the entire community.

The prosperity of merchants depends upon the purchasing power of the mass of the people....

Poverty-stricken people do not eat beef, or mutton, they do not buy woolen clothes in profusion. They have not enough for life's real necessities, nothing at all for books, travel, pleasures, that should accompany national prosperity. Wide and equitable distribution of wealth is essential to a nation's prosperous growth and intellectual development, and that distribution is brought about by the labor union more than any other agency....

The trusts are chiefly responsible for the increase in the cost of living....

It is of course true that the demands of trade unions are not always wise or just.... But the unions at least ask pay for labor which they actually perform. They do not demand extortionate prices for the products of others. And yet unions are subject to more harsh criticism than trusts. For instance, in my business, the producing of newspapers, there came simultaneously two demands. The trust demanded an increase in the price of paper and a union demanded an increase in price of labor.

A number of my brother newspaper-owners gathered in my office and suggested a union of newspapers to prevent an increase in the wages of workers. I asked them why it would not be better to combine to prevent the trust from getting its arbitrary increase in the price of paper, but I could not interest them in that. They seemed to think it all right for a great trust to ask for money arbitrarily, but all wrong for men that work to ask for more money to meet the constantly increasing cost of living.

When William Randolph Hearst met with political disappointment frequently he turned to his mother. Once he wrote,

"I feel about eight years old." In his early forties Phebe Hearst disappointed him and did not pay the young Hearsts a visit in New York, and he wrote to her:

I feel blue that you didn't come. I am getting kind of aged, and so are you. We ought to stop working and worrying and have some fun together before we die. Then there is the baby. I want him to know his grandma. He knows the picture and kisses that, and it can't be very satisfactory just to lick the varnish off photographs. I think he would prefer the real article, and I think you would prefer the real baby.

CHAPTER XXXIII

CAMPAIGN FOR MAYORALTY

CONGRESSMAN and Mrs. Hearst went to Europe in the summer of 1905. Before the editor sailed he realized that it would be impossible for his papers to support Mayor McClellan at the approaching election. McClellan belonged to Tammany, and Hearst and some of the leaders of both parties agreed that McClellan should be defeated by a fusion ticket. When late in the summer the Hearsts returned, the plan for a fusion ticket had been upset. Hearst said that he would not support McClellan who was the candidate of evil forces in both parties. The Republican nomination was being offered to any possible candidate, but none would accept.

The bosses laughed cynically at the situation. The Municipal Ownership League had been formed to bring public utilities under the control of the people. Only the League forces opposed McClellan.

As soon as Hearst landed from the steamer, the leaders implored him to run for Mayor and represent the Municipal Ownership League. This invitation was communicated to Hearst by Judge Samuel Seabury, who in 1932 was to have a large share in ousting Mayor James A. Walker from office.

Hearst wrote a letter to Seabury declining the honor. At a meeting of the League it was read:

I thank you for your kind letter and good opinion, but I don't believe it would be for the best interests of the independent movement for me to become its leader. It does not seem to me that this fight for principle should be encumbered with the introduction of personal hostilities. I am proud of my friends, for our friendship is disinterested; I am almost equally proud of my enemies, for these latter belong to the rich, powerful and unscrupulous class that most people are afraid to have as enemies.

I am not afraid of them. I glory in doing battle with them whenever I see their greedy hands outstretched for the public purse, but I am afraid to array their power and wealth and unscrupulous methods in their most violent form against the movement which means so much for the welfare of the community. I think this movement can best be brought to success under some other man, and I will fight harder than I could fight for myself, and more effectively than I could fight for myself, for any upright man who will make an honest fight against the bosses and the forces of corruption.

I would make any sacrifice to run if I thought it would benefit the independent movement, but I do not think so. I appeal to my friends and associates among the businessmen and merchants, to my friends on the East Side and my constituents on the West Side; to my friends among union labor from whom I have received more favors than I can ever repay, though I shall never cease to try—I appeal to them all to unite against the traitors in office and the franchise thieves back of them. And if my friends would support me, I entreat them to support more enthusiastically whatever conscientious man may be nominated by the independents—a man who will be, I am sure, better fitted in many ways to lead this important movement to success.

In an editorial addressed to the voters Hearst said:

You know what kind of government this city has. Whose fault is it? It isn't the fault of the corporations. It isn't the fault of Murphy or Odell. It isn't the fault of Murphy's puppet or Odell's' puppet. You are like a sleeping giant pillaged by pygmies.

Wake up! Nominate honest and independent men like Judge Seabury or Senator Ford. Elect them, and restore to this city a government of the people, by the people and for the people.

A committee from the Municipal Ownership League waited on Hearst. It was led by Judge Seabury and ex-Senator Ford.

They saw Hearst in his office and said to him, "Mr. Hearst, you're our one hope of victory. If you run, we can win. If you refuse, we'll be defeated."

Hearst thanked the committee, but he did not say whether he would reconsider. Other members of the League called on him and urged him to change his mind.

Finally on October 4, 1905, Hearst wrote Judge Seabury accepting the nomination with this statement, "The situation in the city is so grave, and the condition of the public in the face of organized bosses is apparently so helpless, that a man has no right to consider himself, least of all his personal affairs."

Hearst had in mind the Gas Trust litigation, Death Avenue, the subway that had been given away, and the amazing revelations brought out in the insurance investigation by Charles E. Hughes. He recalled that Doctor Walter R. Gillette, first vice-president of the Mutual Life Insurance Company, testified before the Legislative Committee that his company had set aside a secret confidential fund of two hundred thousand dollars for influencing legislation. This sum was not placed on the books, nor was any record made by the company of the ninety thousand dollars given in the two McKinley campaigns, nor of the forty thousand dollars contributed when Roosevelt ran in 1904. Hearst felt that such a situation demanded all the strength, enthusiasm and power possessed by him, or that he could command in others.

But he recalled also Tilden's crusade against the Tweed ring in the seventies. He felt that gallant warrior's hand still on his shoulder as he said, "Be a good boy, and a good Democrat."

On October 12, 1905, Hearst delivered his speech of acceptance:

My friends: I shall present my principles and purposes to you in a carefully prepared letter of acceptance. I come forward now to thank you for the confidence you have reposed in me, and to assure you that whether I am elected Mayor or whether I am merely retained with the resources I now have, I shall always endeavor to give you my best service and prove worthy of your endorsement.

I was, as you know, reluctant to enter this contest; but I am no longer reluctant. I am in it now, and in it to win. I know I shall speak for all of you when I say we are not here to make a showing, but to win the election. We are not anxious to win because we are politicians scheming for place, but because we are citizens with principles, desirous of seeing those principles put into practical operation for the benefit of our fellow citizens.

Our principles briefly summarized are: honesty and efficiency in office; prosperity and progress for the people of this city; public ownership of public utilities to the end that taxes may be reduced, and service improved, and the conditions of employees bettered.

We want officials elected in whose eyes the welfare of the whole people is more important than the interest of the Gas Trust, the Traction Trust, or any other trust. . . .

Let all legitimate business be welcomed to our city. Let us not permit conditions to exist under which an enterprise may not locate here because it has to pay more for a Board of Aldermen than it has to pay for its plant and equipment. . . . Let the city retain its public properties, and develop their wealth and apply their profits to the public benefit. Let the city prove a model employer, giving good hours and good wages—realizing and demonstrating the fact that prosperity as a whole is simply the sum of the prosperity and purchasing power of the individual citizen.

Hearst developed into a whirlwind speaker. He appeared daily before ten or twelve meetings. The campaign was short but intense. People listened much moved by his sincerity. Their attention was his daily reward for the labor of the campaign. He became a crusader aflame.

At Durland's Riding Academy he spoke to ten thousand workmen. Night after night he denounced Tammany. For these denunciations his life was threatened. Warnings were written to him, "I'll get you Friday night!"

He realized the possibility of a tragic end, but he went on with a fatalistic faith that he was to escape tragedy. A group of armed men was necessary to obtain entrance for him into a building so that he could make a speech.

Sometimes Hearst quietly set out on foot from his residence at Twenty-eighth Street and Lexington Avenue and took a street-car to the hall where he was to make an address. Then he would be picked up by a carriage and driven from hall to hall.

Many times during the campaign Hearst said to his listeners, "I don't want the office of Mayor. I certainly don't want the salary. What I want is your good opinion. Vote for the entire ticket."

At the noon rallies longshoremen cheered for him, as did the men along the North River docks. At night lanterns were strung across the streets. Flowers were showered on his conveyance. In every hall he was given a big floral emblem. East Side audiences rose to their feet and bellowed such hoarse approving sounds as New York City had not heard since Samuel Jones Tilden made his famous campaign against the same kind of grafters as those of whom the voters were now determined to rid themselves. On one occasion Hearst aroused the wildest enthusiasm when he came down to the footlights and said: "The reason I entered this campaign was because I am tired of helping elect men who swear to protect the people, and then break their oaths and betray the people."

The Bowery was Hearst's greatest triumph. Once he set out at Third Avenue and Ninety-first Street and worked his way along the East Side to Chapman Square, stopping several times to speak or bow to crowded meetings without saying a word. People clambered into his carriage, wrung his hand, pulled his coat-tail shouting like Indians. The nearer he approached lower East Side, Tammany's stronghold, the louder grew the cheers and the denser the crowd. Men formed themselves into little groups of escort and ran beside his carriage. When he reached Fourteenth Street he was in the "enemy's country," and bedlam began. At Tenth Street five hundred men formed themselves into a procession, and surrounding his carriage marched with the band. At every block the crowd grew. Turning at Eighth Street he entered the Bowery on his way to Everett Hall.

For the next two hours the thoroughfare was Hearst's own. At 8:45 he spoke to a thousand persons at the Old Homestead at Third Avenue and Ninety-first Street. At 9:05 he addressed the overflow meeting. Twenty minutes later he made a speech at Union Hall. At 9:45 he stopped two minutes at the corner of Second Avenue and Forty-second Street where an open-air meeting was in progress. Without leaving the carriage he shook hands with seventy-five persons who shouted greetings to him. Two hundred more tried to meet him, but failed. At 9:55 he slowed down at the corner of Tenth Street and Second Avenue where his carriage was surrounded by a large crowd of cheering men with flags and torches escorting him to the next place. At 10.15 he spoke to twenty-five hundred persons at East Fourth Street. At 10:35 he spoke to a crowd of four thousand in the Grand Street Opera House while as many · cheered outside. On the shoulders of his admirers he was carried on to the stage. Only ten years before William Randolph Hearst had arrived in New York City. No one but Theodore Roosevelt, who was born there, had ever met with such complete triumph in that city.

Hearst did not repeat his speeches. He had one long address and many short talks. As he went along he coined epigrams against the evils of boss rule, and against the Gas and Traction Trusts.

"There is no difference between Republican decency and Democratic decency. I stand as Tilden stood when he spoke against the Tweed ring in 1871."

Hearst invaded Brooklyn, city of homes and churches ruled by Boss McCarren.

"Does the Honorable Patrick McCarren represent these homes?" he asked defiantly. "Does he represent the church? Does he represent the honesty and citizenship of Brooklyn?"

In Madison Square Garden Sunday night before election

was the largest political gathering ever known in New York City. One hundred thousand people were unable to gain admission. The Garden was filled at 7:15. At twenty-six minutes past eight, Hearst entered the Garden with Mrs. Hearst.

Flags were flung on high, handkerchiefs waved, hats thrown into the air. Coats were stripped off and hoisted over the heads of the crowd. Some men lifted up their chairs and swayed them back and forth. Babies were held in front of the Hearsts when they moved slowly through the crowd and entered their box on the Twenty-sixth Street side of the building. Horns were blown, rattles were shaken, forty thousand feet beat a tattoo on the floor. An orchestra of one hundred and twenty pieces worked madly to drown the noise, but when Hearst's tall figure appeared on the stage applause did not cease for seventeen minutes:

My friends, I do not desire to make a speech. I only want to thank you for your kindness and your friendship. I greet you to-night not as Democrats or Republicans, but as friends. I greet you not as partisans, but as citizens deeply interested with us in the welfare of our citizens and in the progress and prosperity of our great city. I greet you with hope and confidence in the result because I believe implicitly in the wisdom and the patriotism and the conscience of the people. . . .

I am proud of the friends that have rallied around us. They are the people's friends. I am proud of the enemies who oppose us. They are the people's enemies. We will fight those enemies together and triumph over them, no matter how powerful and unscrupulous they may be. . . . We shall say with Jackson, "Let us ask nothing but what is right and submit to nothing that is wrong." We will fight the battle along these lines, and we will win a glorious victory if we will only trust the people.

The day preceding the election was tense. In editorials Hearst gave Tammany what his East Side friends called a "last Kerry wallop." He declared that the Democratic Party of the city, State and nation, could never be successful until the traders and traitors of Tammany Hall had been wiped out of the party.

Hearst called on the Irish to vote as Robert Emmet would vote; on the Jews to vote as Maimonides would vote; on the Poles to vote as Kosciusko would vote; on the Italians to vote as Garibaldi would vote; on the Hungarians to vote as Kossuth would vote; on the Americans to vote as Jefferson and Lincoln would vote.

On election day, Hearst voted before he ate breakfast. Unaccompanied he left home, but by the time he reached the polling place a large number of admirers gathered around him cheering as he walked along, shaking his hand at every step. The voting booth was in an undertaking establishment. Some of his friends spoke jokingly of the place.

"Oh, I am just looking for a coffin for Tammany," smiled Hearst, confident that he would be the next Mayor of New York City.

When the early returns came independent voters rejoiced. About eight-thirty there was a long lull in the bulletins. For more than an hour Tammany did not permit returns to be given out. In the silent hour dark work was done. Ballots were thrown off Brooklyn Bridge; into cesspools. Hearst's manager, Max Ihmsen, knew. Hearst knew.

Wild scenes were at the Hoffman House that night, and at the Municipal League headquarters. Hundreds of witnesses reported tales of fraud to Hearst and Ihmsen. Hearst's lieutenants were excited and angry. They shouted orders to men, breathlessly awaiting to obey. Pandemonium reigned, but Hearst was serene. He said he did not care one whit about being Mayor, but he was going to see that the men who voted for him had their names counted. He told reporters that he would probably be at headquarters all night. In the morning he hoped to get a few hours' rest.

The truth came out. As the Bowery put it, "The election was as crooked as Pearl Street," the crookedest street in New York. Tammany leaders had intimidated voters and ruled out ballots on every possible technicality. Purchased voters were compelled to bring their ballots from the booth unfolded to show that they had kept corrupt agreements. On every hand Hearst workers and watchers were offered bribes, and when it was found that they could not be corrupted they were assaulted and driven from their posts. Organized gangs of repeaters and thugs marched from polling place to polling place, and were allowed full swing by Tammany's election inspectors.

On November 8th, Hearst made the following statement:

We have won this election. All Tammany's frauds, all Tammany's corruption, all Tammany's intimidation and violence, all Tammany's false registration, illegal voting and dishonest counting have not been able to overcome the great popular majority. The recount will show that we won the election by many thousands of votes. I shall fight this battle to the end, in behalf of the people who cast their votes for me, and who shall not be disfranchised by any effort of the criminal bosses.

Meetings of protest were rapidly held. On November 11, more than five thousand persons gathered in Durland's Riding Academy to protest against election frauds and on behalf of Hearst to demand a recount of the votes. Thousands were unable to get inside. They swarmed about the building, marched and countermarched through the streets denouncing Mayor McClellan and Charles F. Murphy.

Hamilton Holt, editor of the New York *Independent*, was chairman of the meeting. On the stage were Senator John Ford, Bird S. Coler and Alexander S. Bacon. Among the vice-presidents of the meeting were Doctor Parkhurst, General James Grant Wilson, S. S. McClure, Ernest H. Crosby and Henry Siegel. Hearst was not present, but Chairman Holt could hardly speak when he tried to read a letter from him. Hats, canes and newspapers were tossed into the air. Speakers referred to Hearst as the "next Mayor of New York." At one time the audience kept the Chairman waiting for more than a minute while they hissed and groaned at the name of Mayor McClellan.

"There is no reason now to doubt," said Holt, "that last Tuesday a deliberate attempt was made to rob the citizens of New York of their suffrage. Now we have come here calmly and soberly to consider the purity of the ballot."

In his letter to the meeting Hearst said: "I am glad that your public-spirited action gives concrete expression to public indignation. I have no doubt of the outcome of the protest that you are to make. I have perfect confidence that the courts will deal with this most serious offense against the whole people speedily and effectively, as they deal with offenses against individuals."

A letter from Dr. Parkhurst was cheered: "The city has reached a crisis. The question is not who has been elected, but who has been juggling with the ballot boxes. . . . Atrocious as seem to have been the performances of last Tuesday, it is nevertheless a boon to the city, for these acts were so depraved that every one must protest against them."

At this meeting Chairman Holt appointed a committee of seventy citizens to collect evidence and prosecute the frauds. A resolution was sent to Mayor McClellan calling upon him to use all his energies to have the votes counted.

Outside of Durland's Riding Academy thousands of persons took part in an open-air demonstration. Sixty-sixth Street was illuminated from the Park to Columbus Avenue. Transparencies lighted up windows. Orators spoke from platforms till midnight. Tammany men tried to climb upon the platform, and there was disorder. Mounted police ended the disturbance.

On the next day Hearst gave out a statement asking his friends to hold no more meetings. There was no necessity to urge Hearst to the utmost effort. William M. Ivins, Republican candidate for Mayor of New York, offered his services without compensation to undertake the conduct of the case proving election frauds. The ablest lawyers in New York were retained. Ample rewards were offered, and the results were encouraging. "The Attorney-General has secured many indictments," said Hearst, "and more will follow within the next few days."

In spite of the opposition of Mayor McClellan an investigation and a recount were ordered. False registrations were numerous. Many votes were cast by "floaters" and "repeaters." Twenty thousand colonizers were brought from Philadelphia, Troy, Newark and Hartford to vote several times that day. The poorer sections of the city were padded thickly with names of men who had no right to vote—aliens, non-residents, fictitious persons. Men were registered from vacant lots, public parks, gas tanks, stone piles. One man voted twelve times. Names of cats and dogs were voted. More men were registered from one lodging house than the entire house ever held.

The vote-brokerage business was well organized and ably directed. Outside the booth stood a judge or candidate for high office. He spoke in a friendly way to the floater or repeater thus guaranteeing protection. No crime was safer. A man was brought from the Tammany agents into a polling place, and although challenged he was given a ballot and prepared to vote. Policemen were called, and the "floater" was arrested. The Tammany man rushed in between the officers, and the "floater" was told to run. If he was captured, the Tammany watcher held a whispered conversation with one of the election inspectors and the prisoner was released. The "floater" disappeared, and he returned in half an hour, dressed differently and—voted again. One man voted as Mason, Hicks, Connelly and Conton.

In one polling place ballots were missing. A man pretending to represent the Board of Elections brought them in from a rear room, and over protest they were counted. In another district four hundred and thirty-one votes were counted, and the ballot boxes were taken away by two policemen. Afterwards its was discovered that the ballot clerk's tally showed that eight hundred and thirty-six votes had been cast. In another district the captain of the Board of Inspectors left the polling place, and the Tammany Captain, a candidate for the Assembly, was in and out of the polling place all day. He was observed giving money to the various people before they entered the booth to vote.

In several polling places in the Sixth Assembly District blue pencils were furnished the voters, and the ballots marked with pencils were thrown out as void. At one place twenty men came together whose names were called off with such rapidity that no one could take them down. All twenty men left the polling place without having their names checked off. When the ballots were counted there were three hundred and forty-two for McClellan and thirty-one for Hearst. Of those counted for McClellan, sixty-six were vainly protested. In one district as soon as the ballots were removed from the boxes, Hearst's watchers were ordered out of the polling places, although they had been duly appointed as watchers. The police refused to interfere.

There was continual shooting, and hospitals were filled with injured men. The average day's earnings for an active repeater were twenty-five dollars. Gas, transportation, electric light, insurance companies, eager to control the Board of Aldermen, supplied the funds. Hearst offered to pay ten thousand dollars for evidence resulting in the arrest, conviction and imprisonment of the first Tammany district leader for fraud against the ballot in connection with the election. There were twenty-four convictions. Two or three nobodies were sent to Sing Sing. Hearst was supposed to have been defeated by about eighteen hundred votes. There was reliable evidence that the fraudulent vote cast by the Murphy machine aggregated fifty thousand.

Out of Hearst's defeat and the exposure of the election frauds, came the Independence League. The Signature Law in New York State was also enacted to make difficult election frauds. This law requires all voters on registering to sign their names on the registration lists, and then, before receiving a ballot on election day, to sign a supplemental record so that watchers can compare the two signatures. This procedure prevents "repeating."

Hearst recognized the similarity between his life and that of Tilden's. Both men had fought for political purity and both had been defeated by chicanery, but for his own personal convenience he was glad he was defeated. He said: "I was counted out. But although I was the victim of election frauds, I shall continue to fight graft and do the best I know for good government as long as I own newspapers and am able to write and talk."

CHAPTER XXXIV

THE SAN FRANCISCO EARTHQUAKE

NEW YORK considered Hearst elected in 1905. Hearst considered himself elected. But his victory lay at the bottom of the river where it was hurled on election night. Hearst, the hero of the city, had new terror for Tammany. The leaders knew his defeat had been difficult and dangerous. They felt that Hearst must be stopped.

The spirit of the Municipal Ownership League lived again in the Independence League. On February 28, 1906, Hearst led a delegation of five hundred citizens to the new Independence League conference at Albany. In the group were professional and business men, and women from all walks of life. Hearst thanked Governor Hughes for his aid in securing cheap gas, and besought his influence for other activities advocated by the League. These were investigations of the Ryan-Belmont merger, the Feth Direct Nomination Bill, the Young Bill for the reorganization of the Rapid Transit Commissions, the Rock Eight Hour Bill, the Harvey Semi-Monthly Payment Bill, and the Raines-Murphy Recount Bill providing for the recount of votes cast at the last city election. Governor Hughes eventually did order a recount, but the election crimes had been committed before the ballots reached the boxes.

The Independence League held a conference at Albany. In his speech Hearst said that:

The fundamental idea of the Independence League is independence—independence of boss rule, independence of corporation control.... The immediate object of the Independence League is to wrest control of the Government from the hands of the powerful financial interests and return it to the hands of the typical American citizen who created it ... and who should control and conduct it.

There can no longer be doubt in the minds of intelligent men that a powerful financial class is now absolutely dominant in the government of this nation.... So long as the corporations control both parties the people have no ... relief except through an independent movement....

I am a Democrat, but a Democrat through principle.... I refuse allegiance to any democracy that is controlled by corporations for the interest of a favored class to the detriment of the whole citizenship. I refuse to sit supinely by while the choice offered me as a citizen is to vote for Mr. Ryan's Democrats or Mr. Morgan's Republicans.

It is clear that the government of the nation ... is no longer a government of the people organized for their own betterment. It has degenerated into a corporation of organized monopoly operating ... for the enrichment of a small predatory class.... Any railroad corporation has infinitely more influence in any department of government than all the human beings that live in the territory that the railroad traverses. ...

The people are weary of detecting the voice of a corporation manager in every political utterance, in the legislature, the Governor's messages, in the expressed opinions of mayors of cities and the Senators sent by the State to Washington, and even in the decisions of judges on the bench.

Hearst recalled the insurance funds of widows and children that had been stolen by both Democrats and Republicans. He protested against taxation controlled by corporations that refused to share the burdens with the citizenship they exploited. He said that the Independence League

invites the advice and support of all those who feel that the time has come to make the Government of the State represent the will of the workers, and not the interests of organized money and tyrannical monopoly.

The plans and purposes of the Independence League are to prevent the private confiscation of public property ... to secure for the State and its inhabitants a government by the majority in the interests of the majority, in place of a government by cliques or corporations; honest elections and ballot reform; direct nomination of candidates; good roads; abolition of discrimination in railroad rates; lowering of farm taxes and aid to the farmer in the transportation of his products; encouragement of labor unions as an antidote to the trusts, as the best agency for the equitable distribution of wealth; direct election of United States Senators; control of life insurance and all moneyed corporations to which savings of the people are confided.

This platform was signed by the Executive Committee; William Randolph Hearst, chairman; J. G. Phelps Stokes, Samuel Seabury, Clarence J. Shearn, Thomas Gileran, Melvin G. Palliser, John Ford, John Palmieri, C. August Haviland, and M. H. Ihmsen.

Great enthusiasm was aroused by the Independence League throughout the State. Hearst was showered with letters and telegrams. Thousands of citizens were indignant at the brazen theft of the Mayoralty of New York City. For the first time since the Civil War there was a spirit of reform in the Republican Party, and President Roosevelt was leader of the movement that stirred young America.

Roosevelt's Attorney-General Moody was far more eager to prosecute corporations and trusts for violating the law, than had been McKinley's Attorney-General Knox. When Hearst presented to the Department of Justice evidence obtained against the Sugar Trust for violation of the law, it was received with great enthusiasm.

The President went over the evidence against the Sugar Trust with Attorney-General Moody. He asked United States District Attorney Henry M. Stimson of New York (later Secretary of State), to take all the papers in the case, summon a grand jury and investigate. Subpoenas were issued for half a hundred witnesses. Each link in the evidence was sound and every scrap pertinent. The Attorney-General asked for the indictment of H. O. Havemeyer, president of the American Sugar Refining Company; A. J. Cassatt, president of the Pennsylvania Railroad; W. H. Newman, president of the New York Central Railroad; W. H. Truesdale, president of the Delaware, Lackawana and Western Railroad; George F. Baer, president of the Delaware and Reading Railroad; Lowell L. Palmer, president of Palmer's Docks Company, Brooklyn; John R. Thayer, Jr., vice-president of the Pennsylvania Railroad; Nathan Guilford, vice-president of the Pennsylvania Railroad; and Charles S. Mellen, president of the New York, New Haven and Hartford Railroad. These companies and others were charged with giving rebates.

The New York Federal Grand Jury deliberated on the evidence for sixteen days. On May 6, 1906, they handed in to the Federal Court seven indictments for violations of the Interstate Commerce Act and the Elkins anti-Rebate Law. The following corporations and the officers were found guilty: The New York Central Railroad; the American Sugar Refining Company; the New York Central and Hudson River Railroad Company, Nathan Guilford, vice-president, and F. L. Pomeroy, general traffic manager of the company; the American Sugar Refining Company of New York; C. Goodloe Edgar and Edwin Earle, these two men being wholesale sugar dealers in Detroit, Michigan, for conspiracy to violate the Elkins anti-Rebate Law.

Indictments against these companies and men for breaches of the Elkins Law were punishable only with a fine. The seventh indictment was for conspiracy for which the penalty was a fine of not less than one thousand nor more than ten thousand dollars, or imprisonment of not more than two years, or both.

In a special message to Congress a few days after the indictments, President Roosevelt said: "The Attorney-General reports to me that the investigation now going on as to the shipments of the Sugar Trust over the trunk line going out of New York City tends to show that the Sugar Trust rarely, if ever, pays a legal rate of transportation, and is improperly and probably unlawfully favored at the expense of its competitors and general public."

Attorney-General Moody said that he had no knowledge or suspicion of the activities of the Sugar Trust until it was furnished his department by a representative of the *American,* owned by Hearst.

The case was brought to trial in November before Judge Holt sitting in the Federal Circuit Court. Joseph H. Choate, later Ambassador to England, was attorney for the Sugar Trust. On November 20, 1906, the jury found the Sugar Trust and the New York Central Railroad guilty of rebating, as charged in Hearst's complaint before United States Attorney Stimson. Judge Holt declared that the crime of the New York Central was deliberate and premeditated and extended over a long period of time. "A crime of this kind is more heinous than the vulgar common crimes that are tried in our criminal court, and which arise from passion and temptation of the moment. This crime is committed by men of high standing in the community; persons who should stand forth as examples of probity."

The men so scathingly characterized by Judge Holt were: Chauncey M. Depew, chairman of the Board of Directors, George F. Baker, Samuel F. Barger, G. S. Bowdoin, Charles S. Clarke, Darius O. Mills, J. Pierpont Morgan, William H. Newman, William Rockefeller, James Stillman, Hamilton Twombly, Frederick W. Vanderbilt and William K. Vanderbilt.

It was shown in court that W. H. Edgar, of Detroit, was granted a rebate annually of $84,000, which enabled him to stifle rival beet-sugar producers. The Sugar Trust pleaded guilty in December and was fined $186,000. The New York Central was fined $108,000, and the traffic manager, F. L. Pomeroy, was fined an additional $6,000.

On February 24, 1909, the United States Supreme Court upheld the verdict of the lower court against the Sugar Trust and the New York Central Railroad.

A few months later Collector Loeb and United States District Attorney Stimson began proceedings that were an indirect result of the Hearst suit. They sued to compel the Sugar Trust to pay the Government $2,250,000 for customs frauds to make good duties out of which the Government had been defrauded by scales that had been tampered with. In his papers Hearst supported this suit, but it resulted in the conviction of only weighers and checkers. The powerful financiers, who had profited by the swindling, escaped.

In the midst of Hearst's Congressional work, his direction of seven papers, his management of the Independence League, his tireless search after rare and beautiful objects of art, his trust investigations, came one of the great shocks of the publisher's life. Early on the morning of April 18, 1906, there flashed over the wire news of the San Francisco earthquake. That night Hearst had been late at the *American* office, and he was in bed asleep when the telephone awakened him.

An anxious voice said, "There has been an earthquake in San Francisco."

"Don't overplay it," replied Hearst. "They have earthquakes often in California." Then he went back to bed.

First came the exaggeration—the city was wiped out—swept into the sea—every one dead—Hearst thought of his mother. Perhaps she was gone—the *Examiner*—his beloved birthplace!

Finally the truth seeped through. At 5:13 the inhabitants of San Francisco had been shaken out of their beds by a prolonged temblor. The privately owned, ill-cared-for-water mains of the city were broken. San Francisco, joyous, Bohemian San Francisco, was being scourged by flames. But Phebe Apperson Hearst was alive.

For three days the fire raged. Two-thirds of the city were charred smoldering ruins. One-third was left standing. Even the water-front was destroyed. The *Examiner*, its buildings and plant, were wreckage. Only its name survived. Hearst's individual loss was more than a million dollars in addition to the temporary loss of a great revenue.

In New York Hearst considered what could be done. Immediately he organized theatrical benefits for his stricken birthplace. By telephone and telegraph he established hospitals. A large relief corps was sent from Los Angeles to aid the city by the Golden Gate. Two relief trains set out from the East.

At first, during the erection of a temporary home for the *Examiner* at Spear and Folsom Streets, the paper was the guest of the *Tribune* in Oakland. Within a week the *Examiner's* new linotype machines were on their way to the Pacific coast. Hearst gave orders for the immediate construction of a larger building than the one destroyed.

On May 1st, Hearst introduced in Congress a joint resolution proposing an appropriation of $4,502,500 for the rebuilding and repairing of public buildings in San Francisco, Oakland and San José. In his newspapers Hearst opened a column to raise funds for San Francisco.

At a Casino benefit in New York City, Mrs. William K. Vanderbilt, Jr., a Californian by birth, occupied with her sister, Mrs. Herman Oelrichs, a thousand-dollar box. The Hippodrome benefit had Madame Schumann-Heink as star. Hearst occupied with Mrs. Hearst and friends a box at the Academy of Music benefit for which he paid a large sum. When he was called to make a speech, at the end of a long ovation, he thanked New York for "help which is not charity, but the loving aid of friend to friend, and brother to brother."

When Hearst reached "the city that was," he presented the victims of the fire and earthquake with a fund of more than two hundred thousand dollars that had been collected by his newspapers. He was thanked by the Governor of California, George C. Pardee.

In Oakland, across the bay from San Francisco, Hearst found that less than one per cent of the buildings had been seriously damaged. Beyond that one per cent the loss came entirely from cracked plaster and wobbly chimneys. At the Hacienda of his mother at Pleasanton not far from Oakland he found that only two chimneys had fallen. There was no other damage.

Hearst began to think that the entire disaster was exaggerated, but in San Francisco, the havoc from the fire appeared. The damage done by the earthquake was greatly overdrawn, but the destruction by the fire could never be adequately described. Nine-tenths of the buildings destroyed by the earthquake were brick. Almost without exception wooden and steel structures passed through the earthquake unharmed. But all the business portion of the city was burned to the ground. The wholesale district, the retail district, the manufacturing district and the water-front were no more. There was a blackened waste with acres of ashes, twisted iron and steel, and jagged fragments of walls. The mighty blaze that raged for two days and nights left only a fringe of houses along the southern limits. The district beyond wide Van Ness Avenue, the western part of the city, and a portion of the Mission were all that was left of San Francisco.

Almost overpowered by the desert of tumbled brick, tangled iron and blackened timbers, Hearst wandered to the district where had been Woodward's Gardens in which he had played as a boy. He was relieved to find that the ancient Mission Dolores was spared. Then he went northward to the bay to see what had survived of the home of his childhood. Strangely enough his hillside home, and that delightful sunny nook of San Francisco, lay smiling in the sunshine wholly unconscious of the city's disaster.

He returned to the ruins of the business section. Women and children were huddled in tents in little parks that had shriveled in the flames. Portsmouth Square, where the American flag had first flown in San Francisco, was crowded with refugees, laughing, singing refugees, already dreaming of another splendid city with a splendid future. The city was under martial law, but overwhelming as was the calamity, Hearst rejoiced that the people were not overwhelmed. He wrote to his newspapers:

Everything has been destroyed except that indomitable American pluck, that unconquerable American spirit which will not be subdued. The past is already forgotten, the future is in every one's mind. The question is not, "How shall San Francisco be restored? But how shall it be made greater than it ever was, greater than it could have ever been except for this fire?"

There is already a rebirth of business activity. One-story buildings are being erected while plans are being made for larger structures. The wholesalers have located out near the railroad shops in the Potrero, the retailers are already beginning to carry on business in some of the private residences left standing to the north of Van Ness Avenue. The newspapers are erecting presses on concrete foundations while the single-story buildings to cover them are being built overhead. The restaurants are opening in the tents. Piles of débris are decorated by signs announcing that certain great business houses will open here as soon as the building can be constructed, and that meanwhile they are opening at such and such places in the outskirts. In a month there will be the beginning of a new and splendid city; in a year it will have assumed shape, and in three to five years it will be built and busy, an example of American progress and prosperity.

If you stood on one of the hills of San Francisco and looked only at the ruins at your feet, you might be discouraged at the prospect, but if you look out upon the glorious bay and see ships from every great port in the world floating upon its satin surface, if you look across the bay and see the long line of railroads from the North and South and East centering there; if you look beyond, over the great valleys teeming with grain and fruits, flowing with milk and honey; if you look further still to the mighty mountains, rich in gold and precious ore, you know that the rebuilding of a greater San Francisco is as well assured as that the sun now sinking above the Golden Gate, will rise to-morrow above the snow-capped peaks of the Sierra.

Again he wrote:

The plain facts are that earthquakes in California which occur at intervals of about twenty-year periods, kill far fewer people than the cyclones in the Middle West, the flood tornadoes in the

South Coast States, and the lightning storms and heat waves along the Atlantic States kill every year.... However, don't understand me as maintaining that earthquakes don't occur in California. They do. About every twenty or twenty-five years an earthquake of some consequence occurs somewhere over our thousand miles of longitude. And that is exactly as if I said that every twenty or twenty-five years an earthquake might occur along the Atlantic coast, either in Massachusetts, or in Connecticut, or in New York, or in New Jersey, or in Pennsylvania, or in Delaware, or in Maryland, or in Virginia, or in North Carolina, or in South Carolina. If that were the situation in the East nobody would stay awake much at night worrying about their friends on the Atlantic seaboard.

Californians don't wholly approve of earthquakes, but they prefer them to cyclones or tornadoes or floods or prostrating heat or lightning storms. The earthquakes don't come so often, and they don't cause so much loss of life. In fact, all of the earthquakes which have occurred in California since it was discovered nearly four hundred years ago have not killed so many people as one or two great cyclones of the Middle West.

A friend of mine, Guy Barham, publisher of the Los Angeles *Herald*, says that California, with all its wealth of gold-mines, oil-wells, fruits, grain, cotton and corn, with its marvelous roads and splendid harbors, its great industries and growing exports, should have some little kind of drawback, or else the people of the United States would be crowding out the Californians, and keeping Californians themselves from making the money they do and should, out of their State's astonishing riches and resources.

Hearst established several hospitals at the time of the earthquake and they relieved much suffering. He turned over the W. R. Hearst Tent City at Adams Point near Oakland to Major James B. Erwin, Ninth Cavalry, United States of America, to be used by military authorities.

Hearst's confidence in San Francisco's future was so assured, that he foresaw the *Examiner* of 1907 as a greater and more valuable newspaper than the *Examiner* of 1905. One year, one month, and ten days after the earthquake, on May

28, 1907, Hearst used red ink to celebrate the first work of the new press. He made the following statement:

> The new *Examiner* salutes its readers. The *Examiner* takes occasion to apologize for the irregularities of the paper since the fire. The biggest, fastest, most effective press that ever came to the Pacific coast printed this issue, and the *Examiner* feels about as a man does moving on crutches, when he finds that he is able to cast aside crutches and walk at his old gait. The *Examiner* feels so good that it is printing this announcement in red.

In 1906, there was a political as well as a terrestrial earthquake in San Francisco. Eugene Schmitz, the musical Labor Union Mayor, who had been elected as the result of the street-car strike, was discovered to be secretly in the pay of the United Railways. The city streets had been delivered by the Mayor to piratical capitalists. In open defiance of the law Schmitz signed an illegal franchise which Boss Ruef planned secretly to make valid. The Mayor and the supervisors attempted to justify this crime under the plea of emergency need. Openly or covertly the legislature would be asked to do all that lay in its power to legalize the seizure of the streets of San Francisco.

Hearst launched into a struggle to help save the Geary Street Railway to municipal ownership. The venal supervisors declared that the *Examiner's* attacks on them would drive capital away from San Francisco and delay the rebuilding of "our beloved city." Within a year, the city fathers had confessed their guilt. They had accepted bribe money, and as partners of Boss Ruef and Mayor Schmitz were engaged in looting the people who elected them.

At this same time Hearst was attacking the Traction Trust of New York City which also owned the United Railways in San Francisco. He said that "they were known as 'Captains of Industry,' but in reality they were 'Captains of Crime.' The real criminals will stay out of jail. The big men of the trusts who furnish the money and instructed the bribe-givers will still go to Europe, sail their yachts, buy their pictures, and continue to rob the people of the country that made them rich, and to bribe the people's elected officials shamelessly, impudently, fearlessly, and above the reach of the law." These words were prophetic; none of the capitalists who paid the money to the San Francisco Supervisors went to prison.

During this same year the workmen of the United Railways made demands for higher wages. Hearst supported them in their strike, and he addressed an editorial to Patrick Calhoun, President of the United Railways, asking him to turn back the strike-breakers that were being imported. At the same time Hearst sided with the printers who demanded better wages, and he helped them win their fight.

Before Hearst left San Francisco in 1906 he wrote a letter to the publisher of the *Examiner* saying:

I wish you would announce to the compositors, stereotypers, etchers, pressmen, mailers, drivers and other mechanics an extra allowance of one dollar a day each, from now until May, 1907. I believe they are entitled to an extra allowance because of the increased cost of living in San Francisco since the fire. I believe that all money spent in extra wages at this time will be distributed throughout the community; will be spent in stores by the families of the men; will be paid to the landlord and will be deposited in the bank, and will tend in every way to restore the utmost confidence and stimulate business in all branches of industry. I advise the *Examiner* to appeal to all citizens to conduct their business in a liberal spirit, and to make San Francisco attractive to those most valuable classes, the wage-earners and the businessmen who depend upon them.

You may say that the *Examiner* doesn't take this action through any access of prosperity, for its heavy losses in the fire were only slightly covered by insurance, but from a firm conviction that such a course, generally pursued, will greatly benefit all citizens of San Francisco at this time.

WILLIAM RANDOLPH HEARST

CHAPTER XXXV

CAMPAIGN FOR GOVERNOR

OF all Americans, probably Lincoln best expresses to Hearst the ideals of America. It was a great satisfaction for the publisher, during the month of August, 1906, to purchase the old farm homestead of Abraham Lincoln consisting of sixty-two acres—historically the most valuable site in Illinois. Hearst gave it to the Chautauqua Association of that State.

Congressman and Mrs. Hearst went to Illinois for the presentation of the gift. Old Salem had never seen so large an audience as that which assembled to hear Hearst speak to that characteristically American and national university, the Chautauqua.

Among other things Hearst said, "I am a deep and earnest admirer of Lincoln. I consider him one of the noblest characters and one of the greatest heroes."

For more than an hour the Hearsts shook hands with the immense audience. Congressman Rainey presented the editor with the Jacob's-staff used by Abraham Lincoln sixty years before in surveying the present site of Petersburg. It was made of hickory and cut by Lincoln from a tree. The Jacob's-staff was in a fine state of preservation, and Hearst has long held it as one of his valued treasures.

During this era one of Hearst's most important battles to many New Yorkers was his conflict with the Brooklyn Rapid Transit Company which had decided to collect an extra fare of five cents for a continuous ride to Coney Island. Hearst was determined that the cost of the pleasure trips of the poor should not be increased. Through his attorney, Clarence J. Shearn, Hearst applied to the State to sue to annul the charter of the Brooklyn Rapid Transit Company on the ground that it exceeded its powers in charging a ten-cent fare to Coney Island. The petition urged that the Attorney-General apply to the Supreme Court for an injunction restraining the corporation from further attempting to collect an extra fare of five cents for a continuous ride.

Justice Gaynor issued a mandate against the ten-cent fare, but he was defied by the Brooklyn Rapid Transit Company. The Attorney-General began action toward the forfeiture of the company's franchise. Assemblyman Robert F. Wagner introduced a Five-Cent-Fare-to-Coney-Island Bill in the Assembly. It passed without debate. The Senate voted favorably on the bill in April. Then it was up to the Public Service Commission to change the rate of fare. This was not accomplished until after a long struggle. On May 1, 1920, the ten-cent fare to Coney Island was reduced to five cents.

Hearst concentrated his activities on his crusades for bettering the conditions of the people and on extending the potentialities of his newspapers. After being unfairly deprived of the office of Mayor, he had no desire again to be a candidate for office. But the nefarious method of the Mayor's election aroused deep indignation that would not subside. Not since the Presidential contest between Hayes and Tilden in 1876 when Samuel J. Tilden after receiving a quarter of a million votes more than Rutherford B. Hayes was deprived of the Presidency, had there been so much excitement over a New York election. Hundreds of thousands of citizens demanded another opportunity to vote for Hearst. These indignant voters vowed that the Independence League should not die. It was their one hope of political freedom.

On March 11, 1906, the new party issued its first call to the voters of the State of New York. It was signed by William Randolph Hearst, Judge Samuel Seabury and Judge John Palmieri. The League protested against government by political bosses and a small predatory class. All reputable citizens were invited to end this disgraceful rule of the corporations. The party welcomed the support of men and organizations that endorsed its principles. Plainly the hour had come for the birth of a new party.

No other man was considered as a possible candidate of the Independence League for Governor except William Randolph Hearst. Although the League convention had not been held, he virtually opened his campaign on September 3, at Syracuse. Speaking at a mass meeting of labor Hearst said he felt that Labor Day would soon be a national holiday.

Eight days later the Independence League Convention was held in Carnegie Hall, New York City. Hearst was placed in nomination for Governor, followed by a prolonged demonstration. For thirty-five minutes they cheered. Three cheers were given for Mrs. Phebe Hearst, three cheers for Mrs. William Randolph Hearst, and three cheers for Master George (Buster) Hearst.

After he was nominated, Hearst said in essence, "I think the lines of this campaign should be clearly drawn between those who are in favor of special privileges, and those in favor of popular rights."

Wherever Hearst appeared he was acclaimed as the next Governor of New York. The Democrats soon realized that in order to be victorious, their party must fuse with the Independence League. Progressive Democrats of New York State declared that they controlled the Democratic Party. Their leaders approached Hearst and said that it would be a political tragedy and frustrate the political purpose of the Independence League, as well as the desires of progressive Democrats, if they should permit the Republicans to win. A fusion of the Independence League and the Democrats would insure victory. So thought the Democrats, and so thought the Independence League. The two groups persuaded Hearst that their judgment was right. On September 27, 1906, he permitted himself to be nominated by the Democrats at Buffalo.

When Hearst accepted the Democratic nomination for Governor he said in part: "I pledge myself to work with others to rid the Democratic Party, and, so far as possible, all branches of Government, of that plutocratic trust element that seeks to rule both parties and to destroy the Democratic Party."

Hearst kept his word. No sooner was he named by the Democratic leaders than he flouted the Murphys and the McCarrens. The hair of politicians stood on end. He was warned that attacks on crooked Democratic leaders might mean defeat, but he would not be silent.

Republicans started slander factories. Hearst bore the campaign slanders with equanimity. Charles Edward Russell said, "If I had as many dollars as they told lies about William Randolph Hearst, I'd go and live for the balance of my life at Shepheard's Hotel in Cairo."

Russell urged Hearst to sue for libel, but the candidate answered with serenity, "Why? If they don't tell that lie, they will tell another."

Mrs. Phebe Hearst was unhappy about the campaign slanders, but Hearst wrote to his mother:

Those articles are outrageous, but don't read them. Any kind of success arouses envy and hatred. The best punishment is to succeed more. I shall try to do that. After a while when people understand what my papers are trying to accomplish everything will be all right.... Don't let us bother about the liars and blackguards. If a dog barked at me in the street, I would be foolish to get down on all fours and bark back.

The Republicans tried to make an issue of their statement that Hearst "wore collars made in Paris."

While he answered that this was not true, he added, "Even if it were true, it is hardly so serious a charge as it would be if I wore a 'corporation collar' made in Wall Street by the corporation party."

One of the first papers to attack Hearst bitterly was the New York *Herald* owned by James Gordon Bennett, Jr. Bennett was the son of the elder James Gordon Bennett, one of the most picturesque editors of his day. When Bennett, Sr., began publishing the small one-cent *Herald* in a basement he said that he "started with a disclaimer of all principles, all parties, all politics." His *Herald* was alive with flamboyant energy. Bennett published the first Wall Street financial article to appear in any American newspaper. In 1846, he was the first to obtain a full report by telegraph of a long political speech. During the Civil War he maintained a staff of sixty-three war correspondents.

His son, James Gordon Bennett, Jr., sent Henry M. Stanley to find Livingstone lost in central Africa. He fitted out the Jeanette Polar Expedition, and with John W. Mackay established the Atlantic Commercial Cable Company. Bennett was feared by New York more than any other publisher ever known in that city. Socially and politically he dominated. Being a subscriber to the *Herald* was almost like being in the Social Register. Advertising rates were of the highest. Bennett felt that the *Herald* was beyond attack, and so for years he shamelessly published a Personal Column so indecent as to border on obscenity. This one column brought him about two hundred thousand dollars a year. Bennett defied the authorities to stop his printing the "Personals," but they did not even try.

Then Hearst asked S. S. Carvalho, publisher of the *Journal,* to assign Victor Watson for one year to be a member of the Parkhurst Society for the Prevention of Vice. Watson's task was to answer *Herald* advertisements. He was to be massaged, manicured, champagne-bathed, to go to every possible rendezvous suggested by a *Herald* advertisement, until he obtained sufficient evidence to convict Bennett.

It was easy to enlist the forces of the Reverend Doctor Parkhurst, for that distinguished clergyman's Society for the Prevention of Vice was already aroused over a personal that had appeared in the *Herald* and which read, "I want a fifteen year old Miss as secretary: Must be pretty and good figure. I am a wealthy, retired bachelor. Splendid opportunity. Write particulars in own hand. Address Matinee, *Herald,* Brooklyn."

Hearst began his crusade against the "red light" column of the *Herald.* By means of decoy letters, the advertiser—an insurance agent, Kit Burns—was caught while waiting for one of his supposed victims. He was arrested and placed under heavy bail. After thorough investigation by the *Journal* the evidence was laid before United States Attorney Henry M. Stimson. The evidence was conclusive, not only of the character of the advertisements, but of Bennett's knowledge of their unlawfulness. A telegram was found in the Western Union files giving an order to the *Herald* from Bennett, "Pay no attention to Hearst. Go ahead with 'ads.'"

Bennett was indicted by the United States Grand Jury for sending obscene matter through the mails. Each indictment contained eight counts, and the penalty on each count was five years' imprisonment, or a fine of five thousand dollars, or both. Bennett kept out of the law's clutches by remaining on his yacht in European waters. He was declared to be a fugitive from justice. Measures were about to be taken to bring him back from France when he suddenly returned, appeared in person in court, and paid the twenty-five thousand dollars in cash.

After Bennett was found guilty he wired Hearst, "I'll never forgive you!"

"I hope you never will!" wired back Hearst.

Bennett's conviction annihilated the influence of the New York *Herald.* Later the paper was sold to Frank Munsey. Bennett seldom returned to this country. With the back of the *Herald* broken one potent active force against Hearst was removed.

It was said that the Independence League movement could not succeed because new parties were seldom successful. Hearst replied that the first new party to obtain success in this country was the Independence Party of 1776. The movement began with the Boston Tea Party. The Independence Party was opposed by the Tory Party. The Tories wished to submit to taxation without representation, to acknowledge divine right of kings, and consent to the oppression of the plain people. The Independence Party elected George Washington President of the United States. Conservatism triumphed in Adams. Then came a new popular movement, the Republican Party, the party of Jefferson now called the Democratic Party. In 1856, arose another new party, the Republican Party. In 1860 the Republicans elected Lincoln President of the United States. Hearst asserted that the Independence League said with Jackson, " 'If there is any power in this country greater than the power of the people, we will destroy it.' Our little League is only local, but we aspire to the spirit of the men of 1776.... Our intention is to restore to government the principles of Washington and Jefferson."

Hearst was attacked by DeLancey Nicoll of New York on the ground that he was not loyal to the Democratic Party. Nicoll was really speaking for August Belmont who accused Hearst of not supporting Judge Parker, Belmont's private candidate for the Presidency in 1904.

Hearst replied, "I did, as a matter of fact, shut my eyes, hold my nose and support Judge Parker as a Democratic nominee; but I'm not proud of having done so.... It is the one act of my political career that I am heartily ashamed of, and if Mr. Belmont can prove I didn't do it, I shall be sincerely obliged to him."

After Hearst was nominated by the Democrats the politicians tried to persuade him that it would be accomplished politics for him to speak at Tammany Hall, but Hearst publicly said:

Murphy may be for me, but I am not for Murphy. I decline to fuse with Tammany Hall. I repeat now that I am unalterably opposed to the Murphys, the McCarrens, the Sullivans, the McClellans, and to the kind of politics they represent. I am opposed to boss rule.... The old parties are infested with the vermin of bosses, corruptionists and rascals in office who mouth empty words about civic righteousness while the dollars of their corporation masters are jingling in their pockets.

About this time an emissary of one of the most important men in Wall Street called on Hearst and said his client offered to contribute one hundred thousand dollars to the campaign fund, and would raise several hundred thousand dollars more if his views were reasonable in regard to honest business. Hearst answered:

Your friends are merely proposing to waste their good money. If I am Governor, wherever business is honest I will promote and encourage it without a hundred thousand dollar bribe. If their business is dishonest, not all the money in Wall Street would influence my attitude toward it. Honest business needs no bribe. The thief well asks to be let alone in his thievery, but the legitimate business man should ask for all the encouragement that intelligent business administration can properly provide.

Hearst set out to campaign in upper New York State. With him went Mrs. Hearst and little George. Frequently they traveled on a special train a mile a minute to keep appointments. With his small son, Hearst often went forward to give cigars to the fireman and engineer, and to let George shake the driver's hand. The candidate visited county fairs. Often with his son and wife he drove from village to village. He spoke in dreary weather, in sunshine, in streets, in tents, in halls, from the tail-end of cars. At stations were good-sized crowds, and usually a brass band. Sometimes Hearst apologized, saying that his voice was "shopworn." He caused laughter by calling Hughes "an animated feather duster." After he had made ten or twelve speeches in one day Hearst declared to his lieutenants that he wouldn't talk again. Then he rested, ate a sandwich or fruit, re-charged his fatigue into activity, and went on.

Throughout New York State babies were named for Hearst,

ten or fifteen a day. His secretary took down the names and addresses of the little William Randolph Jones, Browns, and Snooks. Each infant received a silver cup. During the campaign several thousand dollars were spent by Hearst for silver baby cups. Little George Hearst thought the babies the jolliest part of the campaign.

The *Herald* stated that Hearst would spend a million dollars on the campaign. His answer was: "I guarantee not to contribute more to my own campaign than I did to the campaigns of Grover Cleveland and William Jennings Bryan, in which I was merely interested as a Democrat. . . . I do not want any man's vote that I cannot get by an appeal to his conscience and his reason."

Hearst was trailed from village to village and city to city by an army of pickpockets.

"They expected the candidate to drop a hundred dollar bill every time he turned around," said one of his managers. "They thought they could get rich by looking at him."

From the underworld of New York came the repercussions of the wails of disappointed pickpockets. All they were able to steal from Hearst were fancy handkerchiefs. The candidate carried no money. Cash he obtained from his manager. Much less was spent on these tours than was generally thought. Hearst had able managers, and they made money go far.

Hughes went about in the crowds shaking hands. He did not make so many speeches as Hearst. He called the editor "a menace to business stability." He said he did not believe in government by the New York *American*. Hearst replied:

I agree with Mr. Hughes. No private citizen like the publisher of the New York *American* should be compelled to do what public officials ought to do. Unfortunately, public officials are largely controlled by the very corporations against which they should proceed. They often refuse to protect the rights of the people, and then it becomes necessary for private citizens to step forward and take up the cause of the people as in the Gas Fight. While I do not believe in government by the New York

American, it is better than defiance of the Government by corrupt corporations.

At Elmira, New York, Candidate and Mrs. Hearst and Buster were greeted by two hundred young women from Elmira College. In their enthusiasm the students embraced Mrs. Hearst and kissed George, shouting their college yell, "Rah! Rah! Rah! El-mi-ra! Elmira College! Boom! Rah! Hearst!"

In Buffalo, the Hearsts were met by thousands at the train. Norman B. Mack led the delegation. Cannon boomed welcome. The crush was so great that Hearst could shake hands with only a few in the crowd as he went from hall to hall.

At Utica during the campaign Elihu Root, Secretary of State for President Roosevelt, made an attack on Hearst:

Day by day and year by year, Hearst has been sowing the seeds of dissension, of strife and hatred throughout our land. He would array labor against capital, and capital against labor; poverty against wealth, and wealth against poverty.... He would destroy that respect for law, that love of order, that confidence in our free institutions which is the basis of true freedom and true justice.... He spreads the spirit, he follows the methods, and he is guided by the selfish motives of a revolutionist.

"That's a lie! Take it back! Shut up!" shouted some New York supporters of Hearst in the gallery.

The Secretary of State was disconcerted by this menacing interruption. Turning pale he seemed about to leave the stage, but he controlled himself and proceeded calling Hearst an "insincere, self-seeking demagogue who is trying to deceive the workmen of New York by false statements and false promises." His closing words caused a great sensation, "I speak with the authority of the President."

In reply Hearst said:

I do not believe any one doubts my sincerity. The trusts hate me for my sincerity. There is no possible reason for my wanting to be Governor except one, and that is to accomplish something. I certainly do not want the salary of the office. I certainly do not want any extra work, as I have occupation enough with my business in five cities. I have no pride or satisfaction in mere office holding. I regard office as not an end but an opportunity. I have supported a great many men who promised to do things that I thought ought to be done, who proved faithless to their promises. ... I have but one desire, and that is to be known as the Governor who kept his promises and who stopped the trusts from robbing the people.

Hearst said that as a young man Root was attorney for Boss Tweed, the most corrupt boss of his time. He said that Root was the personal attorney of Thomas F. Ryan, that he was campaigning for Hughes who was the attorney for the Lighting Trust, the Shipbuilding Trust, the Sugar Trust, the Whisky Trust, the Street Railway Trust, the Tobacco Trust, the Insurance Trust, the Steel Trust.

Hughes denied being a corporation attorney. Hearst answered:

I define a corporation attorney as a man who served the corporations before he went into politics, and who expects to serve the corporations after he has gone out of politics. Does any one imagine what Hughes is going to do while he is in politics. ... If Mr. Hughes will stop lying about me, I will stop telling the truth about him.

Wherever Hearst spoke in New York he was met with the same enthusiasm he received when he ran for Mayor. Sometimes when he appeared cars were stalled by his admirers. Once he had to seek refuge in a subway station. He got aboard the train and the crowd escorted him to the door of his residence at Twenty-eighth Street and Lexington Avenue.

As the campaign progressed Hearst daily defied the bosses:

I do not want the support of any boss, any Ice Trust Mayor, or any Gas Trust Mayor. And I will add, of any Standard Oil lobbyists like McCarren, or any Captain Kidds of Industry like Morgan or Perkins, or Ryan of the Traction Trust, or Rogers, or Rockefeller of Standard Oil, or Belmont of the Interborough, or Brady of Brooklyn Rapid Transit, or Vanderbilt of the New York Central. Let Mr. Hughes have them all. I do not want to be elected unless I can be elected by the people alone. Free to serve the people.

In the very heart of Patrick H. McCarren's Brooklyn stronghold, Hearst denounced the Gas Trust Senator. He spoke in the Masonic Temple and as he was preparing to leave the hall, a man in the crowd called out, "Why do you expect Democrats of Kings County to support you?"

Hearst hastily removed his coat and leapt upon a table. A hush fell over the hall. "My friends, a gentleman has asked me why I expect him to support me. It is because I am a Jeffersonian Democrat, and because I do not allow hirelings of Standard Oil to define my democracy. I repudiate McCarren because I do not believe he is a Democrat. I ask the support of all Democrats in Kings County."

In spite of the protests of McCarren and his friends, Hearst insisted that the Independence League nominate a third ticket for local officers in Brooklyn and Kings County. McCarren's messenger told Hearst that this decision would give Kings County to Hughes by seventy thousand votes. Hearst went on denouncing McCarren:

I will not tolerate McCarren after election, whether he is for me or against me. He is a distributor of bribes at Albany, personally a most evil influence in politics. I hope he will be defeated and eliminated from politics, not merely because he is opposed to me, but because he is opposed to the best interests of all honest citizens ... the white slave of the trusts.

In a speech to laboring men Hearst said:

I am attacked on one side by the organs of socialism as an enemy of radicalism, and on the other side by the organs of

Wall Street as an enemy of conservatism. I am opposed by both extremes ... but my program is not extreme, simply Americanism. ... Good wages for good work and ... prosperity for the legitimate business man. ... I do not entertain these ideas for campaign purposes, but have advocated them and practiced them all my life. ... I believe they are for the general good of the general community.

Hearst read a letter that he had written on December 17, 1903, to the International Paper Company. He gave his reasons why the union label should be affixed to the rolls of white paper delivered to his newspapers:

I am personally interested in union labor, and sincerely believe that their organization benefits not only their immediate numbers but the country at large, by increasing the purchasing power of the mass of the community. I consider that through this higher purchasing power merchants and manufacturers are benefited, advertising in newspapers is extended, circulation of newspapers enlarged, and the demand for white labor greatly increased.

From that time 'all rolls of paper delivered to the Hearst newspapers bore the union label.

The Roosevelt Administration and the Federal forces aided Hughes. They knew that if elected Governor, Hearst would be the Democratic candidate for President in 1908. They said that if Hearst were elected, the masses would break into riots. Charles Edward Russell recalls going into the city room of the New York *Herald* about two weeks before the election to see an old friend. The *Herald* man opened his desk, showed Russell a riot rifle, and said that every desk in the office was equipped with guns. Each day more stories attacking Hearst's private life were set afloat.

Just before election there was a great Hearst meeting at Madison Square Garden. Twenty-five thousand could not get into the building. Four hundred policemen were assigned to preserve order. Piloted by twenty officers, Hearst walked through crowded Madison Square acknowledging the greetings of his followers gathered around the gaily caparisoned speaking stands on the edges of the park. Finally the policemen wedged a lane for him into the auditorium. The crowd climbed upon chairs and stood on boxes to wave a greeting.

Two year old Master George Hearst made his first public appearance in New York City at this meeting. When the crowd recognized Mrs. Hearst and her son seated in the box for the candidate's family, Madison Square Garden was filled with cheers. George stood up and waved his tiny American flag. His action carried the audience by storm. Some one shouted, "Three cheers for George Hearst!" The little boy did not know that the commotion was being made on his account. He fell in promptly with the demonstration and laughed gleefully as he waved his small flag.

Flags were everywhere at this meeting. Flags ran up through tier after tier of galleries to the very top light flooding the dome. Flags of all nations were there, and twenty-four Irish flags, and two white streamers representing clubs. Every man and woman waved a two-foot American flag. Newspapers were held aloft on sticks, and so were handkerchiefs, hats, and helmets of enthusiastic policemen. Cow bells were swung. Whistles piped, but above all the crowd roared its friendly welcome. Striding down the main aisle on the south side of the Garden, through a lane of men and women waving flags and attempting to touch him, Hearst reached the stage. Eleven minutes he stood on the edge of the platform waiting for the crowd to exhaust itself. This was probably the most dramatic moment in Hearst's life.

A *World* reporter described the candidate:

Hearst presented a striking figure, the predominant notes of which were the clear pink-tinted complexion of his face, a white Ascot tie knotted under a high, turned-down soiled white collar in which nestled a little brown pin that looked as if it might have cost as much as forty-five cents. His light tawny hair was sleek and brushed over his forehead, a stray lock reaching almost to the brow of his left eye. His tall straight figure was encased in a long, Prince Albert coat that was shiny at the elbows and was long at the sides. His trousers of dark gray stripe had not been recently creased. Mr. Hearst's first act upon reaching the platform was to rub the back of his left hand over his mouth. Then he picked up a beer glass and poured into it a drink of water from a cracked white pitcher that stood on the reading stand.

He turned to Henry A. Powell who had called the meeting together, made a remark, and the corners of his mouth turned up in a broad smile of almost childish pleasure. Then he faced the audience gripping the rail in front of him with both hands, drumming upon it with his fingers. His right foot tapped in unison with the crash of the band of one hundred and fifty pieces behind him. He bowed as each succeeding wave of cheers bellowed at him from the front.

When Hearst spoke he said:

I think this is a revival tent. I am glad to see such a great crowd, for it presages a great popular revival that will redeem the people from the trusts. If the campaign is kept up much longer, none of us will be able to speak at all, because the speakers are hoarse from talking and the audiences are hoarse from shouting and cheering.

Hearst pointed out the unpleasant spectacle of the long line of envious editors viciously howling their lies like dogs baying at the moon, spotted from head to foot with the mire in which they had been wallowing. Frantically they had followed Talleyrand's advice: " 'Throw mud, throw mud, some of it may stick.' Most of it has stuck to the throwers."

The candidate said that newspapers accused the Hearst papers of being a trust. His answer was:

A trust is a combination to raise the price of a product or limit the output. . . . My friends, when I came to this city I did not increase the price of papers. I put my papers at one cent, and I compelled the *World* and *Times* and other newspapers to sell to the public for one-half of their former price.... When I came to New York you were getting ten and twelve pages in a paper. I not only cut the price, but doubled the output so that you are now getting eighteen and twenty and twenty-four pages a day.

Hughes asked scornfully in a speech whether if Abraham Lincoln were in New York State he would be for Hearst. The editor answered:

I say that is not the question. If Lincoln were here to-day Hearst would be for Abraham Lincoln.... I consider office not an end but an opportunity. It is no great credit to a man merely to be Governor, but it is a credit to be a good Governor, to serve the people faithfully, to protect them from the extortions and oppression of the trusts; to employ the power of office impartially without favoritism or discrimination; to promote prosperity and endeavor to secure just distribution of wealth....

In addition, I want to say this to you, my friends, the one thing that gratifies me most is, that I retain your friendship and confidence after all the abuse of the campaign.

In closing Hearst repeated what he had many times said:

I would not give a snap of my fingers to be known as the Governor of New York State, or any other State, but I would give nearly all I possess to be known as the Governor of New York State who actually kept his promises and stopped the trusts robbing the people.... If you think the other man will serve you better, I ask you to vote for him, but if you think I will serve you best, I ask your votes for that reason and for that reason alone.... I firmly believe that we will carry this State, and I hope this time all votes will be counted, by over one hundred and fifty thousand plurality.

Late on election night, Hearst found out that Hughes had been elected by fifty thousand. He recognized that he had made a political error in declining to fuse with McCarren of Brooklyn, and Murphy of New York. They had prevented Hearst's election, but he had no regrets. He said:

I congratulate the bosses on their foresight in defeating me, for my first act as Governor would have been to lift the dishonest officials by the hair of their unworthy heads. . . . I repeat what I said in my speeches. I am enlisted in this fight against the control of government by the trusts and corrupt corporations, and I will fight it out to the end. I will serve in the lead or in the ranks, just as the people desire, and as earnestly and loyally in one place as in the other. The people have decided to retain the Republican Party in power. I will make my fight in the ranks therefore, and as a private citizen do my best to promote the interests of my fellow citizens.

There was a rumor that Hearst would no longer live in New York, but this statement was denied. He set out on a trip to Mexico to inspect his mining properties and his ranches.

On his way back he wrote to his mother, on a double post card:

We have just arrived in God-blessed California. The light is real sunlight—not artificial light. The heat is real sun heat, not steam heat. The Colorado River is real mud. The Yuma desert is real dirt, and the Indians are mostly real dirt, too.

Some people may object to the horned toad, the cacti and the tarantula, but I like them. I like them, not for what they are, but what they may become. The horned toad will soon be replaced by the Eastern tourists, and the cacti by orange groves, and the tarantula by the real estate agents. Most old Californians prefer the horned toad, the cacti and the tarantula, but I am for progress and reform. I think California is the best country in the world, and always will be, no matter who comes into it or what is done to it.

Vive le ranch! I am going to save up and build a cabin down at the ranch just big enough for you and Millie and the baby and me.

CHAPTER XXXVI

STANDARD OIL LETTERS

IN 1907, another son was born to the William Randolph Hearsts. He was an attractive, intelligent, blue-eyed child, his father's namesake, William Randolph Hearst, Jr. When the baby was about a year old he fell ill of pneumonia and the distraught parents feared that he was dying. Mrs. Morrill Goddard, wife of the editor of the *American Weekly,* was a Christian Scientist and very devoted to her faith. She treated William Randolph Hearst, Jr., and he recovered.

The healing of his son brought a new spiritual interest into Hearst's life. From that day the publisher had a friendly interest in Christian Science. When *McClure's* magazine attacked Christian Science and Mrs. Eddy, Hearst sent Arthur Brisbane to write articles concerning the leader of the movement. They proved to be a defense of Mrs. Eddy, and when she died Brisbane was her only pallbearer who was not a Christian Scientist. The healing of his son by Christian Science produced a strong impression on Hearst. From that time, when he had a slight illness, if asked by his wife whether he wished to have a Christian Science treatment he frequently complied and felt better. Hearst has a strong mystical strain that responds to the symbols of religion. He has hundreds of pictures, images and tapestries of the Madonna and the Child. He is greatly devoted to St. Francis d'Assisi, the patron saint of San Francisco, the city of Hearst's birth. When Hearst goes to Italy he always visits the church of St. Francis at Assisi.

Before Hearst went to Europe in 1907 with Mrs. Hearst, one of his last acts during the close of the final session in Congress was to introduce a bill to prevent corrupt practices at Federal elections. It was framed to limit the amount of money used, and it defined any other expenditure of money as bribery. A person guilty of improper use of money was to be punishable by a fine of not more than ten thousand, nor less than two thousand dollars. Half of this amount was to go to the informer together with immunity. A constant reward of from one to five thousand dollars was to be offered for the detection of the improper use of money at elections. Another clause in the bill provided that upon conviction of the accused the informer should secure one-half of the reward and immunity. Jail sentences might also be given. Hearst pointed out that a short time previously Rockefeller had given thirty-two millions of dollars for public education, a praiseworthy and commendable act, and yet there was the possibility of the misuse of great wealth to control the Government under our lax election laws. Hearst's bill would have prohibited campaign contributions and the employment of workers at the polls or for other purposes. Hearst believed that this measure if passed would end vote buying. The bill was referred to the Committee on Elections and ordered printed, but it was never made into a law.

A bill very near to Hearst's heart was introduced in the New York Legislature on January 15, 1907, by Assemblyman Alfred E. Smith who later was to be a candidate for President. Smith's measure continued Hearst's first newspaper crusade begun in the San Francisco *Examiner* in 1887 against the sale of narcotics. Smith introduced the bill as the result of revelations made by the *Evening Journal*. More than fifty thousand signatures to a petition were sent to Albany at the instigation of Hearst asking that the anti-cocaine bill be passed. The measure went rapidly through the legislature and was signed in June by the Governor.

When Hearst went to Europe he was thoroughly tired. From Paris he wrote his mother: "I won't look at a paper, not even French papers. I don't know what is happening anywhere. I have telegrams from the office saying that everything is all right there, but I am not interested in the 'news.' I have the same aversion to news that I once had for stewed pears after having got sick from them. My mental gorge gags at the thought of news."

About this time, Hearst received a special silver medal from the Italian Relief Committee for aiding Vesuvius sufferers. The Pope gave him thanks because his papers had collected funds. But Hearst did not remain long in Europe. The Independence League leaders met at dinner in New York in honor of Jefferson's birthday, April 13, 1907. Hearst urged them not to be discouraged by reverses:

Both Republicans and Democrats are corrupt. The motto of the Democratic Party is, "Anything to get in...." The motto of the Republican Party is, "Anything to stay in...." The Republican Party extracts campaign funds from public plunderers.... It denounces trust promoters and stock jobbers as public enemies, and then invites them to outline its political policies and edit its public documents.

Splendidly representative of this liberal policy stands the Honorable Theodore Roosevelt with a big stick in one hand and a contribution box in the other.

He spoke of the deficit of the postal service in this country, ten millions a year, instead of a profit of that amount made by private express companies in similar business. The railroads were favored because of their campaign contributions. He pointed out how Postmaster General Cortelyou, in 1905, repaid George W. Perkins for his campaign contribution of fifty thousand dollars. Perkins was awarded a contract for his steamship company which paid him five hundred thousand a year more than other steamship lines were given for similar service. This contract extended over ten years and gave Perkins five millions above legitimate profit. Hearst's comment was: "It seems that Mr. Roosevelt and Mr. Harriman are not the only practical men in this practical administration. Mr. Cortelyou and Mr. Perkins appear to be about as practical as men can be and remain at large."

Hearst repeated that neither public control nor public ownership could be successful until faithful public officials were selected. "Choose the manager of your government as you would the manager of your private business."

In Rochester the League combined with Democrats to overthrow Boss Aldrich. In Albany the League joined the Independent Republicans and the Independent Democrats to dethrone Boss Barnes. In Syracuse, Buffalo and Brooklyn, the League put straight tickets in the field. In Manhattan the League joined forces with Republicans to depose Murphy and McClellan. Hearst's political manager, Max F. Ihmsen, ran for sheriff and was supported by the *Journal* and *American*.

Hearst had genuine pleasure in campaigning for Ihmsen and other candidates. He declared that he had permanently retired from politics, and it was joy to talk of some one besides himself. He assailed the "bandits and pirates of politics united under the same black flag." With his old fire and drive he urged the Independence League to press forward to complete victory. He recalled to them what Napoleon asked concerning one of his great captains who had been victorious, "And what did he do next day?"

In the fall of 1907, there were no impressive victories for the Independence League, but during the summer of 1908 President Theodore Roosevelt did what he had often threatened, took "a fall out of that Standard Oil gang."

For the first time in his life John D. Rockefeller took the witness stand. He admitted that he crushed rivals. During the investigation that followed the nation saw diagrammed the methods of Standard Oil. Hectic hatred enveloped the oil octopus. Judge Kenesaw Landis received a national pæan of praise when he fined Standard Oil twenty-nine millions.

With imperial arrogance Rockefeller commented, "Judge Landis will never see that fine paid."

John D. Rockefeller knew the courts better than did the man in the street. Soon it was demonstrated that the oil magnate was a prophet with occult power. When an upper court set aside the fine fixed by Judge Landis, the hatred of Standard

Oil in the United States deepened till it approached a communistic red. It seemed the precise moment for a third party.

In February, 1908, Hearst called a national conference of the Independence League in Chicago. Delegates from all parts of the country were present. William Howard Taft had been nominated by the Republicans, and William Jennings Bryan by the Democrats. As temporary chairman of the Independence League Convention held in Chicago on July 27, 1908, Hearst urged an independent ticket:

The Republican Party is the open and avowed handmaiden of the trusts. It scorns those who will bravely rescue it, repudiates those that reform it, and glories brazenly in its profitable infamy. The Democratic Party is merely envious of its sordid sister's ill-gotten finery. It upbraids her at one election and imitates her the next. The Republicans are political attorneys of trusts and monopolies, the representatives of those giant corporations which have superceded the people in this republic as a source of power.... The Democratic vanguard is the Falstaff army ... officered by such soldiers of fortune as Sullivan, Hopkins, Murphy, McClellan, Tom Taggart, the roulette gambler, Tom Ryan, the Wall Street gambler, and Belmont, the race track gambler. It is composed of such political mercenaries as Bailey of Standard Oil and Williams of the Southern Railway, and Hinkey-Dink and Bath-House John and Red Duffy and Nigger Mike, all harmonized at last, and all marching together in rhythmic cadence strongly suggestive of the lockstep.

Hearst said that even though Mr. Bryan was a great lawyer, an enlightened statesman, an inspired patriot, no decent Democrat could tolerate his companions. He urged the Independence League Convention to make a platform so clear and so sincere that every citizen would understand their position and have confidence in their intentions. Hearst eloquently went on: "Let us nominate candidates from among the many men here present whose lives and deeds are a guarantee of genuineness, a pledge of the sincerity of our profession. Then let us go forth to an honorable effort for a righteous cause, to battle and to victory."

Clarence Shearn read the Independence League platform. It provided for direct nominations, initiative and referendum, and recall. Other planks of the platform demanded legislation against corrupt practices at elections, cessation of over-capitalization, no injunction in labor cases before trial, a jury in contempt cases, removal of organizations of farmers and workers from the operation of the Sherman anti-Trust Law, eight hours' work for government employees, laws against black-listing employees, better protection of lives and health of workers, employer's liability law, prohibition of child and also convict labor, creation of a department of labor including mines and mining, all money to be issued by the government through central banks, tariff revision, better supervision of railroads and physical valuation of their property, effective anti-trust law carrying a prison penalty, government ownership of rail-roads as soon as practicable, immediate government ownership of telegraph lines, parcel post and postal savings-banks, good roads, prohibition of fictitious sales of farm products for future delivery, suppression of bucket-shops, national health bureau, exclusion of Asiatic cheap labor, extension of inland waterways and conservation of national resources, popular election of United States Senators, State and Federal Judges, and a graduated income tax.

Thomas L. Hisgen of Massachusetts, was nominated for President, and John Temple Graves of Georgia for Vice-President. The campaign began.

Hearst delivered a Labor Day speech at Davenport, Iowa, on September 4, 1908. He was in especial demand as a Labor Day speaker because the preceding year he had aided the striking printers of New York in winning their eight-hour day in all job and book concerns. In San Francisco the *Examiner* had championed the telephone girls in their struggle to form a union. The paper had opposed the im-portation of Farley and his strike-breakers who were taken to San Francisco by Patrick Calhoun in an effort to break the street-car strike.

On the occasion of Hearst's Davenport Labor Day speech he said, "I claim to be a worker. I suppose I might have been an idler if I wanted to be one, but I have always had a hearty contempt for dudes and drones, and deep sincere admiration for men who do the useful work of the world. I have always desired to be enrolled in the ranks of the worker, and I am truly pleased when I am invited every Labor Day by union men to appear before them and speak on matters of interest and importance to them."

Hearst called the attention of his audience to the Sherman anti-Trust Act which carried a prison penalty for trust law-breakers, but he said that a court had so construed the law that only labor leaders had gone to jail, and only labor unions had been treated as trusts. Hearst urged a campaign of equal rights for all. He encouraged union men to struggle for higher wages. San Francisco was cited by him as an encouraging example. The city was doing more business, making more money than in the prosperous days before the fire, and prosperity was the result of high wages.

Hearst made the speech notifying Hisgen of his nomination. He spoke of Bryan as a "dangerously new Bryan. . . . I will not follow such a Bryan. I fought corruption side by side with Bryan when he fought it. I will fight it just as far, although the new Bryan has made contact with it. What a sorry picture the Democratic Convention makes with Bryan of political purity enthroned between Murphy and McCarren. We have lost confidence in the Democratic Party, as millions of other Democrats have done. We cannot see in this nomination any hope."

Hearst urged all to vote for the party of independence led by Hisgen and Graves. "Honest Tom" Hisgen was born in Indiana, but most of his business life was passed in Massachusetts. In that State he was known as the "man that Standard Oil could not break." He had run for Governor of

Massachusetts on the Independence League ticket, going about the State in an old-fashioned carryall. His opponent, Governor Guild, traveled in a costly automobile. Hisgen finished in the campaign second, next the Republican, and so he was considered a strong candidate.

Thomas L. Hisgen was one of the four Hisgen brothers who in 1866 began the manufacture and sale of axle grease. The Standard Oil Company manufactured axle grease as a by-product and tried to buy the Hisgen business. The offer was refused, and storekeepers were notified that if they sold Hisgen axle grease, kerosene oil would be withheld from them. When Standard Oil made this threat the Hisgen brothers entered the oil business in competition with the great company. For twenty years they successfully resisted the efforts of Standard Oil to drive them out of business. The Hisgens were among the few who had done battle with Standard Oil and survived.

Hearst and Hisgen opened the campaign in Indianapolis, near the birthplace of the oil man. Hearst was described by a reporter as wearing a long frock coat of fashionable cut, pin-stripe trousers, a high collar, a large puff tie of white held in place by a diamond, and patent-leather shoes. Experienced in many campaigns Hearst used humor with excellent effect. Shouts of laughter came when he declared that "the Republican Party has exchanged its principles for Mr. Morgan's bank checks, and the Democratic Party has cashed its principles for Tom Taggart's blue chips."

The campaign of 1908 was soggy. President Roosevelt had been a dynamic campaigner, but he was leaving for Africa. People were tired of Bryan, the perennial office seeker. William Howard Taft was drearily judicial. The political stage seemed dark, empty.

Suddenly a light flashed. On September 15, 1908, Hearst was about to address an audience at Columbus, Ohio. John Eddy, a stranger to Hearst, called at his hotel and submitted to him what afterwards came to be known as "The Standard Oil Letters." How Eddy acquired these letters is unknown, but they were from the private files of Vice-President Archbold of the Standard Oil Company, parent of the ten thousand trusts in the United States.

Thrilled, Hearst read the letters. One revealed that Archbold wrote United States Senator Joseph Foraker that he was sending him fifteen thousand dollars. Hearst dropped the letter upon the floor, paced up and down the room exclaiming, "These letters are treason. The world must know. I'll read some to the audience to-night."

"It can't be done," protested a companion.

Hearst answered, "George Washington intercepted a letter that cost Major André his life. Washington would have hanged Benedict Arnold if he could have caught the traitor."

The letters involved both Democrats and Republicans. Hearst determined to read them so as to deprive either party of advantage. Both parties were guilty. However, the Republicans had been long in power. Special privileges were obtainable from them. The majority of the letters were addressed to or received from Republicans. Hearst was in a Republican State, Ohio. The first letters were read at Columbus.

The letters were so appalling that Hearst read them quietly without apparent attempt to sway the crowd. He introduced them as he would have presented evidence in a court room.

John D. Archbold, vice-president of the Standard Oil Company, wrote the first letter on February 6, 1900, from 26 Broadway, New York City, to Senator Joseph B. Foraker, who had been considered as a candidate for the Presidency.

"Here is a very objectionable bill. . . . I hope there will be no difficulty in killing it."

Ten days later Archbold again wrote Foraker, "This bill is so outrageous that it is ridiculous. It must be looked after." In March Archbold wrote the Senator, "Make a demonstration against the whole bill. . . . The ninth clause should be stricken out. The same is true of House Bill No. 500, introduced by Mr. Price in relation to foreign corporations. I am glad to hear you think the situation is well in hand."

Archbold paid promptly. On March 17, from 26 Broadway he sent Foraker a certificate of deposit for $14,500. Nine days later he sent $15,000, writing the Senator, "I need scarcely again express our great gratification over the favorable outcome of affairs."

Affairs continued favorable apparently, for on January 27, 1902, Archbold sent Foraker a certificate of deposit for $50,000, "in accordance with our understanding." A few days later Archbold wrote Foraker protesting against a "vicious bill" introduced by Senator Jones of Arkansas, S. 649, intended to protect trade in commerce against unlawful restraint and monopoly.

The Columbus audience listened to the letters read by Hearst. Senator Foraker had been Governor of Ohio before he served in the Senate, and in a few short years he had accumulated a handsome fortune. Hearst read the letters so quietly that the Columbus audience did not sense their importance.

But, the men of the press understood. The letters roared through the United States. Their repercussions sounded in London.

The next day when Hearst stepped from the train at St. Louis, all the newspaper men in America seemed to be present inquiring about the letters.

"How many are there? Who wrote them? What do they say?"

Archbold issued a statement for Standard Oil to the Associated Press: "Such correspondence and relations as I may have had with Senator Foraker were entirely proper and legitimate."

Foraker explained to reporters, "I don't know whether the letters given out by Mr. Hearst are true copies or not. I assume they are. I was then engaged in the practice of the law and was employed by the Standard Oil Company as one of its counsel when it was attacked in the courts and in the Legislature. While I do not recall the details, I remember I rendered this company such service as I could, charged for it and was paid. The employment had no reference whatever to anything pending in Congress, nor to anything in which the Federal Government had the slightest interest." Foraker declared that he was proud of his client, Standard Oil. "It had not then become discreditable, but was considered just the reverse, to be employed by such corporations. That employment ended before my first term in the Senate expired."

Some of the letters revealed that Foraker was asked to oppose bills, but he asserted that the $50,000 check advanced by Standard Oil was to get control of an Ohio newspaper, and that he later returned that money.

Hearst replied that he was willing to believe Foraker's story of the loan, but there was a sum of $44,500 which was not a loan.

President Roosevelt quickly repudiated Foraker. He said that the Ohio Senator had always opposed him and the entire reform wing of the Republican Party. Hearst received a letter at this time from President Theodore Roosevelt asking him to call at the White House. Hearst made the journey from Chicago. When he entered, the President seemed a little nervous. Roosevelt spoke of various public matters, then he said, "Mr. Hearst, you did a great service in publishing those Standard Oil letters. Every one suspected Standard Oil political activities, but you were the first to establish them definitely." The President sat lightly tapping the table with his fingers. Suddenly he asked, "Do any of the letters contain anything about me?"

"Nothing that will harm you," replied Hearst.

The publisher realized that the President had sought the interview in order to ask that one question. Hearst went on across the continent lightly tossing political bombs. He read letters at his meetings written in longhand by Mark Hanna to Archbold. From the United States Senate, Hanna wrote on September 15, 1903: "The election will be no walk-over. We must carry Cuyahoga County. . . . Standard Oil must help the State Committee liberally. . . . I am holding the bag. This is going to be an expensive campaign. I can see where I will land before this thing is over, so I have no doubt I will have to call again. . . . Should Johnson carry the legislature, the corporations will catch it, as I am their representative, so-called. . . . There is more than me interested in this result."

Three times in one week Hanna wrote expressing thanks for enclosures. He also revealed the Hanna technic in collecting two of the greatest campaign funds that America had ever seen.

Archbold wrote back to Hanna that he wanted a man named Bennett defeated for the Attorney-Generalship of Ohio. His crime was that at one time he had accused Standard Oil of offering him a $400,000 bribe while he was public prosecutor. He had also been associated with S. S. Monnett in an action against Standard Oil. Bennett's candidacy was called by Archbold a "danger." Archbold wrote to Hanna, "Ohio is not so poorly off as to take that sort of timber for Attorney-General."

The "timber" for public officials that Archbold liked was shown by Congressman Joseph C. Sibley of Pennsylvania. Hearst read his letters written to Archbold: "I can obtain twenty-five Senators, and I suggest that you obtain 'Senator B.,' Democrat, one of the strongest men in that body. Had you not ought to have a consultation with him? One great man at the proper time would be a tower of strength and safety. If you want to see him, I think I could arrange for him to call in New York."

"Senator B." proved to be Senator Joseph Bailey of Texas.

Archbold wrote immediately to Sibley, "We are anxious to have a talk here at as early date as possible with Senator Bailey of Texas, and I write to ask if you will do us the favor to communicate with him and write when he can be here."

The Brooklyn *Eagle* said in regard to Hearst's exposé of both Republican and Democratic statesman:

"He ran a live wire through the leaders of both Houses."

Bailey was considered by many the most brilliant man in the

upper House, the future leader of his party, but this visit to the Standard Oil offices was the beginning of his disastrous end. For barely $5,000 the Senator enlisted in the service of the company. He was lent thousands more. Bailey had come to Washington from Texas, declaring he would not wear even a dinner coat, but in the scarlet livery of Standard Oil, disgraced and shamed, in spite of his fortune of half a million dollars, he was returned to obscurity.

Another United States Senator, John L. McLaurin of South Carolina, wrote Archbold in a letter read by Hearst: "I can beat Tillman if properly and *generously supported*. There is no time to lose."

Archbold replied, "I will keep a law practice in mind with the hope that something may develop in which I can be of service to you in connection therewith."

McLaurin was of service to Archbold. He warned him that President Roosevelt in the Senator's presence had said, "I hope some day to take a fall out of that Standard Oil gang." Then he added, "If Roosevelt succeeds himself, mark my words, he will try to make good his statement, as he believes it will appeal to the masses and keep him in the center of the stage. I thought it might be a friendly act to give this to you in strict confidence. . . . It will show you anyway that I am not unmindful of your many kind actions toward me."

Hearst read a letter showing that Standard Oil apparently controlled United States Senator William J. Sewall. Archbold asked him to see that the report of the Industrial Commission regarding industrial corporations soon to be made to Congress "should be wisely and conservatively shaped." Representative John J. Gardner of Atlantic City, New Jersey, should be spoken to by Sewall.

The press was not overlooked by Standard Oil. Amidst great excitement and applause letters were read by Hearst in Madison Square Garden. He showed that even an insignificant industrial magazine received a check for three thousand dollars. Another periodical was given five thousand dollars. He disclosed a plan of Standard Oil to control the Associated Press regardless of cost.

Manipulation of judicial appointments was revealed in letters written by Standard Oil's Archbold and read by Hearst. On December 5, 1902, Governor William F. Stone of Pennsylvania, was asked to appoint Judge Morrison of McKeen, to the Supreme Bench of the State:

"Aside from Judge Morrison's character and ability, his familiarity with all that pertains to the great industries of oil and gas, and the important relation they bear to the interests in the western part of the State, make him especially desirable as a member of the court from that section." So wrote Archbold. Judge Morrison was appointed.

Archbold asked Governor Stone for another Judge, on September 5, 1900: "Will you permit me to say that if it seems consistent for you to appoint Judge John Henderson of Meadville, Pennsylvania, to the vacancy on the Supreme Bench caused by the death of Judge Green, it will be a matter of intense personal satisfaction to me?"

Judge Henderson was placed on the Supreme Bench of Pennsylvania.

Hearst pointed out the evolution of another Supreme Court Justice of the State of Pennsylvania. On September 22, 1899, John D. Archbold sent Attorney-General John P. Elkin of Pennsylvania, with a letter of introduction to William Rockefeller, J. W. Winkler, and H. McKay Twombly. A few months later Archbold sent Attorney-General Elkin ten thousand dollars, and in another month five thousand dollars. He asked the Attorney-General to kill a measure pending in the legislature. Later John P. Elkin was elevated to the Supreme Court.

In a letter read by Hearst, the toga of Senator Boise Penrose of Pennsylvania, was spattered with mud. It was shown that he was given twenty-five thousand dollars by the Standard Oil Company. Penrose acknowledged the receipt as chairman of the Pennsylvania State Committee, but he declared that the twenty-five thousand dollars sent him by Archbold was for

Roosevelt. Penrose defied Hearst, "If you have any more letters I hope you will publish them."

President Roosevelt defended himself. He said he wrote a letter to Cortelyou dated October 26, 1904, saying, "I have just been informed that the Standard Oil people have contributed one hundred thousand to our campaign fund. . . . If true, I must ask you that the money be returned 'forthwith."

The President reminded the public that he had caused Standard Oil to be indicted nineteen times in Illinois, in 1906, and ten times in New York, in 1907. Through prosecution instigated by him, Standard Oil had been fined twenty-nine millions in Illinois for rebates. He had denounced the reversal of judgment as a "gross miscarriage of justice." Finally he had the Standard Oil Trust sued under the anti-Trust Act, and a decree of dissolution was entered against it.

"It must be admitted of Mr. Roosevelt," replied Hearst, "that although he received the financial and political support of the Standard Oil Company, he repudiated that institution after he was elected. . . . He can boast of belated honesty."

John D. Archbold frankly declared that in 1904 he gave one hundred thousand dollars to Cornelius N. Bliss, the Republican treasurer, but when he did so he told Bliss that he would not give the money unless it was thoroughly appreciated by the President. He said Roosevelt prosecuted Standard Oil because the company refused to contribute an additional one hundred and fifty thousand demanded by Bliss. At the time this statement was made, Bliss was dead. The truth lay between the veracity of Roosevelt and Archbold.

The President was asked by newspapers to produce the letter he had written Bliss rejecting Standard Oil contributions. Roosevelt could not find the letter.

Another letter written by Sibley to Archbold on January 9, 1904, showed that Roosevelt was having what Hearst called "a flirtation with Archbold for the political support of the Standard Oil Company."

Sibley wrote:

I went to the White House with your letter, thinking that although it was marked "personal" it was meant to show to him. He still wants you at lunch. I told him that inasmuch as now there is a perfect understanding all around that a meeting would not be necessary, thinking that you would probably not wish to come. He wanted me to tell you, however, that he wished you to come over as soon as possible and for me to come with you. ... He told me Aldrich called yesterday and had told him what I had told him as to the friendly attitude of the Standard Oil Company. Aldrich told him also that he did not know as it would do for Mr. Archbold to come over, as it would cause comment. I told him that I thought he, Aldrich, was right, but Teddy seemed determined to have whom he pleased.

Archbold accepted Roosevelt's invitation to lunch at Oyster Bay. In the newspapers the President explained that if Mr. Sibley or any of the other Congressmen desired to bring any friends to meet him, he was always glad to receive them. He said he had met Morgan, Harriman and Rockefeller, and that sometimes he discussed the baseball situation, and sometimes the labor conditions, and at one time the white-slave traffic.

During his tour of the United States while speaking for Hisgen and Graves, Hearst discovered that Kern, Bryan's running mate, lost a railroad pass. The potential future Vice-President of the United States traveled on a pass from the Big Four. Hearst spoke of Kern as a Railroad-Pass Candidate. He called on him to resign from the Democratic ticket, but Kern refused. Hearst asked Bryan to kick out Charles N. Haskell, the paymaster of Standard Oil who, Monnett of Ohio said, tried to bribe him while he as public prosecutor was in action against Standard Oil. Haskell was the chairman of the Democratic National Convention and treasurer of the Democratic campaign fund. In a speech Hearst stated that Bryan dared not kick out Haskell who had passed the hat. Bryan made no sign of a kick.

In San Francisco Hearst and Hisgen spoke to a great crowd in the Central Theater. For the first time San Francisco saw

Hearst in action as a speaker, a mature Hearst inviting assault, welcoming attack, in fierce give and take master of himself.

Probably the political speech made by Hearst that he most enjoyed was on October 10th, in the stately Berkeley Greek Theater that he himself had given to the University of California. Hearst reminded his thousands of hearers that while it was true that monarchies had been destroyed by poverty and republics by wealth, there was no record of any republic being overthrown by honest wealth. In closing Hearst warned, "Do not let corrupting influences destroy this Republic, such as in ancient days destroyed the Republic of Rome."

Hisgen and Graves won a creditable vote, but from the beginning it was clear that theirs was a lost cause. Hearst's discovery and publication of the Standard Oil letters revealing how the Government was run and by whom, was the most significant occurrence of the campaign of 1908. Senators Foraker and Bailey and Congressman Sibley were forced out of public life. Pious John D. Archbold triumphed. He was elevated by the directorate of his company to the presidency of Standard Oil.

William Howard Taft was elected President. On looking at the Independence League slogan of the campaign, "Vote for Hisgen, Graves and principle," Mr. "Fingey" Connors made the epigram, "People don't want no principle, they want to be on the winning side."

CHAPTER XXXVII

· FIRST AIR FLIGHT

EVEN repeated defeats could not blast Hearst's hope of freeing New York from Tammany Hall. Waves of reform had risen, broken and receded, but the rock of corruption was unshaken. This was 1909, the year of election of the Mayor, and already the wolves of Tammany were licking their chops in anticipation of the eight hundred million dollar budget soon to be divided among themselves.

Hearst still hoped for a progressive party. He was told by his supporters that it was his duty to make one more fight. Unless he did the city would continue under Tammany rule. Probably he would not be elected, but so many of the Tammany ticket would be defeated that it would be a partial victory for the League.

When Hearst was assured that his defeat was certain he brightened up. Personally he had never desired to be Mayor of New York City, but he was glad to give a few weeks' service to aid the independent movement. Certain of defeat he yielded to his friends' suggestion. Once more he accepted the nomination for Mayor, and he entered the campaign with these words: "I do not ask you to elect me, but this is one of the most disgraceful Tammany tickets ever nominated in the city. I do ask you to vote for the ticket of able men I have the honor to head, and against the Tammany rogues and rascals whom I have the honor to oppose."

The Independence League nominated most of the fusion ticket in opposition to Tammany Hall. Otto Bannard, the Republican candidate for Mayor, opposed municipal ownership. Hearst cited the city of San Francisco as an illustration of private ownership. There the Spring Valley water rate was four times as much as the New York City rate where the water company was municipally owned. In Chicago the rate for power and light in certain publicly managed districts was one-tenth of what it was in New York under private ownership.

Hearst was urged to modify his Tammany attack and not draw out their bitterest opposition, but he replied, "I have gone up and down New York City for fifteen years, and never once have I been inside of Tammany Hall. I will not change my course."

Hearst and Shearn campaigned together. The editor spoke with his old dynamic energy. Vast East Side audiences thrilled to the recital of his battle against the Gas, Ice, Sugar and Coal Trusts. Hearst thundered defiance at the bosses, "I will not break into office with the McCarren mask on my face and a Murphy dark lantern in my hand."

The candidate promised to build subways. There should be enough schools to provide full-time education for children. He advocated more playgrounds and parks for the youngsters, and recreation grounds for the whole population. He pledged himself to change Blackwell's Island, an institution for the punishment of criminals, to an open-air resort for the health of the people. He advocated the three-platoon system for policemen and firemen; the eight-hour day; a new charter for the city containing the principles of initiative, referendum and recall; the income tax; direct nominations as proposed by Senator La Follette. Hearst urged voters to abandon the fetish of party loyalty. He said it was time for people to combine against both machines.

On election night Hearst received returns by telephone from his newspaper offices. Judge William Gaynor was elected Mayor.

Hearst said:

As for my candidacy, I made an honest effort to win on account of the friends and supporters who desired me to be elected. If I had been made Mayor, I would have, as I said, "served my term at hard labor." I would have endeavored to be a credit to the citizens who believed in me, and to do my full duty to them and to the city. But, obviously, if my sole desire had been to be elected, I would have run on an absolutely independent ticket where all the candidates would have been working and speaking for me, instead of running on an opposing ticket where all the candidates were working and speaking for Mr. Bannard. I hope that Judge Gaynor will make a satisfactory Mayor, and I am certain of one thing, that at least he will make a better Mayor surrounded by an honest and independent Board of Estimate than he would have made if surrounded by the Tammany gang from which we have the good fortune to be delivered.

Hearst's mind never dwells on dead to-day. It always soars toward to-morrow. In this year the publisher found great satisfaction in two court decisions. After more than twenty appeals had been taken in the Eighty-Cent Gas fight, the case was carried to the Supreme Court. Hearst's attorneys were opposed by Joseph H. Choate for the Gas Trust, but the United States Supreme Court decided for Hearst. That same tribunal affirmed the verdict of the United States Circuit Court for the Southern District of New York in imposing a fine of $108,000 on the New York Central Railroad Company for granting rebates to the Sugar Trust.

California, Hearst's home State, in this same year revealed much political progress. After seventeen years' struggle he saw a direct primary measure enacted. The *Examiner's* referendum ballot showed that soon another suffrage State would be added to the Union. Through his mother, Phebe Hearst, the publisher had come to advocate suffrage. In her genuine, but quiet way she had supported the cause. As early as 1896 Hearst had employed Susan B. Anthony to write on suffrage for the *Examiner*. Sympathetic articles on the British militant suffrage movement appeared in the *Examiner*.

"You cannot take a woman's son," said the *Examiner,* "and send him to war to be shot, unless you give her the right to vote about that war."

Hearst insisted that woman should vote not because she is man's equal, but because she is man's superior. In 1911, women received suffrage in California. From its earliest issues in 1900, the Chicago *American* stood for suffrage. In 1911 the *American* sent special representatives to Springfield to work for the passage of the suffrage bill.

Dark clouds appeared in California in this same year. The Japanese were denied the right to own land in California, or be directors of corporations. War was rumored. At the request of President Roosevelt and Governor Gillett the bill was held up by the Legislature for one week. Hearst telegraphed the President urging him to order the fleet back to the Pacific coast. Should that be impossible, he suggested that a special fleet be built for the Pacific. In preparedness for war lay peace.

In 1909, there came a new reason to Hearst for going to California—his third son, John Randolph, was born, a handsome infant with his mother's brown eyes. Phebe Hearst wished to see her new grandson, and the Hearsts went to California with their three boys.

The children were happy in the "Boys' House" built by their grandmother in a grove of oaks near her own Hacienda in the rolling country across the Bay of San Francisco near Pleasanton. Upstairs in the Boys' House were thirteen large rooms for governesses, nurses, tutors and themselves. Downstairs was their playroom, so spacious that they rode around the hall on their tricycles.

In the garden were games, sand piles and swings. The Hearst boys learned to ride at the Hacienda, and became skilled horsemen. Phebe Hearst herself had taught her son to ride by holding him in her arms on her horse's back, and a similar method was devised for the grandchildren. While mere babies they all learned to ride by sitting in a basket chair on their pony Brownie. As soon as they were able to sit alone one of the workmen led Brownie through the garden, and the children never feared horses. When the boys were completely confident they were allowed to ride Brownie seated in the saddle. After they were accustomed to the saddle, each boy was given his own mount. While incredibly young the boys became horsemen able to ride with their father. After Brownie was no longer of service to the youngsters, he was pensioned, and he died at San Simeon at a mellow age.

Often Phebe Hearst during the hottest summer weather took her grandsons to Wyntoon, where she had a German castle on McCloud River in a magnificent wilderness of pine and spruce forests near Mount Shasta in Northern California. The Hearst boys liked the freedom of the wilderness. It was so unlike the high-walled city of New York. The Hearst boys learned to swim at Wyntoon, and perhaps they were happiest there.

With regret the boys left their grandmother, whose dominating thought was to give them pleasure. During their childish illnesses she sat at their bedside and administered their medicine. When the boys returned to their schools in the East, Mrs. Hearst asked that their toys be left lying in the Boys' House just as they had been carelessly dropped. These scattered toys gave the boys' grandmother an illusion that the children were likely to return any minute, and they shortened the distance between Pleasanton and New York. There were many friendly discussions between the William Randolph Hearsts and Phebe Hearst concerning how much time the boys should pass in California. The parents permitted the children to pass their summers in California on condition that they be informed in a daily letter about their daily life.

From Pleasanton, the William Randolph Hearsts went to Los Angeles where Louis Paulhan, the Frenchman, was flying his Bleriot monoplane. One year previously the Wright Brothers soared triumphantly into space, and such an achievement of the impossible lured Hearst. In 1910 the Los Angeles *Examiner* was holding the first international aviation meet. The Hearsts and their two elder sons were in the grandstand watching the great new synthetic birds.

Many of them lighted unexpectedly on their noses, but

Paulhan's Bleriot lifted lightly from the ground, scurried swiftly around the course, rose to great height, departed on excursions into the surrounding country, and swooped back dramatically in front of the grandstand.

Paulhan's manager brought a message from the flyer inviting Hearst to the new adventure of flying.

When the publisher entered the frail monoplane he feared that his two hundred pounds added to Paulhan's one hundred and fifty, would be too much for the fragile machine, but he folded himself into a little space back of Paulhan and put on the heavy woolen cap offered by the aviator.

Paulhan adjusted the machinery and the big propeller swished through the air. The engine gave a musketry fire of successive reports like a racing automobile with the throttle wide open. The men who were running alongside of the machine, let go with a shout of "good-by," and the great bird rose majestically into space.

In writing of the event Hearst expressed a sense of deep serenity and the ecstasy of entering a new and better world. The earth seemed small, always growing smaller. It belonged to the past. Hearst felt gloriously of a new era.

Was he flying or soaring through space? Steadily he rose several hundred feet above the earth, over automobiles below, over people toiling in fields. He felt himself transformed into an eagle.

Then Paulhan turned. The monoplane dipped a little. Suddenly Hearst realized that the surface of the earth had some advantages. He leaned heavily to one side trying to help the machine maintain its equilibrium.

After Paulhan turned he flew boldly into the setting sun. In the distance was San Pedro. Some inlets of the sea reflected the rose reds among the grays and greens of the marshes.

"Shall we go on?" asked Paulhan.

"As far as you like."

Hearst and Paulhan then flew toward the snowy peaks in the east. The air was icy. Hearst was glad when they dipped toward the earth. For four hundred yards it was like shooting the chutes, but without a splash at the finish. The monoplane settled as calmly and gently as a lighting bird.

As a result of this experience Hearst offered a prize of fifty thousand dollars for the first continuous flight from coast to coast. He wrote frequently of the importance of the airship in war. Soon he was unanimously elected an honorary member of the Aeronautic Society of New York. He received the Gold Medal of Merit from the society for aiding the advance of aërial transportation.

No one rejoiced more than Hearst when Charles A. Lindbergh, alone in the Spirit of St. Louis, hopped off from Mineola, New York, on May 20, 1927, and landed in Paris on May 21. On Lindbergh's return he was entertained by the publisher in his New York apartment. The young aviator admired a pair of antique silver globes of the world. Just as he was leaving, Hearst handed Lindbergh the globes asking him to keep them as a memento of his visit.

Later Hearst wished to do something substantial for Lindbergh. His motion-picture company was associated with Metro-Goldwyn-Mayer, and these two organizations proposed to Lindbergh that they do a fact story of his life for motion pictures. The heroic aviator was to receive one-half million dollars and a percentage of the profits. In his New York apartment Hearst presented Lindbergh with a contract, signed and sealed, ready to deliver. Only Lindbergh's signature was wanting.

The aviator read the paper, smiled, shook his head and said, "I wish I could if it would please you. I can't. I said I wouldn't go into motion pictures."

"All right," answered Hearst, "but you tear up the contract. I haven't the heart to do it."

Hearst watched Lindbergh tear up the half million dollar contract and throw it into the fire. He had great admiration for the aviator's magnificent disregard for money.

Before the Hearsts returned to New York they went to Mexico. While in the City of Mexico, Hearst gave interviews to

El Diario and *El Imparcial* in which he said that he thought war between the United States and Japan was possible, but if it could be avoided for twenty years the world would have advanced beyond the period of war and would enter a period of universal peace.

In Mexico Hearst, as the son of the late Senator Hearst, the friend of Diaz, and one of the great landowners of that country, was always most hospitably received and entertained. For several years he had not been in the country. In the City of Mexico he was given a banquet by important citizens. When called upon for the usual speech he paid the usual graceful compliments to President Diaz. On other occasions when he had done his duty by the President his auditors thundered applause and shouted approval. To Hearst's astonishment on this occasion his words were received in silence. The deadly silence was like a blow. For the first time Hearst realized that Diaz was doomed. He was not surprised when one year later Diaz's resignation was forced by Madero.

The Hearsts kept on wandering. They took their sons and went to Europe. They were entertained by Prime Ministers and distinguished people wherever they went. From London Hearst cabled a signed account of the funeral of King Edward VII. The London *Chronicle* spoke of Hearst as "one of the most remarkable of all living Americans. Some go so far as to say, 'the most remarkable of all living Americans.' "

The Hearsts spent some months on the continent. The publisher-collector never wearied of looking at art treasures. Everything interested him, Persian bowls and vases, Della Robbia pottery, textiles, Etruscan plates, English silver, illuminated manuscripts, armor, tapestries, sculpture, furniture, every object of beauty and rarity created by man. Swiftly he went through galleries visiting his favorite masterpieces, closing his eyes to the second rate. Occasionally in driving through Europe he saw out of the corner of his eye something rare displayed in a window. He would park his car, stroll up the street, enter the shop, ask the price of everything, and finally casually inquire about the object that had lured him into the shop. Quickly he bought what he desired and left.

Even in Paris Hearst was pursued by politics. There the story was published and given out in America by the Roosevelt publicity bureau that Hearst, Harriman and Rockefeller were "in a conspiracy" to ruin Roosevelt. Hearst was greatly amused by this indirect charge of Roosevelt which had arisen from the famous Roosevelt letter written to E. H. Harriman. In this letter Roosevelt invited Harriman to come to Washington to help him frame his message to Congress. Roosevelt wrote to Harriman, "You and I are practical men." Harriman thought it indiscreet to go, and so the visit was not made.

In answer to the conspiracy charge made by the Roosevelt press bureau Hearst wrote:

When Roosevelt's letter to Harriman appeared, proving that Roosevelt had been inviting Harriman to Washington to help him edit the Presidential message at the very time that Roosevelt was publicly denouncing Harriman as an "undesirable citizen," I found I had become a conspirator without my knowledge, and much to my surprise. Roosevelt was in dire fear that the Harriman letter would give the people a true insight into his character. So he assembled the correspondents in Washington at the White House, and, after sufficiently inflating himself, he gave vent to the astonishing declaration that Rockefeller, Harriman and Hearst were in a conspiracy to injure him. I have never met Rockefeller or Harriman, but I was a conspirator. I have always made it a rule not to meet men that I might be called upon to criticize, as it is distressing in the performance of an editor's duty to have to criticize one's friends. But still I was a conspirator.

Rockefeller had not written the Harriman letter. Harriman had not written it, he had only received it. I had not written it, but we were all conspirators. . . .

Roosevelt had written the letter. He had privately asked Harriman to Washington whom he publicly denounced to help prepare a public document. Roosevelt himself had written the compromising phrases in the letter, but when compelled to make public the letter he struck out the compromising phrase.

I have never allowed Mr. Roosevelt's childish charge of conspiracy to influence my attitude toward him.

At this time Hearst felt more in accord with Taft than with Roosevelt. Taft was for the fortification of the Panama Canal with the heaviest guns known to war. Taft established the Commerce Court proposed by Hearst six years previously. Hearst felt pity for Taft who he said had to bear the mistakes and burdens resulting from the disastrous panic of the Roosevelt Administration.

In spite of the hostility ever shown by Roosevelt toward Hearst, in September of 1910, before the publisher returned from Europe, he was interviewed by the *World,* and he said that he would support any man for President who sincerely stood for progressive principles.

"Do you mean, Mr. Hearst, that you would support Mr. Roosevelt upon a progressive platform?"

Certainly, I would support Mr. Roosevelt upon a properly progressive platform, but frankly I would much prefer to support some other man in whose sincerity and stability I have more confidence. . . . I like Mr. Taft's policy of quiet effective performance. The big thieves are in much more danger from Mr. Taft than they are from Mr. Roosevelt, while legitimate business is much safer in Mr. Taft's hands than in Mr. Roosevelt's.

Mr. Roosevelt's reckless threats alarm all business interests. Mr. Taft's dignified acts convict the guilty and leave the innocent unmolested. . . . Look at Mr. Taft's indictment of those great criminal trusts like the Beef Trust and the Sugar Trust that are monopolizing the necessities of life and cruelly increasing the cost of living. Look at Mr. Taft's calm, but firm handling of the railroad rates situation. . . . In his own State Mr. Roosevelt deposed Boss Barnes, who was his personal enemy, and installed as boss of the State Republican Party, Mr. Root, who is his personal friend. I consider Mr. Root as a boss much more dangerous than Mr. Barnes. . . . I know that it requires courage to get out of the comfortable though corrupt party and take a cold plunge into strange, but clean waters. Still, I would not have asked Mr. Roosevelt to do anything more than I myself would have done. Mr. Roosevelt is not given to taking cold plunges. He runs promisingly up and down the beach with his bathing suit on, but he does not go into the water.

After Hearst came back from Europe the Independence League nominated John J. Hopper for Governor. Hearst advised against fusion with the Republican Party. In reply to the suggestion for fusion with the Democratic Party he sent the following telegram, "I am not in politics to barter the principles I have advocated for twenty-five years, nor to betray the local friends who have stood beside me through so many hard-fought campaigns. The bribes offered me to support unfit candidates on an unsatisfactory platform I consider merely an insult, not an inducement."

Roosevelt took no part in the New York campaign of 1910, but he spoke in other states. He arrived in his own State only two days before the primaries. When reporters gathered to ask what message he had for the people, his reply was that he could not say anything until he dusted off his clothes.

Dix, the Democrat, was elected Governor of New York, but throughout the United States there were Progressive victories. In New Hampshire was chosen the Progressive Governor Robert P. Bass. In Ohio Harding, the stand-patter, was defeated by Governor Harmon, the Progressive. In Iowa the Republicans were led to victory by Senator Cummings, the insurgent. In Massachusetts the Democrats elected a Progressive, Governor Foss. In California Governor Hiram W. Johnson, a Progressive, won. In Tennessee Cooper, a Progressive, triumphed over machine Democracy.

Even Roosevelt's great popularity could not save the stand-patters that he campaigned for. In New Jersey the Democrat, Woodrow Wilson, was elected Governor by fifteen thousand plurality, the first Democratic Governor to be elected in New Jersey since the first election of Cleveland as President.

In an editorial on the appearance of Woodrow Wilson in politics Hearst made far-sighted comment:

The nomination to the Governorship of Doctor Woodrow Wilson is an event of exceptional significance. Through this interesting personality, as through a deep channel, the university with its high-sourced mountain springs of art and science will have a chance to pour itself upon the arid plains of public life.

For Doctor Woodrow Wilson is no isolated school man descending into the political arena. His accepted mission and the whole meaning of his career as a political historian and college president has been the democratizing of knowledge....Woodrow Wilson may perform before the eyes of politicians a Galilean miracle. That graven image of respectability is likely to walk into the pilot house and lay a commanding hand upon the wheel.

CHAPTER XXXVIII

BUYS MAGAZINES AND NEWSPAPERS

WHILE living in Twenty-eighth Street, Hearst began collecting tapestries. Now he has specimens of this distinguished, royal art everywhere, in museums, in store-rooms at San Simeon and New York, on the walls at San Simeon, on the walls of his New York apartment. Many millions have been spent by him for tapestries. His collection excels any in the world owned by a private individual. Only Spanish royal tapestries equal in beauty, rarity and number those belonging to Hearst.

When the Hearsts moved to the Clarendon in 1907, at the corner of Riverside Drive and Eighty-sixth Street, several partitions were removed, and the entire river frontage was made into one room, but there was not sufficient wall space for some of the publisher's recently acquired tapestries. In 1910, he made such great additions to his collections of art objects that he needed more space to house them. In order to do this properly, Hearst found it would be necessary to remove floors and reconstruct ceilings. Hearst was willing to pay for these alterations, but the plan did not suit the owners of the apartment house. So he purchased the property. By removing floors he created a vast, high, distinguished Gothic hall, gleaming with armor. Here some of his rarest tapestries were suitably placed. The Clarendon residence is a small, choice museum without formality or austerity. No matter how imperially spacious Hearst's dwellings are, they always have a warm hospitable air.

The Clarendon apartments were especially homelike. Hearst became a child again with his children. He was vexed when realistic outsiders destroyed the boys' faith in Santa Claus, but he taught them to believe in the spirit of Santa Claus. He was never too busy to put on a Santa Claus costume and delight the boys by pretending to come down the chimney.

Hearst understands children. Frequently he bought a comic strip because his boys enjoyed it. Some humorists have had their columns accepted because Hearst's sons liked them. He felt that what would please his boys would please other children. He still enjoys playing with type and pictures, trying to create a new and startling effect. He early discovered that sports were a short cut to circulation. Frequently he went into the sporting departments of his newspapers and revolutionized the make-up. Once when he suddenly transformed a page, a sporting editor protested, "Mr. Hearst, you're making the page ridiculous."

The corners of Hearst's mouth curved upward in amusement. "Maybe that's just what I want—to make it look ridiculous."

Competitors imitated Hearst in novel pictures, news thoroughness, attractive features, comic strips, and simple, constructive editorials, so that every newspaper in the United States is in a sense a Hearst paper.

In 1912, another newspaper was bought by William Randolph Hearst. The Atlanta *Daily Georgian* and the *Sunday American* became the eighth arm of his power. In 1913, Hearst acquired his ninth newspaper, the San Francisco *Morning Call,* a conservative journal founded in 1856. It was converted into an evening paper.

So swift was Hearst's success in the magazine world that in 1911 he bought *Good Housekeeping,* an old magazine established in 1885, from the Phelps Publishing Company of Springfield, Massachusetts.

Hearst sent George d'Utassy to Springfield, Massachusetts, authorizing him to buy *Good Housekeeping,* provided he could get it on credit and pay for it out of future profits. D'Utassy offered Mr. Myrick, the owner, $300,000 in bonds, with 10 per cent to be redeemed each year. Myrick accepted the proposal. D'Utassy had lunch, bought the magazine in an hour, and caught the 1:02 train back to New York.

With *Good Housekeeping* magazine came to Hearst the advertising manager, Richard Waldo, now of the McClure syndicate. He founded the Good Housekeeping Institute to test and approve mechanical devices. It was his idea to guarantee advertisements by employing Dr. Wiley to pass on food and medical advertisements. About this time W. F. Bigelow, then just out of college and a reader of manuscripts on the *Cosmopolitan,* was made editor of *Good Housekeeping* and he still occupies the position. *Good Housekeeping* has a fashion office in Paris, and has become the most successful woman's publication in the world with a circulation of nearly two million. It specializes in excellent fiction.

The World To-day, was an unsuccessful magazine bought by Hearst for $25,000. It was renamed *Hearst's International Magazine.* Its circulation was lifted to more than four hundred thousand, and then, the publication was combined with the *Cosmopolitan* under the name of *Hearst's International Cosmopolitan.*

So successfully did *Good Housekeeping* enter nearly every well-to-do home in this country, that in 1912 Hearst became interested in *Harper's Bazaar* which had the prestige of fifty years of the House of Harper. With the coming of *Vogue,* the *Bazaar* had slipped down until it was merely a name. Hearst's agents succeeded in buying the *Bazaar* for $10,000.

Hearst tried a new idea in *Harper's Bazaar.* He had an art editor in charge, and made reading matter secondary to illustrations. Martin Johnson was art editor, and he was assisted by Mrs. Lewis, who supplied the text. *Harper's Bazaar* went steadily ahead until it became recognized by women as the reflection of the style centers of the great world in Europe.

While Hearst was developing lighter magazines, he was carrying on crusades in his daily papers. In 1910, he campaigned against the Milk Trust in New York City which had so lowered prices to the producer that farmers received virtually nothing for their labor. Hearst also made a fight against the Automobile Trust. In Chicago he urged harbor improvements not only for freight, but for municipal bathing beaches. He went to Washington to aid in obtaining the appropriation for the Panama-Pacific Exposition to be held in 1915 at San Francisco, to celebrate the completion of the Panama Canal. Cheers and salvos of cannon greeted President Taft when he broke sod for the San Francisco Panama-Pacific Exposition. San Francisco added five million dollars to the government appropriation, and swung into work. In order to enhance the beauty of the city for the exposition, Hearst offered seven thousand dollars in prizes for the best window boxes and gardens.

In 1911, Hearst carried to success the campaign for Reciprocity. He received thanks from President Taft. About this time he attacked the proposed increase in magazine postage as a serious blow to popular education. He also aided in the election of Carter Harrison, a progressive Democrat, as Mayor of Chicago.

In 1912, Hearst saw triumph a crusade begun by him twenty-five years previously in the San Francisco *Examiner*. Both Houses of Congress passed a resolution declaring for an amendment to the Constitution providing for the direct election of United States Senators.

This was also a Presidential year, and every State in which the Republican Party held direct primaries gave Roosevelt not only the majority of the votes, but the majority of the delegates.

"In view of this very definite expression of public opinion," wrote Hearst, "Mr. Taft should retire from the contest as gracefully as may be, and should permit the nomination of Mr. Roosevelt at Chicago. To repudiate the clearly expressed preference of the mass of the Republican Party for Mr. Roosevelt, is not merely to deny the nomination of Mr. Roosevelt—it is to deny the people the right to make the nomination."

Elihu Root presided over the Republican Convention held in Chicago in June. For days the people thundered to make themselves heard, but they were steam-rollered into silence. President William Howard Taft was renominated. In August, former President Theodore Roosevelt and Governor Hiram W. Johnson of California, were nominated by a thousand Progressives who, singing psalms, launched a new party. Roosevelt and Johnson went forth to the Bull Moose campaign.

Hearst was certain that Taft could not be reëlected. M. F. Tarpey, a Democratic leader from California, wrote him that Speaker Champ Clark of Missouri suggested Hearst as the Democratic nominee. Tarpey offered the publisher the support of the California delegation.

Hearst replied to Tarpey:

There is no honor that I would appreciate so much as an honor that the citizens of my native State might see fit to bestow upon me. But the present situation is too important for any man to be influenced by considerations of personal advantage or by any consideration other than general welfare....

Mr. Clark has led the Democratic Party to victory in the legislative branch of the National Government. He can with equal judgment lead the party to success in its effort to obtain possession of the executive branch of the Government.... Mr. Clark is not only the ideal candidate from the point of view of Democratic policy, but the point of view of democratic principles.... To my mind he is the logical candidate of the democracy for President and should receive the support, not only of the Democratic voters of California, but of every State in the Union.

During 1911, Hearst advocated in his papers Speaker Champ Clark as a Democratic candidate for President. Whenever he was interviewed, or when he made a speech, he mentioned Champ Clark. Early in 1912, Hearst, Bryan, Clark, Governor Joseph Folk and other Democratic leaders met at a Jackson Day banquet. Hearst said that this was the first opportunity since Cleveland's time to restore Democracy.

Hearst went to the Democratic Convention at Baltimore in the latter part of June to bring about the nomination of his friend, Speaker Champ Clark, for the Presidency. He said he did not go as a delegate, but as a Democrat. Bryan was a delegate, and Hearst shared the common knowledge that once more Bryan hoped for the nomination. That was why Bryan championed Woodrow Wilson. Repeatedly he declared, "I don't want to be President. This convention must nominate Governor Woodrow Wilson of New Jersey."

Hearst and Bryan had several conferences. Hearst said, "This convention must nominate Speaker Champ Clark of Missouri. He will be elected, and make the greatest President since Jackson."

Bryan was adamant. Hearst was adamant; he realized that Bryan was trying to deadlock the convention. Bryan's ambition for the Presidency was unkillable. This convention was his last hope. If he could deadlock it long enough, the people would turn to their old hero, the Boy Orator of the Platte, of sixteen years gone. The convention did not turn. At one time the balloting stood five hundred and fifty-six and a half for Clark and three hundred and fifty and a half for Wilson. The convention was dominated by two-thirds rule, and was held in deadlock by the square hands, the square jaw and the square shoulders of William Jennings Bryan.

Hearst and Bryan conferred again. Neither would yield. Doubtless Hearst's mind went back to 1896 when blindly he had risked everything on his faith in the new political savior from Nebraska—prestige, circulation, fortune. How many hundreds of thousands of dollars had been rashly hurled by him into the Bryan campaign of 1896, and again in 1900. Had he not established the Chicago *American* to strengthen his support? After all of Hearst's devotion to Bryan, on a day when the Nebraskan had not the slightest chance of winning, Hearst asked Bryan to step aside for Clark.

But Bryan had forgotten what Hearst had done. Either he or Woodrow Wilson must be President. Bryan had given his pledge. His mouth strengthened, the corners of his lips drooped, his nose lengthened. The delegates might walk over his body; they might crucify him, but he would not yield.

Until the third of July the convention was dead-locked.

Would Bryan hold the delegates there over the Fourth? Tammany saw this opportunity to take revenge on Hearst for all the years of battle waged by him against the Tiger. The Tiger snarled. Tammany broke. New York led the stampede. California went to Clark. The Underwood group did not budge. Bryan had one vote. He changed it to Wilson. It was like the vote of one hundred men. Pandemonium reigned in the hall. Wilson was nominated. Champ Clark's daughter wept. She said she remembered the time when her father was a Bryan fanatic, had gone about borrowing sums of two dollars to contribute to the campaign of the Boy Orator of the Platte.

Hearst was profoundly disappointed by the result of the Baltimore Convention. To-day he thinks that the Clark nomination was lost by timidity and compromise. He wrote editorials, but the Clark leaders begged him not to publish them. This lack of aggressiveness lost the nomination that was expected by the people.

By insisting on the nomination of Wilson, indirectly Bryan precipitated our entrance into the World War to which he was so much opposed that he himself was obliged to leave Wilson's Cabinet in protest.

Hearst and Clark were equally opposed to our entrance into the war. If Champ Clark had been elected President, the United States would have remained out of the World War. America would have had the benefit of the intellect and the brawn of fifty thousand young men who died on the battlefields of France, and of one hundred thousand other young men who were permanently disabled. America would have been able to use for constructive purposes the thirty-two billions and eighty millions that the World War cost the United States. But above all, America would have been spared the hatred, the madness and the fury that poisoned the Nation.

After Clark's defeat, Hearst went to Europe with Mrs. Hearst and wandered through galleries of art, monasteries, and ancient cathedrals. The balm of beauty soothed and healed.

With four hundred and ten electoral votes, Wilson was

swept into power. But he did not have a majority of the popular vote. Roosevelt and Johnson received one hundred and six electoral votes. Taft had only eight.

Despite Hearst's disappointment over Bryan's behavior at the Baltimore Convention, he wrote an editorial later saying, that if Wilson believed that: "Mr. Bryan or any other candidate can render service to the country in a Cabinet position, he should be allowed to select that man without the interposition of any unnecessary objections or obstacles on the part of good Democrats and good citizens."

Even in this year of Presidential election, Hearst sent an automobile, the *Pathfinder,* from coast to coast to campaign for the great automobile highway. The car left Los Angeles in the spring, visited fourteen States, and nineteen Governors were converted to the idea of the coast to coast highway. Governor George W. Hunt of Arizona, Mayor Carter Harrison of Chicago, and Governor Thomas Marshall of Indiana, all wrote enthusiastically of the project. Soon afterwards California appropriated eighteen millions for highways, Arizona, three millions, and New Mexico two millions. The Lincoln Highway was begun.

During this year Hearst saved the United States from a difficult Japanese situation. The Los Angeles *Examiner* discovered that a Japanese syndicate was about to buy land fronting Magdalena Bay. This would have given the Japanese control of one of the best strategic bases on the Pacific coast. The information was verified by an expedition of investigation sent by Hearst. Senator Lodge presented the matter to President Taft. On July 1, 1917, the Senate passed resolutions reaffirming the Monroe Doctrine and opposing the acquisition of any land by a foreign country. The sale to the Japanese syndicate was forestalled.

Again in 1919, there was an investigation by the State Department caused by Hearst. The Los Angeles *Examiner* revealed that the Chandler interests were about to sell a million-dollar ranch across the border in Mexico to the Japanese. The sale was ordered canceled. Because of these efforts on the part of the Japanese to acquire large acreage just over the border from California, Hearst and his California papers strongly advocated the anti-Alien Land Law which would prevent aliens not eligible to citizenship from owning or leasing land in California. The measure was enacted into law by a large majority.

In 1912, many trusts were born and they were attacked by Hearst. Most important and far-reaching of all was the Power Trust with which he battled for nearly twenty years. There was the Brick Trust in Detroit, the Bathtub Trust in New York, and the mighty Traction Trust. To this corporation, in 1912, Mayor Gaynor, Borough President McAney and Comptroller Pendergast, gave complete control of the city's subways for fifty years. Nearly nine per cent profits were guaranteed.

Hearst protested in the New York *Journal*. Gaynor, McAney and Pendergast were alarmed. The question must be settled immediately in order to prevent a popular vote for a referendum on the plan. The settlement must be hastened with both the Interborough Rapid Transit Company and the Brooklyn Rapid Transit Company. Pendergast and McAney reached a secret agreement with the Interborough Company. The Gaynor-Pendergast Interborough Enabling Act was introduced in the State Legislature.

The *Journal* discovered several jokers. The Interborough System and Brooklyn Rapid Transit Company were to have their franchises in perpetuity. They were also to have franchises to all extensions to the Elevated system, or to three-track privileges on existing Elevated lines. This was in violation of law which forbade such franchises. The secret agreement fixed the price to be paid by the city in recapturing transit lines controlled by the Brooklyn Rapid Transit Company and the Interborough System at the end of ten or fifty years at "cost defined in the grant." Usually it was cost of actual construction plus 15 per cent. The Interborough was to have con-

trol of new subways awarded without publicity by secret
contract. This meant that the trust could control extensions
for sixty-five years with the guarantee of 8.76 per cent on its
capitalization, instead of for forty-nine years.

Hearst's exposure of the jokers brought hurried changes in
the Gaynor-Pendergast Bill; it was blocked in the Legislature.

About this time Anthony N. Brady of the Brooklyn Rapid
Transit Company endeavored to see Hearst in his office, but
the publisher left him standing in the hallway. When, after
waiting two hours he departed without seeing Hearst, Brady
remarked to Arthur Brisbane, "It is the first time I ever froze
my feet standing two hours on marble waiting to show a man
how to make a million dollars. Hearst must be queer. What's
the matter with him?"

Brady wished to ask Hearst to join ex-Governor Flower and
himself to buy one hundred thousand shares of Brooklyn
Rapid Transit then selling around eight dollars a share. He
might have taken a profit of ten millions.

When Hearst heard what Brady had said, he sent this message: "Please tell Mr. Brady I don't interest myself financially
in public investments. At any time a newspaper may be called
on to criticize and fight public service enterprises."

After Brady discovered that Hearst could not be tempted
by millions, he brought all possible pressure on the legislature. Boss Barnes, Mayor Gaynor and the minor bosses
helped.

Hearst organized mass meetings. He formed a committee
of protest headed by Clarence J. Shearn and Justice Ford of
the Supreme Court. Labor unions, taxpayer's organizations
and transit associations fought the Gaynor-Pendergast Bill at
Albany.

Hearst pointed out that the measure did not compel contractors employed by the city to keep agreements nor to be
liable for deficiency in their work. The city might enter into
contracts before a permit was obtained for the construction of
the new road. City authorities could lay out future routes for

the next generation. If the city took over the road, it was to pay not only the cost of any betterment, but 15 per cent in addition. The Third Avenue and Bowery Elevated were to be relocated in the middle of the street, and third tracks were to be added giving a perpetual franchise. The Interborough Rapid Transit Company and the Brooklyn Rapid Transit Company could prevent any one else building, and yet these companies themselves were under no obligation to build. Contracts might be let without advertising proposals and permits. New roads might be built as extra work. Dummy construction companies controlled by favored corporations might make huge profits. Shearn computed that the city would owe eighty-five millions in fifty-three years after the transit companies had pocketed five hundred and fifty millions.

Mayor Gaynor was deaf to all protests against the "grab." Governor Dix helped the traction lobbyists jam the bill through the legislature. The new Governor Sulzer did nothing to prevent the passage of the bill, in spite of long petitions of the people.

Hearst appealed to the courts. Justice Hendrick of the Appellate Division of the Supreme Court restrained the signing of the subway operating contract. Mass meetings of protest were held in Cooper Union. Senator Anthony J. Griffin introduced a bill in Albany repealing the Wagner Act which made it possible for the Public Service Commission to treat secretly with the Traction Trust concerning the subway profits of five hundred and fifty millions. As a result of this intensive campaign Hearst forced the Public Service Commission to alter the contract with the Interborough so that taxpayers were saved forty million dollars.

Then the J. P. Morgan Company appeared in the subway "grab." They held a mortgage on the bond issue. The Morgan Company rushed the final details of the subway contract to completion. Litigation was begun on behalf of the minority stockholders of the Interborough Company against the proposed mortgage to the Morgan Company.

On March 13, 1913, the Public Service Commission of the First District closed contracts with the Interborough Rapid Transit Company and the Brooklyn Rapid Transit Company involving financing to the extent of three hundred and ninety-one millions, at that time the largest deal of its kind in the history of the world. The two companies could operate until December 31, 1965, the subways and Elevated lines of the City of New York, in all 629 miles. They agreed to maintain a single five-cent fare, and the city promised to pay one-half of the construction costs and all the equipment charges on the new lines. It also agreed to pay interest on the bonds and to provide a sinking fund for retiring them. The New York Municipal Railroad Corporation agreed to supply thirteen millions and five hundred thousand dollars for the construction of its lines. Its equipment was estimated at twenty-six millions, and it had the same guarantee of redemption as had the Interborough Rapid Transit Company.

Hearst gave notice that he intended to bring proceedings in the court to have the entire action annulled, but on March 15, 1913, the Public Service Commission granted to the Manhattan Railroad Company, owner of the Elevated lines in Manhattan, a certificate authorizing the third tracking of the Second, Third and Ninth Avenue Elevated lines. Now the Interborough Rapid Transit Company and the Brooklyn Rapid Transit Company were masters of the entire traction system of New York City. The firm of J. P. Morgan and Company pocketed in brokerage on the bonds about two millions and four hundred thousand dollars.

Interested as Hearst was in his crusades, collections, and the Presidential campaign, during April of 1912 he had time to send to all his newspapers the best advice of which he was capable as the result of his twenty-five years' experience as an editor:

Have a good exclusive news feature as often as possible.
Pay liberally for big exclusive stuff, and encourage tipsters.

Get reporters with acquaintance.

When a big story must be in all the papers, try to have notably the best account.

Try to get scoops in pictures. They are frequently almost as important as news. I don't mean pictures of chorus girls, but pictures of important events.

Make the paper thorough. Print all the news. Get all the news into your office and see that it gets into the paper. Condense it if necessary. Frequently it is better when intelligently condensed—BUT GET IT IN.

Get your best news on your first page, and get as much as possible on that page.

Don't use up all your page with a few long stories, but try to get a large number of interesting items in addition to your picture feature and your two or three top-head stories.

Of course, if your feature is big enough, it must get display regardless of everything, but mere display does not make a feature.

When you have two features it is frequently better to put one on the first page and one on the third, so as not to overcrowd the first page.

Get important items and personal news about well known people on the first page, and sometimes condense a big news story to go on the first page rather than to run it longer inside.

Make your departments complete and reliable, so that the reader will know that he can find a thing in our paper, and that he can find it right.

The most sensational news can be told if it is written properly.

Make the paper helpful and kindly. Don't scold and forever complain and attack in your news column. Leave that to the editorial page.

Be fair and impartial. Don't make a paper for Democrats, or Republicans, or Independence Leaguers. Make a paper for all the people, and give unbiased news of ALL CREEDS AND PARTIES. Try to do this in such a conspicuous manner that it will be noticed and commented upon.

Please be accurate. Compare statements in our paper with those in other papers, and find out which are correct. Discharge reporters and copy-readers who are persistently inaccurate.

Don't allow exaggeration. It is a cheap and ineffective substitute for real interest. Reward reporters who can make THE TRUTH interesting, and weed out all those who cannot.

Make your headlines clear and concise statements of interesting facts. The headlines of a newspaper should answer the question "WHAT IS THE NEWS?" Don't allow copy-readers to write headlines that are too smart to be intelligible.

Run pretty pictures and interesting layouts, but don't run pictures just to "illuminate the text." If a picture occupies a column of space, it should be as interesting as a column of type. Pictures of pretty women and babies are interesting. Photographs of interesting events with explanatory diagrams are valuable. They tell more than the text can, and when carefully and accurately drawn people will study them. But much space in my papers is wasted on poor and uninteresting pictures. Make every picture worth its face.

Please sum up your paper every day and find wherein it is distinctly better than the other papers. If it isn't distinctly better, you have missed that day. Lay out plans to make it distinctly better the next day.

If you cannot show conclusively your own paper's superiority, you may be sure the public will never discover it.

A succession of superior papers will surely tell. When you beat your rivals one day try harder to beat them the next, for success depends upon a complete victory.

CHAPTER XXXIX

MOTION PICTURES

HEARST became interested in producing motion pictures in March, 1913. Edgar B. Hatrick, then in charge of the "still" photograph department of the Hearst papers, suggested that motion pictures be made of the first inauguration of Woodrow Wilson as President of the United States.

At that time the word news-reel had not been minted, for there was no reel of news. The *Pathé Weekly* was a compilation of short subjects without any attempt being made to reproduce news while it was fresh. Motion pictures of Wilson's inauguration were rushed to New York where a print was made. On the evening of March 5th, a Broadway theater showed the picture. Such a prodigious feat of speed created a sensation. As rapidly as prints could be made they were shown throughout the country. The first news-reel was born.

Hearst recognized its importance. Long interested in photography he easily mastered the processes of the new invention. Again he began taking pictures. Special cameras were made in Europe and imported. Cameramen were trained. He established a news-reel organization to make permanent weekly releases.

In December of 1913, the first news-reel assignments were given out. The Hearst-Selig Company was formed with a laboratory in Chicago. In February, 1914, the *Hearst-Selig Weekly* made its appearance, the first regularly issued news-reel. Ansel Wallace sent pictures from Mexico showing fighting between the Huerta and Villa forces. Wallace was arrested, imprisoned and sentenced to be shot, not for photographing Mexican disorders, but for photographing President Huerta in his palace garden drinking brandy. Wallace was saved from death by the swift efforts of Secretary of State Bryan. The Hearst news-reel has been in existence for twenty years, but under various names. At present it is called the Hearst Metrotone News.

In 1913 and 1914, Hearst began screening popular romances. In association with Pathé he made the first of these serials, *The Perils of Pauline*. Pearl White was the star, and Theodore and Leo Wharton were directors. Other popular film serials followed in 1914 and 1915, such as *The Exploits of Elaine, The Mysteries of Myra,* and *Patria*. Cartoon pictures came later, and feature pictures were introduced. Among the most popular of these were *When My Ship Comes In, Jaffrey, The Girl Philippa* and *The Goddess*.

Both Mr. and Mrs. Hearst became interested in the fascinating new art. They took cameras to San Simeon where they summered. The publisher himself wrote and directed motion pictures to amuse the house-party. Guests, family and animals were actors. The half-completed buildings served as "sets." Evenings the pictures were shown in a large tent.

In 1919, Hearst's commercial motion picture concern, the International Film Service Company, built and equipped its studio at 127th Street and Second Avenue, New York City. There was produced Fannie Hurst's *Humoresque* with Alma Rubens and Ramon Novarro, as stars. *Humoresque* made a large sum, and was the first gold medal winner. Then followed *When Knighthood Was in Flower,* with lovely Marion Davies, which made millions. Two millions came from another of her great successes, *Little Old New York*.

Many other pictures were produced by Hearst, and they were usually distributed by Famous Players-Lasky.

Production activities were removed to Hollywood where a long series of important pictures was introduced and distributed by Metro-Goldwyn-Mayer. These included *Beverly of Graustark, White Shadows in the South Seas, Floradora Girl, The Big House, Chickie, Five and Ten, The Big Six, Blondie of the Follies, Gabriel Over the White House, Peg o' My*

Heart, Operator Thirteen. Hearst also produced *Broadway Melody,* the first of the musical sound pictures.

In 1934, Warner Brothers began distributing Cosmopolitan pictures. *Page Miss Glory, Shipmates Forever,* and *Special Agent* are among the films produced by Warner Brothers for Hearst.

In an interview given in 1927 to Miss Louella O. Parsons, the motion-picture editor of Universal Service, Hearst said:

The way for motion-picture producers to make more money, is to stop trying to rival each other in extravagant productions which have no essential merit of fundamental interest. . . . It is not possible to make a big success merely by spending a big amount of money; but you can, if you are not careful, make a big failure. . . . If you start with a good story, you can make a successful film at a small expense. . . . One of the best films I ever made, *Humoresque,* cost only about one hundred and fifty thousand dollars. Even Metro-Goldwyn's great film, *The Big Parade,* cost, I am told, less than a million. . . . Sometimes the vanity of scenario writers impels them to throw away practically all of a good successful story in order to substitute something original, or rather something of their own which probably is not original.

Hearst was asked about the advisability of buying plays and novels for the screen, and he answered:

When a fiction story has a big sale, nine times out of ten there is a quality of interest that will make a screen version a success, provided that the quality of interest is retained in the scenario. There is less risk in putting on the screen a story which has proved a best seller than in preparing an original story. . . .

Don't try to make a big expensive picture out of even every good story. . . . After a story is pretty well along, if everybody agrees that the picture has the qualities of a big picture, you can add necessary expense to insure it being a big picture. One of my best pictures, *Little Old New York,* was started this way. We started to make just an ordinary good picture out of just an ordinary good play. After we got into it everybody was enthusiastic. We appropriated more money and made a very big picture. In this way *The Covered Wagon* and *The Big Parade* were made. You can't always be sure before you start a picture that it has the essential qualities of a good picture.

Hearst supervises the direction of his productions. Frequently while on a motion picture "set" he writes an editorial and telegraphs it to his newspapers.

The editor is interested in the drama of the cinema, but he is held even more by the drama of life. His papers collected funds for erecting a national monument in memory of 266 men who sank on the battleship *Maine* in Havana harbor, February 15, 1898. Seventy thousand persons were present at the dedication of the monument in Central Park on Memorial Day of 1913. Master George Hearst unveiled the monument which was made by the sculptor, Mr. Attilio Piccirilli. In his speech Hearst thanked the sculptor and the architect, Mr. H. Van Buren Magonigle, and the City of New York which gave the site, and the people of the United States who contributed funds for the monument. Hearst said, "We cannot all be heroes, but we can all be grateful for heroism."

Later on the same day Hearst entertained at luncheon ex-President Taft, Admiral Sigsbee, and Mayor Gaynor.

Hearst's feelings always responded to the struggle of Ireland for Home Rule. He declared that if he were ever President of the United States he would send an Irish-American to the Court of St. James. Once in a speech he said, "There is not the slightest doubt that the vivacity, alertness and beauty of American women are due in a large part to the strain of Irish blood in the American race. I am sorry that I haven't a great deal of Irish blood in my veins, but my son has. I remedied that family defect at the earliest possible moment, and in the most satisfactory manner."

When the Great War came Hearst wrote editorial after editorial vainly endeavoring to save the life of Sir Roger Casement, the Irish patriot who was about to be executed. During that time Hearst was obliged to undergo a minor surgical operation. Mrs. Hearst says that within an hour after he left the operating table he was writing an editorial for Casement. A Boston paper attempted to justify the trial and condemnation of Casement and Hearst wrote to his Boston *American*, "If this Boston paper believes that Sir Roger Casement should be executed for his endeavor to secure liberty and justice for his party, then it must equally believe that those who participated in the Boston Tea Party and threw the tea into the sea as a protest against England's injustice should have been executed; and that John Hancock and John Adams, and other signers of the Declaration of Independence and leaders of the American Revolution, should have been hanged."

In 1913, under the Wilson Administration, Hearst at last saw the consummation of the most important work he did while in Congress. The Parcel Post was established. In this same year another deep satisfaction for him was the passing of the first vessel through the Gatun lock of the Panama Canal. To this end he had struggled since he was a youth of twenty-three.

In the autumn of 1913, Hearst flung himself into the New York campaign for a complete progressive program. He spoke with Governor Sulzer, Bainbridge Colby, and John Temple Graves, and they supported the candidacy of John Purroy Mitchel for Mayor. They advocated the Massachusetts ballot, the initiative, the referendum, and the recall. They spoke at both Independence League and Democratic mass meetings. Mitchel became Mayor of New York by a majority of one hundred thousand.

About this time in his New York and Boston papers Hearst declared war on the management of the New York, New Haven and Hartford Railroad which was being wastefully and criminally conducted. In reality, he challenged the J. Pierpont Morgan Company. He blamed Morgan, and not President Mellen, for the New England Railroad monopoly. The bankers secured a monopoly of a stock controlling a certain commodity.

Then the Morgan Company inflated and over capitalized securities of the monopoly to many times their intrinsic value. High prices were extorted for inadequate service in order to pay dividends on inflated securities. The public had to accept inadequate service and pay extortionate prices, or be entirely deprived of service essential to their business development and existence. So neglected was the trackage of the New York, New Haven and Hartford Railroad, that as a result of a resolution by Senator Norris, the Interstate Commerce Commission investigated the railroad.

It was discovered that one hundred thousand dollars had been spent by the road in molding the opinion of the Connecticut Legislature. Twelve millions had vanished into air. Two hundred and four millions had been wasted in operations during nine years outside of the railroad sphere. The loss of these vast sums was sustained by the widows and orphans of New England.

In the latter part of 1914, twenty-one directors of the New York, New Haven and Hartford Railroad were criminally indicted. Among them were William Rockefeller, and George F. Baker, richest banker in America. They were not charged with wrecking the railroad or looting its treasury, but with violating a criminal statute of the United States.

In the spring of 1914, Hearst was again in California, the happy, golden land. There his fortune ever increased and his policies were speedily being realized. In San Francisco, the Municipal Street Railway was in successful operation, and Hearst hoped it would increase municipal ownership. Already Los Angeles, by more than a two-thirds vote, had decided to own and operate its light and power plant.

Hearst was accompanied by George Pancoast, superintendent of the mechanical department of the Hearst papers. They strolled over to the Panama-Pacific Exposition grounds on San Francisco Bay, in the vicinity of Hearst's childhood home. Various exhibits were being assembled. Soon the Exposition was to open. Suddenly Hearst turned to Pancoast and said,

"George, we are asking the world to come here. What can the *Examiner* show?"

"Nothing, I'm afraid, Chief. It's too late."

"None of the exhibits will be complete on opening day," replied Hearst. "Won't you build one of your presses to exhibit?"

Pancoast explains, "The Chief will forgive a lie, anything except not trying. He says, a man who doesn't make mistakes doesn't make anything."

Hearst ordered a twelve-cylinder Universal Unit press that had been invented and patented by Pancoast. The mechanical superintendent has a gentle voice and manner, but great executive ability. He went to New York and convinced R. Hoe and Company that a press of this type could be built and shipped to the coast in four and a half months. This was accomplished and was a record achievement. In fourteen days Pancoast set up six carloads of machinery.

At the opening of the Panama-Pacific International Exposition the press in the Palace of Machinery on the Exposition grounds printed a special issue of two hundred and fifty thousand copies of sixty-six pages of the *Examiner*. Each day three hundred thousand papers came from the mighty machine, at the time of the Exposition, the largest in the world. Something had been achieved that had been thought impossible. Hearst was happy.

The publisher spent much time at the Exposition. To him it was a fleeting fairyland. He tried to catch its beauty in permanent form, and some of the best photographs made of the Exposition grounds were those taken by Hearst at night.

Hearst lingered over the work in the section on arts and crafts created by Americans. Frank Ingerson, a distinguished artist in enamel, whose work is in Rothschild and Dupont collections, had charge of assembling the display for the Exposition. He says that one day a visitor came with knowledge of virtually every craft. The man understood enameling on metals and porcelain. He knew more about weaving, lace making and embroidered textiles than any one he had ever met. Certain knots in weaving and lace making were familiar to him. He knew wood carving and finishing of wood. He understood porcelains under- and over-glazed. Processes in metal work were intelligently discussed by him. Several times the stranger returned to discuss American arts and crafts. When he began to make purchases, Ingerson discovered that the stranger was William Randolph Hearst.

It was the policy of the Exposition to deliver nothing until the closing day in order that the exhibits might not be disarranged. The publisher asked Ingerson for the "loan" of his purchases for a few hours on Sunday, so that he might take them to Mrs. Hearst for her birthday breakfast, and then return them. Hearst wrote down the names and addresses of the artists and artisans. He said that he enjoyed their work more than he did the fine arts. He was glad Americans were able to produce so much beauty in arts and crafts.

For months before the World War came, Hearst sensed that it was near. George d'Utassy tells of a luncheon at the publisher's Riverside apartment attended by Sir Gilbert Parker and Arthur Brisbane when he heard Hearst make the prophecy.

The explosion, which took place at Serajevo, came like tragic destiny to those who had heard the prediction. Europe crashed when on that quiet summer day of June 28, 1914, the Austrian Archduke Francis Ferdinand and his wife were assassinated. Then came new history, a new map of the world.

On July 28, Austria and Serbia took up arms. The Czar massed twelve army corps along Russia's frontier, and sent Austria an ultimatum. Germany declared war on Russia. On August 3, came war between France and Germany. The neutrality of Belgium was guaranteed by Germany, the unity of France and the integrity of the French colonies, but England refused to remain out of the fray. Then all Europe took flame, armies began to march.

Germany hacked her way through Belgium. Moral law was suspended. War was necessary, righteous. Destruction, carnage began. Civilization sank into barbarism, back to the moral level of the time when prisoners were condemned to perish in gladiatorial shows, when the right hand of the brave was cut off as punishment for self-defense, when captives were thrown to wild beasts, when entire populations were slaughtered.

Hearst realized that no adults of his day would ever again feel secure and safe. The world hurricane beat against the doors of America. Would it force its way through?

Arrangements were made by the publisher for the news service of the London *Times,* and *Telegraph,* and the Paris *Matin.* Leading Italian, Russian and German papers also agreed to supply war news. Day by day stories grew more frightful. Tales arrived of German atrocities such as in modern times had never been heard. They were largely discredited by Hearst, but all that he heard and read determined him to cast the influence of his newspapers into the struggle to keep America out of the war.

More and more revolting became the atrocity stories. Hearst saw that war had transformed rulers of Europe into maniacs, and the countries of Europe into madhouses. There were those with powerful financial European connections who declared that we should enter the war. But one ever present consuming idea guided Hearst—America should not lose herself in the blood madness raging in Europe.

Never was he so much in earnest. His language was as imperious as the declarations of the ancient prophets. No covenant would he make with this perfidious war. If the slaughter went on, it meant poverty, disaster, anarchy in Europe. If America entered the war it would mean poverty, disaster, anarchy for America. When Washington, in his *Farewell Address,* warned the young country to avoid entangling alliances he was the eternally wise statesman. America must remain out of all European wars.

To this battle Hearst was self-dedicated.

CHAPTER XL

BATTLES FOR PEACE

AFTER war broke out in Europe, President Wilson said to his friends, "If Germany wins, it will change the course of our civilization and make the United States a military nation. If the Allies win, Russia will dominate the continent."

The President issued a proclamation urging strict neutrality. He charged the country to refrain from any deed or word that would irritate the warring peoples. So diversified in origin was our population, that it would have been impossible to side with any of the combatants without wounding the feelings of those whose parentage might bind their affections to their homeland. Even as late as September 23, 1914, former President Theodore Roosevelt was neutral when he declared in the *Outlook* that we had not the slightest responsibility for what had befallen Belgium.

Soon it was apparent that belligerents would seek loans in America. First to appear was Germany. American bankers inquired of the Wilson Administration whether the Government would tolerate the making of war loans by Americans to belligerent foreign powers.

Hearst published several editorials approving of the President's response that such a loan "would be inconsistent with the spirit of neutrality." The publisher was glad that Bryan, the pacifist, was the strong arm of the Administration.

When Japan appeared in the European war as an ally of Great Britain, Hearst was greatly perturbed. He saw Europe prostrate, succumbing to possible Asiatic aggression, hastening the end of the white man's civilization.

Hearst sent a cable to Lord Northcliffe of the London *Times*, and to Lord Burnham, publisher of the London *Telegraph,* two of the great forces influencing British public opinion:

Can the war be stopped? I think it can. Both sides must be supremely horrified at the awful death and destruction of modern warfare. . . . I think the press can appeal to the people, to your people, to our people . . . as no other influence can. . . . If it is not stopped, there may be riot and revolution and red anarchy in the centers of government, and the relentless revenge of the masses, resentful of their needless sacrifice. Will the press of England not join the press of America to avert these infinite calamities? Can we not appeal to the people of our country, and the press and people of all countries, to make one mighty, united effort to compel peace and restore happiness to the people of the world?

Hearst received no satisfaction from the English press. The World War was called by him a war of kings. He urged President Wilson to appoint the three most notable men of the nation, Theodore Roosevelt, Taft and Bryan, and send them to Europe empowered to make an immediate peace plea.

Soon Colonel Roosevelt himself swung violently toward England. He demanded that the United States enter the war. He denounced every one who opposed the war, including the President. Wilson was keeping us out of the war. Roosevelt called it a betrayal of civilization. But the people of the United States were with Wilson.

German newspapers urged their armies to spare ancient cathedrals, but a few days after the battle of the Marne, the Cathedral at Rheims was destroyed by German artillery. New horror ran through the Christian world.

Hearst organized peace meetings. One was held in Golden Gate Park, San Francisco. Another filled the Sixty-ninth Regiment Armory, New York City. Everywhere were brilliant flags intermingled with white flags of peace. Madame Schumann-Heink, her great heart ravaged by having sons in both Germany and America, sang Ernest Ball's *Let Us Have Peace.*

Judge Elbert Gary, head of the Steel Trust, was in the chair. He said that fifteen thousand men were being wounded daily, and two thousand five hundred lives were being destroyed. He urged arbitration. Vice-President Marshall spoke against the war. Speaker Champ Clark said that when as a boy he first went to an election in Kentucky he saw four men shot before he got out of town. One was an innocent bystander. "In this World War we are innocent bystanders."

In his address Governor Glynn said, "Woodrow Wilson and William Randolph Hearst stand shoulder to shoulder for the peace of the world." When the audience spied the publisher he received a thunderous demonstration.

Early in the war, President Wilson issued a proclamation urging people to assemble in their accustomed places of worship, to pray that battle-stricken peoples might find peace. But more ghastly atrocity stories came from Europe. Propagandists arrived from England and France to "educate the United States." Ex-President Theodore Roosevelt soon caricatured even his own violent advocacy of war.

In 1915, England began to strangle Germany by shutting off food, and Germany destroyed England's merchant vessels with submarines invented by the Irish-American, John P. Holland. This submarine warfare aided English and French war propaganda.

Stories of German atrocities against women, children, and the aged were circulated. It has since been admitted that the atrocity stories were largely manufactured by the Northcliffe press, who justified their action by what they called their righteous cause. The Allies wished to arouse sufficient hatred in generous, mercurial America to bring the tremendous resources of this country into the war on their side. Hearst vainly warned his readers not to be imposed upon by stories that outrages had been committed upon the helpless, wounded or non-combatants by any of the warring countries.

Embattled European nations placed in this country unprecedented orders for underwear, surgical supplies, motor trucks, horses, canned goods, flour and grain. Factories ran day and night. Housemaids wore silk stockings. Laborers owned silk shirts. The material millennium had arrived. Prayers for peace grew faint.

Emboldened by this apparent prosperity, Senator Henry Cabot Lodge and other Republican leaders fomented an ever increasing war spirit, criticizing the President, opposing his legislation. Theodore Roosevelt declared that the United States should have prevented the German march through Belgium. This country should have blocked the seizure of China's soil. Had he been President, he intimated that the United States would have been in the war.

In an editorial Hearst replied: "A great many other Americans take the same view of the Colonel. . . . Possibly that is why he is not President."

Hearst compared the behavior of Belgium and Luxembourg, two small nations, side by side. Belgium defied Germany to pass. The reigning Duchess of Luxembourg chose not to fight. The army passed. The German Government paid large amounts in cash to Luxembourg for the damaged roads of the country, because of the temporary occupation of the Duchy by the German army. Belgium chose to fight and suffer untold disaster. Hearst complimented Luxembourg's hard-headed good sense, but his papers collected large sums for Belgian relief.

Atrocity stories grew more gruesome. Old men with feet cut off, nuns outraged, mothers gibbeted, babies hacked to pieces, the dead crucified. The more horrible the atrocity tale, the sooner it was believed. Thousands of young Americans crossed the sea and served in the Allied armies. Colonel Theodore Roosevelt thundered against Wilson. When the President's name was mentioned, Roosevelt was like a man obsessed.

Business boomed. Farmers bought automobiles and made the acquaintance of traffic officers. In rural homes Victrolas ground out war songs. Romance-hungry girls joined the Red Cross. War music got into the feet. The nation was singing,

It's a Long, Long Way to Tipperary. Europeans said the battle of America was being fought by them. Americans were yellow, they sneered. "America will not fight." The red rage of war had got into the blood of the world. Men were marching, ever marching, into the underground trenches of death.

In these days Hearst lived at his highest. At times he seemed the only powerful sane man on the mad planet. In all his papers he kept on with his valiant fight to keep America out of the war, and to maintain peace, but always peace grew more remote.

At this time Hearst's minor interests would have exhausted a strong man. He traveled across the continent accompanied by secretaries, dictating dispatches, at every station receiving telegrams. In New York he campaigned against the Bread Trust and had the price of bread reduced to the usual five cents, and saved the city fifty millions annually. In Chicago he campaigned for pure milk, fought for reduction of the cost of lighting, and aided in bringing about the "two platoon" system in the fire department. In San Francisco he contributed his twenty-five thousand profit from the Panama-Pacific Exposition toward the preservation of the beautiful Palace of Fine Arts, and aided in maintaining the building as a living memorial to the inspiring Exposition. In Los Angeles he erected the new *Examiner* Building, at that time the largest building in the world devoted exclusively to the production of a newspaper.

But, Hearst's most intense activity was the battle for peace. In 1915, the United States had become the general provider for Europe. Even the Lord Chief Justice of England came to New York with a commission of financial experts to arrange terms of payment for arms shipped to England. Hearst called upon the Administration to stop shipment of arms. He said that a prayer for peace while the Administration permitted arms to cross the sea was an insult in the ear of God. If the United States wanted the European war prolonged, it was only necessary to supply the ammunition. Europe would supply the men to be butchered.

At the same time England held up more than two hundred American vessels on the sea, declaring cotton contraband. American commerce was being throttled. England was strangling the million-dollar staple industry of the United States by not allowing cotton to be shipped to her foes. This was a distinct violation of the treaty of 1908. Cotton was at the head of the list of articles of commerce exempted in this treaty.

Hearst addressed editorials to the President and urged that England be compelled to lift the contraband decree from cotton. Should England refuse, the United States should permit no other cargo of war munitions to cross neutral seas to fill the guns of England and her Allies. The President set his face like granite against this plea. The contraband decree was not raised. Munitions of war continued to be shipped to England. Men of Wall Street, and manufacturers of weapons of slaughter grew richer. Always wider and deeper flowed the river of blood. It seemed to submerge the entire world.

Early in May, 1915, the German Embassy at Washington warned travelers by newspaper advertisements that they would risk great peril if they took passage on British ships passing through waters declared by Germany to be in the war zone. Some travelers heeded the warning, but more than two thousand, including one hundred Americans of the hazard-loving-sort, set sail on the *Lusitania*. As the giant boat neared England, on May 7, 1915, a torpedo sent one thousand, three hundred and nine human beings to death, and the *Lusitania* was no more. Now would America go in?

President Wilson cut himself off as much as possible from human contact. Most of those surrounding him were for war. Lane, Houston, McAdoo and Redfield thought that the President had no "punch." They were as mad as England; and England, Northcliffe told Ambassador Page, was as mad as hell. Franklin K. Lane in his memoirs revealed the President and his Cabinet as meeting daily with cold, formal conversation. In lonely thought the President moved through the silent corridors of the White House while a nation of one hundred millions awaited his decision. Walter Page, Ambassador to England, bombarded the President with statements of English demands until Wilson ceased reading the Ambassador's messages. What would the President do about the *Lusitania?*

Hearst pointed out that the *Lusitania* was an English naval auxiliary built on admiralty lines, aided by government subsidy, liable for military service. The ship carried contraband articles, and was properly a spoil of war. Cruel and evil as was the destruction of the *Lusitania* with its non-combatant passengers, it was an indictment, not of Germany's war activity, but of war itself. It was wholesale murder.

After the sinking of the *Lusitania,* President Wilson addressed a note to Germany calling upon that country to make reparations and prevent the recurrence of such a deed. Germany offered to respect American rights if England could be compelled to do the same. Against this demand the President stood firm. William Jennings Bryan resigned as Secretary of State. He declared it was unfair to coerce Germany while England went on violating treaties.

Hearst said of Bryan, "Even Mr. Bryan's detractors will not question the sincerity of his devotion."

The jingo Republicans and the jingo politicians clamored for war. Hearst protested, "Not ten sane men in America want to see war with Germany. What sense is there in conduct and speech that might lead to war?"

During the summer of 1915, the head running daily in the Hearst papers was: OUR FIRST DUTY IS TO MAINTAIN PEACE; OUR NEXT DUTY IS TO PREPARE FOR WAR.

Hearst warned that in a world crisis the United States by continuing to send arms and ammunition to warring countries, would find themselves without arms and ammunition:

Where would we get arms to defend ourselves? ... If we were in conflict with England, she controls the seas with her mighty navy, and surely would not allow us to buy them abroad. Mexico will not furnish them. Canada would not furnish them. We would be in the position of poor, incompetent, improvident, impotent

Russia. . . . President Wilson, the only sane and even semi-states-manlike thing to do, is to keep our arms at home. . . . MAKE THE MANUFACTURE OF ARMS IN THIS COUNTRY A GOVERNMENT MONOPOLY. . . . When and thereafter, if we choose to make a few blood-stained dollars by peddling abroad the instruments of slaughter, we can do so in safety if not in honesty and morality.

It seems probable that the phrase, "League of Nations," and the idea itself came from an editorial published by Hearst on July 1, 1915. Entirely as a war measure he gave the following suggestion:

It seems to us that our government is the one government able to suggest and form a LEAGUE OF ALL NEUTRAL NATIONS, an arbitration tribunal composed of representatives of these neutral nations to which our trials with Germany and Great Britain too, might be submitted, as well as any and all matters affecting any and all other neutrals. . . . We think that our government . . . should take immediate steps toward the formation of this LEAGUE OF NEUTRAL NATIONS, and this international board of arbitration.

No League of Neutral Nations was formed. But as late as August 11, 1915, Hearst addressed the following plea to President Wilson:

We make this appeal, Mr. President, with all respect to your high position. . . . It is admitted that we have a right to supply arms to our brother nations who are destroying themselves. We have that right under international law, but have we that right under moral law? . . . The Lord God hath said, "Thou shalt not kill." Does that not mean also, "Thou shalt not help to kill?" The plain fact is that the people of this nation are either in favor of peace, or they are not. If they are in favor of peace, they should be against the supplying of arms to nations engaged in needless, ruthless, purposeless war, when they know that those arms are to be used to increase the murder and destruction of that war. If the people of this country are not in favor of peace, then they should continue to supply arms to the murdering nations and make all the money they can out of murder. . . .

But this paper is in favor of peace, and it believes the people of the United States are in favor of peace. . . . We are not pro-German nor pro-British, Mr. President. . . . We turn to you as the President. . . . Why cannot you supply the just and righteous principle, the civilized principle, the Christian principle, to this matter of the exportation of arms to nations evilly engaged in destroying themselves and the achievements of civilization and Christianity? . . . Mr. President and citizens, let us try to promote peace, and as a preliminary step for the promotion of peace, let us stop the exportation of the implements of war.

But ships went sailing across the sea freighted with death. More silk stockings, more silk shirts, more Victrolas, more automobiles were owned in the United States than since history began. Every one felt like a millionaire.

Among the earliest "scoops" of the Hearst papers during the war was the exposé of the criminal activities of the Captains Boy-ed and von Papen, military and naval attachés of the German Embassy at Washington. Seventeen years later von Papen was to be Chancellor of the German Republic, but the United States Secret Service disclosed that he and Boy-ed spent enormous sums in bribery, instigation of strikes in munition plants and exploding bombs in ships. The New York *American* obtained legal proofs of bribery of American citizens with the design of obtaining false passports for the use of spies sent to this country and to England, and also for facilitating the communication of German secret agents on neutral steamers going between Germany and the United States.

Hearst laid before the United States District Attorney all the evidence obtained, and three dupes of the German agents were convicted. Boy-ed and von Papen escaped. For some months Hearst reporters had difficulty in obtaining news from the German Embassy. After a protest from Hearst, apologies were received from Ambassador von Bernstorff, and reporters were courteously received at the Embassy.

Then the British commission asked for the unprecedented war loan of a billion dollars. The Morgan firm, which was to float the loan, said Hearst, was asking neutral United States to supply four civilized nations of Europe with money and weapons to destroy two other civilized nations. Hearst stood precisely where the Administration did when President Wilson appealed to all Americans to unite in prayer and bring about peace in Europe. With clarity Hearst foresaw the disaster that European war loans would bring to the United States:

Why sacrifice the interest of the country for the benefit of Wall Street? I do not believe that such a loan is for the interest of the country. It is plainly for the special advantage of some financiers who are not noted for considering the interests of this country, or for considering anything but their own profit and benefit.

Over his own signature Hearst wrote in September, 1915:

It is not for the interest of this country to begin lending money to what may be the losing side, and then have to lend more money in the hope of making our first loans good, and finally be overwhelmed in what may be a great financial catastrophe. For, we have not only war in Europe to face, but eventual possible revolution and repudiation. Why send money abroad that we all admit we need here at home? Why sacrifice the interests of this country for the benefit of Wall Street? ...

It is easy to understand why certain big banking houses led by the able and ambitious young Mr. Morgan should want to extend this loan to England. Mr. Morgan is practically an Englishman. He has represented England financially in the United States. He has invested his money with the Allies and he wants to see his investment guaranteed. He is the head of the Steel Trust, and the Steel Trust profits with every gun and shell furnished fighting Europe.

That is the material side of the question. There is the moral side to be considered. ... We have gone into our churches, and in the sanctuaries of our homes and prayed to God to restore peace and revive good-will among men.... God has... made it come to pass that this war cannot continue unless we who prayed for peace shall supply the arms and the money to protract the war.... Shall we go back to our churches and say, "Lord God, we thought we wanted peace ... but we had not estimated the income on the guns and shells to kill our brothers in Europe or the interest on the loan to continue the war.... After we balanced up our books we felt that, like Judas Iscariot, we needed the money."

Citizens of the United States, must we say this?... Let us hope not....

A war loan was made. In October of 1915, the Hearst newspapers printed the advertisement of the five hundred million dollar war loan. In the same issue with the advertisement, run in a "box" at the top of the editorial column, was the following:

This paper disapproves of the loan to prolong the war in Europe and is unwilling to accept any money for advertising such a loan. We do not, however, feel at liberty to deprive our readers of the statement of the American war loan, whether in news, text or advertising. We, therefore, print the advertisement of the loan, but will contribute all the money paid therefor to the Red Cross, in the hope of relieving some of the suffering of the injury that the war loan will inevitably cause.

All of Hearst's intelligence, strength and resources were summoned to preserve the United States from the European struggle. Vainly he quoted Lord Charles Beresford, who said that England would soon be bankrupt if the war went on. He cited the former Lord High Chancellor of England, who warned that unless common sense prevailed England would be little better than a wilderness peopled by old men, women and children. Deaf ears were turned when he declared that war loans would end in the exhaustion and destruction of Europe. Almost alone among the highly placed, Hearst insisted that the United States would render a signal service to the world and benefit itself as well as other nations, by withholding all supplies and all money until negotiations for peace were begun.

Hearst might as well have spoken to the miles of white crosses on the scarlet poppy fields of Europe. More loans were made. The shouting, the recruiting songs, the mad fury of war went on.

CHAPTER XLI

PROTESTS AGAINST ENTERING WAR

WHILE war was devastating Europe and threatening to involve the United States the William Randolph Hearsts were happy because they hoped that a daughter was coming to them. Mrs. Phebe Hearst was especially pleased. She asked that the baby be named Phebe. When the event occurred in New York City, Hearst telegraphed his mother: "Sorry, neither of the boys can be named Phebe."

The twins were named Randolph and David. At first the boys seemed strange to the young mother, like changelings. She was always looking for little Phebe. And so was Mrs. Phebe Hearst. Many years later a little Phebe Hearst did come to the Hearst family. Master George Hearst grew up and married Miss Blanche Wilbur while they were students at the University of California. Their children were twins, George and Phebe. Much of the time of little George and Phebe is passed at San Simeon.

Aside from the birth of the twins, the year of 1916 for Hearst was made up largely of storm and battle. Never did he struggle so hard as he did to keep the country out of war, but nearer and nearer approached the conflict. Vainly he warned his readers that in the wake of the war would follow financial prostration, bankruptcy, revolution and anarchy. He continued to protest against peace-loving Americans subscribing to war loans to create disaster and desolation, but pseudo-prosperity had arrived, and wisdom was silenced by the lure of material things. Thought was benumbed by "two automobiles in every garage." By this time Hearst realized that war would probably come, and he advocated universal military training.

Early in January, a miniature war was fought on Hearst's million-acre Babicora Ranch which sprawls over the mountains at an elevation of seven thousand feet in Chihuahua, Mexico. Diaz, the friend of Hearst, had fallen. The province was terrorized by General José Rodriguez and General Almeida, leaders of a bandit army preying on all of northern Mexico. So powerful were these plundering forces that even the troops of Carranza did not attack them. When they appeared in any community terror reigned.

The Babicora was the scene of several attacks. After property was destroyed, cattle were driven away. Led by Foreman Marquez of the ranch a small army was organized, and one hundred vaqueros gave chase. After following the bandits for one hundred and twenty-five miles the Babicora vaqueros fell upon the outlaws in a surprise attack. Rodriguez and Almeida were captured and executed. Nearly all of their followers were taken prisoner or killed.

On the Babicora Ranch there is a community of more than one thousand, and here were substantial spoils for bandits. Other outlaws returned, and the vaqueros gave battle. When the fighting was over more than twenty of the outlaws had died unshriven. Within a few weeks seventy-five bandits under the leadership of Pedro Castillo and a companion Dominguez, raided Hearst's ranch and made off with their loot in a southern direction. After they had gone one hundred miles twenty-five vaqueros from the Babicora Ranch overtook them and a conflict ensued. Castillo and several of his followers were taken prisoner and turned over to the Mexican garrison. For months the men of Babicora slept on their guns. Many bands of outlaws were fought off by them including those of Francisco Villa.

Because of frequent similar happenings Hearst called upon President Wilson to police Mexico, put down riot and rapine and restore order. Hearst said that no peace could come to Mexico until it was enforced by the United States. The pub-

lisher was accused of trying to bring about intervention in
Mexico in order to protect his property. Hearst replied that
he had his own special officers, but less fortunate American
citizens in Mexico had inadequate means of protecting themselves unless aid was given by our Government. To the great
satisfaction of Hearst, peace was finally restored in Mexico.
From that time he has always opposed troops being sent into
a friendly republic by the United States.

The President permitted ship after ship to sail from the
ports of the United States for Europe, but opinion prevailed
that he would hold the country in the path of peace. People
watched to catch the meaning of every message from the
White House. Many official utterances seemed to indicate that
President Wilson still opposed the war. In February, he wrote
to Senator Stone: "You are right in assuming that I shall do
everything in my power to keep the United States out of the
war. I do not doubt that I shall continue to succeed."

To a delegation of Scandinavians who visited him in March
the President said: "I can assure you that nothing is nearer
my heart than keeping this country out of the war."

When the Democratic Convention assembled President Wilson was renominated by acclamation. Hearst was not enthusiastic about the nomination, because he thought that Wilson
was not sufficiently progressive.

For a few brief moments [wrote Hearst], before the nominating convention of 1912 Mr. Wilson possessed a few radical senti-
ments, but in four years of unrestricted opportunity he put no
radical utterance into actual operation. What has become of
the Presidential primary? What has become of Mr. Wilson's
declarations in favor of the initiative and the referendum? What
has become of the radical provisions of the Democratic platform?
They have all been buried in the crowded cemetery of political
controversy.

At the time of Wilson's second nomination Hearst was
greatly disappointed in the Democratic platform, but he hoped
the President would keep America out of the war.

In June, Hearst attended the Republican Convention in Chicago. There were three conspicuous candidates, Elihu Root, Charles Evans Hughes and Theodore Roosevelt. Hearst was always opposed to Root, because he knew him as the old defender of Tweed. He was indignant that an attorney who made his reputation "protecting rascality and promoting corporation criminality" should be considered for the Presidency of this Republic. Hughes was called by Hearst "exceedingly honest, extremely moral, but not in the least progressive. As Governor of New York his most notable act was the elimination of horse racing. . . . He never put through a single measure to extend popular government. He vetoed a bill for two cents a mile railroad fare, and a bill for five-cent fare from congested New York to Coney Island."

By political heredity Hearst was a Democrat, but he early outgrew party limitations. Now as always he was eager for the creation of a new party without the defects of old organizations. At the time of the Republican Convention he hoped to see progressives gain control of the party machinery. Hearst was in Chicago, and his heart sank as the Republicans jeered down the progressive planks of the initiative, referendum and recall, government ownership and woman suffrage.

In his eagerness to see a Progressive nominated for the Presidency by the Republican Party, Hearst forgot the hostility shown him by Roosevelt. When he met Alice Roosevelt Longworth at the Chicago convention, he asked her to urge her father to come to Chicago. He felt that the ex-President's presence in the convention hall would change the balloting. He sent a message to Roosevelt at Oyster Bay:

I urge you to come to Chicago to use your splendid ability and mighty influence . . . to establish a permanent, patriotic, radical party. . . . Stop wasting your wonderful opportunity and your magnificent energy in an effort to secure the Presidential nomination of the old discredited and discarded Republican Party. . . . If you secure the Republican nomination, you will be defeated because the ultra conservatives would resent you and the radicals would distrust you, and both would vote for Wilson rather than you. Come to Chicago by all means, Mr. Roosevelt, but come to do your real duty, to embrace your true opportunity.... Be loyal and faithful to your highest interests.... Come quickly. Come courageously. Stand boldly for what you know to be right.... Do not waste your time and break your fingers trying to untie the Gordian knot of politics. Cut it through with a sharp sword of determination and decision. Here is the occasion for another Alexander.

Theodore Roosevelt did not go to Chicago. Justice Charles Evans Hughes of the United States Supreme Court was nominated. Concerning the choice of the Republicans Hearst said:

Hughes has the political advantage of being thought to be a Progressive by the confiding masses, and being known to be a reactionary by the privileged classes. He is therefore likely to get the votes of the one and the contributions of the other, and thus may be triumphantly elected.

Hughes began his campaign with a short, masterful letter of acceptance. In 1916, issues and platforms were negligible. There was only one issue, to enter the war or not.

The President did not make any definite promises for the future, but the convention was controlled by a direct wire from the White House. In all nominating speeches it was said that the only way for America to keep out of the war was to reëlect the President. The Democratic slogan during the campaign was: "Wilson kept us out of the war."

The President was reëlected by the votes of fathers and mothers, who thought they were saving their sons from battle and death. His majority was substantial. Hearst commented on the election results:

Mr. Hughes is so much more of a reactionary that Mr. Wilson seems a satisfying Progressive by comparison. I am always glad to see the more progressive candidate win.

Hearst was especially gratified because California, the State where his newspapers had the largest circulation per capita, was pivotal in the election. He rejoiced because no matter whether the Progressives called themselves Republicans or Democrats, they were in an overwhelming majority.

The cause of the Progressives is not lost.... The hull can be kept afloat until the battle is over, until the port of safety can be reached, and the good ship renewed for another campaign.

Hearst's nine papers beat out a daily protest against the conduct of the war. The publisher attacked England not only for her embargo on cotton, but for the abstraction of American mail from neutral steamers on the high seas. British naval officers inspected all mail between the United States and the continent. Diplomatic pouches were taken from neutral steamers, sent to London and held for weeks. Thousands of important communications belonging to American merchants were destroyed, "reducing," as Hearst wrote, "international law not only to a scrap of paper, but to a scrap heap of paper."

Several times Secretary of State Lansing declared that the United States would not permit British violations of international law on the ground of military necessity. Hearst backed up Lansing, and he insisted upon printing the news. In the New York *American* were published stories and pictures of the sinking of the British dreadnaught *Audacious* off the Irish coast. Publication of this news enraged the British censors. The Northcliffe press in London and the Manchester *Guardian* denounced British censorship, but they were not allowed to record military happenings.

Hearst was greatly disturbed by the execution of Sir Roger Casement, the Irish patriot, and his publication of that tragic event and the riots following caused the International News Service and the Hearst newspapers to be excluded by the British Government from the privileges of the cables and mails. On October 9, 1916, a statement was issued by the British Government to the effect that the "International News Service was debarred from the use of mails and cables because it had garbled and distorted the news."

When the Hearst papers were banned by the British censor, the publisher wired J. J. Harris of the International News Service:

I will apologize for nothing, retract nothing, alter nothing. Instead of discharging editors, I would rather raise their salary wherever I find they have honestly and earnestly endeavored to sift the facts out of the mass of misrepresentation which the English censors impose upon this country. The act of the English censors is wholly unjust and unjustifiable. At first I believed that their attitude was based on some actual error of importance in our news service. But I find on careful investigation that the couple of items on which they base their claim were so frivolous as to prove the claim absurd and insincere. I am satisfied that the exclusion of the International News Service is not due to any delinquency on its part, nor on the part of the Hearst papers, but is due to the independence and wholly truthful attitude of the Hearst papers in their news and editorial columns. Therefore, I have nothing to retract or alter in the slightest degree. On the contrary, I wish to assure the English censorship and the English government that the Hearst publications will continue to pursue the same independent course that they have been pursuing, with redoubled conviction of the truth, justice and propriety of that course.

During the month of November, 1916, Hearst learned that his papers were barred from circulation in Canada. If any one was found with one of his papers in his possession a fine not exceeding five thousand dollars, or imprisonment for a term not exceeding five years, or both fine and imprisonment were liable to be imposed. Hearst was put to some inconvenience by these orders of the British Government, but the policy of his papers was unchanged and circulation increased. All restrictions upon cables or mail by the British Government were removed on April 24, 1918.

Before America entered the war the Hearst papers were also excluded from the use of the French cables. Information of this occurrence arrived in the middle of the night. Colonel Joseph

Willicombe, Hearst's secretary, recalls well the bewilderment
of Managing Editor Caleb Van Ham of the New York *American,* when the news arrived. Van Ham did not know what to
do. Willicombe has one unvarying order from his employer.
The Chief must never be awakened for good news. Good news
can wait. Bad news requires immediate attention. Willicombe
knows more about Hearst and what he desires, than any living
person. He acted.

When the news of losing the French cable was given Hearst,
he received it with the same poise that he accepts all difficulties.
On the telephone he dictated an editorial and he wrote the
beginning of the news article to go in all his papers. Then he
went to sleep.

While under the ban of England and France, Hearst contin-
ued to employ the most illustrious foreign writers such as
Rudyard Kipling, Sir Gilbert Parker, Sir Arthur Conan Doyle,
Sir Hiram Maxim, Arnold Bennett, George Bernard Shaw,
Hall Caine, Israel Zangwill, and Mrs. Humphrey Ward.
France was represented by Jean Finot, Jules Bois, Pierre Loti,
Edmond Rostand, Maurice Maeterlinck, Gabriel Hanotaux,
former Minister of Finance, and M. Viviani, later Premier of
France. Italian accounts of the war were given by Gabriele
d'Annunzio, and Guglielmo Ferrero, the distinguished Italian
historian. Hearst had the best and the most authoritative news
from all belligerents. He published four thousand columns of
articles about Germany and ten thousand about the Allies.

Hearst criticized an advertising agency for saying that a
"newspaper should give the American people what they want."
He said that he spared no effort, no thought, no time to get and
print, not only that which is best, but that which is recognized
as best in literature and art:

We have gotten it for the most part exclusively, so that not
only could the best be found in our periodicals, but could be
found nowhere else. Does this look as if I failed to appreciate the
high quality of American taste? ...

In reply to your question, "Was it an editor who gave us Shakespeare or Milton or Goethe or Dumas?" I must say that no editor created them. But if Shakespeare or Milton or Goethe or Dumas were writing to-day, our editors would proceed promptly to secure their writings for our periodicals and exclusively for our periodicals.... Every blundering incompetent, every crass vulgarian who has ever produced an unworthy publication, has apologized for it by saying that he was "only giving the public what it wants."...

The public taste is high, and is constantly being educated to a still higher standard. I have never been able to understand the point of view of some publicists who think they have to write or edit down to the level of public taste. I have never seen an editor who did not have to do his utmost to edit up to the public taste, and after he has done his utmost, there is always a possibility that he had not a sufficiently high standard of excellence. The best editor is the editor who produces the best publication, and the best publication in these days of cultivated public taste eventually and inevitably receives the widest public support and approval. An editor is no bigger than his public. But he must be as big as his public. He must be as big as his opportunity. The public appreciates all that is best in literature and art, in selected paper and perfected writing, but it cannot be appreciative of these things until it sees them....

Good stories, good pictures, perfection of material in mechanical production, do not merely happen in a magazine. All these things do not drop off trees into the lap of an editor while he is asleep. If the editor wants the best for his publication, he must go out and by force of arms wrest it from some other editor and bring it home in triumph for the delectation of his own special clientèle.

An editor must be judicious, discriminating. He must exercise a nice taste, and must cultivate a suggestive and creative faculty. ...He must give the public the best that is in ourselves as well as the best that is in others. Let us give what we have to say in the clearest and most comprehensive manner. Give the public what is best, and what is universally recognized as best by all discerning and discriminating minds.

CHAPTER XLII

THE UNITED STATES IN WORLD WAR

IN 1917, Hearst was called upon by the late Judge John F. Hylan, who asked aid in his candidacy for Mayor. For several years the publisher had noticed the decisions of Judge Hylan. They were conspicuously fair, and had the ring of the early leaders of democracy. Hearst had quoted them in editorials, but until Hylan called, the publisher and the Judge had not met. When Hearst was asked for his support by Hylan he answered, "If you think you can be as good a Mayor as you have been a Judge, my papers will be with you." Hylan said he would try.

Hearst was attracted by Hylan's typically American story; the poor farm boy reading nights, going to New York a laborer; again night study, this time engineering. Hylan became a locomotive engineer. More night study, and he was a lawyer. Hylan conducted the cases of the poor for nothing, went into politics and became a Judge. Hearst made Hylan's campaign and elected him Mayor.

For eight years Hylan was Mayor of New York, and he always had the support and friendship of Hearst. He said that he admired the publisher because Hearst was the only university-bred, rich American, who understood and sympathized with the masses, and battled to protect their rights. Once Hylan and Hearst were in the Waldorf-Astoria dining-room. Looking in at the window was a poorly clad and plainly hungry man. Hearst sent a waiter to fetch the stranger into the dining-room. The man was allowed to order anything he might desire.

On another occasion Hearst and Hylan were traveling in the West and the train stopped. Looking out of the window Hylan saw that there was something wrong with the engine. He went forward to investigate.

"My friend," he said to the engineer, "your driving brakes are jammed down. Back a little and release them, then go ahead."

"By golly, I believe you're right," said the engineer, looking Hylan over. "But who are you?"

"I'm a locomotive engineer."

The engineer followed Hylan's suggestion, and the train moved forward.

Little incidents such as these bound the two men together despite their dissimilar backgrounds.

During the early months of 1917, Hearst continued to demand that the United States refuse to deliver food, funds or arms to any country which insisted upon the protraction of the war. But peace receded on the horizon of America. The war party grew larger. Chanting the hymn of hate were investors who had bought Anglo-French bonds, manufacturers who had sold enormous quantities of supplies to the Allies, the National Security League made up of Eastern capitalists, the old Navy League, many partisan Republicans, and those who loved excitement and an orgy of blood.

At the head of all these forces was ex-President Roosevelt eager to reënact his Spanish War youth by leading the army to France, and then to return to the White House. In a telegram to the New York *World* Hearst said:

I think the President fully realizes that advice from blusterers like Roosevelt is neither serious nor sincere, and furthermore, the man who plunged the country into the worst financial panic of a generation is just the kind of a man who would advise plunging the country into the cataclysm of the World War. I think it is the solemn duty of all loyal citizens to stand solidly back of the President in his efforts to maintain peace.

Several times in 1916, President Wilson was rebuffed in an effort to bring about peace. When the Bolsheviks made public the secret treaties of England and France with Russia, Italy and Japan, by which in advance the spoils of war were divided, it was clear why those countries would listen to no proposal of peace from the President.

In private, President Wilson said he did not wish either side to win. England had the world, and Germany wanted it. England had been ruthless in taking the property of neutrals; Germany had been brutal in taking the life of neutrals. Now the President did what ex-President Roosevelt had done during the Russo-Japanese War. Roosevelt called it "interfering before the knockout blow."

On January 22, 1917, President Wilson went before the Senate and proposed to the world peace without victory, the right of nationality, the right to liberty and self-government, independence of Poland, freedom of the seas, reduction of armaments, abolition of entangling alliances.

The President spoke to deaf ears. More bloodshed was demanded by the war party in all countries. Germany renewed submarine warfare. A hurricane of war swept across the ocean and six American vessels were destroyed. The New York Port stopped the sailing of all ships.

England had blockaded Germany. Now the Kaiser planned to starve England. Hearst wrote:

The seriousness of the situation demands soberness of speed and action.... We are profoundly hopeful that our peace can be maintained.... Mr. Wilson's judgment, his foresight, his statesmanship are equal to the problems of avoiding war, if it can be avoided. ...But if it be his lot to find no other way to walk in honor, except with a sword in hand—which God forbid—then we will all walk loyally in that way with him. And as this paper has always been neither pro-Teuton nor pro-Ally, but always earnestly and with whole heart American, so it will continue to be....If we must fight, let us fight our own war, for our own rights, with our own men, under our own President and under our own flag. ...Let us firmly resolve that under no circumstances will we waste our wealth and slaughter our youth in the wars of foreign alliances.

In a despatch to his New York papers March 2, 1917, Hearst said:

I believe in war, if the people want war. They have to do the fighting. I believe, first, in a referendum to the people, and failing that, a decision by the people's representatives in Congress assembled.

About this time the *Vossische Zeitung*, Berlin, cabled Hearst for an interview on the attitude of the United States toward the war, and he replied:

I believe that the majority of the people in the United States are entirely undesirous of war with Germany. I believe also that the people of Germany are equally undesirous of war with the United States.... Americans have been taught from childhood to regard both Germany and France as their proven friends. We therefore deplore the war between these nations which have contributed so much to the progress and civilization of the world. We earnestly desire to employ the influence of our country, not for the extension and protraction of war, but for promotion of just and lasting peace.

Again in the New York *American*, Hearst opposed the war loan:

Of what use are the I. O. U.'s of the bankrupt? Uncle Sam is buying a gold brick. He has been sold a satchel full of green goods in return for his hard-earned property. We are reveling in mock prosperity and shall find the sheriff at our doors.

And why are we wasting our wealth?... To continue a carnival of murder, to prolong an era of overwhelming disaster, to encourage the destruction of the white race, to tear down the achievements of civilization which has taken ages to construct, to repudiate religion and violate all established standards of decency, morality and righteousness, to prostitute the world to the meanest and basest of purposes. If we persist in doing this we will deserve a heavy penalty which will surely fall upon us.

Let us end these shipments of food and ammunitions to the warring nations of Europe for their sakes and ours.... Let us end the war and the wastage of war.

Vainly Hearst wrote and spoke. Families of international social position who spent half their time in Europe, returned with tales of how unpopular and discredited Americans were abroad for remaining out of the war. If the strongest man is he who stands most alone, then Hearst was the strongest man in the United States. Of all living Americans of his wealth and position, he was most alone, as alone as was LaFollette in the Senate who was denouncing England and declaring that the Administration had not pursued impartial neutrality toward England and Germany. Hearst insisted that the Administration would not dare call for a war referendum, for it would be defeated ten to one. On this isolated peak of righteousness Hearst did not feel lonely. Abuse and calumny did not touch him.

On his return trip from California, Hearst was met in Utah by a messenger bearing a round-robin signed by his ablest executives. They said that if he did not alter his attitude on the war, they would resign. The corners of Hearst's lips curved upward in his most boyish smile as he answered, "Sorry, I hate to lose good men." He did not lose the executives, and he never held it against them, because swept along with the madness of the moment they tried to force him into the war.

When one of his editors behaved with disloyalty and publicly placed Hearst in the wrong, it was assumed by the General Manager of the organization that the Chief would immediately dismiss the editor.

"Mr. Hearst," he said, "whom shall I get to take Blank's place?"

Hearst was surprised. "Why should I dismiss an able man because he can't help being a liar?"

Another employee was discovered in graft and dishonesty. He was transferred to a position where Hearst thought he could still be of use. "I think he'll be all right now, he knows I'm watching him." Hearst smiled, "You must trust somebody, unless you intend to spend all your time distrusting people."

Even in this trying year of 1917, when executives sent Hearst the ultimatum, he purchased two more newspapers, the Washington *Times*, and the Boston *Daily Advertiser*. Now he had eleven daily voices. In 1921, the Boston *Record*, which was established in 1844, was bought by him and combined with the *Advertiser*, one of Boston's oldest papers, founded in 1813. The *Advertiser* was merged with the *Record* on May 18, 1921. Its Sunday rights were consolidated with the Boston *Sunday American*, and the two papers were issued as the Boston *Sunday Advertiser*. The new *Advertiser* became a tabloid, and in 1929, its name was changed to the *Record*.

During the excitement preceding the war, certain Congressmen charged that some American newspapers were subsidized to support the Allies. Hearst wrote to his editors:

Please make vigorous denials denouncing those ignorant Congressmen who accused any newspaper of being subsidized to support the Allies and to promote war with Germany. Even any moderately informed person knows that this charge is as absurd as it is outrageous.

The standards of newspaper ethics are the highest of any business or profession in the world, certainly higher than the ethics of politicians who are for the most part lawyers. A lawyer will take a fee to represent any side of the case, ... but no newspaper man of any position would be influenced directly or indirectly by money or by favor ... to do or advocate anything that he did not believe to be right.

There are some black sheep in every profession, and there are some in the newspaper profession, like the unspeakable thing who posed as a war correspondent in Germany and sold himself to Northcliffe as a paid spy; or like those conscienceless reporters who peddled tips to stock speculators from news received in confidence for the legitimate information of their newspapers. . . . These are isolated incidents. . . . The bigger men in the profession have the most exalted view of the ethics and duty of their business. . . .

After the astounding Zimmermann note to the German representative in Mexico revealed that Germany would make an alliance with Mexico and Japan and partition the United States among the conquerors, Hearst realized that war was inevitable. He had always dreaded Japan's covetous eye on the Pacific coast. Now he visualized the United States set back one hundred years to a period before the Mexican War. In an editorial in the New York *American,* he said:

Citizens, prepare! The hours are short, the days are few in which you may make your defence. The indications of the impending struggle are plain. The time of our supreme national test is fast approaching.

In February, Ambassador von Bernstorff received his passport. On March 3rd, Hearst wrote that we faced the gravest situation ever encountered by the United States. It was the duty of the new Congress to provide universal military training. The day before war was declared Hearst said in an article that the conduct of the conflict should be dictated by President Wilson. "Many counselors are good in time of peace, but undivided authority and responsibility are necessary in war."

Probably no one will ever know the crucial circumstance which caused President Wilson to plunge the United States into conflict. Many forces swayed Wilson, but according to Colonel House, the President himself desired to play a masterful rôle on the international stage by launching the United States into war.

On the evening of April 2, 1917, Wilson became the world leader, and a new era in the United States began. The Sixty-fourth Congress was drawing to a close. President Wilson left the White House for the House of Representatives, passing through crowded streets. White searchlights revealed the Stars and Stripes floating in the breeze under the clear blue sky. Two troops of United States Cavalry in dress uniform guarded the entrance to the House of Representatives. Thousands cheered the arrival of the President's automobile at 8:30. Each Senator carried a red, white, and blue handkerchief as the Senate walked slowly from the north end of the House to the Capitol.

The Supreme Court came, all the United States Government, and diplomats, to listen to the President, nervous and pale.

Fewer than fifteen hundred persons heard his address, but the House of Representatives was filled. The President's fingers trembled as he turned the pages of his message and in a low tone, spoke. Benumbed by the impressiveness of the occasion, the audience remained silent until he uttered these words:

There is one choice we cannot make, we are incapable of making; we will not choose the path of submission and suffer the most sacred rights of our nation and our people to be ignored, or violated. The wrongs against which we now array ourselves are no common wrongs; they cut to the very roots of human life....

Spontaneous applause came from the listeners.

Four days later on April 6, 1917, President Wilson declared to the world a state of war against the Imperial German Government. George Creel, a close friend of the President and later the head of the Board of Public Information, accompanied the President to the Capitol and back to the White House after war had been declared. He says that President Wilson was so greatly moved that when he reached the White House he buried his face in his hands and wept.

But whistles were blown in the navy yards and throughout the national capital. They were caught up throughout the nation. Hearst was heartsick, but he desired his country to carry the Stars and Stripes proudly, serenely forward to the redemption of the affairs of mankind. He wondered whether the star of Ameria had sunk below the horizon.

Pictures of the President surrounded by flags in colors appeared on the first pages of Hearst's papers. An army of a million men was suggested by him, the largest increase that could be made in the navy, innumerable air- and sea-planes, increase in the supply of food, and above all universal service. Every man and woman must serve in some capacity, in fields, factories, arsenals, at forges, or bearing arms. There was a task for each in the winning of peace.

At first many Congressmen and Senators opposed conscription. Representative Claude Kitchin, the Democratic leader of the House, declined to introduce the Universal Service Bill. Speaker Champ Clark also publicly condemned conscription. Hearst went to Washington and personally interceded with his old friend, Speaker Clark, urging him to desist from his opposition to Universal Service. In the Washington *Post* Hearst published a four-column signed article:

Gentlemen of the Congress of the United States who put us into this war, it is your duty now to give us sufficient means of making war. If the folks at home did not want you to go to war, it was your duty to think of that before you declared war. It is in no way right or reasonable or wise or patriotic for you to project the Nation into war, and then in unfounded fear for your own future, deny the Nation the method best qualified and calculated to make victorious war.

Hearst pointed out that Jefferson, the great pacifist, opposed the draft, but in the war of 1812, he advocated universal service. He also declared that without universal service at the beginning of the war, France would have ceased to exist as a nation.

All the Hearst papers published a petition for universal service. Within a week one million and a half signatures were on their way to Washington. Another million soon followed. Representative Kahn of California presented the first instalment of signatures to Congress. The Selective Draft Act was passed, and when Hearst heard the news, he shouted, "Hurrah!"

In order to aid recruiting, Hearst erected stations in the principal cities in the Union. More than half the enlistments in New York City were made at the New York *American* station. Hearst imported the official French film production, *Fighting in France,* to quicken war interest. He caused the French cinema to be exhibited in the best theaters in the United States, and gave the profits to the charitable societies of France, England, Italy, Serbia, Belgium, and other Entente Allies. He distributed hundreds of thousands of copies of President Wilson's speech, printed in color, in which he declared war. He devoted three thousand columns in his papers to the free promotion of Liberty Loans, but he asserted that the untaxable Liberty Loan was unfair because it placed the burden of taxation upon active productive capital and allowed non-productive capital to escape. He printed thousands of colored posters, placarding them throughout the United States and supplying them free to the Liberty Loan committees. When the Red Cross drive was on, Hearst directed all his papers to give their editorial pages for six weeks to articles and cartoons for the Red Cross printed in two colors. Extra pressmen and extra color-cylinders were required. The editions published exceeded four million copies daily, and were issued at the expense of one hundred and fifty thousand dollars.

Hearst personally and the members of his staff subscribed for more than a million, four hundred thousand dollars' worth of Liberty Bonds. During the first six months of the war, one hundred and thirty-three men from Hearst's New York papers entered the army and navy. Under the second draft many registered. Five died in service, and a score of men were wounded.

In the early months of the war Hearst opposed the Espionage Bill on the ground that it was only the Alien and Sedition Act in another form. He urged no censorship beyond news of military and naval value to the enemy. Hearst recommended Herbert Hoover for Food Director, and the appointment was made.

Since his early days on the San Francisco *Examiner*, Hearst had opposed the saloon and the sale of whisky. Once he said to an editor, "You can't do me a better service than to have a daily editorial against whisky. I want my sons to carry on the fight after I am gone." He advised all his publishers that whisky advertisements, and advertising of ardent liquors were to be rejected. In this order Hearst included whisky advertisements masquerading as medicine. Soon after the war began,

Hearst rejoiced when he thought he saw the doom of the whisky traffic. In the Universal Service Bill before the Senate there was a bone-dry army clause that he felt would end the traffic in brandy, gin, and rum in the United States. In each issue of the Hearst papers appeared a temperance petition to be signed and sent to Congress. Hearst pointed out that while there was whisky in the land it would be sold to soldiers. It was as great a menace as any foreign foe. Hearst had editorials of rejoicing when the saloons were no more.

Never was there such power given any President as that wielded by Woodrow Wilson. Despairingly a United States Senator lamented: "We haven't a President, we have a King." In truth, the President, with the consent of Congress, fixed prices for commodities, distributed necessities, took possession of mines, factories, packing houses, steamships and railways.

In these new functions of government, Hearst saw the realization of policies for which he had always battled, government control of railroads, and regulations of trusts. Hearst hoped that the railroads especially would never return to "all-the-traffic-will-bear" private ownership. He expressed this hope in an editorial: "Sixty-nine of the seventy-eight nations in the world operate their own railroads. How long are we to remain behind?"

Hearst also hoped that now the trusts would be controlled by the Government. The price-fixing power granted to President Wilson by Congress in September of 1918 was a fulfilment of a prophecy made by Hearst at the age of thirty-six when he wrote:

We are advancing towards a complete organization of which the Government will be the head. It will be the trust of trusts.... When a productive business affecting the life and welfare of the community becomes sufficiently organized to fix the price of its product, it is undoubtedly right, and it will undoubtedly become the duty of the Government to interfere on behalf of the consuming public.

Later Hearst added: "No one believes that having been adopted as a war measure, price-fixing will ever be wholly abandoned in the days of peace that are to come."

During the summer of 1917, the Kaiser was still the great Wilhelm on the throne of Frederick the Great. Arrogantly he declared that there should be no peace without annexation and indemnity. Hearst immediately telegraphed his papers that this declaration should cause the Kaiser to lose his throne. He said that the United States went into the war in spite of the fact that the Democratic President and the Democratic Congress were elected on a pledge of peace. We must genuinely democratize the Teutonic powers and the Allies. He urged peace without annexation or indemnity:

Such peace can probably be secured within a reasonable time by pressure brought to bear by the United States on the various combatants, while a peace of aggression and aggrandizement can only be secured after years of war in which millions of young Americans, the pride and promise of our country, will lose their lives. . . . I deeply desire to see Belgium and France freed from German occupation. . . . I sincerely and firmly believe that peace without annexation or indemnity is the best terms that the Allies can get under the present distressing conditions, and that if they do not take these terms now, they cannot get as good later.

Hearst deplored the wastage and woe of war, the destruction of the best specimens of the human race and he asked:

How long before the Government will be changed here? . . . How long before Socialism will take the place of democracy? . . . I am not considering myself or my properties. I am thinking of our . . . splendid young men who should not die on foreign battlefields but should live and labor here to preserve at home and to bestow abroad the conditions of liberty and enlightenment, of peace and prosperity which we have made for our country. . . . If it is commendable for our nation to be in this war without selfish purposes, it is desirable for other nations to be in it with purposes unselfish and altruistic as our own. And surely it is desirable and commendable for citizens of any country ... to urge peace without victory which our President himself lately urged ... which the Russian democrats demand, and which I dare to hope the rest of the world will accept.

At that time Russia was a new democracy, and that country alone agreed with President Wilson's lofty proposals of peace without indemnity or annexation. Hearst urged that the United States and Russia agree that they together would fight Germany so long as the Kaiser insisted upon annexation or indemnity of any character. Russia and the United States should together cease fighting if Germany would abandon her terms of annexation and aggression, even if England insisted upon carrying on the conflict:

Hearst said, that the "United States alone out of her great wealth could restore France and rebuild Belgium at a lesser cost, whatever it might be, than the cost of war, and with a saving of the priceless lives of her sons."

Hearst besought the United States to demonstrate the peace and virtue of democracy, to glorify it in the minds and to enthrone it in the hearts of all the peoples of the world. For the sake of humanity, and for their own sake, all belligerents should accept President Wilson's wise and just peace terms.

Former President Theodore Roosevelt talked and wrote day and night against the President. His conduct was fairly representative of that of the regular Republican leaders. Hearst had opposed our entering the war, but after we had joined the Allies, and he declared for peace with no indemnity or annexation, his popularity in fashionable circles was at its lowest. Now, since the world sees the unhappiness and disaster that befell America for entering the war, he appears as the most farsighted man in a position of great power at that time in the United States. He says that frequently he is right at the wrong time, and his attitude on the war is a conspicuous example of that tendency.

In war time it was the vogue to be bloodthirsty and militaristic. All those proposing peace were called pro-German. During the campaign for the reëlection as Mayor of the late John F. Hylan, Hearst was frequently accused of being pro-German, and so was Hylan. One of the slogans of the Republicans was, "A vote for Hylan is a vote for Germany." Slanderous stories reflecting on the loyalty of Hylan and Hearst were concocted and circulated.

About this time it was discovered in Paris that Bolo Pasha, part owner of *Le Journal,* was in the pay of Germany. Eager to reëlect Mitchel, defeat Hylan, and destroy Hearst, the political scandal-mongers of New York broadcast that when Bolo Pasha had been in New York eighteen months previously, Captains Boy-ed and von Papen, and Hearst had met Ambassador von Bernstorff at the publisher's residence, and that Hearst had attended a secret dinner at Sherry's given by Bolo Pasha. It was even said that Hearst had a secret exit from his apartment house, the Clarendon, by which the Germans made their departure.

Hearst published Bolo's background. The Parisian journalist was a brother of Monsignor Bolo, a distinguished French prelate of the Roman Catholic church. A large fortune had been made by him in the Far East where he obtained the title of Pasha. He was co-owner with Senator M. Humbert of the Paris *Journal,* and was introduced to Hearst by Charles F. Bertelli, representative in Paris of the International News Service. Bertelli made a steamer acquaintance with Bolo on his way to New York and quite naturally fraternized with him as the proprietor of an important French newspaper. Hearst did not dine secretly with Bolo, but met him at dinner in a public dining-room at Sherry's together with Jules Bois, the well-known lecturer; Julian Gerard, brother of Ambassador Gerard; Carr Van Anda, Managing Editor of the New York *Times;* Mrs. Van Anda; Owen Johnson; C. F. Bertelli; and Adolph Pavenstedt and others. During the dinner Bolo Pasha told Hearst he was having difficulty in obtaining print paper for his Paris *Journal,* and he desired to have a talk with him about procuring a supply from America. Three or four days later Bolo Pasha called at Hearst's residence on Riverside Drive to ascertain how he could get print paper in this country. Hearst and he chatted for a time. The publisher gave his visitor a letter to the principal paper manufacturers.

After Bolo Pasha was revealed as a spy in Paris, it developed that he had distributed much money in the United States. He had even bought a daily paper in New York City. The J. P. Morgan Company and the Royal Bank of Canada had handled more than a million, seven thousand dollars of the spy's money without investigating who he was.

"If anybody was to blame in this whole situation," wrote Hearst, "it was the House of Morgan and Company, whose duty it was to know something about the source and use of the money which they were handling in war time."

The so-called secret escape from Hearst's Clarendon apartment which had sounded to the public thrillingly melodramatic and pro-German proved to be a fire escape. The attempt to brand Hearst and Hylan as pro-German, failed. Hylan was reëlected. Hearst hoped that the Bolo Pasha matter was over, but the propaganda against him continued. The publisher was made aware of this hostility while in a New York restaurant. A strange woman hissed at him, "*Boche!*"

Courteously Hearst removed his hat, made a low bow and said, "You're right, Madam. It is all bosh."

CHAPTER XLIII

WAR PERSECUTION

NAPOLEON is said to have invented modern publicity, but even he never developed it to such a degree as it was used in the United States in 1917 and 1918 when the Government was "selling the war" to America. Children, women, teachers, motion-picture houses, theaters, industrial plants, banks and churches combined to force each issue of bonds "over the top." Women sang, urging the public to buy. People were besought to "buy until it hurt." Pictures of bloody hands of Huns were shown on the advertisements of war bonds. Speakers shouted, "Wipe out the Huns." Blocks and blocks of bonds were sold—twenty-three and a half billions! People who refused to buy were black-listed and enrolled in the Department of Justice as traitors.

Any criticism of the Wilson Administration was made illegal in May 1918 by the Sedition Act. Newspapers were silenced. Several Senators told Hearst that his own papers were under consideration as disloyal. Critics of the war, or of the Wilson program, were sent to jail. Some were held without bail, and in one case an adolescent girl was sent to prison for several years. Long lists of citizens were branded as traitors by a nation-wide spy system with thousands of employees and millions of money. Spies were planted among organizations of humble working people, and instructed to incite them to unlawful acts. Two hundred thousand private citizens were enrolled by the Department of Justice to inform against their neighbors. Extra pennies were turned by many who became keyhole listeners. Teachers were dismissed and professors were expelled from universities. Clergymen were sent to prison. The war made an excuse for people to get even with their enemies. Salem, 1692, was once more in America.

When Hearst criticized the conduct of the war as Northcliffe did in England, people remembered the struggle he had made to keep the United States out of the conflict, and called out against him, "pro-German." It did not enhance his popularity that he urged the recognition of Russia.

In 1918, Hearst wired the editor of the *American:*

Why are we in this war? We are in it for democracy. Then, for heaven's sake, why not recognize a democratic government? We recognized the imperial government of Russia, but when Russia secures a democratic government we have so far not recognized it. Does not this seem to discredit our professions of war for democracy? If the imperialistic government of Russia could be restored, we would not hesitate to recognize that. . . . We must not lose the ideals of war. We must not lose the opportunities of war, because if we do, we will lose the war—as far as our American objects are concerned. . . . Let us recognize the truest democracy in Europe, the truest democracy in the world to-day.

One long stride toward democracy was at this time made in the United States, women were given suffrage. Horace Greeley had called woman suffrage a "logically defenseless abstraction that would not be deserved by women until they freed themselves from the thraldom of etiquette." When the constitutional amendment of woman suffrage was before the Senate, Hearst advised that body "to confer credit upon yourselves and upon your country by passing the woman's suffrage amendment to-day." The voice of the President aided, and with the passage of the amendment all women builders of civilization triumphed—spinners, weavers, soap-makers, candle dippers, factory workers, teachers, housewives and mothers. There were Abby Kelley standing for free speech; Sarah and Angelina Grimke, for freedom of slaves; Lucy Stone for education; Elizabeth Blackwell, the right to practice medicine; Antoinette L. Brown, the right to be a minister; Susan B. An-

thony, the right to vote; and valiant Alice Paul and her followers besieging the gates of the White House finally to open
them in victory. In 1875, Susan B. Anthony had drafted the
suffrage amendment. It was ratified August 18, 1920, a day
of glory for women.

In 1918, Hearst launched a movement for rebuilding and
rehabilitating the ruined villages of France. On the committee
to supervise the reconstruction of the devastated cities were
Mayor John F. Hylan, Cardinal Gibbons, Governor Charles S.
Whitman, Senator James W. Wadsworth, James W. Gerard,
Mrs. William Randolph Hearst and Madame Sarah Bernhardt.

Vice-President Thomas R. Marshall wrote to Hearst: "Like
the returned exiles to Jerusalem, we fight with sword in one
hand and a trowel in the other. While we wage war against injustice we spread the cement of brotherly love in kindness and
in building homes."

At this same time, Marshal Foch sent a letter of thanks to
Hearst for the large edition of the San Francisco *Examiner*
published on July 14, 1918, commemorating the fall of the
Bastille. Madame Sarah Bernhardt, who was in San Francisco
for the last time, posed for the picture of the woman holding
aloft the French flag, printed in the red, white and blue of
France.

During the war, Mrs. William Randolph Hearst suffered
under the attacks made on her husband's loyalty, but it was
at this time that her public activities became noteworthy.
Mayor Hylan appointed Mrs. Hearst chairman of the Mayor's
Committee of Women on National Defense. This position included activities in emergency relief and civic aid. Immediately
Mrs. Hearst established in convenient localities canteens where
food was served by volunteer workers for army and navy re-
cruits, overseas men and officers. In the Edison Building were
a rest-room and a library for enlisted men, and at Forty-second
Street and Fifth Avenue were the officers' headquarters. Here
also were sold Liberty Bonds. At this time, Mrs. Hearst was
chairman of the Distinguished Guest Committee, and she as-

sisted in planning receptions for American and foreign visitors.

While engaged in civic work, Mrs. Hearst's attention was arrested by the large number of undernourished children in New York. She became the founder and president of the Free Milk Fund for Babies, Inc. Through her financial aid and personal efforts from 1918 to 1936 more than seven million quarts of milk have been supplied to undernourished and sick babies in their homes. During summer months pasteurized milk is dispensed from milk booths to anæmic children in the congested areas.

At the beginning of the depression, the Millicent Hearst Emergency Fund paid the rent of one hundred of the neediest families in Manhattan for one year. In 1931, under the auspices of the Free Milk Fund for Babies, free hospitality tents were opened where coffee and sandwiches were served to unemployed men and women. During two years nearly seven hundred thousand visitors were aided.

In January, 1933, Mrs. Hearst established a clothing center where needy families made their wants known and were supplied with wearing apparel. She gave aid not only to individuals, but she took part in procuring social welfare laws for the good of women and children. She was one of those who aided the enactment of the bill creating the Child Welfare Board in New York, which made it possible for widowed mothers to keep their children at home instead of confining them in institutions.

Among the obnoxious by-products of the war, were suspicious citizens who saw a German plot in the way that the neighbors hung out the washing, and who never took a car ride without discovering German spies behind the trolley post. Mrs. Hearst found these super-patriots in her house one day when she entered the library and discovered the new butler rummaging among the family papers. She reported the matter to Mr. Hearst, saying that she was going to dismiss the butler. He asked her to delay. When he had investigated the man, he found that he was a secret-service agent who had been placed in the house as a spy. There was nothing in the Hearst library to discover, and so after a few days the man left.

But secret-service men returned. Frankly they said they wished to investigate the system of signals of colored lights reported as flashing from the windows of the Clarendon. The puzzled publisher gave his callers the freedom of the house. For sometime the men turned on and off the electric lights. The meaning of the colored signals was revealed. Hearst owns the most important stained-glass collection in the world, and some of these windows were in the Clarendon apartments. Shining through the stained glass the electricity reflected a variety of bright colors visible from the street. These were the so-called disloyal pro-German signals. When the head officer discovered the flimsy foundation for the investigation, he was so disgusted that he said, "Oh hell!" Greatly humiliated he led his men out of the house.

One of the disseminators of the disloyalty stories was Attorney-General Lewis of New York. Later he admitted that his information came from an ex-prisoner named Charles Hubert Jerome, who had been employed as a servant at the Clarendon. When Lewis was threatened with prosecution, he apologized.

Usually Hearst is in extraordinarily good health, but during the war he had so many vexations that his physician sent him to rest at Mt. Clemens, Michigan. But the fight against him went bitterly onward. Opposing him were the big interests that had suffered from his activities since his arrival in New York; all those who owned legislatures as well as railroads, city councils as well as traction lines, public commissions as well as gas companies. These forces fused, tried to destroy Hearst and curtail his power. They were led by ex-President Roosevelt. He wrote a rambling letter of ten thousand words to Senator Poindexter, accusing President Wilson of being incompetent, playing vicious politics, suppressing free speech and printing, being a tyrant, tolerating and encouraging disloyalty and sedition in the interest of his personal ambition. Roosevelt attacked the President for not suppressing the

Hearst papers before we went into the war. At the most critical stage of the war Roosevelt caused this diatribe to be printed in the *Congressional Record* and to be distributed broadcast.

Hearst newspapers were again thrown out of clubs as at the time of McKinley's assassination. Sometimes they were burned in the streets. News-stands would not sell them. People left their friend's houses if they saw there a Hearst paper. It became the fashion to berate the publisher as pro-German.

·The motive of the attacks by ex-President Roosevelt was at this time unconsciously supplied by the late Theodore Douglas Robinson, a Republican New York State Senator, nephew and confidant of ex-President Roosevelt. Robinson made the indiscreet but illuminating statement that his uncle would be a candidate of the Republican Party for President in 1920. From the Mt. Clemens hospital Hearst answered Roosevelt. The publisher declared that the ex-President attacked the President and his Cabinet for partisan and political purposes:

What was worse, he did it for pay ... to aid and advertise those magazines and newspapers which pay and support him, and to reflect upon those magazines and newspapers which do not hire or admire him.

Hearst criticized the former President for being a "scold." He spoke of the ex-President's effort to form a division of volunteers and personally lead it to France, adding:

Although his military experiences have been confined to shooting a fleeing Spaniard in the back on the slopes of Kettle Hill in Cuba.

Hearst reproached Roosevelt not because of his attack upon him and his papers but because in war time, out of partisan hostility, he persistently attacked the Government of the United States:

No other conspicuous American public man would behave with such squalid selfishness.... The ex-President is out of power, and he is greedily eager to get back into power. He does not scruple at any methods, no matter how unfair to the Administration nor how harmful to the country, in order to accomplish his purely selfish political purposes.

Hearst pointed out that the *Metropolitan Magazine* which hired Roosevelt at a dollar a word as the "professional vituperator of the President," was owned by the Whitney estate, and administered by Harry Payne Whitney, a grandson of Henry D. Payne, the Standard Oil magnate.

As to the charge that he was pro-German, Hearst replied that he would not be silenced by the epithet. Any American who at the beginning avoided taking sides, was pro-German. Any American who said that the peoples of Europe were not responsible for the war, was pro-German. Any American who said that British treatment of neutrals was unfair, and that they violated international law and rights, was pro-German. Any American who said that the European belligerents should fight out their own war, was pro-German:

We shall perform the bounden duty of an American newspaper by defending with all our legal might, any citizen who is made the object of legally or morally unjust assault. We shall defend the freedom of speech, freedom of printing, freedom of individual opinion against any and all assailants as long as our papers are printed.

Château-Thierry, Belleau Wood, Saint Mihiel—and the world tragedy ended. On November 11, 1918, came the great day. This new day was ushered in by blowing of whistles, ringing of bells, men hugging each other and shouting, and crowds dancing in the streets. Women wept for the thousands who would never return. These bitter tears were dried, and there were tears of joy that the slaughter was over—sons, husbands, lovers were coming home. Peace had come.

The soldiers did not return as soon as expected. Hearst made a campaign to have them brought home with pay for six months. He was chairman of Mayor Hylan's military committee to receive guests when the soldiers returned from the war.

Although among the common people of the world since the day of the Armistice there had been good-will toward all, Mayor Hylan was bitterly attacked for having Hearst on the committee, receiving guests. Some members refused to serve with Hearst. Mayor Hylan said that the publisher came to his office and said, "I don't wish to embarrass you. I want to help. Here's my resignation."

Mayor Hylan answered, "I shall be greatly embarrassed and grieved if you insist on your resignation being accepted."

When the Twenty-seventh New York regiment returned from the World War, Mayor Hylan asked Hearst to review the troops from the Mayor's stand while they paraded through the city. The Mayor missed Hearst from the grand stand. He was told that the publisher was viewing the parade on a side street opposite the grand stand. Immediately Hylan sent a messenger asking Hearst why he did not come to the grand stand. Again Hearst did not wish to embarrass the Mayor. He begged to be excused. Hylan sent a police inspector to escort him to the grand stand, but Hearst watched the parade alone.

The war was over, but the hatred of the pro-German propagandists was not subdued. A meeting was arranged by them for the purpose of denouncing Hearst and Mayor Hylan. The organizers of the meeting called themselves the National Security League, but Hearst changed it to the National Scurrility League. The humble folk who had not forgotten Eighty Cent Gas, and the other crusades in which Hearst had engaged, appeared in great numbers at the Madison Square Garden meeting. President James P. Holland of the New York State Federation of Labor, said these attacks on Hearst were not directed against him personally, but against the progressive policy for which his publications stood. When speakers attacked Hearst, they were almost mobbed by the thousands present who resented the malice of the meeting.

The passions and hatreds released by the war were difficult to subdue. Professional patriots continued their attacks on Hearst long after peace was declared. Early in 1919, a mass meeting, nominally to welcome New York's returning soldiers, was held in Madison Square Garden. The plan was to assemble a crowd of sailors and soldiers, and then have speakers attack Mayor Hylan and Hearst. The Rev. Dr. Manning of Trinity Church garbled Hearst's statements on the *Lusitania* tragedy. Charles Evans Hughes urged sailors and soldiers not to read the Hearst papers. James M. Beck, a highly paid railway attorney, spoke for two hours, but when the attacks on Hylan or Hearst began, all uniformed soldiers and sailors cheered. Finally the chairman demanded that every one not in sympathy with the speeches about Hylan and Hearst, at once leave the hall. Thousands of uniformed men filed out of the meeting cheering Hylan and Hearst.

Then the speakers went on uninterrupted, but in the autumn they were answered by the people. Mayor Hylan was reëlected.

The Hearst papers throve under these attacks. An interviewer said to the publisher that it was said that he desired to own one hundred papers. Hearst's answer was, that he had in mind no fixed number. When a man had a paper that he wanted to sell, he came to him. If Hearst thought the newspaper worth buying, he usually added it to his chain.

In 1918, Hearst bought the Wisconsin *News* at Milwaukee, and in 1924 he acquired the Milwaukee *Sentinel*. In 1918, he also obtained an option to purchase the Los Angeles *Herald*, but the option was not exercised until 1922. Three papers came to Hearst in 1921, the Boston *Record*, the Detroit *Times*, the Seattle *Post-Intelligencer*. The Washington *Herald* was purchased by him in 1922. Mrs. Eleanor Patterson, granddaughter of the late Joseph Medill of Chicago, and the only woman editor with a million dollars a year in her own right, is in charge of the *Herald*.

About this time Hearst sent to his publishers and editors additional instructions concerning management of his newspapers:

Be perfectly fair in the news. Print an unbiased account of every proceeding, especially political proceedings. Please bear in mind that it is our policy to be conspicuously fair, not merely negatively fair. Go out of your way to be fair.

Pay less attention to merely routine news, less attention to routine duties, less attention to anything ordinary, and concentrate all your force and energy on the big things, the lasting things, the fundamental things, consistently with general supervision and watchfulness. I do not care if you are beaten on some small stories, or miss some second rate thing or writer, or artist. But you must never be beaten on a big thing, or the best thing, or the best writer, or the best artist.

I would not have you make ten suggestions a day to your sub-editors, even though all suggestions were fairly good, but instead, by more intense concentration of thought and initiative, produce one striking idea a day, making the hit of the day, or curing one fundamental defect completely.

Your search for talent must be incessant and sleepless. Remember that if you can discover one new man or woman of talent, you have secured a continuing, permanent advantage or improvement to the paper running three hundred and sixty-five days in the year, and worth much more than a news "beat" that lasts a day, or an advertising contract that lasts a few months. The talent will secure both the other things, but the other things cannot secure the talent.

Nothing is more important than continuing ideas and writers of real excellence, for they make our papers different and distinctive from all others.

You ought to have some fight or crusade for the public welfare always in progress, and you ought to fight hard for it. If you are lukewarm, you will achieve nothing. If you are not deeply interested, you may be sure your readers will not be. The best causes excite the greatest opposition and meet the most obstacles at first.

You ought to post on the office bulletin board frequently articles of prolixity, of verbosity, taken from your own paper as concrete examples of what is to be avoided.

Sometimes a very interesting story is put under a dull headline. Ten times as many people read headlines and "boxes" as read the news in detail—fifty times as many as will read a long story. A good newspaper cannot be made by clever headlines, but it can be spoiled by bad ones. Select every day from your own paper, or a competitor's, a good headline or a well-written terse news story, post it up in the office, and invite the whole staff to excel it if it can.

Never criticize without giving an example and intelligent reasons which will be helpful to the copy reader, the reporter and everybody else that has anything to do with the matter.

Pictures are of increasing importance. Every single one should tell a story, excite interest, wonder, curiosity, or the pleasure that beauty always awakens within us. The picture should be a bull's eye, a magnet to the eye. A feature that entertains the average right thinking reader is more valuable than any academic discussion of the statesman for instance.

A small staff of the best reporters is essential. Good reporters get the facts about all matters of public concern, and dissipate the paid propaganda now more rampant than before.

Finally this mandate to all editors:

Make an effort to secure greater unification and harmony among the Hearst papers so that all may benefit by the variety of talent in each one of them. There is, I'm sorry to say, sometimes a lack of that spirit of unity which ought to prevail, without subordinating any individual newspaper. There ought not to be separation and cold indifference. It is as killing to enthusiasm as jealousy or distrust.

CHAPTER XLIV

OPPOSES LEAGUE OF NATIONS

SOON after the Armistice was declared, William Randolph Hearst began what he considers the most important of his many campaigns during his life as a journalist—the battle against the League of Nations. "Other editors might have carried on my other campaigns," said Hearst to the writer, "but there was no one else with so many newspapers actively interested in defeating the League of Nations. I am a pacifist in the sense that I always try to keep the United States out of war. If it had not been for my papers, this country might, through the League of Nations, have become involved in war."

Senator Hiram W. Johnson also said, "Without the campaign made by Hearst, the United States would probably have been in the League of Nations."

From Hearst's youth, the warning of Washington, "No entangling alliances," has been the compass of his political life. In the tempestuous days of January, 1918, Wilson went before Congress and proclaimed his Fourteen Points of Peace. They were: open diplomacy, freedom of the seas, removal of destructive trade barriers among nations, reduction of armaments, adjustment of Colonial claims in the interests of the populations concerned, fair treatment for Russia, restoration of Belgium, righting the wrong done to France in 1871, adjustment of Italian frontiers on principles of nationalism, more autonomy for the peoples of the Austro-Hungarian empire, restoration of Rumania and Serbia, an independent Poland, reorganization of the Turkish empire, and finally an association of nations to uphold a peaceful world order.

Such was the creed of Wilson, probably suggested by the Fourteen Points of Jeremy Bentham's Plan for Universal and

Perpetual Peace written in 1796. Wilson's Fourteen Points went ringing through the world. At first they were loudly acclaimed, but Hearst knew that he could no longer walk the way of the President. He saw the mischief in the fourteenth point of Wilson's peace proposals which was the League of Nations, an entangling alliance. During the following summer and autumn Senator Henry Cabot Lodge and ex-President Roosevelt expressed their opposition to the League of Nations.

President Wilson was held by the world to be the spiritual leader of the war, and so he held himself. The President regarded the opposition of Hearst, Lodge and Roosevelt to the League of Nations as a challenge to his leadership.

Again and again during the World War, President Wilson had said that the United States warred not against peoples but against autocracy. Germany deposed the Kaiser, laid down her arms and appealed for peace. The Germans were promised that Wilson's Fourteen Points of Peace would be accepted as a basis for peace discussion. They trusted the President of the United States to obtain for them a just and magnanimous settlement.

It was a departure from all precedent for a President of the United States to go to Europe. It is now generally conceded that Wilson made a blunder in crossing the ocean to treat with the warring powers. Three weeks after the Armistice, the first passport ever issued to a chief executive of the United States was given to President Woodrow Wilson. On the steamer *George Washington* he set out for Europe, accompanied by Mrs. Wilson, Colonel House, four commissioners chosen by him, and an army of secretaries and experts in history, economics and diplomacy. The President took with him no member of the Senate, no leader of his own party, not one of the Republican majority necessary to the ratification of any treaty.

On Friday, December 13, 1918, President Wilson arrived in Europe from the West as a man of destiny, the hero who saved the Allies, the prophet who held the heart and hopes of mankind. He came to succor the Old World.

When Wilson reached England that nation was crying out for the execution of the Kaiser. The spiritual world leader reminded Europe of forgotten ideals of mercy and justice, and of the purpose of the great "war to end war." President and Mrs. Wilson drove through the streets of London and were received with the rapturous ecstasy accorded only royal sovereigns.

In Rome and Paris, the President with Mrs. Wilson at his side was hailed as the great peace-maker of his nation. So determined was he to be just, that he would not visit the battle-fields of France, lest his sympathies be overwrought. On January 18, 1919, he engaged formally in the high diplomatic combat with the most astute politicians in the world. Like a white knight of democracy he rode into the entanglement of European nationalism, secret agreements and secret treaties as represented by the thirty-two peace delegates in the hot, gorgeous rococo conference-room at Versailles where had dwelt the ill-fated Bourbons.

He entered the palace as a wide-eyed idealist, but he found leaders of nations plotting for power. There were Lloyd George, the English firebrand, and Orlando, whose crafty Latin mind was experienced in subterranean activities. In the middle of the semicircle of peace delegates wearing a substantial, black broadcloth frock coat, his square gloved hands clasped in front of him, eyes closed, parchment face impassive, sat enthroned on a brocade chair that cynical, aged imp, Clemenceau. He carried no papers, no portfolios. He had no personal secretaries. With him were ministers and officials, but he held the reins of power. He alone spoke both French and English. In his youth Clemenceau had lived in America, and he understood the demands of Europe and America.

There was no place in Clemenceau's philosophy for sentimentality in international relations. His mind had only one purpose, the supremacy of France. For the rest of the world he felt indifference or amused contempt. France was his sovereign. The glory of France was his goal. When he thought of France he envisioned the France of 1870. That France should be restored. For nearly half a century Clemenceau had cried out for *revanche*. Now it had come.

Clemenceau was a man without religion, but his idea of a personal devil was a German. With his sophisticated, cynical smile Clemenceau looked at Wilson. The President ceased being a prophet, the new Deity of 1918. He became merely a provincial professor with a book of psalms. When the atheistic French Clemenceau looked at the devout American Wilson he expected the Presbyterian President to pray. And all others in the conference saw Wilson with the eyes of Clemenceau.

Soon the world realized that Wilson played one kind of game, and the Allies another. Among these thirty-two delegates who sat round the green baize-covered table at the Peace Conference there was little idealism. Here were leaders of nations who preached hatred, clamored for revenge and schemed for power. From them Wilson asked nothing for his country but the League of Nations, and that he was asking for humanity. Against the other delegates he stood alone. In a droning voice without cadence or drama Wilson read his Fourteen Points. Clemenceau chortled, "God gave us his Ten Commandments, and we broke them. Wilson gave us his Fourteen Points—we shall see." To Clemenceau the League of Nations was an evanescent dream.

Soon it was decided that the important business of the conference would be transacted by the representatives of the United States, Great Britain, France, Italy and Japan. As soon as Japan was assured of the possession of Germany's Shantung, she dropped out of the conference. Angered by Wilson's refusal to meet Italy's demands Orlando withdrew. It was left for Lloyd George, Clemenceau and Wilson to shape the treaty of peace.

It became apparent that in another direction Wilson played a different game from the representatives of the Allies. With him were several delegates, mostly men of his own Democratic Party, but they were regarded and treated by him as dummies.

American newspaper men were not informed even semi-officially concerning the American position. The Premiers of England, France and Italy shared knowledge of their aims with the journalists of their own countries. Wilson had not been developed in the political school of working politics as had Orlando, Lloyd George and Clemenceau. He was always a schoolmaster whose authority forbade the teacher making a confidant of a pupil.

Wilson was slow and unadaptable, unaccustomed to the give and take of swift, personal encounter. He could not compete with the subtle, rapid intrigue of the Old World. Wilson was opposed to secret treaties, but he yielded to France the great advantage of having the negotiations secret. He played in darkness when he should have insisted upon light.

Lloyd George was inclined to generous compromise with Germany which would have led to modifications of extreme demands of France, but he was obliged to manipulate a reactionary House of Commons, and he shifted perceptibly to peace with vengeance. Clemenceau believed that a German should not be conciliated, only bullied.

For months Wilson sat in the poisonous air of the conference room and heard demands that Germany's economic system built on coal, iron and exports should be destroyed, that she should lose colonies, European territory, trading bases and banks in all parts of the world, merchant marine and navy. When Wilson protested that Germany had asked for the Armistice on the basis of the Fourteen Points, Clemenceau and the other Prime Ministers of the Allies adroitly made him feel that he was pro-German. Clemenceau was a realist. He made no pretense of being bound by the Fourteen Points. Openly he declared that they would only hasten Germany's recovery, and enable her once again to hurl her superior resources and greater numbers at France.

Slowly before his eyes Wilson saw his own child, the League of Nations, strangled. At times he felt that there was no hope for the future peace of the world. On one occasion the President ordered the *George Washington* to stand in readiness, and he made a feint of setting out for home. Had he done so, he would have been welcomed by his followers, but the Prime Ministers would have accused him of being pro-German, eager to prolong the war.

Soon Wilson realized that the blaze of his popularity was dimming. He was losing control. England was cool and ducal. Already there were articles in the Paris press insidiously criticizing the President, and censorious of the behavior of American soldiers. The Fourteen Points which had been thundered from the White House as from Sinai were becoming fantastic. Europe could not understand that Wilson desired only things spiritual. Europe desired things material—economic advantages, military guarantees, boundaries, balance of power.

And yet Wilson could have held the conference in his hands. He was the commander of the great American army of two millions disciplined and equipped. Already Europe owed more than she could pay, and more loans would be required to save her from bankruptcy and starvation. Utterly she depended on the food supply of the United States. All weapons were at the hand of the President, but he would not use them. He did not think that a threat of force would be ethical, and so, in the end he was defeated by his own conscientious will.

France made the most exact and extreme proposals. Clemenceau let it be seen that he would accept the League of Nations —but he must have barter. For the League of Nations Wilson traded Germany. He dismembered Austro-Hungary. He took Alsace-Lorraine from Germany and the highly developed mineral wealth of those provinces. He stripped Germany of her coal-fields in the Ruhr, Upper Silesia and Saar. He seized her colonies. He swept from the seas her mercantile marine and her navy. He agreed that Germany should be pledged to pay thirty-three billions in gold dollars; but in February, when President Wilson left Paris for Washington, he believed that he had done what was just and right. He carried with him the

Covenant of the League of Nations which was to him a guarantee of Utopia.

Before sailing for the United States, at the suggestion of Colonel House, President Wilson cabled inviting the Republicans as well as Democrats of the Foreign Relations Committee of the Senate to confer with him concerning the Versailles Treaty. When the President returned to the White House he believed that eighty per cent of the people of the United States were for the League. Even in its imperfect form, the President thought it was permanent. To him it established new principles in world government, new justice in international relations. He thought the centuries would look back on the Peace Conference of Versailles as the foundation of a civilization never again to be rent and scarred by war.

Republicans as well as Democrats of the committee of Foreign Relations met President Wilson on the morning of February 19th at the White House to discuss with him the League of Nations. The President began the conference with a detailed, able exposition of the League. Then he stated that he would welcome questions. There followed a long gruelling interview during which Lodge, Knox, Johnson, Harding, Brandegree and others questioned the President. Articles X, XI and XIV were discussed. Special interest pertained to Article X which dealt with the abolition of force in international relations. Senators made it clear that in their opinion there could be no peace without force. It might take the form of "boycott," "refusal to trade," "breaking off relations," or "embargo,"— they all meant force. Then would come war inevitable.

Senator Hiram W. Johnson described to the writer with what patience and ability President Wilson met the barrage of barbed, tormenting questions. Only once did he show lack of self-mastery, and that was when Senator Warren G. Harding of Ohio spoke. So clearly uninformed was Harding that President Wilson grew impatient and irritable.

The President reluctantly went on with his efforts to win the influence of the Senators for the treaty. Some Senators were irked that copies of the treaty found their way into the hands of journalists and bankers before having been read by the Senate. Finally the President made an effort to disarm his critics in the Senate by inviting Republican Senators, singly and in groups to confer with him. He addressed the Senate on the treaty and said, "It has come about by no plan of our conceiving, but by the hand of God who led us into this war."

In March, just before the President sailed for Europe the second time, the Republicans circulated a round-robin in the Senate. More than one-third of the members of the Senate served notice on the world that the Versailles Treaty of Peace in the form originally agreed upon would not be ratified. The President was dazed. He could not understand that his cherished Covenant of the League of Nations could be inhospitably received. The League provided for three international agencies: a Secretariat to be located at Geneva; an Assembly to be made up of one deputy from each nation, dominion and self-governing colony; and a Council consisting of representatives from the United States, Great Britain, France, Italy and Japan, and four other representatives to be elected by the Assembly. All these powers bound themselves to respect one another's territorial integrity and to coöperate in preserving it against aggression. Every dispute that could not be adjusted by diplomacy was to be submitted to arbitration or inquiry by the Council. Never were the members of the League to resort to arms until three months after the decision of the Council. In case the verdict was unanimous the members of the League were bound to abide by it. Retaliation could be lawfully invoked against any member that declined to abide by its decision. Refusal was an act of war against the League. The trade of any offending member could be cut off. Then the Council could recommend to the associated governments to adopt military measures. President Wilson considered this super-government a World Parliament to enforce peace. His vision had become reality.

But when the President set out for Europe the second time,

behind him lay all his glory. Vainly he had tried to explain the League of Nations to an angry, disillusioned people. On the second journey he carried with him a pocketful of amendments to the Covenant. In June of 1919, the Treaty of Versailles was signed. When the President returned in July he said the heart of the world would break if the Covenant was not accepted by the United States. Lloyd George, Orlando and Clemenceau had obtained their coveted balance of power, their indemnities and their annexations, but Wilson still had his vision.

Now the struggle of the President was for the ratification of the treaty. Already in the elections of November, 1918, the President had lost the Democratic Congress. The Senate was Republican. A two-thirds vote was necessary, according to the Constitution, to ratify a treaty. How could the ratification be brought about?

Hostility to the treaty grew. When the liberals of the world read and analyzed the Versailles document they realized that "making the world safe for Democracy," "self-determination" and "rights of small nations" were discarded. A treaty of peace had been written that was unparalleled in greed. Then the League of Nations was adopted. For all time it perpetuated the wrongs of the inhuman treaty of peace, a complete betrayal of Germany.

Hearst led those opposed to European entanglements for the United States. He saw a super-state invading the domestic interests of this country. It might meddle with immigration laws, obligate this government to take part in the wars of Europe and Asia. It would impose a moral obligation of other countries to concern themselves with the affairs of the Western Hemisphere.

With alarm, Hearst saw the reversal of the foreign policy adhered to by the United States during the whole of its existence as an independent nation. Would Wilson divert the course of the United States to a new channel? In an editorial Hearst said:

After being elected by the campaign slogan, "He kept us out of the war," Wilson spent thousands of millions of dollars for America's part in the war. . . . How are we to know that Mr. Wilson's pledges are any more trustworthy to-day when he is campaigning for the League of Nations, and perhaps for its Presidency, than they were three years ago when he was campaigning for the Presidency of the United States?

And if there are still some who believe that Mr. Wilson's promises are sincere and his policies founded on fixed determination, how are we to know that his judgment is any better than it was three years ago when he declared that his election meant peace?

In all his newspapers Hearst assailed the League of Nations. In the *Evening Journal* he wrote:

A League of Nations is of no real value. . . . There was a League of Nations after the Napoleonic wars, and the object of that League was to end war forever. But within a very few years the very nations that composed the League were at each other's throats.

There were two Leagues of Nations before the war—the Entente and the Triple Alliance. The war between these nations was precipitated by the disposition of these two Leagues to meddle in Balkan difficulties. The League of Nations will not establish peace. In fact, the real danger is that it will drag the United States into war that it would otherwise have no connection with.

Nothing that I know of will establish world peace at present. The abolition of war is like the abolition of slavery, a matter of education and civilization. But peace for our own country can be secured if we retire behind the greatest navy in the world and attend to our own business. The object of the League is good. The intention of the framers is good, but I am seriously afraid that the League will develop complications which would be a distinct injury to our country, and which will lead us to depart from the very wise principles of the founders of this Republic who warned us against mingling in and meddling in European complications and conflicts.

The League of Nations means that we together with other

members of the League would be compelled to take an interest in, and to a certain extent, to take part in the various quarrels of minor European nations and even major European nations. This we ought not to do. . . .

The League of Nations also means that European nations constituting a majority of the League will proceed to interfere in matters affecting this Western Hemisphere of ours. This means an abandonment of the Monroe Doctrine, the submission of our inter-American questions to a court, the majority of which will be disposed to decide matters against the interests of the United States. I cannot see how the Democratic Party can be willing to abandon the Monroe Doctrine, a doctrine which has proved to be of such great advantage to this country and to the whole Western Hemisphere.

Hearst said he was opposed to the League of Nations not because he did not love peace. He fought the League because it was not a league of peace, but a league of international financiers and greedy European nations, counting upon the whole world to guarantee them the spoils of the European war.

Senators Johnson and Borah of the Republican Party, and Hearst's close friend, Senator James A. Reed, the Democrat of Missouri, campaigned against the treaty and the League. Through his newspapers Hearst reached millions. On September 26th, he wrote to the editor of the New York *American:*

Will you please write editorials urging that the question of the League of Nations be referred to the people to be decided by referendum vote. Three questions should be submitted: First, the question of ratifying the covenant as it shall be amended by the Senate. Second, ratifying the covenant with reservations. Third, the question of rejecting the whole proposition. . . .

The people should be given an opportunity themselves to decide whether or not they want to depart from the policy of no entangling alliances established by Washington, endorsed by Adams, Jefferson, Madison, Monroe, Jackson, Lincoln, Cleveland, and practically all the great men in history, but rejected by President Wilson.

...As a matter of fact, the question of deciding on declaration of war and making peace should rightly belong to the people themselves, and should not be delegated to any representative who may through vanity, or arrogance, or prejudice, or family association, or sectional affiliations, or racial or religious bigotry, decide vital questions on some other basis than the best interests of the people, and the greatest security and prosperity of the nation. Furthermore, there is no wisdom so great as the collective wisdom of the people. They can best decide these questions, and should in a genuine democracy be allowed to decide on the League of Nations.

In the Senate the League of Nations had not a majority. There were Senators called the "mild reservationists," and there were the "irreconcilables." When Senator Hiram W. Johnson returned from California in the autumn, he was shocked on discovering that in his absence Chairman Lodge had appointed a committee from the Committee on Foreign Relations to meet with the committee of those who favored the League. The purpose of this was to effect a compromise on Article X. The compromise had been agreed upon, and the United States would have been in the League, but for the fact that President Wilson would have no compromise.

Immediately Johnson sent out a hurry up call to the "irreconcilables" for a meeting in his office. Soon sixteen Senators assembled. Among them were Medill McCormick of Illinois, Fernald of Maine, Knox of Pennsylvania, Moses of New Hampshire, Sherman of Illinois, Brandegee of Connecticut, and Borah. Excitedly the Senators stalked up and down Johnson's office. Senator Moses was despatched to fetch Chairman Lodge.

Senator Knox was strutting up and down the room when Senator Lodge entered somewhat amazed and flurried to find such an atmosphere of fury. "Mr. Lodge," said Knox, "I do not appreciate the fact that after I have worked a year you appoint a committee to oversee my work."

Another Senator threatened, "If the League of Nations goes

through, there will be new Republican leadership in the Senate. We won't stand for it!"

With his customary Boston courtesy Lodge asked, "What shall I do?"

"Kick the committee into a cocked hat," was the answer. That was the end of the meeting.

President Wilson daily realized that he was losing control of even his own party. The newspapers published reports of defections of Democratic Senators. Reed of Missouri was a missionary among the Democrats. The President decided to go to the American people to make what he called an "appeal to Cæsar." Physically he was failing. Doctors advised against the effort. The President was determined, so certain was he that he could sway the people.

No sooner did President Wilson leave Washington than he sensed that there was a shadow between himself and his aloof, questioning audiences. In all his newspapers, Hearst kept up the crusade against the League of Nations. More Democrats declared against the Covenant.

Although the President had represented the United States at the most momentous conference ever held between governments there was nothing stirring on his tour. As he moved toward the West street crowds were not enthusiastic. There was occasional hand clapping, sometimes a cheer. The President abandoned prepared speeches and plunged into extemporaneous addresses. Constantly he exalted American ideals and sympathies. When he was not speaking he strolled into the club car trying to convert newspaper correspondents. In his speeches he said that when the League of Nations and the Versailles Treaty were enforced, soldiers need never again cross the sea to fight. He called the League of Nations the League of the Fine Passions of the World. He talked of a visit to a French Cemetery where American soldiers were buried, and he spoke of a promise there made by him to the dead that there should never be another war. The President said that he would gladly die to bring about the peace of the world.

Mrs. Wilson looked anxiously at her husband. Men and women in the audience wept. Coughing, President Wilson went on with his travels appealing for understanding. Through Ohio, Iowa, Missouri, Nebraska, Montana, Washington, Oregon, California, Utah, and finally into Colorado the train bore the President. In Denver he could not sleep. His nerves gave way. On September 26, 1919, the World War claimed its most distinguished victim: President Woodrow Wilson broke down at Wichita, Kansas. He was rushed back to Washington. The remainder of his life was spent as a semi-invalid.

Congress convened and six Democrats in the Senate under the leadership of Hearst's friend, Senator James Reed, changed their vote and opposed the treaty. On the 19th of November, 1919, on the anniversary of Lincoln's address and the battle of Gettysburg, the Senate rejected the treaty and the League of Nations. Twenty-three Democrats deserted the President. Only twenty-four Democrats stood with him for the ratification resolution of the Versailles Treaty. The final vote on the Versailles Treaty was taken in March, 1920. The Republican Party in the Senate stood thirty-four for ratification, with the Lodge reservation. Fifteen desired neither treaty nor League of Nations.

In March, 1920, the treaty was formally sent back to President Wilson with the Democratic Party split in twain. Only a handful of Southern Democrats stood with the President to the end. Senator Hitchcock of Nebraska, and Senator Johnson of South Dakota, were the only Senators north of the Mason and Dixon line, or from the West, who supported the position of the President in the last count. During the second week of April, 1920, President Wilson met with the Cabinet for the first time in eight months.

In June the National Democratic Convention at San Francisco failed to give the President even a complimentary nomination. Governor James M. Cox of Ohio was chosen as Democratic nominee. The approaching election was considered a referendum to determine whether the American people were for the League or against it.

Hearst in all his newspapers urged not only the defeat of the League of Nations, but suggested a new party. He called upon Governor Cox to shake off the heavy load of Wilson and Wilson policies, and to take a stand for true Jeffersonian policy. Hearst desired to have a new party made up of progressives dissatisfied with the Republican platform, and Democrats who saw that their party provided no medium through which they might express their views.

Senator Hiram W. Johnson had been overwhelmingly elected in California when he campaigned in the Republican primaries against the League of Nations. In many States where there were direct primaries Johnson received instructions of the delegates. Hearst proposed Johnson as the candidate of the Progressive Party. Johnson would not lead the Progressive ticket, but at the Chicago Convention he was offered the nomination for the Vice-Presidency. At the suggestion of Senator Warren Harding himself Hearst conveyed to Johnson the invitation to the California Senator to be the running mate for the Senator from Ohio.

Although Republican success was assured, Senator Johnson declined. As a Progressive, Johnson felt that he could not consistently accept a nomination to be the running mate of a reactionary Presidential candidate. And yet, had he accepted, Hearst's wish might have been fulfilled, Johnson would have been the first Progressive President. With the death of President Harding, there would have been President Hiram W. Johnson.

At that time the Presidential current was running swiftly toward Johnson. Friends of Knox tried to interest him in the candidacy of Knox and Johnson, but the Californian was seeking the Presidential nomination himself, and had no interest in second place. And yet, that nomination, which he could easily have obtained, would also have made Johnson President. Before the four years were over Knox had died.

President Woodrow Wilson considered the election of 1920 a referendum to determine whether the American people were for the League or against it. The election of Senator Warren Harding, that Ohioan whose conspicuous misinformation on international questions had so painfully disturbed the scholarly serenity of President Wilson during his meeting with the Foreign Relations Committee of the Senate, was a great blow to the President.

At the time of the election Hearst was in Los Angeles, and from there he wrote:

Mr. Wilson wanted a referendum on the League of Nations, and he has had it. This overwhelmingly Republican election is not a victory for the Republican Party, although the Republican Party will make the mistake of thinking that it is. Nor is it a defeat for the Democratic Party.... Bryan was right when he said, "At the end of Wilson's term of office there will be no Democratic Party. There may be a Wilson party, but there will be no Democratic Party."

In his valedictory to Congress, President Wilson made answer to the election returns when he said, "I have not so much laid before you a series of recommendations, gentlemen, as uttered a confession of faith, the faith in which I was bred, and which it is my solemn purpose to stand by until my last fighting day. I believe this to be the faith of America, the faith of the future, and of all the victories which will await national action in the days to come, whether in America or elsewhere."

How completely Hearst was right in his attitude toward the League of Nations, was demonstrated in 1924, when Mussolini bombarded one of the Greek islands belonging to another member of the League of Nations. In 1932, again Hearst was demonstrated as wise in opposing the League of Nations; Japan without apology resigned from the League of Nations in order to fight her neighbor, China. Protesting warlike words were thundered from Geneva, but Ministers of Foreign Affairs of powerful members of the League declined to interfere in the armed strife. In 1933, Hearst's attitude toward the League was again shown to be right when Paraguay and Bolivia both resigned from the League of Nations in order to carry on a war. The Covenant of Versailles could not maintain peace between even two minor South American republics.

Hearst took the same attitude toward the Republican Kellogg Pact and World Court that he had maintained toward the League of Nations. He wrote that

The Republican Administration took up the remains of Mr. Wilson's League of Nations and refitted and refurbished it, called it by a different name, and went before the public for a mandate to meddle in European affairs and allow Europe to meddle in our affairs through the medium of the so-called World Court.

In the election of 1926 the World Court was an issue of the campaign. Nearly all Senators opposing the World Court were elected. The American people had learned the lesson from sending two million people across the ocean to fight for something that did not concern them and from lending billions of dollars to their competitors, who repaid them by calling them usurers.

At this time a question arose as to whether the United States should collect from Europe the billions due this country. Hearst wrote the New York *American:*

It is ridiculous of France and England to talk about the United States canceling a part of their actually incurred obligations to the United States, provided France and England canceled part of their unprecedented, impossible demands upon Germany.

It would be more reasonable for France and England to say that the United States should cancel her demands upon Germany in proportion to the degree that France and England should cancel their demands upon Germany; but the United States has made no demands on Germany—it has, in effect, already canceled its demands not in part, but entirely. It is the one nation that has gained nothing and asked nothing for its sacrifices in the war.

The money owed by France and England to the United States is not imaginary money. It is actual money, actually borrowed and actually due, and actually used by the Allies to save themselves from defeat and destruction.

Finally the United States would advise the nations of Europe to abolish their excessive armament. We would advise England to reduce her naval and aërial armaments.... We should advise France to abolish her excessive military armament, to a point equaling those of England and the United States. There is no country in Europe at present threatening France or able to threaten France, if she minds her own business and progresses in a peaceful democratic way, resisting further imperialistic adventures and further attempts to plunder Central Europe and annex territory there.

We should advise Germany to pay a reasonable indemnity, maintain her democracy, and refrain from again becoming a menace to Europe.

In an interview given to Cornelius Vanderbilt, Jr., on this subject, Hearst said:

My idea of the attitude the United States should take toward the debts with foreign nations is simply the attitude taken by business men toward any individual debtor. The obligation of the individual debtor is to pay his debts, or go into bankruptcy and repudiate them. The obligation of the individual debtor, even if he goes into bankruptcy, is to pay as much of his indebtedness as he can, according to his assets or ability.

England is not going into bankruptcy, so let her pay her honest debts, dollar for dollar, especially since the money that was lent by the United States and the aid that was given by the United States meant the preservation of her very existence, not only as an empire, but as a nation. She cannot repudiate such a debt without dishonor and she will not repudiate.

It remains merely for us to collect what is due in a proper manner. France is in the same condition as England. She can pay her debts and should pay them....

France talks about the losses she suffered, but she says nothing about rich provinces gained, of Alsace-Lorraine, of the coal-fields of western Germany. She says nothing of colonies gained, and of the great actual and potential wealth and power that these gains mean to her as a nation.

England talks of the debt that is owed her, but she says nothing of the German colonies she has acquired, of the German ships she is operating, of the oil-fields she has possessed herself of, of the many additions of wealth and power to her empire.

The United States has gained nothing. We spent billions to save civilization ... to establish peace and make democratic institutions secure as we thought and hoped ... but democracy has not been established. France is as militaristic as Germany was at its worst, and both France and England are more imperialistic, more contemptuous of the rights of weaker nations than any empires have been since the days of ancient Rome. The autonomy of weaker nations and the self-determination of smaller nations are ghastly jokes. Most of the subject nations of the world are under the heel of English despotism, and the mailed fist of European imperialism has been transferred from the hand of Germany to the hand of France.

The money we give Europe is used to finance war and promote oppression. The money we forgive Europe will be used for the same purpose.... Let us keep out of Europe's political and financial complications. Let us maintain our full rights to the moneys that Europe owes us, and let us demand full payment of debt and interest.

We did our full duty to Europe when we paid the price of our participation in the war, and when we won the war for France and England that they could not win for themselves.... They owe us everything, even to their very existence. Let them pay their honest debts or stand pilloried as dishonest debtors.

CHAPTER XLV

ENGLISH PUBLICATIONS

IN October and November of 1921, Hearst inspected his Mexican properties, the oil land at Ojinaga, the Campeche Ranch, the hardwood forest at Vera Cruz, the Babicora Ranch, the San Luis silver-mine, and the Guanacevi gold-mine. The superintendent of one of Hearst's Mexican mines said to the writer, "Senator Hearst used to call our mine the 'little mine' because we made only twenty-five thousand a month."

After the fall of President Diaz, Hearst's Mexican buildings were burned and his employees killed. The publisher went to Mexico to put an end to the turmoil prevailing on his properties.

Warned that the El Paso and Chihuahua Railroad was in bad condition and infested by bandits, he chose that route. Not a bandit was in sight. Hearst found the road-beds to be on the average as good as those in America.

At various towns such as Aguas Calientes and at Queretaro where Maximilian met defeat, Hearst traveled in street-cars and talked with the people. He wrote: "As none of them rose in protest at my bad Spanish, I felt justified in concluding that they were at least a patient and peaceful lot."

In Mexico City shops were busy, newspapers were lively and filled with advertisements, and streets were thronged. Theaters were well patronized by the increased population.

Apparently there was no more crime than in New York or any other big city. While he was in Mexico City a pay car on one of the railroads was robbed and seventy-five thousand dollars were stolen. In twenty-four hours the police captured the thieves and recovered the money. Before Hearst left New York City, there was a mail robbery of five hundred thousand dollars, and those thieves had not been arrested.

The publisher motored over the mountains to Cuernavaca, land of Zapata, the Indian bandit. Hearst found that for a year Cuernavaca had been quiet.

On returning to Mexico City, Hearst had an interview with President Obregon who was a wise diplomat and a powerful executive. On the advice of the President, Hearst visited remote parts of Mexico, traveling on small railways and making horseback trips. In Uruapan, Guadalajara, and Colima restoration was in progress and people were developing rice-fields, and coffee and banana plantations, even at the base of the great volcano. Through the solitude of sub-tropical jungles, Hearst traveled unmolested hearing from groups of horsemen or plodding peons a courteous "God be with you, Señor!" or Adiós, Señor!" The publisher's aged guard looked like a bandit, but talked and acted like a caballero. When Hearst gave his gun to his guide in appreciation of his service, the Mexican said that if Hearst ever had need he would gladly use it in his defense.

Hearst saw railroads being extended and improved; highways built into mountain districts, telephones being installed, electric lighting systems, power and irrigation districts developed, hospitals built, farming and manual-training schools established, and fifty million dollars a year spent on education, six times the expenditure of any preceding administration. Many Mexican youths of the upper classes educated in American schools and colleges, imbued with American ideas of political freedom, had returned to Mexico and brought about a revolution, so Hearst was told by Governor Ignacio Enriquez of Chihuahua. Hearst wrote:

There was ample reason why the United States should not recognize the government of Carranza which was authorized protracted anarchy. Why should we not recognize the government of General Obregon which has restored law and order and offers friendship and encouragement to citizens of the United States and Mexico which have been so long denied them?

The United States should recognize Mexico, and Mexico on its part should withhold no right from our citizens in Mexico which it would not wish withheld from its citizens in the United States.

This is the plain principle of the Golden Rule applied to international politics, and it applies as aptly to politics and diplomacy as it does to religion, morality, business activity and all phases of human society.

Hearst informed the Harding Administration and offered to establish the fact that Lamont submitted to the Mexican government the proposition of securing recognition by redeeming, at one hundred and twenty dollars, a vast quantity of Mexican bonds which the International Bankers had bought at an average of approximately forty dollars. Hearst stated that the revolution had freed the people from a dictatorship like that of Russia under the Czar. During this revolution there had been excesses, but these should be charged to the oppressors who precipitated the revolution. He said that President Obregon, Minister de la Huerta, and General Calles compared favorably with the leading statesmen of any of the leading nations of the world.

"Why is the friendly, orderly representative government of Mexico not recognized?" repeatedly asked Hearst of the Harding Administration. Largely through the publisher's efforts Mexico was recognized.

One year after Hearst returned from Mexico, when he was fifty-nine years of age, he said: "I never plan any extensions, but newspapers seem just naturally to keep coming to me to be taken over. I am not as young as I was once, and the older we get the less likely we are to set out to conquer the world."

Hearst's greatest activity in publishing followed this statement. Once he said that without newspapers he would not know what to do for enjoyment. He derives much pleasure from building up a magazine or a newspaper, of the same sort that an architect feels in constructing a fine house. Some of Hearst's executives declare that he is never greatly interested in a wholly successful paper.

In 1922, Hearst bought the Rochester *Journal*, the Oakland

Post-Enquirer, the Los Angeles *Herald,* and the Syracuse *Telegram.* The name *Telegram* was dropped when he bought the *Journal* in 1925, and the *Telegram* became the *Journal.* He took over the Baltimore *News* in 1923. The Albany *Times-Union* became a Hearst property in 1924, as did the San Antonio *Light,* and the Milwaukee *Sentinel.*

In July of 1922, he established in New York the *Daily Mirror,* a condensed newspaper of miniature size, commonly called a tabloid. Hearst had long been interested in an intelligently condensed newspaper. Lord Northcliffe told Hearst that he modeled his own *Daily Mail* largely on the New York *Sun* of Charles A. Dana, who was the founder of this form of journal. While Northcliffe was still Alfred Harmsworth, on one of his trips to New York in the nineties, he published a special edition of the New York *World,* condensing all articles in order to illustrate his idea of an intelligent tabloid. The newspaper men smiled patronizingly and continued to make voluminous papers.

The *Daily Mirror,* the first London tabloid, was something of an accident. Harmsworth planned to print a daily newspaper for women, and the result was the *Mirror.* It did not succeed, and so he transformed it into a general newspaper without changing the small size of the page. This gave him better opportunity for condensation than he had found in the *Daily Mail.* The popularity of condensation was speedily demonstrated in the astonishing growth of the *Mirror.*

When Hearst established the *Mirror* in New York, he engaged as editor Phil Payne, managing editor of the New York *Daily News,* owned by Joseph Patterson and Robert McCormick of Chicago. The *Mirror* circulation grew rapidly and Arthur Brisbane is its present editor.

By this time more than three million people in the United States bought a Hearst newspaper every Sunday morning. Never in the history of the world was there such an audience as that held by the New York *American,* Boston Sunday *Advertiser,* the Atlanta *Sunday American,* the Chicago *Herald and*

Examiner, the Los Angeles *Examiner,* San Francisco *Examiner,* and Washington *Times*. They were really one great American paper. About this time the profits of the California newspapers alone in one year were five million dollars.

As the years flowed on, less and less did Hearst engage in conflict with competing newspapers. He learned not to read attacks. However, one of his publishers told him that an opposing newspaper had been particularly ugly, and advised Hearst to retaliate. Now was the time. The man had been connected with a bank failure. The public was indignant. Hearst could easily have won sympathy. He declined to declare a newspaper war. "No one is interested in what I think of my competitors, nor in what they think of me. Our opponent has an especially mean disposition. He quarrels with his wife, his children, his business associates. He would enjoy a quarrel with me. We ought to feel sorry for any one with such an ugly nature."

No large successful business was ever conducted with such generosity as that of the Hearst enterprises. Charles Edward Russell says that his hardest task as publisher of the Chicago *American* was to keep Hearst protected from people seeking assistance. He usually gave, even though the case seemed unworthy. When he found a person in real need, he would say triumphantly to Russell, "Even you can't find anything wrong with that case." Hearst was so frequently imposed upon by members of his staff who drew their salary months in advance, that he was requested by business managers to cease advancing salaries to employees. The new order was sent out. Shortly after it was received one of his most irresponsible Bohemian borrowers lay in wait for him and requested an advance of five hundred dollars. Hearst complied and returned to a conference with the publisher, who reproached, "Mr. Hearst, remember your new rule against advancing money."

With a whimsical smile Hearst answered, "I didn't advance that five hundred dollars. I gave it."

In spite of Hearst's generosity his business expanded not

only in the United States but in England. In December, 1910, he entered the English publishing world by forming the English company known as the National Magazine Company, Ltd., and this organization published the first number of *Nash's* magazine under his direction.

During the next few years Hearst sent a succession of American editors and art editors to edit *Nash's,* but it was too American for England. Then a brilliant Irishman, J. Y. McPeake, was engaged, and *Nash's* circulation rose to a number seldom known in England. There appeared in its pages some of the finest work of Rudyard Kipling, John Galsworthy, H. G. Wells, Arnold Bennett, George Bernard Shaw, W. J. Locke, and Sir Hall Caine. Among American authors who appeared in *Nash's,* were Robert W. Chambers, Bruno Lessing, Edna Ferber and Fannie Hurst. Harrison Fisher's covers were so popular that reproductions were sold by the thousands.

After the great success of *Nash's,* Hearst decided to bring out the English *Good Housekeeping.* McPeake spent two years preparing the foundation for the magazine. The profits of *Nash's* were used to increase the staff, and the National Magazine Company, Ltd., moved in 1921 from 69 Fleet Street to 1 Amen Corner, a quiet backwater in the shadows of St. Paul's Cathedral. In March, 1922, the first number of English *Good Housekeeping* was issued, and it was an instantaneous success. Launched with an advertising campaign costing only seventy thousand dollars, even the third number showed a profit. English *Good Housekeeping* quickly outgrew the premises at 1 Amen Corner, and in the summer of 1924, the magazine was moved to its present building, 153 Queen Victoria Street. Hearst also opened the Good Housekeeping Institute for the testing of household appliances at 49 Wellington Street, Strand. Enough money was earned by English *Good Housekeeping* during the first few years so that Hearst was enabled in 1925 to purchase St. Donat's Castle, Wales, from its profits. For some time Hearst had cast longing eyes on the *Connoisseur,* a fine art publication of great interest to antique dealers and collectors. He bought this magazine in June, 1927. An English edition of *Harper's Bazaar* was established by Hearst in 1929, and it has steamed ahead in spite of the depression. In 1924, Managing Director McPeake died, and Miss Alice M. Head, an American, took his place temporarily. When Hearst went to England, Miss Head prepared for him a list of men who might fill McPeake's place. The publisher read the list and said to her, "Who is running the magazines now?"

"I am."

"You're doing well. Keep on running them."

Miss Head was overcome. "Mr. Hearst," she said, "don't you know that no woman has ever been at the head of a large magazine in England?"

"Then it's time one was."

Miss Alice M. Head became the first woman to direct a large publishing property in England.

In England as well as in the United States Hearst insisted that:

The principles and the policies of the advertising department should be just as firmly established and just as well known to every one in the business office as the news and editorial policies are known to the news and editorial departments. We can hope to build advertising only on reliability of statement. No man who misrepresents facts should be allowed on our newspaper. Honesty is a form of common sense.

Employ men of brains, breeding and acquaintance. Character counts in advertising as in all other things. Only men of intelligence and initiative can fully comprehend that advertising is a science of human service. Pay good salaries, and see that the salary is earned. Advance men who advance their own record.

Encourage small advertisers. Ten regular users of ten-inch space are preferable to one user of one hundred-inch copy. Give the small advertiser service. Make his advertising make money for him. Advertising which does not pay the advertiser will not make profits for us.

Encourage your advertising representatives to map out definite campaigns and sell "copy." Good copy is more effective in closing a sale than conversation. Every call made should be accompanied with an idea. Businessmen are always willing to give time to a salesman with ideas. Coöperation is the most far-reaching word in the English language.

Our newspapers must sell advertising only by their printed rate card. If your rate card is wrong, change it. If it is right, live up to every letter of it. There should be no double standard of morality involving buyer and seller of advertising. Cut rates, special concessions and secret rebates are boomerangs, which return to cripple progress when they are least expected. Men who make "gentlemen's agreements" are not wanted.

When position is demanded for advertisements, we must demand that position rates be paid. People who prefer the extra advantage of Pullman cars are willing to pay for this privilege. In the make-up of the paper, preference should be given to those advertisements which lend prestige and dignity to the advertising columns of our newspaper.

Do not accept any advertising which is detrimental to the public welfare. Questionable financial, objectionable medical, clairvoyants', spiritualists', fortune-tellers' and fake advertising of any and every description have no place in the Hearst newspapers. Every one of our newspapers should keep a testimonial file. Careful record of all advertisements which produce unusual results should be made. Such records should be placed in the hands of your local advertising representatives, as well as your foreign representatives.

Foreign representatives of the Hearst organization should at all times be active in advising other Hearst publications of new accounts which "break" or are about to "break."

It is the policy of the Hearst newspapers to coöperate with national advertisers in establishing selling agents and securing window displays, but in no circumstances should the expense of mailing out promotion matter be paid. This is merely another way of cutting rates. Our newspapers should not sell the products of advertisers. The business of advertising salesmen is to sell advertising space, not merchandise.

Special editions, scheme pages and similar lines of so-called advertising should be discouraged. The same energy devoted to the development of a regular advertiser will, in the long run, prove more profitable.

The custom of soliciting business for a single day is wrong. Our papers are published daily because people have daily wants. Merchants keep their stores open six days a week for the same reason. They do not employ their clerks for big days only, nor do they dispense with their services when it rains, or is unpleasantly cold, or unusually hot.

A merchant or manufacturer should be sold advertising on the same basis that he develops other salesmen. Develop advertising for every day in the week, and unusual advertising will come automatically on unusual days.

A head of the advertising department should sum up his newspaper every day to find wherein it is better or fails to be better than other newspapers. If it isn't distinctly better, you have missed that day. Plans should be made to make the next day's and the next week's and the next month's business distinctly better. The succession of superior pages will tell in advertising influence. Much advertising is placed on the basis of volume. Therefore, strive to make your paper the leader every day in the week. Success depends upon a complete victory.

Put the right principles into practice in your advertising department. Persistently push your work and unusual records will result. Definitely decide what your organization is to accomplish. Then determinedly accomplish it. Plan your work, then work your plan. Remember that in advertising, as in all other things, success has no foe but fear—no limitations save those of your own.

On June 14, 1924, Hearst was asked by *Editor and Publisher* if his intention was to possess one hundred newspapers in the United States. He answered: "I have no intention to possess any given number of newspapers ... nor take on any more work or trouble."

The interviewer asked Hearst if he believed it was good public policy for one mortal man to possess the great power inherent in the control of so many newspapers, and he received this answer:

There are twenty-five hundred newspapers in the United States, and I have twenty-three. No very menacing monopoly in that proportion, I should say. There are ten times as many newspapers as I possess owned by reactionary and predatory interests that endeavor to use them in their schemes to exploit the public.... It is exceedingly beneficial from the public viewpoint to have a few groups of newspapers like the Scripps-Howard papers and mine owned and operated in support of progressive policies and to protect the public's properties and privileges.

In the third place, no newspaper has power for long, if it is misused. This is a saving situation in the possession of newspapers by public exploiters; and perhaps too, with respect to any individuals or interests. Newspapers do not form the opinion of the public; but if they are successful, they must express the opinion of the public.

Hearst was asked how it was possible for him or any man to delegate authority which will guarantee an administration of a newspaper in a distant city which will be fair and just to readers in local matters concerning which he could not possibly have full information, and he said:

The assumption that I cannot find able men in the community to conduct a newspaper as well as if I were on the ground is a piece of stupid conceit of which I am not guilty. I organize our papers with the best men available in the community. They consult me in general matters, but endeavor to carry out the desires of the community in all community matters.

Hearst was asked when he bought a newspaper what he paid for—circulation or character?

Opportunity [he answered] ; the character and circulation of a paper are what you make them. The opportunity is determined by the field and the relative excellence of competing newspapers.

When questioned as to what a newspaper must yield from its business and editorial departments to meet his minimum requirements Hearst replied:

I have no minimum or maximum requirements. I expect a newspaper to make as much profit as is compatible with giving the public a good newspaper, and making subscribers and advertisers feel that they are getting full returns for their money, and excellence in service.

I spend a lot of money in making my newspapers. As a matter of fact, I put back into the making of my newspapers over ninety per cent of the money these papers take in from subscribers and advertisers. . . .

Hearst was asked to estimate the capital value of a regular subscriber, and he replied:

I don't know. I don't think you can estimate the value of a satisfied subscriber merely in terms of money. The power of a newspaper depends not merely upon the number of its subscribers, but upon the confidence its readers repose in it. That confidence is earned by intelligent and unselfish service, by a long record of effort for the public good as the editor sees it. The power of a newspaper which has deserved and won the confidence of its readers is considerable, but the American people do not follow blindly the lead of any newspaper, even though they may entirely respect its motives.

As to whether the political influence of the American press was declining, and why—he answered:

I rather think that the influence of the American press is on the whole declining. This, I believe, is because so many newspapers are owned or influenced by reactionary interests and predatory corporations, and are used selfishly to promote the welfare of those reactionary interests rather than the welfare of the public. . . .

Furthermore there are other agencies of publicity which divide the field with the newspapers nowadays. There are motion pictures and the radio.

When asked why he gave so much time to motion pictures he answered:

I think they are important as publications and agents of publicity, both for instruction and entertainment. ... It looks at present as if the radio were likely to be controlled by a few large corporations and employed in great part for their propaganda. However, there may develop a wide field for radio in connection with newspapers and news services.

When asked if circulation was a test of merit he answered:

To a degree circulation is a test of merit. If any manufactured article sold more, and at a higher price than any other similar article, you would naturally infer that the one which sold the greater amount at the higher price was the better—or, at least, that it pleased the public better.

Hearst told the interviewer that advertising rates are too low when they give the advertiser a great profit, and the newspaper little or no profit, which it is often the case.

Advertising rates are seldom too high, if an advertiser knows how to employ advantageously the publicity of a well distributed and well established paper.

When questioned as to what were the correct proportions in a newspaper concerning advertising, news, opinion and entertainment Hearst replied:

The correct proportions of news, advertising, opinion and entertainment is what every fellow must figure out for himself. News, opinion and to a certain extent advertising must all come under the head of entertainment to a reasonable degree, or they will not be read. People do not like to be bored. They read to be interested. Unless we can make our material and every department interesting, it simply is not read. In this case we would be like the chap who winked at the girl in the dark—we would know what we were doing, but the public would not.

CHAPTER XLVI

CRIME

WHEN Hearst was twenty-four he became interested in prisons. In the *Examiner* he made a campaign to improve the city prison of San Francisco. He protested against the management of San Quentin.

As the years ticked on Hearst's interest in crime and its causes grew. He was especially concerned with saving the young from punishment. In September of 1919, two boys were given three hundred thousand dollars in bonds to deliver in New York City. They stole and sold some of them. Hearst had five sons of his own. In an article he said that employers, trying to save a little money in wages, had hired boys to carry thousands of dollars in money and securities. The employers themselves should have been compelled to pay for their thoughtless conduct in tempting the boys, then ruining them by having them prosecuted and sent to jail.

"Under proper circumstances," he said, "the boys might have grown up to be useful men with at least as much honesty as the average financial magnate."

In the *Post-Intelligencer* at Seattle, Hearst campaigned to save twelve year old Herbert Nichols, a child who shot and killed Sheriff John R. Wormell when surprised in a robbery of a grocery store in the little town of Asotin, Washington. Although a *Post-Intelligencer* reporter discovered that the child's father was in an insane asylum, and Father E. J. Flannigan rose from a sick bed to plead with Governor Roland H. Hartley to parole the boy to him, the Governor sent the boy to a life term in the Walla Walla State Penitentiary.

Hearst was greatly disturbed in December of 1929, when newspaper accounts reported that a seventeen year old boy had been stabbed to death in the Sing Sing prison yard by other convicts. In an editorial he asked: "What is a seventeen year old boy doing in Sing Sing prison?"

He said that the population of American jails was increasing 10 per cent a year while the criminal population of other countries was decreasing.

It is time for the American people to give thought to the problem of poverty, the problem of ignorance, the problem of crime. Anger will not solve the problem. Revenge will not, nor will cruel and unnatural punishment, nor jail penalties for small offenses. Shot-gun murders for trivial infractions of unjust laws, associating children with hardened criminals, herding erring brothers into jail until the prisons are packed with twice the population they are supposed to hold, until the President frantically cries to Congress for more prisons and more criminals, will not solve it. No penal or political system which multiplies the population of the prisons at the rate of 10 per cent every year will solve a problem which is growing to be more and more of a danger to the moral and social life of the nation. If you ask, "Am I my brother's keeper?" The answer is, "You are."

During recent years Hearst was especially aroused by prison fires at Auburn, Folsom, Colorado and Columbus. In an editorial he said that all the atrocities of the Spanish Inquisition would not equal the shameful horror of the burning by incapacity and brutality of three hundred and eighteen helpless fellowmen who, after all, had offended against our social organization less than it had offended against them.

On June 29, 1930, Hearst sent a signed editorial to his newspapers of which the following is a portion:

The prison system of the United States is an unendurable disgrace to a civilized country. . . .

An investigation was made of the prisons by the New York Commissioner of Correction, and it was discovered that some of New York's penal institutions were fire-traps. Unbelievable medieval conditions existed in the Tombs. . . . Mayor Walker found that the Welfare Island city penitentiary and workhouse was "archaic, inadequate and impossible." Rated as a model institution the New York City Reformatory was so overcrowded that prisoners slept on cots in corridors. State and city penal institutions were called "crime colleges." Seated as hero worshipers at the feet of hardened malefactors, youthful offenders were graduated in crime.... We've got to have fewer convicts. We've got to create a social system which will make more good citizens and fewer criminals....

A few weeks ago a woman was sent to a state prison in New York for stealing a coat. Yesterday in St. Louis two men were sent to prison for making themselves an alcoholic beverage. Every day more laws are being passed making more misdemeanors criminal offenses, and imposing jail penalties for every trifling infraction of every oppressive statute. Everything is being done to punish crimes and misdemeanors and even innocent errors, and nothing is being done to prevent such errors and evils.

As far back as March 20, 1899, Hearst made in the *Evening Journal* his first editorial protest against capital punishment. He tried to save the life of Martha J. Place, who murdered her stepdaughter, but he failed. In 1925, Hearst began a campaign in the *American* against capital punishment, and over his signature he wrote in the *American*:

What is murder in the first degree? It is the cruel, calculated, cold-blooded killing of a fellow man. It is the most wicked of crimes, and the State is guilty of it every time it executes a human being. There is no logic in the argument that murder must be punished by murder. Such punishment is nothing but legalized revenge, and revenge does not suppress crime. It stimulates crime. Furthermore, an eye for an eye, a tooth for a tooth, and a life for a life is not the teaching of Christ and should not be the law in a Christian community. Nor is there logic in the argument that frightful punishment prevents crime, through fear of consequences. Crime is suppressed by civilization, not by savagery. Education, enlightenment and improved social conditions eliminate crime which is generally born of ignorance, poverty, evil circumstances and vicious surroundings. Crime calls for cure, not for cruelty.

A few years ago men were blinded for killing a deer and were boiled in oil and broken on the wheel and torn asunder by wild horses for various offenses. . . . Cruel, calculated, cold-blooded killing has no place in the practice of a civilized community, and that murder in the first degree by the State belongs to the savage class.

Hearst made a campaign against the hanging of Gerald Chapman for murder, April, 1926. A portion of an editorial said:

The other day Gerald Chapman was hanged by the neck until he was dead, and that meant that he writhed for some nine or ten minutes in a horrible agony and frightful convulsions before at last death came to him. Gerald Chapman had taken life—at least the State was convinced that he had, although he denied it —and the State took Gerald Chapman's life . . . in order to prove that the taking of human life was wrong.

But first, Gerald Chapman was educated and graduated by the State as a criminal. His father and mother died when he was young, and he was at least morally, a charge of the State. When sixteen years of age he stole five hundred dollars' worth of jewelry and was sentenced to the Elmira Reformatory under a ten-year sentence. Here he received the ordinary course of education in cruelty. When he graduated from his course he worked as a conductor on a street-car. He stole some money from the company and was sentenced to ten years in Sing Sing prison. He graduated from there in due course with all that institution could teach him, and became the arch criminal who has just paid for his crimes with his life. How much of the fault of his failure was Chapman's? How much is the fault the State's? How much of the fault is the lack of practical Christianity in the life and law of this Christian nation?

"An eye for an eye and a tooth for a tooth" has failed—has always failed. It fails every day. In fact, on the very day on which Chapman was to be hanged for killing an officer of the law, another officer of the law was killed by another criminal. There is no deterrent in the menace of the gallows. . . . Greater severity does not prevent crime. It merely seems to promote crime.

The time for the State to protect itself against the criminal is before the criminal is made. Most criminals are not born, they are made. Crime is merely a matter of education . . . in decent directions. . . . What a State really punishes in a criminal is its own neglect, its own failure to do its duty to the citizens.

It has been said that dirt is merely matter misplaced. Criminality is merely misdirected mentality. The boldness, the cleverness, the resourcefulness of a criminal, are misplaced, misused. Many of the qualities that go to make a bad criminal might make a good citizen. . . .

You cannot cure murder by murder. We must adopt another and better system. We must try not merely to punish crime, but to prevent crime, to cultivate good citizenship, to create good citizens, the right kind of circumstances, the right kind of education. That is not only the duty of the State; it is the safety of the State; in fact, it is the salvation of the State and society.

Hearst's editorial on the hanging of Chapman drew to him wide attention. Among the many letters received by the publisher was one from Justice William Harmon Black of the New York Supreme Court. Justice Black praised Hearst's article, and the publisher asked the Judge to appoint members of a commission to meet and study the crime situation.

The American Crime Study Commission met for the first time at Chicago on May 28, 1927. Hearst was the honorary president. Members of the Commission were: Justice William Harmon Black of New York; Miss Jane Addams of Hull-House, Chicago; Sanford Bates, of the Commission of Corrections, Massachusetts; Manuel Levine, presiding Judge of the Ohio Court of Appeals; Frank Murphy, Judge of the Recorder's Court, Detroit; Carlos S. Hardy, Judge of the Superior Court of Los Angeles; A. C. Backus, former Judge of Wisconsin; W. W. McCrory, Judge of District Court of San Antonio; Charles S. Whitman, former Governor of New York, President of American Bar Association; William C. Boyden, President of American Bar Association; Rush C. Butler, President of Illinois Association for Criminal Justice; and Judge

Ben Lindsey of Denver. Each member spoke on the great problem.

The late Jane Addams of Hull-House described Hearst's earnestness. His listeners were moved as his voice broke when he spoke. He said that criminals could be divided into two classes: those who were criminals through inherited character-istics and those who were criminals through the force of sur-rounding conditions and circumstances:

The idea that we are free agents is not tenable.... We are free agents only within the strict limitations of our inherited characteristics and our modifying experiences.... We are no more actually independent of our antecedents and our influences than a leaf which drops from a tree on to the surface of the flowing river. The character of the leaf is determined by the tree from which it drops. The course of the leaf is determined by the cur-rent of the river.

Certain individuals, because of inherited characteristics... lack impulses to commit crime, or else possess self-control which restrains such influences. Other individuals, inheriting more of the primitive qualities, when subjected to evil influences have the impulse to commit crime, and lack the self-control to restrain those impulses. These latter individuals are criminals, or at any rate, are likely to become criminals....

We must remember that primitive men were criminals accord-ing to the moral standards of to-day. Plunder was part of their means of livelihood. Murder was part of their methods of com-petition and survival.... A veneer of civilization may hide these savage qualities, but they are always likely to break through the veneer and control the action of the abnormal individual. Ab-normal criminals are therefore, obviously more or less incurable. ... They are defective in the human machine ... subject to frac-ture under stress.

Such criminals, it would seem to me, should not be cruelly punished because of the abnormalities for which they are not responsible.... They should be merely deprived of opportunity to inflict injury upon society.

Criminals of the second group consist of more or less normal persons who are subjected at an early age to demoralizing influences, and whose criminal characteristics have been confirmed by criminals either in or out of penal institutions.

It seems to me that if normal twins were reposing in a maternity hospital, and one of these twins was reared under beneficial educational conditions, this twin would turn out to be a worthy and moral citizen; while if the other twin were taken by a criminal family and reared in evil surroundings it would turn out to be a criminal and a menace to the superior social organization which included its brother twin. . . .

The question then arises: "How far should a normal personality be punished for characteristics due to evil influences at an impressionable age, for which influences he is not as much responsible as is the social organization which permits them to exist?"

Hearst said that from time immemorial we have practiced punishment for crime without having eliminated it. He compared crime and disease. He spoke of the *Microbe Hunters* and how it was shown that yellow fever was eliminated by heroic American scientists, not merely by helping the patient, but by eliminating at its source the cause of yellow fever. Hearst asked:

Cannot the same scientific method be applied to the cure of crime by eliminating at their sources the causes of crime? . . . It seems to me the scientific principle for the cure of crime is the Christian principle, whether all who consider the question from this point of view are Christians or not. Whether they are inclined to consider Christ a divine being or merely a great teacher, all must realize that His teachings have gone hand in hand in the progress of civilization. . . .

Are we civilized enough to make a wider and better application of Christianity to the cure of criminals and the prevention of crime? Are we civilized enough to abandon the ancient discredited disproved policy which Christ disclaimed, of "An eye for an eye and a tooth for a tooth"?

Christ preached forbearance, forgiveness, brotherly love. . . . The exponents of the policy of cruelty sought to suppress His principle of sympathy and mercy while nailing Him to the cross. But cruelty here, as everywhere, defeated its object, and the result of their act was merely to aid in disseminating the principles of Christianity throughout the world.

Should we not apply the Christian principles of forbearance, of helpfulness, of hopefulness, to the treatment of criminals? Should we not apply the scientific principles of removing the cause of crime rather than treating the effects?...

Hearst outlined a plan for cure of crime. He said that the State should cease to commit murder—capital punishment should be abolished. Any abnormal or insane person who proved himself a menace to the community, should be deprived of the power further to injure the community. Conditions which create crime should be studied and as effectively eradicated as conditions which create disease. Those young in crime should not be sent to penal institutions to associate with hardened criminals, any more than patients afflicted with measles should be sent to a pesthouse to mingle with patients afflicted with smallpox. Punishment considered necessary as a deterrent to crime should be imposed promptly so that the effect of the deterrent—if there is a deterrent, should be as great and immediate as possible. It was his hope and the hope of all, that, just as brutalizing punishment diminished in the past so retaliatory punishments would diminish and disappear in the future. Crime would then be confined to those unfortunates whose mental and moral deficiencies and deformities made it possible for them to comprehend and conform to the customs and systems of civilized society.

Hearst printed thousands of columns in his newspapers in opposition to capital punishment. In California, Hearst papers supported an anti-capital punishment bill which passed the Assembly in 1932 and 1933 and was campaigned for most effectively by Noel Sullivan, a young San Francisco philanthropist. In Michigan, an effort was made in 1926 to restore capital punishment, and Hearst's Detroit *Times* vigorously supported the opposition which was led by Judge Frank

Murphy, later Mayor of Detroit and Governor-General of the Philippines. The bill was defeated but in 1928, the legislature voted in favor of capital punishment. Hearst called upon the Governor to veto the measure, and he responded.

During 1933, in a signed editorial Hearst again buckled on his armor to save the life of a woman, Ruth Judd of Phœnix, Arizona. He said in part:

Ruth Judd, convicted murderess in Arizona, tried to commit suicide in her cell, but was prevented from doing so by the authorities who proudly published the fact. Why do civilized or semi-civilized people interfere with a suicide in order to have the savage satisfaction of hanging a woman?

Let us assume that Ruth Judd is a murderess and was properly convicted.... What is to be gained by subjecting a woman to the horrible, brutal, savage death penalty of hanging? Shall we say that it has a deterrent effect upon other criminals? Apparently not, because in the State where they have no death penalty there are fewer murders than in the State where they have the death penalty....

The woman murdered in a frenzy of anger, or jealousy, or fear, or hatred. She had been raised in a good Christian family. She had been a harmless person during her life, apparently law-abiding, but overcome by some storm of the emotions she committed murder.

But the State murders in cold blood, and it murders with deliberation, premeditation, and intent to kill.... It insists upon killing with savage methods rather than allowing the woman to put herself out of the way....

The custom of hanging has survived from earlier, darker days. Is it not about time for modern States to emerge from the dark ages and discard the customs of the dark ages? Let hanging follow the unavailing cruelty of flaying and boiling in oil. Let Arizona be one of the civilized States to discard the survival of savagery.... Surely the men of Arizona would not hang a woman.

In recent years, Hearst was asked by a reporter his opinion concerning the part the press should play in the war against crime sponsored by him in many cities, and he said:

The duty of a newspaper is to record the events which happen in the world, the good occurrences and the bad occurrences, the achievements of worthy people, the mistakes and failures of the unfortunates, and the evil deeds of the unworthy. It records also the rewards of the deserving, and the penalties of the undeserving.

The general effect of this record to the reasoning mind must necessarily be that . . . education and intelligent effort secure the things that are desirable in the world, and that evil deeds bring unhappiness and disaster.

A newspaper should be as impartial in its publication of crime news as it is or should be in its publication of political news or any other kind of news. If it prints an accusation, it should also print a defense. . . .

A newspaper which fails to print any important class of news in which the public is interested would not be considered a complete newspaper. The New York *Times,* which is a very thorough paper, printed more words on the Snyder trial than any other newspaper in New York. . . .

The fact stories which appear in newspapers—such as romance, adventure, melodrama, comedy and tragedy—all these elements enter into human lives and all interest living human beings. There is no reason why any of them should be excluded from the stories of facts that are recorded in newspapers, any more than they should be excluded from the stories of fiction which appear in literature and the drama.

In dealing with these facts of life, the editor, however, must exercise good taste and good judgment, just as the playwright or novelist must. As a matter of fact, the editor generally exercises more discrimination than the novelist or the playwright, because he has a larger and more varied audience; because his product goes into the home and to all members of the family, every day of the year. Such great and all pervading influence must be kept wholesome and beneficial. In fact, it must even be exercised in a way to compel literature and the drama also to be wholesome and beneficial.

CHAPTER XLVII

BUYS ST. DONAT'S CASTLE

HEARST purchased St. Donat's Castle in Wales in 1925. Adventure, tragedy and high romance have dwelt in this medieval castle with its moat, drawbridge, portcullis and crenated battlements. The moat has been transformed into a croquet lawn. The keep is also green with grass. Cavalry stables flank a field on which knights in armor once engaged in friendly jousts, but the ghost of Lady Anne yields neither to modern improvements of Americans nor to time.

Lady Anne's ghost is not to be laughed at. It lives mostly in the tower. Once twelve pirates were gibbeted in the tower, but no pirate's ghost haunts St. Donat's. The pirates played hide-and-seek with death. They lost. They are as dead as dust, and they sleep the sleep of dust. It is Lady Anne of St. Donat's, the lady of unhappy love, who in dead of night when the storm howls along the coast up from the black raging sea, ever wrings her hands and wails as she wanders over the walls and up the stone stairways to Lady Anne's Tower where she died.

Legend tells how Lady Anne died and why. While her Lord was absent in the war she became enamored of a page boy. The Lord of St. Donat's returned from battle to discover his wife's guilt. In the torture chamber he himself tortured her to death. If you do not believe it, there are gulleys shown you to-day where once Lady Anne's blue blood streamed red. Since the day unhappy and tortured Lady Anne was sent to death, she has haunted St. Donat's. Few people will sleep in Lady Anne's Tower. Eleanor Glyn declares that once the ghost of Lady Anne came into her room at St. Donat's and tried to choke her.

During Hearst's last visit to England when he occupied St.

Donat's for a few weeks, three sturdy London chauffeurs were placed in Lady Anne's Tower. The next morning they were all found in one bed shivering and shuddering. They made an insurrection and demanded new quarters. Back to Lady Anne's Tower they would not go. All these adventures add to the picturesqueness of St. Donat's. Any one can buy a castle, but not every one buys a ghost.

Hearst first came in touch with his Welsh medieval fortress through purchasing several antique chairs and tables from the Castle. He was shown by an agent of New York antiquarians the photograph of a room in the Castle.

He studied the photograph closely and said, "That's a lovely room. Where is it?" He was told it was a room in St. Donat's Castle, Wales.

In April, 1925, when Miss Head, managing director of his English company, visited America, Hearst said to her that he had set his heart on possessing a castle in England. He mentioned that if either Leeds Castle in Kent or St. Donat's in Glamorgan ever came into the market, he would like to be informed. In August of that same year St. Donat's was advertised for sale in *Country Life*. For the first time Hearst saw a picture of the Castle. He was delighted. Immediately he sent a cable to Miss Head, "Buy St. Donat's Castle."

That day Miss Head made contact with the agents. Richard Pennoyer, an American, owned St. Donat's. Miss Head inquired regarding the acreage, and whether the property was freehold. Finally she made an offer giving a time limit for its acceptance. At twelve o'clock one morning she opened negotiations, and at half-past two in the afternoon the agent returned to her office saying, "The Castle is yours."

Miss Head had not seen the Castle. Hearst had not seen the Castle. Nobody connected with its purchase had seen it. To all concerned the acquisition of the Welsh Castle seemed like the acquisition of a small fairyland.

St. Donat's is an historic fortress near the village of Llandwit-Major in the Vale of Glamorgan on the Glamorganshire coast. Of all castles that still raise their proud walls along the blood-stained coast of Wales the most dramatic in size is St. Donat's, standing in a wooded glen on a high cliff gazing out on the Bristol Channel, across to Exmoor and its vast sea walls. The site of the castle, defended on two sides by a declivity and a stream, was a fortified camp from the time of the Roman invasion. St. Donat's has the largest wall enclosure of any castle in England. St. Paul is supposed to have been driven by storms into the Bristol Channel. Legend says he landed there and held service under a tree. On that sacred spot is the village chapel.

St. Donat's was the original stronghold of Fitzhamon's follower, Esterling. It dates back to 1080, and is said to have been given by William the Conqueror to one of his Knights, Sir William de Esterling, in reward for military services. The Esterling family held it until the eighteenth century. From the Esterlings it passed to the Butlers, from them to the de Haweys, and later it passed to the Stradlings. The castle had many owners, and finally was purchased by Mr. Williams of Aberpergwn in the Vale of Neath. Enriched by mineral assets of the family estate, he devoted money and years to restoring the Castle to the medieval and Tudor style. He never disturbed its aspect of looking like a stronghold of a border baron. The walls are grim, but the surroundings are charming and bosky.

High on the hill in St. Donat's Park, across the stream a watch tower rears its imposing height above the forest. At the time of the Stradlings it was ostensibly a beacon, and from the restored watch tower they kept a close eye on the Channel. It is claimed that the Stradlings lured ships to their destruction and possessed themselves of the wreckage when pirates were bold enough to sail along this becastled coast. The sea robbers' trade included the capture and ransom of coast magnates.

Once they secured the person of the Lord of St. Donat's himself. He was carried down to the Channel and held until the Stradling family paid a ransom. The sea robbers obtained

Photograph by International News Photos

WILLIAM RANDOLPH HEARST AT ST. DONAT'S CASTLE,
HIS HOME IN WALES

the ransom, but years afterward the same rover was prowling along the Glamorganshire coast, and on the scene of his former exploit he was caught by a storm and dashed upon the rocks. The Lord of St. Donat's was looking on. He drew in the big haul of the drenched but living robber who had been his captor and strung him up on an oak.

Two carriage drives lead to the arched entrance to St. Donat's, and thence to the early English Gate-house, complete with portcullis and guardroom. The outer bailey is enclosed by a battlemented curtained wall upon which a wide walk leads around the ramparts. St. Donat's of to-day shows no trace of the early building.

The present Castle appears to be of fourteenth-century structure with Elizabethan additions, and some good and careful Victorian restoration.

The supposed builder was Sir William Stradling of the time of Edward III. It has an irregularly shaped courtyard with three-storied buildings of good style surrounding a velvety green lawn, somewhat reminiscent of college quadrangle at Oxford. The windows are Elizabethan or Jacobean. On the west side the Castle overhangs a steep ravine. From the south side descends a series of pleasant terraced gardens to the shore of the Bristol Channel.

The Stradlings were furiously patriotic royalists in the great Civil War, mainstays of the King's cause in South Wales. During their four centuries of occupancy of St. Donat's they passed through many vicissitudes. Some of them died in prison. Others were exiled to Ireland. While they were fighting, St. Donat's Castle gave refuge to the fugitive Archbishop Usher who abode there for more than a year after Naseby. His study is still shown, for he devoted his enforced leisure to writing.

The Stradlings endured until 1738 when the last male heir made dramatic exit from life. While traveling on the *grand tour* he was killed in a duel at Montpellier. His body was brought home, and for a day and a night lay in state. Flambeaux placed around it caught some of the funeral trappings, and set fire to the family pictures which lined a great gallery. The portraits of five generations of Stradlings looked down on the burning of the last of their line, and then they themselves caught fire and with their chieftain made a funeral pyre.

For the first three years after Hearst owned the Castle nothing of importance was done with it, although he employed Sir Charles Allom, a distinguished antiquarian and collector, who had redecorated Buckingham Palace, to make the Castle temporarily fit for occupation. Hearst kept a skeleton staff of servants at St. Donat's, and had gardeners keep the beautiful grounds in order. In 1928, he went to England, largely to see his newly acquired property.

Immediately he went down by train to Cardiff, motored to the Castle and arrived there about ten o'clock on a silver moonlight night. So enthralled was he by the ancient structure that until he had inspected St. Donat's he could not even be persuaded to sit down to a ten o'clock dinner. With a lantern he viewed the battlements, the dungeons and every dark passage. Miss Head described him as emerging from the medieval dungeons covered with cobwebs, but happy as a schoolboy. At last he dined.

To Miss Head the most remarkable part of his visit was that after only one night's stay at the Castle he was able to carry away so complete a mental picture of the buildings that he found it possible to describe in great detail from America the restoration he desired undertaken. He was always able to identify in his own mind any given room or passage or courtyard about which Sir Charles Allom wished to consult him. Originally the Castle consisted of one hundred and thirty-five rooms, and its plan was somewhat haphazard, but Hearst remembered each room. The outer form of the Castle has been kept intact, but changes in the interior have been made.

Most essential was the reconstruction of the bathrooms. Even to-day English ideas of bathroom comfort are primitive when compared with American standards, and it is an exception to find more than four or five bathrooms in large English

country houses with twenty bedrooms. There were few bathrooms in St. Donat's in spite of the one hundred and thirty-five
rooms. Those already in the castle had been placed in most
inconvenient spots. One was next door to the dining-room, and
the other was in a passage leading to the kitchen. To-day St.
Donat's Castle is famous in England for the American luxury
of its magnificent bathrooms. Even in the Gibbet Tower where
a series of bachelor bedrooms was made, bathrooms were cut
out of the very thickness of the walls.

In the north court Sir Charles Allom constructed nine bedrooms. When necessary two or three rooms were thrown into
one, passages were built, and all rooms were made convenient
and accessible. After the bedrooms of the north court were
completed Hearst ordered the new wing extended by the addition of a large bay window with a delightful view overlooking
the woods and the estate chapel which lays claims to being the
oldest house of worship in England. A magnificent banquet hall
has been built by Hearst and enriched with a splendid Gothic
stone screen. The chimneypiece which came from a château
at Beauvais is of fine carved stone. Another impressive feature of the room is the carved ceiling from Boston Stump.
Over the banqueting hall is the new armory with a Gothic oak
screen and a minstrel gallery. There is also a new library which
has some of the finest linenfold paneling in existence, taken
from Ellenhall. Over the new armory and the new library is a
magnificent suite of a bedroom, sitting-room and bathroom with
views up and down the Channel. Each morning while at St.
Donat's Hearst spent hours with Sir Charles Allom over the
plans for paneling the armor room. This apartment contains
most of the large collection of armor, to which the editor is
ever adding. A room from Gilling Castle and the best features
of Brankstone Abbey will be incorporated within the old stone
walls.

In the older part of the Castle there had been little reconstruction. The old hall had been virtually left as it was, except
for the installation of an ancient carved chimney-piece. By

means of stone archways the hall had been joined to the gun-room. The Stradling bedrooms have been refashioned, and those in the Mansell Tower. The servants' quarters and kitchen accommodations have been entirely modernized.

The Castle has been filled with priceless period furniture which looks as if it has been in these great rooms since the days of the Stradlings. Hearst has preserved the atmosphere of the place and left untouched the beautiful terraced gardens, the cavalry barracks and the tilting ground where Cromwell stabled his horses in the Civil War.

In 1931, for the first time Hearst spent several weeks at St. Donat's. Meanwhile the Castle had been made into a rare museum by Sir Charles Allom and his staff who were directed by cable and letter from the publisher. Collectors speak enthusiastically of the extraordinary Elizabethan silver at St. Donat's. Particular interest centers around Hearst's own room which contains a collection of priceless Charles the Second, lacquer cabinets. There is a particularly beautiful one of scarlet lacquer with figures and scenes in blue on a cream ground. This cabinet is mounted on a silvered stand which is elaborately pierced and carved. The room itself is a study in scarlet with deep red paneling and red upholstered furniture. The bed is an historic piece, and one reads on the carved silver panel at the foot that Charles I slept in it in 1645. Another superb Charles II cabinet is lacquered inside and out with pagodas, birds, flowers in gold and silver on a mottled tortoise-shell-colored ground. The silvered stand to this cabinet is also carved with great wealth of detail. The massed effect of these five or six cabinets is extremely impressive.

In all the bedrooms are rare historic pieces of furniture. In the Stradling room there is a magnificent Elizabethan carved oak four-post bed, formerly in the possession of Lord Curzon. The Craven bed from Combe Abbey is another memorable piece, and so is the Chippendale state bed from Lord Vernon's collection. From the Duke of Bedford's collection comes a beautiful Charles II walnut cabinet with ivory and mother-of-pearl inlay.

Hearst never tires of collecting. Each day while he is at St. Donat's fresh crates of antiques arrive at the Castle to be unpacked, and the contents are opened for his inspection. Many of these purchases have been made for him by agents after his selection of them from catalogues. Some were made by Hearst in person in London auction rooms. A guest may arrive for breakfast to find an entire table strewn with medieval slippers, massive medieval locks and keys, curious internally painted rolling-pins of glass, grotesque and unique bronzes captured in Benin by an English punitive expedition, manuscripts, or first editions.

When the Master of St. Donat's is at the Castle he has English delicacies served at luncheon—mutton and hot-house fruits. Later comes tennis or croquet. Long walks are taken along the cliffs that line the shore. When the tides are safe there is swimming. For cooler weather he has added a large swimming-pool.

Hearst follows the English custom of afternoon tea. The circular oak table in the library is set with a lovely old Chamberlain Worcester tea-service. Hot water is brought in a gorgeous Paul Lamerie George II tea-kettle for the guests to make their own tea.

After tea, Hearst disappears to confer with Sir Charles Allom or to work with Secretary Willicombe. Cables, telegrams, and long distance calls radiate from the Castle. It is rumored that when the exchange operator at Llandwit-Major received her first request to call Los Angeles, she fainted.

Dinner at St. Donat's is picturesque and like a page out of the time of Elizabeth. A great fire leaps on the ancient hearth. The dark trees peer in through the leaded panes of the windows. The table is ablaze with flowers and silver equal to a king's treasure. When set for guests the silver on the table is worth a quarter of a million dollars. On either side of the centerpiece are delicate nautilus cups, the work of contemporaries of Benvenuto Cellini, one Elizabethan and one Italian. One is worth eight and the other ten thousand dollars. The great Queen Anne monteiths are priceless, and so is the Charles II wine cooler. In order to obtain his collection of Elizabethan and Georgian tankards Hearst has made new price records for old silver, but the collection was worth the effort.

Evenings at St. Donat's are informal. Hearst and his guests indulge in games of cards, charades and other simple amusements. Occasionally Welsh choirs compliment the Master of the Hall with concerts of the early, plaintive songs of ancient days in Wales.

Hearst takes seriously his position as lord of the manor. He is a member of and a contributor to the agricultural and sport clubs of Llandwit-Major, Pontyprid, Cowbridge and other villages in the vicinity. He offered a prize for the Cowbridge agricultural show and also for that of Llandwit-Major.

When Hearst is in America antiquarians and naturalists are frequently given permission to inspect the grounds at St. Donat's. One of the enthusiastic visitors at St. Donat's was David Lloyd George. Three or four years before the Great War, Mr. W. T. Stead, who was an important journalist of Great Britain at that time, told Lloyd George that W. R. Hearst was in London and that he ought to see him because the American publisher was one of the few men to be reckoned with in the United States. Lloyd George was then Chancellor of the Exchequer, and he asked Mr. Stead to bring Mr. Hearst the following morning to his residence at 11 Downing Street.

At that time Hearst was regarded as an anti-British influence in the United States, and Lloyd George received him with a patriotic bias against him. From expected hostilities a real friendship developed. When Lloyd George became Prime Minister he again entertained Hearst. After Hearst bought St. Donat's, Lloyd George became his guest, and he said that when the alterations are completed there would be nothing equal to St. Donat's as a medieval residence, except perhaps Windsor Castle or Arundel.

Lloyd George in making this statement was not aware that when his host was ten years of age and drove through the park at Windsor he said, "I would like to live there."

CHAPTER XLVIII

CRUSADE AGAINST NARCOTICS

FORTY-NINE years ago, William Randolph Hearst attacked a world vice and began a world crusade against narcotics. What the youth of twenty-four set out to do Hearst at seventy-two still carries on. To-day he visualizes as vividly as he did in 1887 the victims of narcotics with their hollow eyes, pasty countenances and shaking hands. They must be protected against themselves and their stealthy exploiters. Hearst still sees America aroused, the world aroused to the common danger.

California was so near the Orient that many addicts among the Asiatic population entered San Francisco. From the drugs and dregs of Chinatown came social misfits, drunkards, prostitutes and habitual criminals. Young messenger-boys were corrupted by degraded women and became criminals. Terrifying tales were told of opium smokers in Chinese dens. Dreadful and unsolved crimes were committed by those under the influence of narcotics brought into this country by every trick and device; in boots, books, hollow chair legs, and even in innocent fruit.

In an editorial Hearst said that no nation alone, however great its vigilance, could erect a barrier high enough to keep out narcotics when opium is grown or drugs are manufactured without limitation or restriction. The nations of the world must be aroused to coöperate against the world danger.

And yet, when morphine was discovered in 1806 by Chemist Hamlin in a little German village, it was hailed as a blessing in the sickroom. Fifty years later the hypodermic needle was invented by Alexander Wood, a Scotchman, and the curse began; many craving the sweet ease of the drug used morphine with the needle.

California addicts became victims not only of opium, but of codein, cocaine, heroin, alpha eucaine, alta eucaine, morphine, chloride hydrate, preparations of hemp, or loco weed. Marihuana is the Mexican name for loco weed—the American hasheesh from a little weed that grows in Texas, Arizona and Southern California. Most of the strange crimes of the southern Pacific coast come from marihuana.

When Hearst began warring against narcotics, nine-tenths of all the opium used in San Francisco was smuggled. Customs officials quarreling over prize money revealed an opium smugglers' ring in the Customs House. Then there was another wholesale smuggler, William Alexander Whaley, on his ship the *Halcyon*. An opium·factory in Commercial Street was seized in 1892. Two years later the *Examiner* criticized Warden Hale of San Quentin prison for owning a large interest in a patent opium cure.

Cocaine became a new evil to be fought, for in 1901 the price was lowered four-fifths. From the beginning Hearst tried to have laws passed prohibiting importation of opium. Nearly every important anti-narcotic law passed in the United States has been suggested or supported by Hearst in his newspapers.

The Japanese sold opium by the millions of ounces every year, but only physicians might buy it in Japan. They disposed of it to China and the United States, and they also dealt in morphine, heroin, cocaine and codein. England permitted the manufacture and sale of narcotics in her far-eastern provinces and made an enormous revenue growing the poppy in the Straits Settlement and in China. In India, there were two semi-annual public auctions of narcotics with all the world present and bidding.

Hearst argued that it was not right to sell narcotics to anybody. He protested against the double standard, one for the East and one for the West. He said that all the nations with interests in the Pacific should meet and see what should be done to control the opium traffic.

The first international movement against narcotics was the Shanghai Opium Conference called by President Roosevelt in 1909. It was hardly more than a pious discussion of narcotics, but out of it grew the various international opium conferences at the Hague, culminating in the opium convention in 1912. The nations of the world pledged themselves to restrict the sale of narcotics to medical and scientific purposes, and to eliminate traffic arising from smoking opium.

There were hundreds of thousands of narcotic victims in the United States, and because of them Hearst had enacted the Harrison Anti-Narcotic Law of 1913. It gave the Federal Government a weapon for combating opium traffickers, but there was a weakness in the fact that it was a revenue measure.

Then followed the Jones-Miller Act regulating the imports and exports of opium and narcotic drugs. Only sufficient opium may be brought legally into the United States to supply the country's medicinal and scientific requirements. Manufactured drugs may not be imported. Heroin, deadliest of opium derivatives, may not.be manufactured in the United States.

European factories continued to turn out tons of poison for American victims. During the first ten months of 1919, licensed manufacturers in this country purchased two hundred and fifty tons of crude opium when physicians legally needed only one ton. During this short period the United States imported ten times more crude opium than did the populations of Germany, France and Italy. There were about eight grains of "dope" per capita for every man, woman and child in the United States. This did not include contraband "dope."

Hearst called upon the civilized nations to do two things: limit the manufacture of drugs to legitimate, medical and scientific needs, and restrict the cultivation of the opium poppy to the fulfilment of those needs.

Already in 1916, experts had prepared for him two bills that were introduced in the New York Legislature. One bill was directed against alcohol in patent medicine, or a compound containing more than 10 per cent of alcohol, unless recommended by a physician's prescription. The second bill was against the sale of patent medicine containing opium, morphine, heroin, codein, chloral or their salts or derivatives. Violation of this law was a felony.

In 1922, under instructions from Hearst, the Chicago *American* launched a secret investigation of the narcotic traffic in the United States, and this resulted in the introduction of the Porter Resolution in Congress. From that measure came the call for the meeting of nations at Geneva for the purpose of reducing the supply of narcotics bartered through gigantic underworld organizations.

In 1929, the New York *American* revealed the perfect organization of the dope ring, the network of peddlers in the city, the sudden death that came from the betrayal of their secrets. Dope was sent by them to a small railroad junction in the State of Missouri and transferred to the dope ring in St. Louis. There were at least a half-dozen organized dope rings in Chicago.

The *American* revealed narcotic peddlers coming out of doorways, drug-stores, saloons. Some impersonated bill-collectors and carried bill-folds. Narcotics were smuggled from Mexico to Florida, from Canada into northern States, and brought by Pullman porters onto trains, and distributed throughout the country.

After the World War the Peace Treaty gave control of the international opium traffic to the League of Nations at Geneva. The United States as an outsider and a driving force compelled the League in 1925 to establish regulations of control. Another advance was made—for Europe. The treaty fell far short of remedying America's narcotic conditions, and our delegation, headed by the late Representative Porter of Pennsylvania, withdrew from the conference before the convention signed its pledge.

In her book called *Dope,* published in 1928 at the suggestion of Hearst, Winifred Black pointed out that the United States used twice as much dope as France, three times as much as England, eight times as much as Italy. She warned America against the vice that choked the life of China. She asserted that the World War revealed that the United States had hundreds of thousands of young men rotten with dope.

When Hearst learned in 1928 that in the State prisons as well as the Federal prison at Leavenworth, 60 per cent of the prisoners were addicts, he realized that here was a medical and pathological problem.

"Let us not shut up these unfortunate people in jail and prison," he wrote, "only to turn them out to go back to the drug. Let us help them. Let us call science to our aid."

Hearst suggested Federal farms. Congress approved of his plan, and the bill authorizing the farm colony was passed. The first appropriation was made in 1931, and the cornerstone of the first farm located near Lexington, Kentucky, was laid July 9, 1932. The second farm is to be near Fort Worth, Texas. Addicts in Federal prisons will be transferred to farms for cure and rehabilitation.

In 1930, Hearst suggested an independent narcotics bureau headed by an expert, and a bill creating a separate bureau of narcotics was introduced by Representative Porter and passed. For the first time the Narcotics Bureau was separated from the Bureau of Prohibition.

In 1931, there was another international narcotics convention at Geneva, and Hearst sent Winifred Black to report proceedings. Her keen eyes detected the chicanery at the International Narcotics Convention, and her articles telegraphed back to the United States helped solidify the American position. The new treaty was dictated by the American delegation of which Harry J. Anslinger, United States Commissioner of Narcotics, and Dr. Walter E. Treadway of the United States Public Health Service, were the controlling members. The United States was the second signer of the new treaty. Among the other signers were Turkey and Egypt, at one time distributing centers of the illicit traffic. The treaty is not perfect, but it marks advance.

In his papers Hearst is carrying on a nation-wide campaign for adoption by the States of a uniform narcotics law to replace the hodgepodge of forty-eight different laws dealing with traffic in narcotics. He seeks to drive out of the medical profession unscrupulous practitioners who debase their calling by dealing illicitly in dope. Under the proposed Federal legislation, ex-convicts and addicts must be registered before they can buy narcotics. When all States adopt the uniform law Hearst has faith that the illicit narcotics traffic will be annihilated. The struggle has been long, and at times seemed forlorn, and that is why the cause has been especially cherished by William Randolph Hearst.

The world goal now sought by him is the limitation of the sowing and growing of the beautiful flaming poppies that produce narcotics. Hearst feels that the day is drawing near when the opium traffic will be outlawed by civilized nations, as has been slavery.

CHAPTER XLIX

BUSINESS EXPANSION

I N the magazine world Hearst continued to widen his field and interests as he did in daily journalism. The Hearst magazines cover every phase of human activity except agriculture. Their contents are devoted to science and invention, fashions, dress, sports and recreation, travel, education, art, business and human affairs. Many of the changes in our methods of living are directly traceable to the influence of the Hearst magazines. Their editorial pages have helped to bring about a higher standard in sports, homemaking, literature, and they have influenced legislative measures for better living. They have played a large part in the development of better types of homes and created more attractive and practicable architectural designs. The better furnishing of homes in America to-day is due largely to educational work carried on by these magazines, the editorial columns of which taught the public how to arrange their dwellings for efficiency, comfort and ease.

Town and Country was acquired by Hearst in 1925. It is the intimate authentic record of the Social Register life of America. For many years it has reflected the activities of society, and it is now the accepted reporter for the ultra fashionable.

Home and Field became a member of the Hearst family in 1929. It was developed from the distinguished old publication, *The Field*. It contains a timely and complete exposition of unusual and correct architecture, decoration and gardening. *House Beautiful* was purchased in 1933 and combined with *Home and Field*.

In 1929, Hearst also acquired the *American Architect*. This publication has broken away from old traditions, and it places major emphasis on many features equally important to a successful architect. It enjoys unique prestige, and has a large circulation among leading architects, engineers and equipment specialists.

In its own field the *American Druggist,* acquired by Hearst in 1927, has become the most influential magazine. Its scientific articles are practicable and immensely useful. It has the largest number of paid readers of any magazine in the druggists' field.

In 1927, Hearst bought the Pittsburgh *Sun-Telegraph.* In this new paper he campaigned for bond issues enlarging school facilities, and for the installation of radios in every school-room. He held a George Washington bi-centennial essay contest, in which more than fifty thousand school children submitted essays on Washington's *Farewell Address* for the cash awards and medals offered by him. The *Sun-Telegraph* exposed election frauds, and at the suggestion of the paper, Pennsylvania adopted a Constitutional Amendment authorizing the use of voting machines as a substitute for paper ballots. The *Sun-Telegraph* also made a campaign against the Mayor of Pittsburgh and his former director of supplies who were convicted of malfeasance in office for plundering tax-payers by awarding contracts to high bidders. Hearst was also instrumental in the establishment and improvement of the Allegheny County municipal five-million-dollar airport.

In 1928, the Omaha *Bee-News* became a Hearst possession. The next year, in 1929, the publisher bought the San Francisco *Bulletin,* one of the most respected newspapers in the West for its reform and civic activities. Like the *Call,* the *Bulletin* was a part of the history of San Francisco. The two papers are combined under the name of the *Call-Bulletin,* and it dominates the evening field in San Francisco. In 1931, Hearst bought the Los Angeles *Express,* and the *Herald-Express* now controls easily the Los Angeles evening field.

Wherever Hearst has acquired newspapers his publications have led crusades. In 1922, the Washington *Times* started a campaign for pure milk. Now no milk is permitted to be sold unless it comes from a dairy approved by the health department. In the same year the *Times* exposed the common custom of obtaining illegal divorces secretly in Alexandria without notifying the wife or husband. In 1923, a crusade was conducted by Hearst for public ownership of the hydroelectric power plant, the Washington phase of his national crusade for public ownership of all hydroelectric power plants. The *Times* also brought about standard weight for all loaves of bread and a three-cent fare for children going to and from school.

In 1924, Hearst's Boston *Advertiser* published powerful editorials demanding hard coal and plenty of it, at a reasonable price in New England. The price of coal was so greatly reduced that the poor were able to secure the fuel needed.

In 1926, the *Advertiser* drove the Ku Klux Klan out of New England, and in 1929, the *Record* saved the shoe industry by battling for a protective tariff on women's footwear. Hearst received the deep gratitude of the long list of labor unions thereby benefited. The *Record* also led in the movement to raise funds for rehabilitating the *Constitution,* the glorious old frigate whose name and fame are a leading part of the history of the country. For thirty-four years the *Constitution* had lain at a wharf in a Boston navy yard. Its keel was laid when George Washington was President, and it fought in the Wars of 1812 and 1861. In 1931 the venerable sea fighter was put in commission with appropriate ceremonies, and it has made a tour of the ports of the United States. The *Record* led the fight against closing the Boston navy yard in 1931. As the result of an investigation by the *Record* in 1931 and 1932, it was found that young girls in sweat shops in Fall River, Lowell, Lynn and other industrial centers were being paid as low as one dollar a week by New York manufacturers. In 1921, the Boston *Sunday Advertiser* opened an employment bureau for World War Veterans. In the same year the *Advertiser* made a crusade and the Milk Trust loosened its grip on Boston's throat. At Christmas time the price of milk was lowered.

In Seattle, the *Post-Intelligencer* carried on a campaign for an airport, and brought about the Beeler Anti-Narcotic Law of 1923. The paper was also active in the recall of Mayor Frank Edwards. Following Hearst's policy from the beginning of his career as a journalist, the *Post-Intelligencer* advocated a municipally owned city lighting plant. It exposed attacks cruelly inflicted in wholesale fashion on epileptic and mentally deficient patients in the northern State Hospital. In 1930, a unique campaign by the *Post-Intelligencer* disclosed the abuses of the Alaska reindeer industry. The Eskimos, wards of the United States, were losing their deer because several private companies organized to breed reindeer were confiscating the natives' herds. One million reindeer were involved in the controversy, and a special commission was established in Alaska to administer reindeer affairs.

In 1922, the *Post-Enquirer of* Oakland began the movement for public ownership of water. A public utility district was created. Arthur P. Davis, formerly of the United States Reclamation Service, General George W. Goethals, chief engineer of the Panama Canal, and others found in the Sierra foot-hills an available water supply sufficient for a city of at least three million five hundred thousand people. In 1924, the *Post-Enquirer* succeeded in carrying the thirty-nine-million-dollar water bond issue, and a bond issue of nine millions, six hundred thousand for new school buildings. In 1925, the *Post-Enquirer* campaigned for twenty-five miles of city waterfront for the port of Oakland.

Detroit has seen many notable campaigns carried on by Hearst through his papers. The *Times,* in 1923, stood alone against and defeated four Judges who had been conspicuously cruel in their sentences. In 1924, it prevented an increase in the gas rate. In true crusading spirit it secured an injunction against the rate that the local gas company tried to impose upon the people. The *Times* also forced a reduction of gas rate amounting to one million dollars a year. It fought the telephone company and saved the public three millions a year. Through its columns the *Times* raised twenty-five thousand dollars for construction of a permanent "shell" to house the Detroit Symphony Orchestra on Belle Isle, the city-owned park in Detroit River.

In 1930, when there were thousands of unemployed in Detroit, the *Times* was the only newspaper to back Mayor Murphy's campaign for solving the unemployment problem. A free shelter was founded, and a free employment bureau. The *Times* originated the idea that every well-to-do family should take care of at least one unemployed family. In 1931, because of a campaign by the *Times*, reëstablishment of capital punishment was defeated by a one-hundred-thousand majority.

Soon after Hearst entered Baltimore the *News* and the *American* led the local boycott against the American Sugar Refinery Company, which was attempting to raise the price of refined sugar to an extortionate figure, from seven to eleven cents a pound. When the Chesapeake and Potomac Telephone Company, a subsidiary of the American Telegraph & Telephone Company, attempted to increase their rate, Hearst and his papers opposed the increase. The company modified its demands and millions were saved the city. The Baltimore *News* took part in the war nationally waged by Hearst against the narcotic traffic, and many of the "dope" peddlers left Baltimore. Through his papers Hearst supported the policy of conserving the national resources of Chesapeake Bay, which had been depleted by too much fishing.

From 1922 to 1928 in Rochester, New York, the *Sunday American*, by supplying scholarships totaling forty thousand dollars, enabled more than five hundred boys and girls to complete their public school education and supplement family incomes. In that city Hearst also carried on an anti-narcotics campaign. He opened a bonus bureau for the Monroe County World War Veterans, and in 1927 advocated and promoted the establishment of a municipal airport. In 1930, more than five hundred public and parochial school children were outfitted with warm second-hand wearing apparel to keep the children in school. The *Journal* and *American* had an emergency clothing depôt for school children, where volunteer women workers gathered to sew, mend and alter.

In Albany, New York, Hearst through the *Times-Union* called attention to the fact that Albany, the second oldest city in the United States, had no free swimming-pools or beaches within easy reach for those without automobiles. Hearst suggested a swimming-pool in one of the parks. In 1932 a municipal golf course was opened to the public. The *Times-Union* was also the first advocate of deepening the channel of the Hudson River so that vessels from the Atlantic and Pacific seaboard and from foreign countries could bring cargoes to and take cargoes from port. The Federal Government deepened the channel of the river to twenty-seven feet and supplied half of the funds required.

Atlanta saw Hearst make a special crusade through the *Georgian* for new school buildings. In 1932, the people voted ten to one for the bond issue in Fulton County for public school buildings to take the place of dilapidated fire-traps. A similar campaign was made by Hearst in San Antonio, Texas, where in 1924 he purchased the San Antonio *Light*. He made a dramatic campaign for a bond issue to erect new school buildings and enlarge others. Many of the pupils were on a half-time basis. In the stirring campaign women took part and the city bosses were defeated. Four million two hundred and fifty thousand dollars were voted for the erection of new school buildings.

In August of 1927, came a great tragedy to Hearst in connection with a transatlantic flight undertaken to advance aviation. Hearst had entertained Colonel Lindbergh and was filled with enthusiasm for aircraft by the daring young hero. Philip Payne, managing editor of Hearst's New York *Mirror*, was manager of the flying expedition to Italy of which the principal plane was *Old Glory*. Hearst did not realize that Phil Payne, his gallant editor, was to make the venture. In fact, he opposed the expedition's setting out unless the ship was in perfect condition and the air currents were propitious. On September 2, 1927, Hearst sent the following telegram to E. D. Coblentz, editor of the New York *American*, with a copy to be given to Phil Payne:

I do not think *Old Glory* should start except under the auspices of and with the full approval of the Government. In view of the recent disasters, I will not assume responsibility, but will proceed only if the government will assume authority and responsibility. The flight is not undertaken for promotion purposes, but to advance aviation, and it is doubtful whether in the light of recent events these flights do advance aviation. These numerous disasters may retard it. Therefore, I wait sanction of the Government.

W. R. HEARST

On the following day Hearst received the following reply:

Secretary of Aviation Trubee Davison and Department of Commerce pronounced *Old Glory* the finest ship to attempt the transatlantic flight. In addition, Mr. Coolidge has sponsored flight by putting letter on *Old Glory* to the King, while Secretary of State Kellogg has sent message to Mussolini. No plane has had such official sponsoring as *Old Glory*. The two pilots would rather give up all money in the world than forego their flight. Rest assured they will succeed. Best regards.   PHIL PAYNE

Two days later Hearst sent this telegram to Payne:

DEAR PHIL:
Please think of my situation. I have had one aeroplane lost and two fine men drowned. If another such disaster occurs effect would be terrible, not only on my peace of mind, but on public opinion. I telegraph you all this to have you get pilots to accept prize and give up dangerous adventure.

W. H. HEARST

From Old Orchard, Maine, on the following day there came to Hearst this message:

DEAR CHIEF:

The pilots appreciate your magnanimous offer, but insist they be allowed to fill their contracts to fly. Weather ideal to-day, and further delay ruinous to morale of pilots. Every possible precaution taken. Army and State inspectors went over *Old Glory* this morning and gave written approval to flight. You have been a great Chief to work for. I honor and love you, and I know you will forgive any mistakes I have made.

Affectionately,   PHIL PAYNE

Payne's final sentence in his telegram revealed to Hearst for the first time that his brilliant young editor was to make the fatal venture. At the last moment Phil Payne hopped off on *Old Glory* and he sleeps somewhere in the Atlantic. On board the plane were Philip Payne, Lloyd Bertaud and J. B. Hill, the pilot. There was hope that the men would be picked up in mid-ocean, but they were never heard of again.

In 1929, Hearst largely financed the world tour of the dirigible *Graf Zeppelin*, commanded by Dr. Hugo Eckener. As the great silver bubble floated down over California from San Francisco to Los Angeles it dipped in salute over San Simeon Ranch. In Los Angeles, Hearst gave a banquet on the evening of August 27th to Dr. Eckener and the passengers of the Zeppelin, in celebration of its safe arrival and in honor of the courageous men and women who ventured around the world in the dirigible. In his speech Hearst recalled that Magellan, first to sail around the world, took nearly three years to make the journey. The Zeppelin had gone faster than even Jules Verne's hero of fiction. During the evening, President Hoover congratulated both Hearst and Eckener. The *Graf Zeppelin* made its tour of the world in twenty-one days and seven hours.

In 1928, the Hearst newspapers outgrew the Rhinelander Building at 238 William Street, New York City. They now occupy an entire square block facing the East River at 220 South Street.

Once Hearst was asked by an interviewer if there was any justification for publication of private scandal:

None whatever [he answered], if it is private, and if it is scandal. News about the actions of private people ceases to be private when it gets into the public courts. I once sat next to a man at dinner in Washington, and he kept annoying me by telling me what some of my papers had published about his brother's divorce. I told him it was deplorable, but I would make a compact with him. If he would keep his brother out of the police and divorce courts, I would keep him out of my newspapers, because as far as I know his brother had no other claim to newspaper attention.... A newspaper's right and duty are to print public facts in which the public is interested, whether the individuals concerned are public or private.

Hearst was asked if he thought the entertainment side of newspapers was being exaggerated, and he replied:

I don't think so. The public demands in the newspaper both information and entertainment. Entertainment is not entirely supplied by features. It should largely be found in the news. Good writing is the important part of a newspaper's attraction. Every editor knows the value of human interest stories, the news item with a touch of humor or a touch of pathos, the news item of romantic character. News is not altogether hard facts. News is what the public wants to know about. Important facts are always news, but they are not all the news. The human side of life interests the public in a newspaper as it does in a play. The romance and tragedy of life figure largely in the news and always will, just as they figure in literature and in the drama. In fact, they have an additional appeal in the news of being true.

During the depression, Hearst sent to his newspaper staffs who were assembling at Atlanta, Georgia, the following message:

Progress is always possible. In good times it is more or less easy. In dull times it can be accomplished just the same, with a little more effort, a little more resourcefulness and a little more determination. Progress in dull times is even more valuable than progress in good times, because in dull times our competitors may not be making progress, and may be satisfied with the explanation that times are not good.

To reach an objective in spite of difficulties should therefore bring us the greatest results and give the greatest satisfaction.

Hannibal, Charlemagne and Napoleon crossed the Alps to victory.

Overcoming obstacles, or rather, not even recognizing obstruction as obstacles, is the surest way to success.

Therefore, whether we have good times or dull times, I know our papers can progress.

The man, not the conditions, makes success.

CHAPTER L

CAMPAIGN AGAINST THE POWER TRUST

DURING the decade preceding the World War, Hearst saw that the Power Trust was reaching out for every stream in the United States that could be seized, and he became the unrelenting foe of the "grabbers." The trust had lured away some of the Government's ablest officials, captured the National Conservation Association, and assembled a powerful lobby at Washington to direct water power legislation. As early as 1915, eighteen companies controlled the country's developed water power, and Senator George W. Norris of Nebraska was alarmed because he saw in the making what he called "the most gigantic, far-reaching and comprehensive monopoly ever devised by the mind of man."

During the World War the merits of the power controversy were obscure. On grounds of expediency a large section of the press supported the claims of the power companies. Hearst's eyes were not clouded by the smoke of battle. His editors were instructed to report all water power legislation. The force of his editorial warning increased. When the Shields Bill was proposed, Hearst pointed out that it turned over the last great natural resources to private interests under so-called leases which were virtually a grant in perpetuity. He succeeded in blocking the bill.

The power interests were filled with wrath. Their press denounced Hearst for his vigorous and alert news concerning their activities, and his editorial policy founded upon this information. It was called "sensational."

Hearst made it more "sensational." He asked and reiterated through his columns: "Why do the Americans pay six, eight and ten cents more per kilowatt for household electrical energy than the people of Ontario in the Dominion of Canada who buy this same energy from their publicly owned plant for less than two cents?"

Hearst decided to install an electrical plant to serve his own and surrounding buildings in Chicago. When he obtained permission to do so, the Insull interests grew panicky. They did not care to have Hearst reveal the actual cost of producing electricity. They gave him a new contract to supply current at about half the prevailing rate. Hearst accepted the contract, but into the agreement he insisted should be written a stipulation that every other consumer in Chicago using a like amount of energy should be supplied at the same reduced cost.

This experience with Insull only intensified Hearst's interest in public ownership of utilities. In 1920, Arthur P. Davis of the United States Reclamation Service, recommended in his report that a high dam be built to control the Colorado River flood waters with power to be developed to help meet the cost. He stated that borings in Boulder Canyon showed that site to be feasible, and that borings had been begun in Black Canyon twenty miles down the river.

The Southern California Edison Company read Davis's able, detailed report. They made an investigation and soon the company gave the newspapers a page story; they were going to build a dam at Glen Canyon on the Colorado.

Hearst read the news in the Los Angeles *Examiner*. He wired the managing editor a message that burned. He opposed the Edison Company's Glen Canyon scheme. The walls of Glen Canyon were of soft sandstone and would not hold the mighty dam. Besides, the canyon was too far away for commercial transmission of power. Above all, Hearst did not believe in private ownership of the natural resources of the United States. Hearst declared himself for the Davis project, and from that moment the *Examiner* in Los Angeles fought for it. The dam was really located at Black Canyon, but it bore the name of Boulder Canyon.

For many years Southern California and the Imperial Valley

region had agitated for the control of the Colorado River flood waters, and now the way to develop the Southern California empire was clarified. This new campaign became the purpose of Hearst's Southern California newspapers, the Los Angeles *Examiner* and the *Evening Herald.* Hearst said to George Young, publisher of the Los Angeles *Examiner,* "Keep at it till you put it over."

Young utilized every resource and showed much ability in the crusade. The *Evening Herald* backed up the *Examiner.* The two San Francisco papers, the *Examiner* and the *Call,* gave aid.

The project was fought by the Mexican Land Syndicate. The Los Angeles *Examiner* and *Herald* campaigned for congressmen favoring the measure, and for Mayor and councilmen, who were friendly. The papers opposed hostile judges in the Imperial Valley. The Hearst press helped recall all officials opposing the measure. Governor Friend Richardson, enemy of the project, was defeated by its advocate, C. C. Young.

The first actual step toward Boulder Dam was the passage in 1920 of the Kincaid Act. Then the Lower Colorado River region was surveyed. Frank E. Weymouth, chief engineer of the Reclamation Service, supervised the survey and recommended a dam in Boulder Canyon at least five hundred and fifty feet high. The Black Canyon site was chosen, but the name Boulder Dam remained. Senator Hiram W. Johnson of San Francisco, and Congressman Phil D. Swing of Southern California, introduced the Swing-Johnson Bill providing for the construction of the Dam and its accessories. Long hearings were held in 1925, 1926, 1927 and 1928.

Strong and able opposition appeared in Congress. Samuel Insull spent millions buying newspapers throughout the country to defeat the Dam. The press, politicians, railroads, gas companies and individual power companies were solidly against the project. Hearst instructed all his newspapers to play up Boulder Dam.

The lobby fighting the project was the mightiest ever assembled in Washington—it represented seven billion dollars in invested wealth. So boasted Samuel Insull's chief power lobbyist. He also declared that the United States Government would never be permitted to build Boulder Dam. A four-hundred-thousand-dollar "war-chest" was raised to defeat Boulder Dam, the Norris Muscle Shoals plan, and the projected investigation of the power industry. Every conceivable pressure bore down on Senators and Representatives to force them into line against "unsound and dangerous" measures.

Even President Coolidge did not believe that the Swing-Johnson Bill would pass Congress.

"Mr. President," said Hearst's representative who was calling on the President, "I am sure you will sign this bill before your term expires. I am so confident that I am going to ask you to send me the pen that you sign it with."

The President requested his secretary to make a memorandum of the pen.

So violent and far-reaching was the opposition of the Power Trust lobby in Boulder Dam that, in 1928, Hearst began one of his most important crusades, an investigation of the Power Trust. The nation depended upon that combination for heat, power or light, and Hearst felt that the people should be made to realize the sinister influence of the trust. Staggering amounts of securities were being offered to the public by the power and light industry, and people must be protected from buying these securities.

The late Thomas J. Walsh of Montana offered the resolution to investigate the Power Trust. It was said that there would be no campaign funds for the next Presidential election if power and light companies were investigated.

In the columns of his newspapers Hearst thundered:

Is the Senate afraid to disclose payments on the part of the Power Trust to political parties for further corrupt control of individuals in public life? Is the Senate afraid that more exposure of political crookedness will ruin the Republican Party? If the American people cannot have their policies cleansed by the Republican Party, they will put at the head of the Democratic Administration a man like Senator Reed or Senator Walsh who is able and willing to do the job.

The Walsh Resolution called for an investigation by a special Senate committee. The power lobby demanded that the investigation be made by the Federal Trade Commission. This body was thought by the power lobby to be their creature, but the appointment of a new commissioner had changed the attitude of the majority. Soon it was shown that the Commission's inquiry was more deadly in its revelation than the Senate committee would have been.

Hearst papers throughout the country revealed that huge sums of money had been spent stealthily by the Power Trust. Advertising was dangled before newspapers. Speakers were sent to clubs and civic organizations. Schools were invaded. They had a slogan prepared by Insull, "Get together for public utilities."

Insull's agents taught the wonders of electricity, its uses, the defects of public ownership. They employed professors of economics in colleges. The University of Colorado gave extension courses in the utility business by mail and charged thirty cents a lesson. Seattle, Tacoma and Los Angeles were pointed out as especially dangerous localities because of their success in municipal ownership. Samuel Insull himself lectured at the University of Illinois. His address was broadcast by two radio stations. He said that he wanted to keep children from starting life with the wrong point of view regarding public utilities. It was declared that 90 per cent of the textbooks affecting public utilities were written by socialists and advocates of public ownership. Any one opposing private ownership of utilities was called a demagogue, theorist, pink, red, radical, socialist, communist, Bolshevik. Even the Progressives were accused of working for destruction of government, and were designated as "mauve."

It was revealed that attractive sums were paid the friends

of the Power Trust. Two Oregon brothers with a large syndicate dealing in "canned" editorials distributed throughout the country, received eighty thousand a year. Two former United States Senators, Irvine L. Lenroot of Wisconsin, a Republican, and Senator Charles S. Thomas of Colorado, at one time a Bryan Progressive Democrat, were in the pay of the trust for a handsome sum. Because of their former positions both had freedom of the floor of the Senate. Insull even invested in candidates for the United States Senate. Republican Frank L. Smith of Illinois received one hundred and twenty-five thousand dollars, and Democrat George E. Brennan had fifteen thousand dollars.

These revelations were made by the Federal Trade Commission and the Hearst newspapers displayed them conspicuously and made frequent editorial comment. When the vote came in the Senate on the Swing-Johnson Bill, few senators were willing to stand publicly and conspicuously with the Power Trust—only eleven. The measure had already passed the House. President Coolidge signed the Boulder Dam Bill on December 21, 1928. He kept his promise. The pen used by him in signing the bill hangs on the wall of the office of the publisher, George Young, in the Los Angeles *Examiner* Building.

Later came the crash of the Insull Power Empire. Samuel Insull lived several years in Greece, but when he returned to this country and was placed on trial, he was acquitted of wrong-doing.

Boulder Dam will be seven hundred and thirty feet high, the largest dam in the world. The project will probably be completed in 1938 and will cost one hundred and sixty-five millions, apportioned as follows:

Dam—$70,000,000
All-American Canal to distribute water to the Imperial Valley —$31,000,000
Power plant and machinery—$34,000,000

Other expenditures including interest during construction—
$30,000,000

These sums will be returned to the Government of the United States, the builder, under power contracts in fifty years. With ample contracts on hand to guarantee repayment of the cost of the project to the Federal Government, the construction contract was awarded to the Six Companies, Inc., on May 11, 1931, by Secretary Wilbur of the Department of the Interior.

Boulder Dam will supply domestic water for seven million five hundred thousand more people in Southern California, or approximately the population of Belgium. This would be equal to water one foot deep over the entire State of New York. It will also irrigate several hundred thousand acres in Arizona and an equal additional area in California. The States of Nevada and Arizona will have 18¾ per cent of all surplus revenues from sale of power, and will also have certain power rights. Even the Southern California Edison and Southern Sierra Power Companies which opposed the Dam will get current for their customers. California, Nevada and Arizona fought over the dam because each imagined that it owned more of the Colorado River than it did.

Conspicuously active in the fight for Boulder Dam and aiding the Hearst press, was a valiant little band of legislators representing western States, the Progressive group in Congress. The story of their victory over the forces of massed and predatory wealth is one of the fine chapters of political history.

Another project fostered by Hearst in Los Angeles, the Colorado River aqueduct, rivals in magnitude its parent enterprise, Boulder Dam. The Metropolitan Water District, comprising a number of California cities headed by Los Angeles, to bring water from the Colorado River to Southern California municipalities, is the builder.

The cost of this project ranges somewhere between two hundred, and two hundred and twenty millions. The district organized to build it voted bonds. The aqueduct approximating two hundred and sixty miles in length, is designed to furnish a water supply for Los Angeles sufficient for a population of about seven and a half millions.

Hearst always welcomes municipal, State or Federal ownership of utilities. Throughout the years he has advocated that the mighty River of St. Lawrence be harnessed for the benefit of the people of New York State. In his publications he has also supported Government ownership of Muscle Shoals, which Senator Norris long and courageously espoused, and which has been given effect by Congress and President Roosevelt.

CHAPTER LI

HEARST AS A FATHER

IN May of 1922, Hearst went to Europe for the first time in ten years. With him were Mrs. Hearst and their three oldest sons, George, William Randolph, Jr., and John Randolph. Hearst always felt grateful to his mother for acquainting him at an early age with the art and beauty of Europe. His own life had been so tempestuous, in fact he had lived so many crowded lives, that sometimes he reproached himself for not having given to his sons more of that personal attention received by him from his mother, and which had been for him definite enrichment of existence. And so Hearst planned this European journey especially for his sons.

In the party were the Guy Barhams of Los Angeles. Barham was the publisher of the *Herald*, and one of Hearst's boyhood friends. To Barham, William Randolph Hearst always remained "Will," as he did to Orrin Peck and Fred Moody, and as he does to Eugene Lent, Will Tevis, and the friends of his early youth. To his later friends he is "W. R." or "the Chief," and to his acquaintances he is "Mr. Hearst."

When Hearst arrived in London he had a long talk on the Irish situation with Arthur Griffith, President of the Dail Eireann, and Michael Collins, head of the provisional government of Ireland. Griffith and Collins were in London conducting negotiations with the British Government arising out of the development of the treaty situation. Mrs. Hearst, who is partly of Irish extraction, took a deep interest in the Irish cause. The Hearsts were received by the delegates at the Metropole Hotel.

Later the publisher and his wife were entertained at luncheon by the British Prime Minister, David Lloyd George, and his daughter, Miss Megan Lloyd George, at No. 10 Downing Street, the historic home of British Premiers. Then they were the guests of Lord Beaverbrook, one of the leading publishers of Great Britain, at his country home, Leatherhead, in the Surrey hills. Mrs. Hearst and her sons were conducted over the House of Parliament by the Lord Chancellor, Lord Birkenhead.

Hearst told a London interviewer that he did not go to Epsom to see the Derby because he was not interested in racing. While on a previous journey he had gone to the Derby to see the people, instead of the races. In fact, before the great race was run he left. On his way back to London men ran out of the houses along the road to ask who won the Derby. When told that he did not wait to find out, the questioners thought him demented.

In London, Hearst was interviewed by Sir Hall Caine, who wrote of him this description:

The personality of William Randolph Hearst is a staggering surprise. Seen at close quarters across the width of a table, it gives the lie direct to nearly every preconceived idea that has been formed of his life.

He is a tall, powerfully built man who must, one would say, have spent many of his early years in a health-giving life of open-air. His face is large and strong. In repose, he is intensely serious. In conversation it is lit up by a smile of extraordinary winsomeness, and even charm. His voice is soft and almost gentle. There is no excess of emphasis, no violence and no vehemence. His manner is pleasant and conciliatory. When strong opinions are expressed, they are put forward without any suggestion of infallibility of judgment.

"Well, yes, that is my opinion," is a phrase frequently on his lips. The last thing you would say of Mr. Hearst in meeting him is that he is, in the ordinary sense, a hustler. If he controls great enterprises, one would say that he does so without fuss.

His speech and his movements are almost leisurely. There is nothing of the political fanatic about him, and nothing of the revolutionary. If his convictions are deep, they make no noise— in conversation at all events. If he has prejudices, he must reserve them for the press.

Hearst told Sir Hall Caine that he believed England's policies to be misguided, and that England's disposition to interfere in American affairs was to the disadvantage of America. He said that the attempt of England and other nations to cancel their debts to the United States was a very good example of how Great Britain and other foreign nations used the United States to their own advantage and to the disadvantage of the United States.

Hearst did not remain long in England, for his friend Guy Barham died suddenly in London. He escorted the widow and daughter of his dead friend to America on the *Olympic*. From this time Hearst's interests in California increased. His newspapers were vastly profitable, and he himself was extensively producing motion-pictures in Los Angeles. When the Hearst boys returned from Europe with their mother, they were reentered in California schools.

In the summer of 1922, Hearst Hall, the gymnasium and assembly-room given to the University of California by Phebe Apperson Hearst before her death, was destroyed by fire. Hearst Hall was the largest structure for the exclusive needs and the recreational activities of the women students of the University of California. Hearst realized how great a loss to the university was the destruction of this gift of his mother's, and so in her memory he offered to rebuild Hearst Hall at the expense of a million dollars.

Hearst Hall was not merely a woman's gymnasium. It was designed by Mrs. Hearst to express to the women of the campus the beauty of interior decoration, and to enable all to share the charm and grace of social life.

President David P. Barrows said of the new building: "All that Mrs. Hearst's generous and gracious nature bestowed on the University of California is now to find permanent expression in the devotion of her son. There could be no action so full of benefit to this great institution which for more than a quarter of a century had Mrs. Hearst's unceasing care and service."

When the memorial gymnasium was dedicated on April 9, 1927, in reply to the congratulatory messages by Governor C. C. Young, President W. W. Campbell and members of the Board of Regents, Hearst said that he was not one to find anything to criticize in the rising generation:

I think it is a wonderful generation, the most wonderful generation the world has ever seen. The fact that these young people differ from their elders in some things is not necessarily an indication of error: it may be the exact measure of their superiority. ... To them this building is dedicated. I built it to take the place of the hall which my mother built, and which was burned to the ground. It is devoted to the same purposes and it is built as nearly as I know, as she would have built it if she had been here.... We all hope that this structure dedicated to-night is suited to its purposes, and that it will suit and please the young students to whom it is devoted.

To the University of California came Hearst's two older sons, George and William Randolph, Jr., and later Randolph, one of the twins, entered as a student. Hearst's mother and father were his closest and most cherished friends, and he has kept in close contact with his children. Even when they were small he did not like to have them humiliated by practical jokes. In order to amuse himself at the expense of Master George Hearst, a servant once put on the boy's coat wrong side out. Grown people laughed, and the child was humiliated. Hearst did not like to have the boy's dignity wounded.

Both William Randolph and Millicent Hearst are instinctively democratic, and George grew up a natural democrat like his parents and grandparents. After he left the University of California he took a minor position in the circulation department of the *Call* at San Francisco in order to learn the business. Good humoredly he acted as pinch-hitter for various departments. In the rush of going to press he was at times taken for an office-boy, and he acted as messenger for the reporters. With a broad grin and great friendliness he complied. Later he entered the business office of the *Examiner* and afterwards became its publisher.

George Hearst, Jr., was one of the first to become deeply interested in aviation, and he travels in a tri-motor plane. A few years ago he became the hero of the Mother Lode country near Sonora by risking his life bucking dangerous currents of air in order to find a small boy who had been missing for a week, but who later proved to be drowned. In 1933, Governor Rolph appointed George Hearst naval commander of California. The Governor also gave away the bride when George, in June of 1933, married Mrs. Lorna Velie at San Simeon, California.

When William Randolph Hearst, Jr., was at a military academy in San Rafael he wrote some letters to his father that greatly pleased the publisher. Hearst kept the following letter:

DEAR POP:

I received the editorial the other day, and this is the first time I have had time enough to tell you about it. I read it over several times and have thought about it quite a lot.

I realize that us kids are handicapped by too much money. We cannot realize the feeling that we *have* to work to keep alive. You have taken such good care of all our needs and whims that we do not know what the word "want" really means. I don't think that we are spoiled, or that money has turned our heads. If it had we would have been told about it sooner. At least, I would, because the boys at Berkeley are not the least bit shy about telling a person what they think of them. I saw this in the paper this morning, "Count your friends, it won't take long." This is true about rich kids. But I really have some good friends in Berkeley, and I have made some here. Mr. Brisbane says that money kills ambition. Not necessarily. Necessity makes a person work a lot harder, that is true. But if it is a worthy ambition, it takes more than money to *kill* it. I'll tell you what my ambition is. It is to be able to help you in your business, to be capable to do my part, and then some. I have tried to prepare myself in my school work with subjects that would help me in journalism, such as all the History and English I can get. I read

MR. HEARST CELEBRATED HIS SEVENTY-FIRST BIRTHDAY BY
PLAYING TENNIS WITH HIS THREE ELDEST SONS

From left to right: William Randolph Hearst, Jr., President of the New York
American; William Randolph Hearst; John Randolph Hearst, Vice-President of
the International Magazine Corporation; George Hearst, President of the San
Francisco *Examiner.*

a good deal, as you know, and I try to pick out useful books. You may think I am just saying this to please you, but it really is the 'truth. All of us kids hate society because those kids are sissies. They wouldn't work if it was the last thing to do in the world. They think people who work are below them in "social standing" and therefore, inferior. Out here the kids work all summer, some in lumber camps, other on ships to Hawaii, or to the Orient. And these fellows are real good guys. If they are your friends, they will stick by you. I'll bet that a lot of people in New York wouldn't do a thing for us if we went broke. And how those people stick around and flatter you and Mom. That is kind of off the subject, but what I meant to say was, we don't shirk work. All of us appreciate what you have done for us, and I am sure that we are not made of the stuff of a fellow that will not work if he does not have to.

Well, Pop, I'll have to close as taps are going to sound in a few minutes, and I still have to undress. I got a letter from Mom saying she was going to Europe, but would be back soon. I've had enough of that place for years.

If you ever have time, please drop us a line, as it is kind of lonesome here.

But we hope to see you at Christmas time,

Your loving son,

BILL.

In one of Hearst's letters sent to William Randolph, Jr., the father tried to develop his son's belief and pride in the form of Government of the United States. He inclosed a dispatch showing that in nine months the German Government had five elections. Then he added:

DEAR BILL:

Brisbane says it takes a good mind to resist education. He is perfectly right. There is a lot of so-called education that ought to be resisted and rejected. Most college professors teach that the political systems of Europe are superior to our own.

You said the other night that you thought they **were**; at least, you asked me if I did not think they were.

I do not think so. I think our own system is the very best that has been devised. You should study it more carefully and know accurately what it is. You cannot intelligently criticize the political system till you know what it is—what its virtues are and what its defects are. You did not know how long the representatives of the lower house served. They serve two years. The whole House of Representatives is elected every two years. That is not too long for Congress to be in office. It takes a certain time to organize, and a certain time to discuss and consider the various problems of government, a certain time to familiarize themselves with recent developments in economics and political situations, a certain time to pass advisable legislation. Two years are not at all too much, and it is well to have a stated period in which Congress will have a reasonable time to do the necessary things before it.

If you want to see some of the difficulties of the European system, please read the enclosed paragraph. This is only September, and there have been four elections in Germany this year, and they are now preparing for a fifth, to be held on November 6th. Imagine what our country would be if we had elections spattered over the political situation with that frequency, or with anything like that frequency. Elections are disturbing, not only to political peace of mind, but to business. A Presidential election every four years disturbs business to a degree. We do not want a Presidential election oftener than four years, nor a Congressional election oftener than two years.

Affectionately,

Pop

Later Hearst sent a telegram to his son congratulating him on becoming a member of the New York City School Board:

San Simeon,
California,
February, 26, 1932.

W. R. Hearst, Jr.,
    The American,
        New York, New York.

Congratulations, Bill, on your appointment, and particularly on your fine talk. There is certainly no way in which you can do more service to the community than in building up the public school system. Furthermore, there is no city in which public schools are more important than in New York, the great melting pot of the nation where good schools will transform immigrants into good American citizens. I am very proud of you, son, and I feel sure you will make a fine record. Please thank Borough President Levy and Mayor Walker on my behalf for their kind action.

POP

To the same son Hearst wired birthday congratulations:

DEAR SON:
I hope you have a happy birthday. Twenty-five years old. That seems mighty old to you, I suppose, but mighty young to me. Gosh! You have a lot of good years ahead of you, and you have done very well indeed, with the years you have had. I am very proud of you. Affectionately,

POP

In response to a telegram from William Randolph, Jr., on his seventieth birthday Hearst wired:

DEAR BILL:
Thanks for your telegram. Geeroosalam! There seems to be a health depression as well as a financial one. Hope you will be well soon. When you get well you have got to stop burning the candle at both ends and in the middle. Meanwhile get yourself in shape. So you are actually missed at the office. I did not think anybody would be missed but myself, but I am glad I was wrong.

POP

William Randolph Hearst, Jr., is president of the New York *American* and director of Hearst Consolidated. In 1933, he married Mrs. Lorelle McCarver at Palm Beach.

When John Randolph Hearst, third son of the publisher, was at a military academy in San Rafael, California, with his brother William, he wrote a letter when he was only fourteen that greatly pleased Hearst.

DEAR POP:

I was very glad to receive your letter. I've got that editorial tacked up in my room. It sure is a good one. You and Mom have given us enough nice things to get spoiled over, but I think we understand the right way to use them, and also the value of getting the nice things.

I think we both will turn out to be hard workers. We are small, but we understand the necessities and work of life. I have thought a lot about what you said about work, that you could never work and work right on a thing if you did not like it.

Next summer after school I am going to work on the *Examiner* for a month or so, just to learn one end of the business young. If I do go to work, I will go to work in the linotype department under direction of Mr. McNeery. He offered me a job one day while I was up there putting the different news on different hooks, and marking the different ones.

My birthday is on the twenty-sixth of this month, and I guess George and Blanche will come out and take us to dinner. I sure hope so. . . .

Hearst took his letter from John Randolph and placed with it the letter written at the same time by William Randolph, Jr.; and sent them to Mrs. Hearst with this message:

DEAR MILLIE:

Aren't these two lovely letters from these two kids? I almost cried over them. It is wonderful to think they have such high purposes and such good views. It shows they had a good mother anyway.

W. R.

Hearst was especially pleased with John Randolph, who is now vice-president of the *Cosmopolitan Magazine* and Assistant Manager of the Hearst organization, because when he was a child he showed a great interest in collecting samples of quartz. He thought he saw in the boy the instinctive love of geology that his own father, Senator George Hearst, displayed early in his boyhood. The manager of the Homestake Mine sent John Randolph samples of quartz which the boy added to his collection.

Like his father, John Randolph Hearst has great physical courage. He leaped overboard from a yacht at sea, and although completely dressed he was able to save the life of his drowning dog. John Hearst has the democratic spirit of his parents and brothers. When a small boy in New York he collected in the streets a dozen or more lads and brought them as his friends to the Gothic apartment on Riverside Drive. Hearst received them as if they were highly placed children, treated them to ice-cream and cake, told them their parents were worried about them, and had them escorted to their homes. Hearst shares the friendships of his sons. Once he provided schooling for a lad that John casually became acquainted with and had made his friend.

In 1927 and 1928, John Randolph was a student at Oglethorpe University, at Oglethorpe, near Atlanta, Georgia. In February of 1933, he married a southern girl, Miss Gretchen Wilson, a great-granddaughter of General Stonewall Jackson. The wedding took place at San Simeon.

In May of 1927, Dr. Thornwell Jacobs, president of Oglethorpe University, placed the purple hood of Doctor of Laws around the shoulders of William Randolph Hearst. The publisher was greatly pleased with this honor, for he had great sympathy for Georgia, youngest of the Colonies founded by the great philanthropist, General James Edward Oglethorpe, as a refuge for unfortunate and worthy indigent classes of Europe. This colony was the home of German Lutherans, Piedmontese, Scotch Highlanders, Swiss, Portuguese, Jews and Englishmen.

The purple hood was given Hearst with this simple accolade: "William Randolph Hearst, counselor of millions, lover of America, exponent of perpetual peace entente among the English-speaking nations of the world."

In his Baccalaureate address the publisher spoke of the

great discoveries and inventions of the nineteenth century and then said:

The most important achievement of all would seem to me the abolition of the utterly uncivilized and wholly savage institution of war. . . . In ancient times war was in the nature of a business adventure. Each side went into the conflict in the hope of defeating and plundering the other side and returning home with the spoils of conquest. In these days there are no spoils of war. There are only debts and taxes. . . . The victorious nations are as impoverished as the defeated nations. . . . War brings nothing but disaster to the individual nations concerned and demoralization to the business of the world. It is doomed to die. Then how can we best approach the abolition of war . . . or the establishment of universal peace?

To my mind . . . the time is ripe to advocate the coöperation of the English-speaking people of the world to maintain peace. I do not mean by this any "entangling alliance."

Hearst explained that the plan he had in mind would exclude consideration of India, Egypt and such subject peoples, and would mean that the United States, Great Britain, Ireland, Canada, Australia, New Zealand and South America would coöperate to insure peace among themselves and maintain the peace of the world. "We are all pacifists in America, in that we are all opposed to war and in favor of peace for ourselves and for the world."

Hearst said that the advocates of the League of Nations need have no hope of the United States ever becoming a party to any League or World Court where the representation of the United States would be in a minority. His proposed compact among English-speaking nations was on the basis of equality between the United States and the British Empire.

In 1929 Hearst gave to Oglethorpe University the four hundred-and-forty acre wooded tract of Silver Lake Park. This gift, in addition to several sums of money, was of great assistance to the new Oglethorpe University which was established by Dr. Thornwell Jacobs. Old Oglethorpe University was founded in 1827 at Milledgeville, Georgia, but was buried in the ashes and invasion of battle during the Civil War. Dr. Jacobs resurrected the old and established the new university.

Hearst himself has worked since the age of twenty-three, and although he has given his sons every luxury, he wishes them to take life seriously, to realize that achievement comes only to those who give everything within themselves to the task. When the boys fell behind in their school work, he was always the first to reprove them. Once he discovered the twins, Randolph and David, passing through a phase of idleness and lagging in school. He sent the boys this night letter:

Randolph and David Hearst,
Riverside Drive,
New York.

You have had a good time at Palm Beach and we try to give you a good time as often as possible; but you cannot always be merely having a good time, and your mother and I expect something more of you than to be playboys. This is not a good period in the world's history for playboys. Things are too serious. Situations are too dangerous, and I want you two boys who are now getting to be men, to begin to take a man's view of life. You will have to work, and work hard. You might as well be learning how to work now. You have got to get an education that will make you able to take care of yourselves. No one knows whether you will inherit anything or not; but if you are not able to make money, you will not be able to keep money. If you are not trained for the contest that is ahead of you, you are likely to bring up in the rear of the procession.

Instead of getting better and better as you get older, you get lazier and lazier. The master of the school complains that you do not work. If he had said you do not succeed, I would not have felt as badly as when he said you do not even try to succeed. I said in the beginning, "We try to make your lives happy. You owe us something in return." Consequently, if you do not want to do anything for yourselves, you should do something for us. I think I have said enough for any boys that have any filial feeling or any sense of gratitude, or any common sense.

I want you to go to work and make a good record this coming session at your school. If you do not do this, I do not want you to come out West. I am going to send you to a summer school somewhere. You have got to learn something, and you have got to go out into the world trained and equipped to do something. Get that firmly into your mind and stop wasting your time. I want to see what you can do when you really work, and I want a monthly report on what you are doing during the coming term.

That Hearst is able to take a philosophic attitude about mischievous youngsters, and that he respects the personalities of his sons, is shown by a letter that he wrote Mrs. Hearst concerning the twins.

DEAR MILLICENT:

I have read the master's letter about Randolph, and I suppose David, too. There is nothing very surprising in this. These boys are simply behaving as the others did. We may not approve of their behavior, but it is characteristic of the clan.

They do not take kindly to education. This is probably a defect, but Brisbane says, "It takes a good mind to resist education." Anyway, a certain kind of good mind does resist education. The boys seem to have active and independent mentalities, and perhaps are cut out to be good businessmen. I wish they would learn something, but apparently they will not. It is not the fault of the school. We used to think it was. We sent John and William to various schools. The lack of result was always the same.

I suppose the school is a good one, but I imagine it is a little trying on boys of the character of Randolph and David. The school is probably too strict with them. They do not submit tamely. They have no particularly bad habits, no evil tendencies. They are simply more or less untamed and untamable. I always rather let John and William have their own way. I thought it would develop character and self-reliance in them. I imagine we will have to do pretty much the same with Randolph and David. At any rate, I would not worry about them. There is really noth-

MR. AND MRS. WILLIAM RANDOLPH HEARST WITH THEIR TWO
YOUNGEST SONS, DAVID WHITMIRE HEARST AND
RANDOLPH APPERSON HEARST

ing to worry about. They are good boys. They may not be the kind of boys that you would like to see them, but they are nevertheless, good, thinking, well-behaved youngsters. That they resent too much discipline may be a good quality. If they do not get along at that school, we will put them in another school and give them all the education they will consent to absorb. Randolph and David will probably be no better than William and John; but I will be satisfied if they are as good.

Mrs. Hearst tells a story of Randolph and David who went to a military school together. Randolph was placed at the head of his company and given the title of captain. One day 'Mrs. Hearst said to David, "How does it happen that your brother Randolph is the captain, and you are only a private?"

Quickly David replied, "Mother, let Randolph glorify the family name. I enjoy being a private."

Hearst often addresses the twins in a jovial humorous way. On March 22, 1930, he wired the boys:

Randolph and David Hearst,
Riverside Drive,
New York City, New York.

I am glad to get your love, but I would like to get some letters too. Hope you have a good time in Florida, provided you write me. Otherwise, I hope you have a bum time.

POP

When the twins sent Hearst birthday gifts in 1932 he telegraphed to David:

Gosh! Those were swell ties. I can now burst into bloom, just like the flowers in the garden. How's everything? Love,

POP

To Randolph, Hearst wired the same day:

Thanks a lot for the handkerchiefs. They are pippins. I am going to catch cold, so I can wave them around and show everybody. Love,

POP

When the twins wired congratulations to Hearst on his last birthday he replied in a telegram:

Thanks for birthday greetings. Why don't you close up that school and come West? We have a pool here, and it doesn't cost anything to keep it open. I am afraid you are studying too hard, especially David. You should have been here for the birthday.

POP

Hearst is never very censorious of his sons. He recalls his own boyhood filled with daring mischievous pranks, rebellion against authority. He believes in the future and in the young people to come. To some college students at Marquette University in 1925, he wrote:

I do not believe in the "good old times." The old times when people were ignorant and violent, and for the most part dirty and dull . . . were the bad old times. . . .

Mankind has improved, constantly and consistently throughout the ages. This, we must admit, or history and science alike are fantastic falsehoods. And, if mankind has so constantly and consistently improved, what reason have we for assuming that it will not continue to improve? What vanity prompts us imagine that we are the pinnacle of such improvement, and that from our supreme elevation mankind will proceed to deteriorate through the succeeding generations, and that we will have cause to pity our grandchildren because they are not the perfect creatures that we are? It seems to me that our grandchildren will have more cause to pity us. . . . Their lives will be largely the realization of the hopes, the fruition of the efforts of the generation of to-day and the many generations that have gone before.

CHAPTER LII

EXPULSION FROM FRANCE

IN the summer of 1930, Hearst went to Europe with a large party of friends and business associates to whom he was giving a holiday. For a time he remained in London, then on July 26th the Hearst party crossed to Paris. As usual the publisher stopped at the Crillon. Beauty and art occupy an increasingly greater place in his life, and as usual he added to his vast collections. On July 30th the party departed for Bad Nauheim where Hearst and some of his executives planned to take the cure.

When the publisher follows a health régime he proceeds with conscientious thoroughness. After he had observed for four weeks the rules prescribed at Bad Nauheim Hearst received from his physician this suggestion, "Now, Mr. Hearst, you must pick out some nice quiet secluded spot and take another four weeks of complete rest. That will be the after-cure."

Paris was selected by Hearst. He thought he could rest well at the Crillon. On his way to Paris he was interviewed by the Frankfurter *Zeitung*. He told the interviewer that in the early part of the World War he had done his best to have America remain neutral because the war was entirely European, and not especially the affair of the United States. He thought it desirable for the United States as a nation to maintain friendly relations with all the peoples of Europe. He spoke of Washington's counsel to this country to keep free of "foreign entanglements." He repeated that the United States entered the war "to make the world safe for democracy and ensure the self-determination of peoples."

He said that now Germany and Central Europe were democratic. He deplored the fact that the Versailles Conference had failed to ensure the self-determination of the peoples, and that the Teutonic peoples had been delivered to the domination of Belgium, France, Italy, Yugoslavia, Czechoslovakia, Poland and Lithuania. He asserted that it was unjust for nations to be under foreign domination:

I think if the nations of Europe actually desired permanent peace and mutual friendly relations, they would allow the peoples of the various ceded territories themselves to determine by plebiscites to which nation each one desired to belong, and to bestow its allegiance.

The principle of self-determination which President Wilson enunciated was a good one and a sound one and a just one. It is a worthy policy for Americans to have had as its inspiration in the war. It is too bad that this noble principle was neglected in the Versailles Conference and forgotten by Mr. Wilson. It is, perhaps, not too late to have that splendid principle revived and eventually established as the firm basis of European peace. Until it is so established, there will be nothing but the continual menace of war. If that principle were firmly established in actual practice, then Mr. Briand's idea of the United States of Europe could probably be put into successful operation.

Hearst said that no United States of Europe was possible while so many countries were living in a condition of rankling injury and injustice. He tried to clarify the European situation for Americans by an imaginary dismembering of the United States and dividing it up among Canada, Mexico, and Spain. He pointed out that had such a subdivision of this country followed the Great War, the United States would not have rested until the injustice was rectified either through peaceful measures or through war. Hearst said:

Personally I do not think there need be another war. I believe that the moral sentiment, the intelligent opinion of the world, could easily proceed along Mr. Briand's plan of a United States of Europe and by rectifying injustices here and there, establishing a United States of Europe which would persist, because it would be based upon mutual satisfaction and self-interest. A democratic United States of Europe is the peaceful and permanent solution of the European problem.

After making this statement on the injustice of the Versailles Treaty in which France had so great a share, Hearst went to Stresa on Lake Maggiore, and from there to Paris, where he stopped at the spacious, tranquil Hotel Crillon to rest for four weeks in order to complete the Nauheim cure.

Just before luncheon on the day of his arrival, Hearst received a call from a polite Frenchman with a flowing mustache. Although the visitor was wearing civilian clothes, he proved to be a French official with a message for Hearst. He suggested that they go upstairs to talk.

Hearst told the visitor to say what he pleased, no secrecy was necessary. In the foyer of the Crillon, Hearst was informed by the official that the French Government requested him to leave France within four days. If he did not go, he would be escorted to the border. If he returned without permission of the Government he would be subject to imprisonment to be followed by an escort to the border.

Hearst was presented with a paper stating that the French Government had the right to expel visitors considered inimical to the best interests of the nation. The order came from the French Sûreté Générale, a department of the Minister of the Interior.

The official statement of what occurred was announced in the newspapers:

The President of the Council communicates the following: "William Randolph Hearst, proprietor of numerous papers in America, has been expelled from French territory. This measure taken upon the order of the President of the Council, Minister of the Interior, had its origin in the rôle played last year by Mr. Hearst in obtaining and publishing a secret document relating to the Anglo-French naval negotiations."

Quickly the reason for his expulsion came to Hearst. A few weeks previously he had been in Paris for several days and had not been molested. It was not until he gave the interview to the Frankfurter *Zeitung* that he became an undesirable visitor in France. He was being expelled for announcing his disapproval of the Versailles Treaty.

When Hearst received the order to leave France he was with E. D. Coblentz, editor of the New York *American*, his own secretary, Colonel Joseph Willicombe, and Harry Crocker. Hearst turned to Coblentz and said, "I have been ordered to leave France. Isn't that childish?"

"Damn silly," answered Coblentz.

"I'll not wait four days," said Hearst. "I'll take the first train."

Harry Crocker said, "Chief, if France doesn't want you, I don't want France." He decided to leave with Hearst.

The luggage was packed, and Hearst went to the Gare du Nord. Coblentz relates that Hearst walked up and down the station platform eating peaches while they waited for the train. On his way out of France, Hearst sat in his compartment on the train writing in longhand the story of his expulsion which he knew would be asked for by the London press. It was written with a light, humorous touch that had a Gallic flavor. While Hearst wrote, his companions, Secretary Joseph Willicombe, E. D. Coblentz and Harry Crocker read and played cards.

The secret document referred to by the Department of Interior of the French Government and which served as a pretext for expelling Hearst, was one that was obtained two years before by Harold J. T. Horan, correspondent of the Hearst papers in Paris. This document revealed in detail an agreement between the French and British concerning the construction of ships suited to the needs of those two nations. The agreement totally ignored the United States, and was greatly opposed to the Naval disarmament stand taken by the American diplomats at that time. One of the reasons given by President Wilson for the entry of the United States into the World War was to end secret diplomacy. This document obtained by Horan disclosed that France had resumed secret diplomacy, thus making future wars certain.

After Hearst made public the proposed treaty, it was never consummated. Hearst said that information of the existence of the Treaty was not obtained by devious or indirect methods, but by good, direct, "Go-and-get-it" American methods. Two prominent Frenchmen, government officials, M. de la Plante, and M. de Noblet, were arrested by the French Government for conspiracy. Hearst was accused of complicity. De la Plante and de Noblet were dragged before the French Court and prosecuted, but acquitted.

Harold J. T. Horan was arrested under spectacular circumstances by agents of the French Secret Service in the Rue de la Paix. He was given an alternative of leaving France, or facing a term of five years' imprisonment for alleged theft of secret documents. Horan preferred exile to imprisonment, although he was wholly innocent of obtaining the documents by unlawful means.

At the time of the difficulty Hearst immediately informed the State Department and Secretary Kellogg that he personally assumed full responsibility for any blame that might be attached to the publication of the documents. Hearst felt that in making public the treacherous diplomatic negotiations he had done a real service to France. On September 21, 1928, he prevented the return of secret diplomacy by exposing the proposed naval treaty between France and England.

When Hearst arrived in London he went to the Savoy. He was received like a hero, and banquets in his honor were arranged. To an *Evening Standard* reporter who interviewed him on September 2nd, he gave a statement of what had occurred in Paris, and it was conspicuously published in the paper:

I have no complaint to make [wrote Hearst]. The French officials were extremely polite. They said I was an enemy of

France, and a danger in their midst. They made me feel quite important. They said I could stay in France a little while longer, if I desired, and they would take a chance on nothing disastrous happening to the Republic.

But I told them I did not want to take the responsibility of endangering the great French nation, that America had saved it once during the war, and I would save it again by leaving it. Furthermore, I was like the man who was told that he was going blind, and who said he did not mind, as he had seen everything anyhow. Similarly, I had seen everything in France, including some very interesting governmental performances. Then I asked M. Tardieu's emissary to express to M. Tardieu my immense admiration for his immense alertness in protecting France from the peril of invasion, and we parted with quite elaborate politeness. It was a little bit foolish, but extremely French.

The reason for the strained relations—to use the proper diplomatic term—was the publication of the secret Anglo-French Treaty two years ago by the Hearst papers, which upset some international "apple carts," but informed the American people; and of course that being the reason, the French Government was entirely right in leveling its attack at me and quite wrong in its action toward Mr. Horan, who was only my agent.

I think, however, that the general attitude of the French press toward our opposing the United States entrance into the League of Nations, or any protective pact to involve our country in the quarrels of European powers, is mainly responsible. Also there might have been some slight irritation at the occasional intimations in our papers that France, now being the richest nation in the world, might use some of the German indemnity to pay her honest debts to America, especially because if it had not been for America she would now be paying indemnity instead of receiving it.

But being a competent journalist and a loyal American makes a man *persona non grata* in France. I think I can endure the situation without loss of sleep. In fact, the whole affair reminds me of a story of a rather effeminate young man who went to call on his best girl and found her in the arms of another young fellow. The effeminate youth went into the hall, took up his successful young rival's umbrella, broke it, and said, "Now I hope it rains!" You see, for the French national policy of revenge to be entirely successful, we will have to have rain.

(Signed) WILLIAM RANDOLPH HEARST

The publisher sailed for the United States on the *Europa,* arriving in New York Harbor on September 15th. He found himself acclaimed by the press of the nation. He was greeted by a notable gathering of World War veterans, public men and citizens. Tears came into his eyes when he saw the vast throng greeting him.

After visiting Boston as the city's guest of honor at the Tercentennial of the founding of the metropolis of New England, Hearst journeyed to California. Chicago made him her guest. In San Francisco, Oakland and Los Angeles he was received as a national hero.

For the first time Hearst spoke over the radio. He said:

Perhaps, fellow citizens, some of you will say to me, "Why did you not sue the French government?" And I say, "First, because I did not want to magnify the incident, and second, because I had the simplicity to believe, fellow citizens, that somewhere among our paid servants at Washington there might be found some public official with backbone enough and American spirit enough to defend the right of law-abiding citizens sojourning abroad, and to vindicate the validity of an American passport, and to maintain the liberty and dignity of American citizenship. . . ."

If Theodore Roosevelt had been alive, or if Grover Cleveland had been alive, you would have heard little of W. R. Hearst, for he was of no importance in this situation; but you would have heard much about the value and validity and inviolability of the American passport, and of due and necessary respect for the rights and liberties of the American citizen. Theodore Roosevelt and Grover Cleveland are dead. But let us hope that American spirit and American independence and American loyalty to the rights and liberties which we inherited from our fathers, and desire to hand down to our sons, did not die with these two great Americans.

The Hoover Administration did not take up the matter with France.

The publisher spoke of the persistent effort made by France to seduce the American press. Her most effective means of seduction was the widespread distribution of the little red ribbon of the Legion of Honor. Hearst said:

The great Napoleon who devised the Legion of Honor, knew human weaknesses and recognized the irrepressible inclination of the citizens of a republic to covet the titles and insignia their democracy teaches them to disdain. All men are created equal in one respect, at least, and that is their desire to be unequal. . . .

Many American newspaper men have been caught by this little red ribbon as guilelessly as bull frogs are hooked by a bit of red flannel, but I have never allowed any member of my organization to accept civic decorations from any foreign nation, or to put themselves and my papers under obligations to any foreign government. Indeed, I think Congress should forbid the wearing of foreign decorations by American citizens, except military decorations honorably won in war.

If our *bourgeois* aristocracy want some recognition of achievement . . . let Congress create a Right Royal Brotherhood of Super-Americans, and confer blue ribbons like prizes at horse shows, and so keep American loyalty at home. . . . I know what France expects in return for her little red ribbon, and feel that loyalty to France above all else, which is properly the highest honor and greatest glory to her Frenchmen, might easily be the deepest dishonor to an independent American journalist.

In Los Angeles, at a civic banquet in his honor at the Hotel Biltmore, Hearst said that they must be careful not to exaggerate the importance of the incident of his expulsion from France. It was of no interest to him except in so far as it indicated France's attitude toward America and Americans:

France resents America for two very human reasons: first, because of the service we rendered her, which she does not like to acknowledge; and second, because of the money we loaned her which she does not like to repay. France has the largest gold supply per capita of any nation in the world, but she does not want to use any of it in paying her debts to America. In fact, she does not even like to have that obligation called to her attention. The situation reminds me of the gambler who came home to his wife in great indignation and said he had been accused of cheating at cards. His wife answered, "but you do cheat at cards, don't you, dear?" And the gambler replied, "Of course I do, but I don't like to have any one speak about it." . . .

France likes to think that she won the late war all alone, while the truth is the victory was secured for her largely by the Americans and the English. France likes to think that she bore the whole burden of financial sacrifice during the war, while the truth is that the money to maintain the American and British armies was spent in France, and the money to maintain the French army was loaned to France with small hope of its ever being returned.

Yet in fairness to France, it must be said . . . she dislikes England quite as much as she dislikes America. . . .

But there is little in the history of the past, or the probabilities of the future, to make us believe that any other European nation with France's military power and wealth of plunder would not act substantially in the same way. The conditions abroad which we deplore . . . are characteristically European. . . . Our fathers left Europe because they wanted to get away from wars and hatred and persecution, from intolerance and bigotry, from injustice and tyranny. They wanted new life in the new land. They wanted freedom from political and intellectual servitude. . . . They wanted freedom of assembly. They wanted freedom of the press because they realized that on vigilant publicity all other rights and liberties depend. They wanted a chance to develop a practical political application of the Christian principle of the brotherhood of man. They wanted to build a nation based on brotherly love and extending liberty, equality and opportunity to all mankind. . . .

Let us not turn back to mingle in the affairs of Europe, to

become part of the intolerable conditions our fathers endeavored to avoid and endured so much to free us from. This land of liberty and humanity is our field of action and opportunity, and the best service we can render the world is to show the hating, warring races of Europe that these same races here in America, in the light of liberty and under the glorious flag of freedom can live eternally in peace and happiness and brotherly love.

Hearst's last speech on his expulsion from France was made in Oakland, California, on October 18th. He closed by saying:

Now, I am going to board a train and go down to my ranch and find my little hide-away on my little hilltop at San Simeon, and look down on the blue sea, and up at the blue sky, and bask in the glorious sunshine of the greatest State of the greatest nation in the whole world. You know, my friends, it is about time I finished my Nauheim cure.

CHAPTER LIII

CAMPAIGN AGAINST PROHIBITION

HEARST'S faith in the people ever deepens. In 1919, he advocated nominating and electing Cabinet officers and even Federal Judges by popular vote. The initiative, referendum and recall should be applied to Federal affairs. The President should be shorn of his power to control Representatives and Senators by use of patronage. A Congressional committee, instead of the President, should have power to make appointments. The President himself should be nominated by popular vote. All public officers should be as nearly as possible under civil service.

In the New York *American* in 1923, Hearst advocated direct nomination of all Judges by popular vote.

They revoke laws by declaring them under one pretext or another unconstitutional. The word unconstitutional now means that such laws meet the disapproval of the judiciary.... An ever increasing number of judges are corporation lawyers—corporation lawyers before they became lawyers, corporation lawyers while they are judges, and living in hope of being corporation lawyers when they cease to be judges.... There will never be complete protection to the public from the encroachment of these corporation lawyers in judicial rôles, until the people have the power of recall. A bad judge is no more sacred than any bad official.... Back of the corporation judge is the boss who nominates the judge, and back of the boss is the public plunderer who subsidizes the boss. The people vote for one or another corporation lawyers, nominated without their consent, elected by corporation contribution, and controlled after the election by the public plunderers who own the bosses. Restore direct nominations to the people, and give the people power of recall, and you make the people the masters whom the judges will serve.

In the welter of corruption following the World War Hearst discovered that thirty warships formerly belonging to Germany were to be sold for twenty-eight million dollars. At the time of the proposed sale they were valued at three hundred millions. John Barton Payne, attorney for many railroads dominated by the Morgan group, had been appointed by President Wilson as head of the United States Shipping Board. Payne had charge of three and one-half billion dollars of ships. For a nominal consideration he was about to transfer the ex-German warships to the Ship Trust, owned largely by England. As a tax-payer Hearst sued in the United States Supreme Court to prevent the sale. It was found that neither the President nor the Shipping Board had any legal right to sell the German ships to the foreign Ship Trust.

In 1919, Hearst declared that we should stop lending money to foreign nations, already in bankruptcy or on the verge of it. The enormous war expenses were exhausting even our immense resources. The war expenses continued, and as late as 1921 Hearst as a tax-payer brought suit against the Secretary of the Treasury, David F. Houston, asking that he be restrained from further disbursements to foreign governments including Czechoslovakia and the defunct Kerensky régime. At the same time, Hearst urged that American troops be brought home from abroad.

Hearst has frequently been called inconsistent because he has written on two sides of the same question. This accusation arises from his unhesitating alteration of opinion about men or measures when he discovers that he has been misinformed. At one time he opposed the sales tax because it was advocated by Otto Kahn, the New York banker, as he thought, in the interest of financiers. Several editorials were written by Hearst condemning the sales tax. After he studied the question he admitted that he was on the wrong side. He had misjudged the motive of Otto Kahn. He became an advocate of the sales tax in the United States. A trainload of Congressmen was sent by him to Canada to study the tax question, and many returned supporters of the sales tax.

In an interview given in 1922 to Cornelius Vanderbilt, Jr., Hearst said that no matter where the tax is laid, it is in the last analysis paid by the consumer. The price of an article is the price of the cost of material, plus taxation, plus 6 per cent profit. All these costs are paid by the purchaser. If taxation came out of profit, there would be no profit, and consequently no investment. Since the consumer pays all taxes along with other costs, how much better it is to have in his own hands the power to regulate by his purchases what that tax shall be:

If it is a desire to lift taxation from those least able to pay it, then the sales tax need not be placed upon the necessities of life and consequently will not fall upon those who buy only the necessities, such as plain food and simple clothing. With this modification the sales tax is most beneficial to the family of modest means. It relieves them of the burden of taxation, and is least hampering to the development of industry. The development of industry means employment and general prosperity.... The high cost of living means nothing more than the high cost of taxation. Any program to reduce taxation is a benefit to the whole community.

Hearst discussed the sales tax with President Harding the last time that he and Mrs. Hearst lunched with President and Mrs. Harding. The publisher suggested to the President the sales tax as a means of meeting payments of the soldiers' bonus.

"Yes," said the President, "the sales tax is one of the best forms of taxation."

Hearst replied, "It is one of the least bad forms of taxation."

President Harding agreed with Hearst that all forms of taxation were a burden, but to a certain extent a necessary burden. Hearst campaigned in his newspapers for a national sales tax. In California, the publisher's five newspapers are read by more than 50 per cent of the population, and in this State the sales tax has been enacted into law and is in successful operation.

Although Hearst endeavored to keep America out of the World War, when the country was once committed to the war his attitude was to prosecute it to the utmost in order to bring it to a victorious conclusion as soon as possible. After the war was over Hearst, in 1922, advocated payment of the bonus to the World War veterans. The Republican Party which controlled Congress had declared in its national platform in favor of the bonus, and went before the country with that as one of its main issues. If Congress failed to carry out its platform pledge, Hearst said that Senators and Representatives would be in the contemptible position of having confessed patriotic sentiment which they did not feel in order to secure votes. They would be charged with repudiating preëlection pledges. He pointed out that Civil War soldiers received a bonus. Even Congressional opponents of the bonus like Senators Knute Nelson of Minnesota and Francis E. Warren of Wyoming received a bonus without protest. George Washington was given a large bonus of public land for his services during the Revolutionary War.

When Hearst was interviewed by Cornelius Vanderbilt, Jr., he said:

Already England and France and most of the Allies engaged in the World War have given their soldiers bonuses. To be sure, they came out of money borrowed from us. . . . Why should we not use some of our money to pay our soldiers a bonus, instead of providing liberally for the soldiers of the Allies? During the war the average wage was at least five dollars a day. Soldiers in the trenches received only one dollar a day, while some soldiers at home working in factories received ten dollars a day. It was poor and inadequate compensation to give men who fought bravely, who ran so much risk and endured much hardship and privation. . . .

Hearst criticized the financial leaders who had clamored for the war, made millions out of the conflict, and after it was over did not wish to give up any part of their profiteering to the soldiers who had risked life "in order to uphold the honor of their country and win the war which had given such profit to profiteers and patrioteers."

Senator Underwood of Alabama led the fight against the bonus. During the last interview that Hearst had with President Harding, the President said he felt certain that Congress would pass the Bonus bill and pass it, even over a veto. President Harding's prediction was fulfilled. When the bonus was voted May 19, 1924, President Coolidge vetoed the bill, but Congress passed it over his head.

Only one-half of the bonus was paid, but it was promised by the Government that the remainder would be ready by 1945. In July of 1932, many World War veterans were out of work. Ex-soldiers demanded the promised half of the bonus to meet emergency needs, but deaf ears met their demands. Straggling, tattered, hungry men, women and children marched on Washington. Two hundred veterans took up their quarters in an old deserted building in sight of the Capitol. Thousands were encamped on Anacostia Creek. These men insisted that three billion, four hundred and ninety-two million dollars be paid to the veterans of the World War.

President Hoover answered that there was no money in the treasury. The Government must borrow from the Reserve Security Fund or impose further taxation.

The encamped veterans held out. "Reds," "agitators," they were called in the White House. It was even doubted that some had served in the World War. They were asked to break camp and leave. They refused. The District of Columbia police attacked them, but were beaten off by the veterans. The encamped men defied the Administration.

The President sent a tank corps to drive away the veterans. Gas was used by the Government. There was a fight. Two veterans were killed and several were injured. A piercing pain shot through the United States.

Hearst was indignant. On July 9, 1932, he sent the following private telegram to E. D. Coblentz, editor of the New York *American:*

I do not care if every paper in the United States comments favorably on Hoover's action. I think it was the most outrageous piece of stupidity, if nothing worse, that has ever been perpetrated by the Government. If the idea is to develop Bolshevism in this country, there is no better way of doing it. Certainly the action of the Government cannot be excused or explained, if it had any other purpose in mind.

The whole situation could have been avoided if the Government had paid the veterans their bonus, now when they needed it, and not at some time in the future when they do not need it so badly.

Mr. Hoover may explain why he ordered out the forces of government to have the veterans shot down, but no true American with gratitude in his heart for the service of the veterans will feel that such action was wholly justifiable, or that it would have been committed by a Lincoln or a Jefferson, or any of our patriotic Presidents of any party. That is the way I feel about it, and I think our editorials should temperately express that view.

I asked Mr. Brisbane early in the day for an editorial. If he delivers his editorial for the evening papers, I wish Mr. Colby would write an editorial for the morning. If you think turning the rules is too hysterical, do not do it. But I feel like mourning not only the death of the veterans, but mourning the passing of American sentiment and democratic principles. I am afraid this despotic action on the part of the Government will tend to precipitate further conflict between Communism and Fascism which is already developing in the country and which threatens to eliminate the patriotic and Republican principles on which this nation was built.

For forty years Hearst attacked whisky, gin, the saloon and all phases of intemperance. In 1902, he ran a series of full-page editorials against the saloon. Editors of his papers were instructed to write on the subject of the suppression of strong drink as often as they could without becoming monotonous or seeming to be fanatical. This crusade against strong drink is the only one that Hearst ever expressed the desire in print for his sons to carry on after he departed. So effectively were these editorials written against the saloon that temperance organizations distributed them widely as propaganda.

And yet, when heated war excitement was at its height, and
there was a demand for nation-wide prohibition, Hearst in all
his evening papers on July 28, 1917, protested. Ten million
workers would be dissatisfied if deprived of beer to which they
were accustomed:

> The President has enough problems without a nation-wide pro
> hibition fight to bother him. . . . Prohibition would not "prohibit"
> any but the milder but relatively harmless stimulants. It would
> again put this nation on a whisky basis as it was in the days of
> Jefferson, who advocated government encouragement of light beer
> brewing as the only remedy for the "poison of whisky."

When prohibition was jammed through Congress, on January
17, 1919, Hearst printed an editorial in the New York *Journal*
saying:

> One hundred per cent efficiency has been added at one stroke
> to the people of America. . . . Half of the misery of half of the
> people has been abolished. Three hundred thousand saloons have
> been eliminated, three hundred thousand traps have been closed
> into which a considerable portion of the youth of the country fell
> every year; fell to degradation and to vice and to crime. . . .
> Strong drink has destroyed more each year than the World War
> destroyed. . . . The suppression of the drink traffic is an expression
> of the higher morality upon which we are entering. . . .

Hearst stood staunchly for the Eighteenth Amendment, in
spite of the crime wave in California one year after the enactment of the Volstead Act. He wrote to Winifred Black of the
San Francisco *Examiner:*

> I do not believe that crime and immorality . . . can be evaded
> by opening the saloon and dispensing vicious alcoholic drink. . . .
> A crime wave occurred after most wars, and it was apparently
> due to the demoralization engendered by the hate and hysteria

of war, and by the disturbed social and economic conditions which follow in the wake of war.... Prohibition has not failed as yet....

One year later Hearst began to question whether prohibition prohibited. He opened an essay contest offering a prize of one hundred and fifty dollars limited to one hundred and fifty words in answer to the question, "What has prohibition accomplished up to date?"

More and more each year Hearst questioned prohibition. In 1926, he asked editorially:

Has the younger generation profited by prohibition? Are they drinking less than formerly? Are they drinking more? Are the elements in the community drinking less or more, or drinking other worse liquor than before prohibition?

Hearst deplored the defiance of the prohibition law which ended in general disrespect for all laws. With despair he observed bootlegging and hijacking. In one big city, nine thousand saloons had been replaced by twenty thousand speak-easies. The police head of Chicago testified that more than half the police force were engaged in bootlegging. Rich men were breaking the laws and their example was followed by an army of gunmen, bootleggers and rum-runners, who came up from the poor. Hundreds of millions were made annually in the bootlegging business. In an editorial Hearst wrote:

Converted, denatured alcohol has become the drink of the American people, and they drink millions of dollars' worth of it annually, as the undertakers will show to their profit in a few years.

Arthur Brisbane said in an editorial:

Gradually it seems to be dawning on some of the population that bootleg whisky which sometimes makes you blind, sometimes kills you, and always poisons you, isn't such a great improvement on old whisky.

Editorials in the Hearst evening papers grew in emphasis and results. Men like Dr. Nicholas Murray Butler, president of Columbia University, on every possible occasion demanded that the prohibition amendment be ripped out of the Constitution.

Early in 1929, at an Associated Press luncheon in New York, President Hoover said in an address:

Respect for law as law is fading from the sensibilities of our people. Twenty times as many people in proportion to the population are lawlessly killed in the United States as in Great Britain. There are fifty times as many robberies. Life and property are relatively more unsafe than in any civilized country in the world.

Hearst said editorially that the "noble experiment had become an ignoble failure." Over his own signature he added:

Everybody knows that the law ought to be respected; just as everybody knows that women ought to be respected, and that women are respected by every decent man. But occasionally there is a woman who is not respected, who is not respectable, who does not respect herself, and who no one in his heart can respect, no matter what outward observance of respect he may render. And so occasionally there are laws which cannot be respected, no matter how much they are respected by good citizens. And there are lawmakers who cannot be respected—such, for instance, as gentlemen who impose dry laws upon the land and carry whisky flasks in their hip pockets.

The Volstead Act had been in force ten years, and Hearst enumerated some of the results in an editorial:

Wholesale bribery of officials, supposed to enforce prohibition; wholesale bribery of police, coast guards, frontier guards; increase in the use of deadly drugs; contempt for the Constitution and the law; corruption of high school youngsters with whisky flasks seen at dances of children in their 'teens; crime organized; blindness caused from bootleg whisky and poisonous alcohol. . . . What solution is possible?

Some said that the only solution was to let the thousands who were drinking bootleg liquor go to an early grave; law enforcement was impossible.

Then Hearst wrote E. J. Clapp, formerly one of his valued editorial writers, later of Durant Motors, Inc., New York City:

I do not believe that prohibition ever will be or can be enforced. After four more years of shooting, spying, key-hole peeping and interference with fundamental rights and liberties by fanatics and professional busybodies, the country will be ripe for a revolution against un-American conditions of this oppressive and offensive kind. . . . There is no use preaching as we all do that crime does not pay, when it so obviously pays big enough dividends to provide for the creation and employment of gangs and gunmen and thugs and murderers and bootleggers and hi-jackers, men who have beome rich and consequently almost respectable.

Hearst observed that the most popular Christmas presents displayed in shops were hip flasks and cocktail-shakers. And this had all come about because in a fever of war excitement without giving the people as a whole an opportunity to express an opinion, the Government decided that it would immediately get rid of alcohol. Hearst asked what was the way out? He offered a twenty-five-thousand-dollar prize for the best plan to repeal the Eighteenth Amendment.

A few months later Hearst spoke over Collier's radio hour from a National Broadcasting station. He quoted what Abraham Lincoln said in discussing the temperance question:

"The American people cannot be driven to do anything they do not want to do. The way to promote happiness is by moral suasion and not by force."

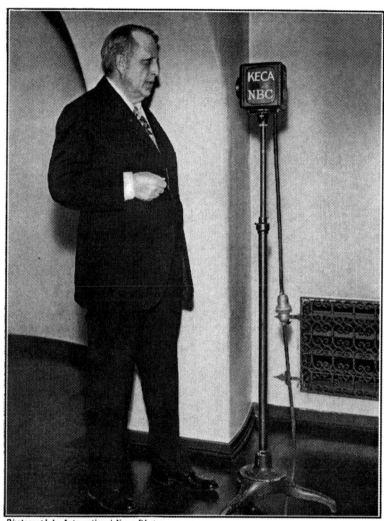

Photograph by International News Photos

WILLIAM RANDOLPH HEARST BEFORE THE MICROPHONE

Hearst said that prohibition had "corrupted the judiciary and made a racket of justice." He advocated restricted manufacture of alcoholic beverages under Federal licenses; Government monopoly of distribution of alcoholic beverages maintaining a high standard of quality and price; sale of such beverages, preferably light wines and beer, in limited quantities to licensed restaurants, hotels and homes, but not to any institution or any individual whose license should have been revoked because of abuse of its privileges. Hearst said that this plan had been successful in Canada and Sweden. He declared that from this plan "the country would have the immediate benefit of genuine temperance; the reëstablishment of law and order; an increased governmental income for greater works and needs; establishments of great industries, and greater sense of satisfaction and content in the nation with less likelihood of serious political, social and economic disturbance."

In 1930, a young girl died in Gary, Indiana, during a drinking party. Five youths were held for murder. Hearst asked:

What is to be gained by a policy of prohibition which makes vicious drunkards of young innocent children and causes them to commit dreadful crimes? Is it not about time for the country to wake up and put an end to prohibition and prohibition parties? ... Young people could not go into saloons, but they can go into speakeasies.... Prohibition has filled our jails with youth. Prohibition has corrupted our police until in many cases they are active allies of the law-breaking elements of the community. It has made our Federal enforcement officers sometimes murderers. It has made our President a dictator executing an unpopular law by force of arms.

Is it not time that the calm conservative portion of our people took stock of prohibition and determined whether this policy is worth all the trouble and all the evil that it costs? We have heard enough of fools and fanatics. Let us hear in the coming election from the sound and sane portion of the American people.

As the election approached in the autumn of 1932, many important voices spoke with authority against prohibition,

President Ernest M. Hopkins of Dartmouth College, President Farrand of Cornell University, President Hibben of Princeton, and Governor Byrd. No opposition to the Eighteenth Amendment occasioned greater surprise than that of John D. Rockefeller, Jr., a lifelong abstainer, a man who had always battled for prohibition, but who now declared himself an advocate of repeal.

Soon the voice of America was heard on the Eighteenth Amendment. A political revolution occurred. Governor Franklin D. Roosevelt of New York was elected President of the United States, and the Volstead Act was soon to be no more.

On February 16, 1933, the United States Senate voted to repeal the Eighteenth Amendment. Four days later the House of Representatives gave the Senate overwhelming support. Then State after State spoke. At last on the 11th of September, 1933, Maine, the parent State of prohibition, voted for repeal, and the Volstead Act which Hearst called "the great American tragedy" came to an end.

CHAPTER LIV

SAN SIMEON

SOUTHWARD and to the West from the old Mission of San Antonio de Padua, fifty miles along the Pacific Ocean, stretches the San Simeon Ranch of William Randolph Hearst. The range of Santa Lucia Mountains runs diagonally through the entire property.

Modern San Simeon began in 1919. When it belonged to the Mission of San Miguel Arcangel it was called El Rancho de San Simeon a la Playa, and here roamed the herds of the padres. After Mexico ordered the Mission secularized in 1934, the Government granted the ranches to important Spanish-Californians, who in turn sold these properties.

Several were bought by Senator George Hearst. One was the Santa Rosa, a cozy little California ranch of three thousand acres owned by the Estradas. Don "Pancho" Estrada, son of the last owner, has most of his life been employed by the Hearsts. He is a picturesque figure at San Simeon, wearing a broad-brimmed sombrero, riding a horse, seated in a Mexican saddle holding the reins of a woven horsehair bridle. To-day he occupies a handsome concrete house in the village of San Simeon, with a gay little patio and a tiled roof built for him by William Randolph Hearst.

After acquiring the Santa Rosa, Senator Hearst bought the ranches of San Simeon and Piedra Blanca. These three ranches, together with all the Senator's possessions in the Counties of San Luis Obispo and Monterey, came to be called San Simeon, perhaps because they encircled the Bay of San Simeon. To this remote, romantic ranch Senator Hearst brought his son and his friends for fishing, hunting and camping. On the crest of what is now called the Enchanted Hill, the Senator erected a cabin, and the elevation was known as Camp Hill.

William Randolph Hearst recalls as a boy going up the mountainside so steep that he was obliged to cling to his horse's tail. Now the ascent is made easy by a wide, well-graveled road that curlicues up the slope, with another road for descent to avoid collisions.

Camp Hill has become the Casa Grande on the Enchanted Hill of San Simeon. Here in remote grandeur, forty-three miles from a town of any size, and two hundred miles from a large city, William Randolph Hearst, this invisible Charlemagne of the mountains, seems to his twenty million readers almost like a myth. Few have seen him, save in the news-reel.

In 1919, Hearst gave to San Simeon a new meaning. The forty-five thousand acres inherited from his father became the nucleus of what has grown to be an imperial domain. Here, with the clarity of isolation, the publisher on the crest of his mountain range surveys his fifty miles of coast line on the Pacific, and edits forty-one newspapers and magazines.

Impelled by his boyhood memories, Hearst brought his wife and sons to San Simeon for summer holidays. They wished to escape stuffiness of buildings, and so on this tawny mountain crowned with oaks and laurels under the sapphire skies, the Hearsts lazed away their summers in their camp. The publisher relaxed in khaki, rode with his sons, taught them how to shoot. Away from telephones and telegraph wires he shut out cites.

A huge henna-colored portable canvas tent with a floor stood in the center of the camp. Here were comfortable seats, camp chairs and a long dining-table appetizing with fruits, jams, marmalade and condiments. Paper napkins were always used. Music, games, and later motion pictures supplied the evening entertainment for the family and guests who assembled in the large tent. The three comfortable guest tents each had four rooms and a bath. So many smaller tents were occupied by servants and attendants, that they seemed like a tented village under the greenery of oaks.

When the Hearsts departed for New York the venetian-colored tents with their gay awnings were folded up. Floors were taken to pieces, and all was packed till spring. During the winter there was much destruction from the elements or rodents. Labor and repairing were necessary to put the Camp in order for summer. In 1919, Hearst said to Miss Julia Morgan, the architect, that he would like to have plans drawn for a permanent camp of spacious, cool, comfortable concrete buildings with tiled floors, where he could place his large collection of Indian rugs. He wished to avoid the annual seasonal set-ups and repairs entailed by portable tent houses.

Early in 1919, Mrs. Phebe Hearst fell ill. So concerned was her son for his mother that he was unable except intermittently to concentrate on building projects. He passed much time in California, but occasionally was called East. Hearst's spring and summer were divided between Mrs. Phebe Hearst's Hacienda, Camp Hill, Miss Morgan's San Francisco office, his editorial rooms, trains and New York City.

One April day Dr. Ray Lyman Wilbur, later Secretary of the Interior under President Herbert Hoover, came from Mrs. Phebe Hearst's room and gravely said, "No one ever died more bravely than Mrs. Hearst."

It was the most melancholy day in Hearst's life, but it was an especially desolate day for the hundreds whose lives had been brightened by Phebe Hearst's friendship and generosity. A great emptiness fell upon the University of California. To that institution Mrs. Hearst had given manuscripts, paintings, prints, scholarships, salaries for professors, foreign travel fellowships, scientific apparatus, concerts for students by the Metropolitan Opera Company, basketball courts, tennis courts, swimming pools, and archæological museums. Two hundred thousand dollars had been given by her to defray the cost of the Hearst International Competition for permanent plans for the grounds and buildings of the university. In memory of her husband, the late Senator George Hearst, she had erected the Hearst Memorial Mining Building, and for the women of the university, Hearst Hall. Her contributions to the university exceeded six millions.

The regents of the University of California placed upon their records the following memorial to Phebe Apperson Hearst:

By native instinct she followed the quieter paths, but the possession of power and rare gifts of mind opened before her a duty to her fellowmen that she did not evade. To bring light and love into the lives of others, that was her burning desire. To forward every good enterprise which helped young people gain their birthright, this was her open door to the obligations of public service. Her early experience as a school teacher led on through one trusteeship after another to the Regency of the University. She rejoiced in the continuous tides of young life which refreshed the brook-beds of the college as from some fountain of perpetual youth; she gladly heard the voices of children. Art and love of beauty, as hand maidens of order, commanded her zeal; and her first interest lay in those early arts of human life which represent the emergency of human culture into the light. One of her last desires, expressed on what proved, alas, to be her deathbed, was that she might live to build here on the University grounds the first unit of the art museum which she had planned for her rich collection already given to the University.

In those later days her mind was singularly clear. She was always thinking of the many things she had yet to do, the messages to send, the last injunctions to give—so much to do, and the hour so short. It was a full, rich, abundant life that she lived, abounding always in care, often in pain, but a great life, gloriously worth while, because she so lived that the community is greatly bettered thereby. Phebe Apperson Hearst: gentlewoman and public servant, a blessing to her day and generation.

With his mother gone, Hearst realized that his home in California had ceased to exist. He decided to create a new home on Camp Hill. The plans for the permanent summer camp were enlarged. Hearst now desired a residence with spacious living quarters, having the informality and hospitality of the summer camp. The large main building was to have two towers. Encircling this structure on the same sites occupied by the guest tents were to be several spacious guest houses, retaining the most pleasing view of the surrounding country. This search for beauty of vista created by accidental design the most extraordinary country place on the continent.

When they planned San Simeon little did Hearst and Miss Morgan realize that after seventeen years they would still be developing this ever-evolving, magnificent group of buildings. Ambitious as was his project, Hearst had little conception of whither his sense of beauty, knowledge of art and passion for perfection would lead. Like the world's great builders, Charlemagne, the Louis, and the Popes, Hearst has the patience and means to follow his vision and ceaselessly to build. Always he sees the entrancing to-morrow.

Miss Morgan says that Hearst appreciates, encourages and develops creativeness in others. He knows more about architecture and ornamental design than any one of her acquaintance. She does not call herself the architect of Hearst's buildings.

"Mr. Hearst and I are fellow architects. He supplies vision, critical judgment. I give technical knowledge and building experience. He loves architecting. If he had chosen that career he would have been a great architect. San Simeon is Mr. Hearst."

In reality, the publisher is greatly interested in all kinds of architecture—the Egyptian pyramid, medieval, Spanish-Californian, and even the terraced towers in the skyline of New York, expressing in their daring beauty the originality, the indomitable spirit of American progress, aspiration and freedom. He likes the architecture of New York because it is not an imitation of some other period, nor a modification of some other type. It is new and distinctly American.

But Hearst's dwelling on the mountainside was to be Spanish. In November of 1919, the work began, and since that time as many as one hundred and fifty men and as few as twenty-five have been steadily at work in construction at San Simeon. And what work! Blasting foundations out of the solid rocky mountaintop. Excavating with picks. The broken rock was crushed and mixed with cement, and with sand from the shore of San Simeon Bay, made into concrete. Quarries were later developed on the place.

When Hearst began building there was no road up the mountainside, and there were no fences. In the winter truck drivers could hardly find their way for the cow tracks in the unfenced pastures. Water for the workers' camp was supplied by a spring. The men lived in tents and used oil lamps. At night, large fat tarantulas sometimes shot out of the bedding. Sleep was broken by the whoo-whooing owls in trees, and coyotes ya-ki-ooing like screaming women in the moonlight. Daytime was rendered interesting by hissing rattlesnakes.

Steel, iron and cement arrived by the coast steamer, landing once a week at San Simeon. Building materials were carted up the hill in large trucks pulled by four horses from San Simeon, five miles distant. The road was washed out by the rains several times, and vanished in mud. So difficult was it to get materials for work that construction did not go forward much that first winter. Then a road was built and graveled so that the pioneering experiences of the winter of 1919 were never repeated.

Excavations were made and foundations laid at the same time for the three guest houses on the steep slope of the mountaintop. Architecturally the houses were called A, B and C. Later A, looking out on the Pacific, was named La Casa del Mar—The House of the Sea. B was called La Casa del Sol —The House of the Sun, because it faces the setting sun. C, which confronts the Santa Lucia range, is known as La Casa del Monte—The House of the Mountain.

The guest houses are entered from the upper level. They drop down the mountain side, the lower stories being reached by outside stairways and winding stepping stones in mossy

paths through tree ferns. The guest houses are characteristically Spanish with plain white wall surfaces. The wide windows, openings and cornices are richly ornamented with stone.
The ceilings are carved in deep relief. Each room has a huge
carved mantel from one of Hearst's great collections.

La Casa del Monte was completed first. Then came La Casa
del Sol, and later the Hearsts' own house, La Casa del Mar,
where they lived until the great house was constructed. This
third house was longest in building because it was in the steep-
est place. Toward the sea it has three habitable stories.

From his New York collections Hearst sent carloads of
rugs, hangings, tapestries, pottery, statues and furniture for
furnishing La Casa del Monte. To-day on the mountaintop are
designed gardens, but in 1921 when the first truck loads of
furnishings arrived the contents were emptied upon the burnt
summer grass of the rocky field. When the first art objects
were unboxed, the late Senator James D. Phelan was a guest
of Hearst. As the Senator watched appearing heads of young
Roman emperors, ancient Venetian settees and medieval beds,
he asked, "How can these heterogeneous objects all be placed
together?" Later the Senator returned to marvel not only
at the ambition and energy of Hearst that had overcome difficulties of construction, but he was amazed to see La Casa del
Monte with the harmonious, tranquil, deep atmosphere of
an ancient Mediterranean palace.

Here were hangings of the fourteenth, sixteenth and seventeenth centuries together with furniture which museums had
competed with Hearst to possess. Such art in arrangement had
been employed by Hearst and Miss Morgan in relating un-
relatable objects that all these furnishings of different periods
seemed to have been created for the present day uses of La
Casa del Monte which is largely of the Spanish Renaissance.
The rich red and gold furnishings are of the fifteenth century.
In La Casa del Sol the colors used are blue, silver and Spanish yellow. Here are Spanish-Moresque tiles, blue and silver
luster, Persian pottery and Persian books. In the overhanging

dark carved balconies of the tower is a tiled frieze in the cornice. Italian and Spanish furnishings are fused harmoniously in La Casa del Mar. Perhaps Italy rather than Spain dominates this building.

Hearst is especially fond of some columns of porphyry brought from Jerusalem and incorporated in the loggia of La Casa del Mar. As he looks toward the Pacific he touches these columns of reddish purple porphyry and senses the thousands of hands that through the centuries have worn them smooth.

While creating San Simeon, Hearst was so absorbed that when in 1922, the Brooklyn *Eagle* telegraphed to ask if he would be a candidate for Governor or United States Senator in New York he replied, "I am a rancher enjoying life on the high hills overlooking the broad Pacific. If you want to talk about Herefords I will talk with you, but not about politics."

In the beginning of the work at San Simeon lights were generated for the houses by an elaborate electric battery plant, but it was replaced by a hydro-electric plant consisting of a turbine engine run by water from Pine Mountain. To-day electricity supplied by a public utility company from San Joaquin Valley does all the heating, cooking, lighting and refrigeration.

The spring water for the camp was wholly inadequate, and in the early days of construction five miles of pipe were installed to bring the hilltop water gushing from the side of Pine Mountain thirty-five hundred feet high, directly in the rear of Camp Hill, to a reservoir holding a million and a half gallons, back of and above the summit of the hill. From this reservoir water is distributed by gravity wherever needed.

After the water system was completed San Simeon's garden came into existence. People told Hearst that flowers would not thrive at San Simeon, a rocky mountaintop with clay soil rendered sterile and shallow by a greedy, thirsty network of oak roots close to the surface of the ground. Hearst recalled the quaint, little, blossom-draped, ship-shaped house of Don

Pancho Estrada in the village of San Simeon, and he answered, "If Don Pancho can grow flowers, so can I."

Indeed, the garden was developed only by removing the soil, then by digging out two feet more of rock and filling with four feet of rich soil brought from the lowlands. Hearst's enthusiasm throve on surmounting difficulties, and with delight he saw his first large garden come into being. Mrs. Phebe Hearst had created a beautiful garden at the Hacienda with spacious lawns, but in her son's new garden a lawn was out of the question because of the formation of the mountainside. Hearst's San Simeon garden was inspired by the memory of the garden of his grandmother, Mrs. Apperson, at her sunny ranch in Santa Clara County. The spirit of that spot of beauty had always remained with him, a fragrant mingling of clove pinks, lemon verbena, heliotrope, lilacs, hollyhocks, roses galore, with red, white, pink and yellow cacti scrambling to the roof.

Hearst's San Simeon garden has passed through many phases. Lavender lantana and pink ivy geraniums festoon the stone walls of the terraces. Red, white and yellow roses riot up tall palm trees transported from a place owned by his mother in Berkeley. Magenta Bougainvillæa vines several years old were brought from Berkeley to cover the guest house with the Persian tiles. Zinnias, gladiolus and dahlias supply gorgeous accents of Oriental color. Camellias, hibiscus, jasmine, daphne and hybridized heathers give an exotic aspect. But through the well designed, fastidiously cultivated joyous garden of San Simeon shines the gay spirit of the simple ranch garden near Santa Clara. That is why the garden at San Simeon sings.

In planting, Hearst produces swift, dramatic effects as in his newspapers. Overnight gorgeous beds of multi-colored tuberous begonias are created by transplanting blooming plants from hot houses. One of his garden surprises with a touch of mystical magic came on an Easter morning when the guests at San Simeon awoke to find the ground under the oaks covered with tall, white Madonna lilies. All night by electric light a large corps of men had worked to prepare for the celebration of Easter at dawn.

During the early construction of buildings it was necessary to cut down an oak. Senator Hearst always treasured this clump of oaks, and his son regretted the destruction of even one tree. The massacre of the sturdy mountain giant troubled Hearst and he vowed no other oak should lose its life on the mountaintop. In widening the terrace in front of the new Casa Grande he transplanted several oaks at an expense of thousands of dollars, and will transplant more. Not one tree has been lost.

A few years ago Hearst found a row of cypress that were to be felled near Paso Robles. The trees were thirty feet high, and he decided to buy them and take them to San Simeon. The first year a box was built around each cypress. For another year each cypress was watered and cared for until established in its new box. The third year the trees were brought to San Simeon where they stand on the terraces, magnificent sentinels.

To-day visitors pass from the guest houses through Italian gardens romantically rich with fountains, lily pools, rose arbors and ancient statuary in perpetually blossoming beds of flowers. They ascend through brilliant gardens under the oaks and reach the broad terrace of La Casa Grande bordered with marble and alabaster standard lamps with indirect lighting. Deep marble seats are framed in fragrant myrtle. On this terrace in easy garden chairs just before dinner, guests sit surveying the twilight sunset over the sea on the right, or the peak of Santa Lucia on the left, while silvery carillons sound from the high towers.

By the countryside and frequently by the guests at San Simeon this ivory-towered building is called "The Castle," but to Hearst it is La Casa Grande. He says it is not a castle. In the Wyntoon wilderness near Mount Shasta Mrs. Phebe Hearst had a castle, and in Wales Hearst has the castle of

St. Donat's. Both are very different from this cathedral-like structure of the Renaissance.

La Casa Grande is a nave-like building of concrete with the front vestibule flanked by two stone towers of the Spanish Renaissance, the romantic period of Spain. At San Simeon, as in all Spanish architecture, there is intent flexibility of design. The Spanish never found it necessary to define distinctly their periods as do the logical French. San Simeon's Casa Grande is of that transition time when the Gothic and the Renaissance came together in picturesque union.

The antique ornaments and motif of the main doorway are Gothic. The iron grille comes from a convent in the South of Spain built during the Renaissance. The floor of the entrance hall is of ancient tessellated mosaic, such as was excavated in the Roman Forum and at Pompeii. Choir stalls from Italian churches form the paneling of the assembly hall. At each end of the room is a wide window. Four Flemish tapestries portraying the history of Scipio Africanus, and originally belonging to the Spanish royal family, are on the old ivory walls. Tapestries designed after Rubens' drawings are over the windows. In this room, as in all rooms of the Casa Grande, are ancient carved ceilings. Here, too, are many figures of the Madonna. At San Simeon the Holy Mother and Child are in tapestries, needlework, marble, terra cotta, glass, pottery and oils. It is Hearst's favorite art subject—youth, maternity.

On Christmas Eve of 1925, the Hearsts took their first meal in the Casa Grande. They came for the occasion with their sons from New York. Hearst set up two Christmas trees for the twins, David and Randolph, then eight years of age. As yet lights had not been installed, but those of the construction camp were gaily borrowed. Great logs blazed in the early French carved sixteenth century fireplace. The refectory was not yet finished, and dinner was served in the assembly hall. After Santa Claus paid his visit to the Casa Grande the Hearsts returned to New York.

The assembly hall is the heart of the hill. Here at half after seven each evening Hearst meets his guests. Dress is always informal. Evening dress has been worn only once by the publisher on the hill, and that was in honor of President and Mrs. Coolidge.

After the assembly hall was completed, next came the refectory running at right angles with the larger room. To this long, noble, high refectory Hearst brought some of his choicest art treasures. Of all rooms in the Casa Grande the refectory is his artistic pride. The ceiling is of his vast collection of carved ceilings, and came from a north Italian sixteenth-century monastery of the Renaissance. The figures are of more than life size, each representing a saint with his or her symbol. One of these saints holds a building in his hands, and by the workers is named Saint Simon. If things go well with them they say, "Saint Simon is on the job."

In the refectory is an early French Gothic mantel room-high that looks as if it might have been made for a royal palace. In the winter logs burn in the opening which is higher than a tall man. Two Gothic tapestries depicting the history of Daniel hang on the walls. Choir stalls from the ancient Cathedral of Seo de Urgel in Catalan panel the walls. The bishop presiding over the Catalan cathedral had a modern soul, and he was depressed by surrounding antiquity. To the displeasure of ecclesiastical authorities he sold the choir stalls, but the ancient seats seem entirely serene and supply grave dignity to the San Simeon refectory.

The austerity of the choir stalls is relieved by an occasional crimson damask cushion, by the red brocade of the Savonarola chairs, and especially by the silken Sienese palio banners softly fluttering from each side of the walls between the high windows. Each banner bears the crest of a noble family or ward at Siena. On palio days the banners were taken into the cathedral and blessed. After the races the winner returned the banner to the cathedral where it was kept. Of every conceivable color, blue and white, red and yellow, green and white, green and red, the banners supply a festal center of interest to this stately refectory.

On the long Spanish and Italian refectory tables which extend nearly the full length of the room are, according to the traditions of the camp, always fruit, jams, marmalades, and condiments, retained because of the days in tents. Paper napkins are a survival of tent life which Hearst clings to in memory. He uses the simple pattern of blue willow china and the silver that belonged to his mother. About forty guests usually sit down to dinner at the week-end, although the refectory easily accommodates one hundred. At half after one a buffet lunch is served in the refectory.

William Randolph Hearst is probably at his happiest when he becomes "W. R.," and abandons newspapers, politics, motion pictures, architecture and even antiques. He places his dog in his motor, and he himself mounts his horse, and sets forth with Don Pancho Estrada. The *caballero* of new California and the *caballero* of the old, lead a house-party up and down mountains, one hour's drive to the picnic grounds by the brook with banks of wild flowers, on the new private road to the far end of the ranch beyond the Mission of San Antonio de Padua forty miles distant. Already they have been preceded by a truck-mounted kitchen manned by several efficient San Simeon servants. Potatoes have been roasted, beef has been barbecued. On rough board tables a baronial feast is spread. Lunch is self-served, picnic style.

In the evening at La Casa Grande motion-pictures are the distraction. At first they were shown in the refectory, and later during the summer the guests gathered out-of-doors and saw the pictures against the courtyard wall. The new left wing of La Casa Grande now contains a theater that might easily seat two hundred. The walls are hung with an antique, crimson, Italian *brocatelle*. Huge caryatides, walnut and gold, hold the lights. The audience sits in roomy, downy chairs. Each night there is a new picture. Many plays are flown up from Hollywood, and before being released are here previewed. Hearst says to the guests, "If you don't like the play, you can go to sleep."

A secret panel of the assembly hall opens to a carved elevator which takes one to Hearst's library, to his Gothic study, to the cloisters and nearly to the towers. Tucked away in these two stone towers is the blue and gold "Celestial Suite" connected by a large sitting-room. The "Celestial Suite" overlooks the guest houses in the front and has a vista of both the ocean and the Santa Lucia Mountains with their pine-covered peaks.

The library on the second floor was not large enough to house Hearst's collection of books, and so he built on the third floor a Gothic study as large as the assembly hall, and the walls are lined with books. Here have been placed two high carved chimneypieces and an ancient carved ceiling. In the windows will be installed some of his famous collection of stained glass.

At San Simeon work progresses in all directions. Between La Casa del Sol and La Casa del Monte is an out-of-doors swimming-pool of white marble faced with Vermont verd-antique marble. The pool is large enough to sail a boat on, and the water which is unceasingly filtered is kept at a temperature of seventy. At one side has been installed a fountain as large as the splendid fountains of Michelangelo. A covered colonnade encircles the pool with white marble columns leading to an ancient Greek temple.

On the left of La Casa Grande, as you go to the tennis-court, you pass the wire-enclosed aery which houses eagles. Here on a lower level to the left is the tennis-court and underneath is the last building Hearst has erected at San Simeon, a gymnasium with an indoor salt water swimming-pool. On account of the winter winds there is at times a tendency to avoid the out-of-doors pool, but in the salt water pool one may swim comfortably every day in the year. In excavating under the tennis court, Hearst also had the idea of producing a mysterious grotto-like effect. At present the salt water is created by adding sea salt to fresh water, but in time to come water will be pumped from the Pacific for this pool which is eighty-four

SAN SIMEON FROM THE AIR

Photograph by H. W. Truesdale

feet long, forty feet wide and twelve feet deep. Extending from the deep pool like the stem of the letter T, is another large pool for children and the timid, varying in depth from three to six feet. About ten feet above the large pool, and directly opposite the entrance, is a gold mosaic gallery from which swimmers dive, a luxurious evolution of the springboard. Both deep and shallow pools, the paneled walls, and the floors are of Venetian mosaic in hues from pale blue to a gorgeous Byzantine cobalt through to deep blue with gold for relief. Each square foot contains one hundred and forty-four pieces of mosaic set by Italian artisans.

In the "sweet dead city" of Ravenna, where Dante died, and Byron and Teresa Guiccioli loved, Hearst found inspiration for the indoor swimming-pool. On one of his many pilgrimages to European shrines of beauty, he journeyed to Ravenna to see the fifth-century mosaics of the mausoleum of the Empress Galla Placidia, the first of Roman royalty to marry a Gothic invader. Breathless he stood before the lapis lazuli and gold mosaic on the vaulted ceilings above the marble walls of the last resting place of the romantic princes. The publisher has an imagist mind. He never forgets that which pleases him. Years had passed since Hearst first saw those mosaics, but they gave him the motif of his new salt-water pool.

The famous factories of Murano near Venice manufactured the tiles for the mosaics. The gold squares were made of glass gilded with gold leaf, fired again, and then covered with glass so that water could not dim the gold. Murano is so far from San Simeon that when the mosaic tiles gave out, it was difficult to obtain others of the precise shade of blue. But all colors were so rearranged that even errors in manufacture were transmuted into new beauty. Artisans worked three and a half years completing this pool which seems to be of liquid lapis lazuli and gold, and cost nearly a million dollars.

Hearst is one of those fortunate beings who have visions of splendor, and who realize these visions with magnificence. He will erect another guest house at San Simeon, and an office and utility building. He would like to house comfortably sixty guests. Then he will build an armor and tapestry room large enough for balls and banquets, which will extend from wing to wing in the rear of the Casa Grande. Here will be hung more of his tapestries and with them will be placed his royal armor.

For the staff of San Simeon Hearst has already re-built the little fishing village and is replacing worn-out ranch buildings with modern structures. The standard wage prevails. A large dining hall in the workers' camp accommodates one hundred and fifty. Motion pictures are provided twice a week.

Hearst seeks work as avidly as other men pursue pleasure and sport. While concentrating on building plans he often works eight hours without cessation. Colonel Joseph Willicombe, his secretary for twenty-one years, keeps from Hearst meaningless telephone calls, but there are those so important in his organization that their questions must be answered. Frequently he speaks by wire with Chicago, Washington, New York or London, and again he returns to his work-play of creation. No one ventures to interrupt him. But his little black and white Boston bull terrier, Buddy, when he was alive, used to scratch at the door of Hearst's work-room all unmindful that the great, fair, lordly figure bending over blue-prints with Miss Morgan was more than his beloved master. Hearst never failed to interrupt his work to open the door for Buddy, take him on his knee and go on with his building plans.

William Randolph Hearst has developed not only the buildings at San Simeon, but he has vastly increased the acreage. He owns nearly in compact body about two hundred and forty thousand acres in Monterey and San Luis Obispo Counties, a ranch about half the size of the State of Rhode Island. One agent is said to have bought for him twenty-three ranches in one day. His property surrounds the old Mission of San Antonio de Padua founded by Padre Junípero Serra in 1771. Hearst has offered to restore the crumbling Mission, and probably his offer will be accepted.

Within a mile of the Mission at the far end of his ranch, formerly called the Milpitas, he has erected a Spanish California
ranch-house with a frontage of two hundred and twenty-five
feet, so like the Mission in construction that frequently it is
mistaken for San Antonio de Padua. This ranch was formerly
the property of the Atherton family, and here Gertrude Atherton came many years ago as a bride. Frequently Hearst brings
a party of guests to this ranch-house. Often he rides, sometimes
he comes by motor, but of late he has flown the forty miles in
ten minutes.

About six miles from the ranch-house is one of Hearst's
unique possessions, La Cueva Pintada, an Indian cave at the
head of Pine Canyon near the top of the hill forming the eastern wall of the San Antonio River. Archæologists study this
cave with its mysterious fresco in black and red, the vermilion
of the exhausted New Almaden Quicksilver Mine far to the
North. On the wall of this cave is an Indian cross with a human
figure, a turtle and the sun. The arms of the cross are adorned
with the sun and moon, evidently the work of Salinan Indians.
Is this the same cave that Padre Junípero Serra wrote about
when he founded San Antonio de Padua, the cave where the
Indians confessed they kept their idols? La Cueva Pintada
opens toward the rising sun. Is it a sun temple?

If Hearst's newspapers should cease to exist, if the public
should forget his services in bettering conditions in America,
he would still be remembered as the greatest private collector
of art ever known. His art objects occupy a block of store-
houses on One Hundred and Forty-third Street in New York
City, vast warehouses in San Francisco, and a two-acre store-
room underneath La Casa Grande at San Simeon. He likes
conversation with connoisseurs, and even in his crowded life he
finds time to study auction catalogues which are sent to him
from all over the world. He is not interested in art objects for
their commercial value. Beauty makes the first appeal.

But he has a collection of early Grecian and Egyptian pottery important for its archæological interest as well as its

beauty. He has more Gothic mantels than any man living. In his Gothic hall in New York City are six tapestries probably inspired by Cardinal Wolsey. One of the masterpieces owned by him is a Straganoff tapestry that once belonged to the Vatican. No private individual ever assembled so many superb tapestries. His collection of old silver is unequaled. Some of it belonged to Queen Elizabeth. He has the finest collection of Majolica or Hispano-Moresque plates. No one has so much antique furniture nor so many paneled rooms as Hearst, particularly English rooms, Elizabethan, Georgian, Jacobean, Tudoresque, and of the time of James the First. Perhaps the most unusual room ever taken out of England is in his possession. It belonged to Queen Elizabeth. In it Will Shakespeare is supposed to have read his manuscripts to the Queen.

Hearst owns more stained glass from the thirteenth to the seventeenth century than any one else. In his magnificent collection of sculpture is a Hermes that comes from the Island of Samos. It is his rarest possession in marble. He has also many fine examples of the early Grecian and classical periods, Byzantine, Romanesque and Gothic. Much sculpture of the *moyen âge* as well as of the eighteenth century is owned by him. In his collection of paintings are works of Rembrandt, Gainsborough, Frans Hals, Greuze, Boucher, Van Dyck, as well as the work of many early Italian painters. He employs an armorer to care for his vast collection of armor. In his collections Hearst has not overlooked assembling the finest American furniture and works of art in existence, as well as a vast collection of silver-mounted Mexican saddles.

Perhaps his possession most interesting to the public is that of sixty species of grazing animals and thirty species of jungle animals. Hearst does not like to have noise or commotion made by people passing through the animals' habitat which is a preserve of two thousand acres enclosed with a woven wire fence ten miles long and eight feet high.

On the road up the mountaintop there are signs, "Beware of Wild Animals," "Reckless Driving Will Not Be Tolerated," and "Animals Have the Right of Way." The animals are tractable and friendly and never disturbed visitors when they used to alight from their motor-cars to manipulate the grasshopper gate. The first field animals obtained by Hearst were the spotted deer from India.

There are black buffalo from Montana, warring yak from Tibet, fighting emu from Australia, musk oxen from Greenland, great-horned elk, prong-horned antelope, and kangaroos ever waging battle with the camel. Several years ago Hearst cabled Miss Head, the business director of his English company, to buy two giraffes. Miss Head sailed for Africa, bought the giraffes and shipped them to San Simeon.

Two of the most recent and admired acquisitions of animals at San Simeon are white polar bears, who surprised every one by adjusting themselves easily to the temperate climate. Their pit, formerly occupied by lions, is visible to all passers-by on the road descending from the Casa Grande. In hot weather they wallow in their big pool. In the Arctic white polar bears live on fish and seals, but at San Simeon they are content with the same diet that the native bears thrive on. The average black bear at San Simeon consumes daily two quarts of fresh milk, six quarts of cooked cereal, six large carrots, two heads of lettuce, and several times a week a little meat. For a few months in the year the grazing animals at San Simeon are able to maintain themselves, but the rest of the time they are fed once a day. Four men look after and feed the animals.

About a quarter of a mile in the rear of the Casa Grande dwell caged animals. Joseph Schenck, the motion-picture producer, once gave Hearst a pair of baby lions, and they were the beginning of the publisher's collection of jungle animals. Visitors never tire of seeing the cheetahs, cockatoos, eagles, South American spider monkeys, sacred monkeys from Japan, Java and India, the orang-outang, the spotted leopard, the sinister black panther, the friendly she-elephant, snarling wildcats, and the Californian lions ever impatient of restraint, charging back and forth in their cages. Human beings are always fascinated by their intelligent cousins, the chimpanzee and gorilla.

Hearst makes an effort to exclude all predatory animals. Wild life is being preserved and permitted to increase. He seldom allows hunting in the mountains or fishing in the streams. When the hunting season comes, it is said that neighboring wild deer make for San Simeon as a refuge. Students of nature from academies of science go to San Simeon to study the habits of birds and animals.

Mountain lions and wildcats alone are hunted at San Simeon. They make their way into the animal preserve by leaping from the limbs of trees.

Hearst has not only brought animals and masterpieces of art to San Simeon, but everywhere is evident his love of trees, especially blossoming trees. The village of San Simeon itself is parked with eucalpyti gorgeous with yellow-red rosettes of bloom. More eucalypti form an avenue as one passes the flying field toward the hill.

In the wild animal preserve are native shrubs, young oaks, pines and redwoods protected by high, woven wire fences from animals that enjoy snipping off tender, young green leaves. These trees have made astonishing growth, but many of them will not reach maturity for one hundred years. Hearst is not disturbed. San Simeon belongs to the centuries to come. As the Casa Grande is neared there are more eucalypti, red-berried pyracanthas, fragrant pittosporum, oleanders, plumbago, groves of oranges, lemons and grapefruit.

Still nearer to the Casa Grande is approached, on the left, a wide pergola with concrete columns curving for a mile around a lower summit. Here promenade energetic guests, who at the same time enjoy every kind of fruit and nut that flourishes in California. Vines and trees are trained over the columns. In the spring the pergola is an avenue of blossoms. An automobile might pass through its wide reaches.

San Simeon may be reached by airship, by freight steamer, by motoring over hills from Paso Robles, or northward along the coast for forty-three miles from San Luis Obispo, and then five miles up the hill. The Hearst private train, arriving at San Luis Obispo, has two sleepers and a diner, so that the repose of travelers may not be disturbed till morning.

Many demands come from the public to see this combination of museum and palace. Hearst is willing to share San Simeon with lovers of beauty, but during the construction period, in order to avoid injury to visitors, he has guards at the entrance to keep out sightseers until San Simeon is completed.

For several years the State has been building from Monterey and Carmel to San Luis Obispo one of the world's great scenic highways. This road follows the seashore for two hundred miles, and with a titanic struggle much of it is being blasted out of the mountain by prisoners. They receive for their toil a shortening of their terms of imprisonment and some money. Right of way for the new scenic highway was freely given by Hearst.

In 1937, the Monterey-San Luis Obispo road will be completed. When tourists from the North pass the little town of San Simeon they will look to the left, and there on the very highest peak of the enchanted hillside will be visible the ivory-colored towers of La Casa Grande.

CHAPTER LV

SEVENTY AND AFTER

W ILL HEARST of Harvard became proprietor of the San Francisco *Examiner* at twenty-three. The paper had twenty-three thousand circulation. Now William Randolph Hearst has forty-one newspapers and magazines and he speaks to an audience of twenty-one millions. He sells features to twenty-two hundred newspapers in the United States, and in ninety countries and in thirty-two languages. He has more than thirty-one thousand employees and a pay-roll of more than fifty-seven million a year. He is the greatest spender of money the world has seen. San Simeon alone cost twice his inheritance from his mother. He has created the second largest fortune in America, distributed great largess, become a leader and molder of national and world events.

With the eyes of youth and the daring of youth Hearst came. He cared more for men, women and children than for tradition and money. Often disregarding his own profit and loss, unheeding personal safety, his deepest concern was for America. He has always believed in the genius of America. Sometimes he seemed to believe too much; but like Jefferson he did not think that he could have too much faith in man. From the day he entered the *Examiner* office in 1887, the common man had a voice for the first time in California. When he went to New York, America had a new voice.

Hearst knew that the *Examiner* could live, that he himself could survive only through material success. Circulation, advertising, with these he would fashion a mighty weapon for the war he was to wage against entrenched evil in public life. He entertained his public, he instructed, he led, but he never deviated from what he held to be the well being of America.

He believed that the American public would respond to a newspaper faithful to its interests, and his confidence was well placed. The voice of the *Examiner* swelled and expanded until the voice of Hearst is the most powerful journalistic voice ever heard.

No man ventures to become a candidate for the Presidency of the United States without trying to learn whom Hearst will support. Before he was nominated, Herbert Hoover motored to Los Angeles and obtained an interview with the publisher. Hoover explained to Hearst what his plans would be if he were elected President; magnificent highways, new inland waterways in the East, Columbia River development in the northwest, water and power dams in the southeast, a gigantic system of flood control of the Mississippi River and its tributaries, water and power conservation in every part of the country. These were projects that Hearst desired to see developed. Long since unconcerned about party lines, it mattered little to Hearst that Hoover was a Republican. He gave the power of his papers to Herbert Hoover.

The crash of 1929 came. Millions of the unemployed were hungry. Hearst called on President Hoover to carry out his splendid program of public works. The United States had lent eleven billions to European nations. Why not a five billion dollar peace loan to unemployed Americans to stimulate prosperity? In all his papers Hearst urged the loan. He advocated government control of manufacture and distribution of alcoholic beverages. In his campaign to aid the unemployed and bring back normal business, he said in a letter to the New York *American:*

I think we should declare vigorously for a six hour day. I have no doubt that if we make a survey, the majority of employers will be against the six hour day. But we are supposed to lead public opinion, not follow it. If we had polled the country on the election of Senators by the people, or on woman's suffrage, the vast majority would have been against it. There is nothing revolutionary in the six hour day. Improvements in modern machinery and advance in modern methods of mass production have so reduced the cost of production that shorter working hours are inevitable. Hours decreased from fourteen hours at the beginning of the nineteenth century to eight hours a day at the beginning of the twentieth century. It is time for another reduction of hours.

Hearst further developed the same subject:

Prosperity must be built from the bottom. . . . It must be dug out of the ground, hoed out of the furrows, plowed out of the fields, woven out of the warp and woof of the loom, hammered out of iron, beaten out of bronze, crushed out of rock, hewed out of the forest, shaped at the mill. . . . It must be gathered from the farms and the mines and fabricated in the factories. The wealth which our statesmen burned up in the war and our high financiers so recklessly threw to the four winds of Europe must with bent back and strained muscles, be laboriously rebuilt by the workers. The first duty of this government is to give the workers work. They will give trade to the shops and orders to industries. They will pay rents, buy shoes and clothing and put money into circulation.

In June of 1931 Hearst spoke over the radio. He said that the collapse of 1929 was caused by over-speculation and over-capitalization:

Leaders must be reminded that business exists for the service of men. . . . The maladjustment in industry, glutted markets on one hand and undernourished people on the other, constitute a serious indictment of management in the large.

The Hoover Administration made no effort to bring about the six-hour day. The five billion dollar loan was not made. American money went into what Hearst called "amalgamated cats and dogs"—foreign bonds, on which international bankers received a heavy commission.

In February of 1933, the United States Senate Finance Committee asked Hearst to appear and give his views on measures to alleviate the economic depression. The publisher did not appear before the committee, but he wrote a statement which was read.

He urged that the Government make exceptional expenditures in public works in all times of depression to be paid for by bonds redeemable in good times when it would be less a burden in taxation to the community. He advocated increasing currency and paying excess of expenditures over government income with this currency rather than by excessive taxation. After recovery was established and credit again expanded, a superabundance of currency could be retired to prevent excessive inflation.

The income tax was declared by him to be a "racket." The Government plundered the public under coercion to the point of confiscation, and the rich disloyally evaded taxation and took refuge in tax exempt securities. A sales tax should be substituted for the income tax.

American home markets should not be flooded with cheap foreign products made by war-pauperized labor under a system of depreciated currency which decreases the manufacturing cost of goods. Cheap foreign imports would reduce the standard of living in America.

He declared that the Government should finance the farmer at a low rate of interest and insure him in the possession of his farm over sufficient time to nullify destructive effects of periodic, unfavorable economic conditions. In the interest of the farmer as well as of the consumer there should be government ownership of railroads, that weighty and bulky farm products could be reasonably transported.

Hearst was deeply disappointed in President Hoover's failure to carry out his public works program, and he was weary of office holders who would not keep their promises. He recalled Speaker John N. Garner of Texas, with whom he had served in Congress—an American of the rugged homespun type, opposed to the League of Nations. He believed that Garner could be trusted.

During the summer of 1932 Hearst declared over the radio for Speaker Garner for President. Until the publisher suggested the Texan few had thought of Garner for President. Suddenly the Speaker's name was everywhere. Texas was for Garner. So was California. Garner was placed in nomination at the Chicago Democratic Convention.

Before balloting began James Farley, Governor Franklin D. Roosevelt's manager, claimed six hundred and ninety votes. Al Smith declared that Roosevelt could not get the nomination. Under the two-thirds rule, seven hundred and seventy votes were necessary. On the first ballot Roosevelt received six hundred and sixty-six and one-quarter votes. Ninety and one-quarter votes were for Garner. On the second ballot Roosevelt gained ten and one-half votes. On the third ballot ten more came. If there was another ballot, Manager James Farley knew that Roosevelt would be defeated by the two-thirds rule. He would lose Mississippi and some other States. Farley realized that the moment was crucial. He telephoned John Francis Neylan of San Francisco, brilliant counsel for all the Hearst papers and second only to the publisher in their direction.

Neylan is Hearst's political representative in California. He is a dark, tall, handsome, burly, swift man of action. He telephoned Hearst who was in Los Angeles, "Roosevelt must have California and Texas now." No one understands politics better than Neylan, for as the head of the California Board of Control he was the right hand man of Governor Hiram W. Johnson. "If California does not go to Roosevelt," Neylan urged, "the swing will be toward Baker."

Hearst has complete confidence in Neylan's integrity and judgment, and he replied, "Baker is League of Nations. Worse, he is attorney for many corporations including the Power Trust."

Already Hearst had an agreement with Mayor Cermak of Chicago that Illinois and California should vote together. With

Illinois would vote Indiana. Roosevelt's nomination hung on Hearst's word.

Hearst gave the word to the California delegation. From Los Angeles he called Garner on the telephone and asked him to release Texas to Roosevelt. Garner agreed. Illinois, Texas and California swung to Roosevelt. For the first time Hearst named a President.

Although William Randolph Hearst virtually made Franklin Delano Roosevelt President, he has differed many times from the Administration, but often he has been in accord with the President. Controlled inflation—what is it but the great silver battle of 1896?

Hearst's most decisive opposition to the Roosevelt Administration was when he criticized the NRA:

... with its nonsensical ... interference with national and legitimate industrial development. We should understand that extravagant employment by governments must be only temporary, that permanent employment must come from industrial development and increased and expanded business activity. Remove restrictions on industry. Lighten the burden of business. Reduce taxation. Abolish political bureaucracy and governmental extravagance.

On another occasion he said that the Government seemed to think that business instead of being the great benefactor of the Nation, was Public Enemy Number One, and it is the duty of democracy to destroy it.

The trouble with the Administration is that it is composed of gentlemen who have had no practical experience in business and no practical knowledge of economics. They have an idea that business is rather a wicked thing that accumulates money which properly belongs to others. They do not realize that business creates wealth and creates employment, and that industry distributes wealth and good wages—the only sound and legitimate way in which wealth can be distributed....

Give business its head. Take off the hobble of government restraint. Lift the backbreaking burden of Federal, State and city taxation. Let the Government do its part; and its principal part is to help business help the country.

Hearst differed from the Administration concerning taxation. Many articles on the subject were written by him. In one of them he said:

All production is hampered and handicapped by taxation. All products are increased in price in exact proportion to taxation. People have just so much money to spend, and if things cost more they buy less of them. When people buy less, less things are made. When less things are made, less labor is employed. High taxation blights the farmer and all producers of raw material, cuts down the consumers' purchasing power, falls ruinously upon labor, destroys foreign trade because high prices make competition and foreign markets impossible. Japan, without the burden of foreign debt, is underselling us in electric bulbs that we read by and in making American flags. The most important thing is to reduce expenditures, reduce the national debt, reduce taxation, reduce burdens upon business and upon labor, and increase the purchasing power of the community by allowing people to retain and spend the money they earn instead of turning it over to the Government to be wasted in useless expenditure and in the support of parasitical politicians. This is the A B C of economics; but unhappily there are a lot of people in Washington who do not know their A B C's.

Hearst advocated the recognition of Russia, but when Stalin announced that the Communist Party in America must be Bolshevized and real revolutionary leadership developed in America, the publisher was disturbed. When he learned that many college professors were Communists and that students in universities were following their teachings, Hearst grew alarmed lest in these dark days of depression democracy might be destroyed. He foresaw that the despotism of Fascism might be raised up to combat the despotism of Communism, and liberty might be crushed to dust and dissolution. In all his newspapers Hearst protested:

Communism is not a new system, but an old, discredited, discarded system.... The Communist party is largely composed of agitators with greed for power, position and property, but without the ability to acquire them except by criminal violence, and certainly without the ability or will to exercise them for the general benefit....

This is the day of the demagogue. Always some one can be found willing to be more of a demagogue, willing to make a more violent appeal to the frenzy of the mob, willing to wave the red flag more vehemently or apply the torch more destructively. When the flames of Bolshevism have once been started it will be difficult to arrest them.... Why should we advocate Fascism or Communism or Socialism or Bolshevism, or any of the oppressive tyrannies which are harassing unfortunate people of foreign lands? Communism in Russia is as much a tyranny as the old régime, merely a different class. Fascism in Italy is tyranny, Fascism in Germany. Neither Fascism nor Communism permits liberty, tolerates freedom of thought or of action. There are enough Lenins and Hitlers abroad, we do not want any at home. We want leaders and not dictators. We have striven to make the world safe for democracy, and not for despotism.

There never will be a Fascist movement in this country until Communism compels it. The menace of Communism develops Fascism in Europe. We must not let it become necessary in this country. We must not allow our Communists to get control of the machinery of the Government and give our people a government based on class prejudice fortified by violence.

Hearst reminded his readers that in Russia people were shot or sent to Siberian prisons for stealing bread or trying to save from the Red army enough of their own grain to preserve themselves from starvation. He recalled to them that the Soviet Government had starved millions in order that seventy million bushels of grain might be exported to obtain foreign money.

We do not want to resort to a Fascist class government in order to prevent such misgovernment. We do not want class government at any time.... In Italy the Fascist government has suppressed all freedom of thought and expression, has dragooned all independent industry out of the country, and has utterly impoverished the people in order to gratify the government's imperial ambition to maintain a nation in arms.

In Germany all liberty is lost, and all modern ideas in thought and speech and publication are ended. The Nazi government has revived medieval methods of execution and political practices of wholesale assassination.

Earnestly Hearst warned his readers against the resulting chaos when violence meets violence. On March 3, 1935, he wrote:

There can be no victory except for tyranny—the tyranny of Communism, or the tyranny of Fascism. Either tyranny means the loss of our liberty, the end of free thought, free speech, free trial, destruction of the fundamental rights of free men, regimentation of free society into a subject state with a scepter held in the bloody hands of despotism. Then the desolation of the Dark Ages will be here again.

In this free America of ours, in the wholesome hearts of our understanding independent people, lies the best hope of the survival of enlightenment and liberty and for the conservation of civilization.

We must be worthy of our great opportunity, our great obligations. Our duty is not only to our people, but to the world. We must keep the torch of freedom aflame to light the feet of humanity, weary of oppression, back to civilization, back to the free exercise and enjoyment of the human rights of life, liberty and the pursuit of happiness.

Hearst seldom reads what his adversaries and critics write, and so his smiling lips still curve upward, but his achievements have aroused envy and his crusades have met with hostility. His repeated articles against Communism stirred great bitterness. His property was threatened and even his life. A boycott of the Hearst papers was under way, and in July of 1935 the publisher defiantly reiterated his policies:

The Hearst papers are American papers published for the American people. They support the American system of government, the American Constitution, American institutions and American ideals. They labor to maintain the American standard of living. They are opposed to the various forms of tyranny which our American forefathers came to this country to avoid. They are in favor of American independence, American rights and liberties, free speech, free assembly, freedom of thought and action, and freedom of the press. . . .

They are opposed to Communism, Fascism or any form of despotism. They are opposed to race prejudice and class conflict. They believe in opportunity for all and equality before the law. They believe in the creation of wealth through industry and the distribution of wealth in wages. They are opposed to any form of politics and economics which endeavors to grade down the more prosperous to the level of the lowest; and they believe ardently in the American system of politics and economics which for a century and a half has successfully raised the lower strata to a nearer level with the upper.

They believe in deportation of alien cranks and criminals, particularly those who came to this country to find freedom of speech and remained to abuse it; who came to this country to gain the liberties which they are unable intelligently to understand and employ; who came to this country to find prosperity and who are trying to create in this country the conditions which have brought adversity to other lands.

The Hearst papers are opposed to any government by clique or class. They believe in genuine democracy and the rule of the majority. They believe America should be for Americans and that Americans should be for America. Those who do not approve of these policies had better not take these papers, because these are the policies which will be adhered to as long as these papers are published.

On April 29, 1933, William Randolph Hearst turned seventy. It was a busy day for his super-secretary Colonel Joseph Willicombe, who has been with the publisher more than twenty years. Willicombe knows his employer better than any other living man, and is as devoted to him as a brother. By some he is called Hearst's third eye. Willicombe and the under-secretaries and telegraph operators spent the day receiving and reading congratulatory messages coming over the wire for the Chief. San Francisco, Seattle, Chicago, New York, Mexico City, Paris and London spoke on the telephone. Hearst answered some of the two thousand messages, but as usual he played tennis, as usual he swam, as usual he supervised building construction, as usual he advised concerning advertising contracts, fiction to be obtained for magazines, editorial policies, New York real-estate leases, motion-picture production, radio stations to be purchased, conduct of orchards, direction of ranches, and mines distant as Peru.

As usual, at half after seven the Chief stepped from the elevator and came through the carved door opening in the choir-stall paneling and entered the assembly hall of La Casa Grande. He could have been no other than the creator of San Simeon, William Randolph Hearst. Kindly time has given the publisher few gray hairs. His skin is unwrinkled, and he seemed in the late fifties as he greeted his sixty guests costumed as in the Days of Gold. As soon as he received their congratulations he retired and reappeared dressed for riding.

Later in the stately refectory where guests were seated under the brilliant fluttering *palio* banners of Siena, musicians in the minstrel gallery sang songs of Forty-Nine. Arthur Brisbane had come from New York and he made the greeting of welcome. William Randolph Hearst, Jr., who delights his father by writing thoughtful articles, rose and read an entertaining prophecy written by William Curley of the New York *Evening Journal*, one of Hearst's ablest and most appreciated editors.

After the mountainous cake, bearing seventy candles, was placed upon the table Hearst rose and said, "I am not thinking about my seventieth birthday. It is much like any other day. My mind is on my hundredth birthday. I am glad you came to-day, and I thank you. I invite you all to dine here with me in 1963."

After dinner Hearst withdrew and until early morning in his

Gothic study filled with his choicest possessions, he went on with the work of editing his far-flung newspapers and magazines. On his seventieth birthday he asked the question ever on his lips, "What shall we do to-morrow?"

When will he retire? Already he has answered that query, "The time to retire is when God retires you, and not before."

At nearly three and seventy William Randolph Hearst has no idea of retiring. Few men have lived so greatly as he, and with so much happiness. Always he has done the work that gave him greatest pleasure—editing a newspaper, molding public opinion.

On the occasion of the opening of the new building of the Los Angeles *Examiner* which is the greatest money-maker in his entire chain of papers, Hearst expressed his feeling for journalism:

The newspaper is a moral force second only to the church. It is a political power superior to parties. It is an instrument of justice coequal with the court. Its representatives sit in the councils of rulers and march with the armies of nations. Its columns record every act of importance, every thought of originality, every word of wisdom. A great newspaper is the sword of the people, the shield to protect them from their enemies. It is the banner which leads the march, the lamp which lights the path for popular progress. It is the torch which Liberty holds aloft for the enlightenment of the world.

No matter where Hearst is, on the Enchanted Hill of San Simeon, at Wyntoon by the roaring, gray McCloud, looking out on the stormy Bristol Channel from St. Donat's, Wales, he always hears the intoxicating music of the presses of his newspapers. He still sees through the eyes of youth, and likes to associate with youth. Time has not dulled his sense of news. He wants to make people laugh, cry, to stir them with his own eagerness for news and his passion for the greatness of America.

Hearst does not seek a tranquil life, he says. He would rather be worried than bored.

"Who wants to hang like a sloth under the limb of a shady tree," he asks, "and blink all day at the beautiful green leaves, and fleecy clouds, and the blue sky? Not I. No one except those who are weak and weary, and those who are getting old."

Hearst's life has always sung and danced. It is still singing and dancing. He is wary of tranquillity. He says that about the time anybody really desires tranquillity he gets it permanently—in death. Hearst's Utopia is action.

In the year that he became seventy he wrote to his editors:

We seem to say to the reader, "There is the news, but it does not interest us. Perhaps you will be interested. That is your affair."

I think *we* ought to be more interested in the news, more excited about it. In ancient time McEwen said that he looked at the first page and remarked, "Gee whiz!" At the second page he said, "Holy Moses!" At the third page, "God Almighty!" Vibrate, respond to the news. Feature news more. Pick out news stories. Develop them. Write them well. Illustrate them. Make them better and more readable than any other paper. Make the paper distinctive by handling the news. A paper stands or falls by its news interest. Print all the news, but see more in the news than other editors do. To interest, be yourself interested. To excite, be yourself excited over the news. Get young people around you. Get rid of the *blasé* crowd. Then give them a chance. Let them get excited. Let them be young. Let them do things. Let them make a few mistakes. Maybe the public will like the mistakes. Maybe we are making the big mistake by not being vital enough.

I am getting old, running down, going to sleep like a top before it keels over. Don't let the papers run down. They must not go to sleep. Get in a lot of youngsters who don't know it can't be done. They will surprise us by doing it. In daily council we should ask just where and in what the paper is better than its competitor the day before. If we have not made its superiority noticeable, we have missed a day. Then take up the paper of the day and see what we can do to make it outstanding. I guess we are not too old to do something. Let's try.

WILLIAM RANDOLPH HEARST KEEPS IN TOUCH WITH HIS VAST
ENTERPRISES EVEN WHILE ON VACATION AT WYNTOON

Hearst was younger than his youngest editors and publishers. Within a few weeks he was revolutionizing the pictures
in his papers. He introduced the "candid camera" from England which enables photographers to make unposed indoor
pictures in any light. He installed picture editors. He told them
to study moving pictures.

Get a good picture and see that it is brilliantly printed. A half-
tone does not mean a mud-tone. Bring out the contrast of light
and shade. Have a cleanly printed newspaper. There is lots of
work for the publisher in this pictorial plan and lots for the
editor. The picture editor must have an artist and technician. He
must know his business. The editor must consult and coöperate
with him and give him every opportunity to make his presence
felt. Let the Hearst papers be what once they were, the best
illustrated before the public.

In the editorial columns Hearst was as alive as he was
nearly fifty years before in San Francisco when he advocated
the new charter and municipal ownership of water, opposed
prize-fighting, demanded improved schools, exposed maladministration of prisons, called for a Merchant Marine, compelled
the Southern Pacific Railroad to pay the Funding Debt, urged
the Panama Canal, proposed the income tax, called for the
popular election of United States Senators, fought for municipal ownership of street railways.

Hearst was as alive as he was in New York when he de-
manded freedom for Cuba, supported Free Silver and Bryan,
crusaded for eighty-cent gas, exposed the Ramapo Water Com-
pany, sent relief trains to Galveston, Texas, attacked the Ice
Trust, smashed the Coal Trust, established the parcel-post,
brought relief to stricken San Francisco, fought Tammany
Hall, read Standard Oil letters, ran for the Mayoralty of New
York, campaigned for the office of Governor, opposed the Milk
Trust, prevented the Japanese Syndicate from buying land in
Mexico, fought to stop the World War, brought about Uni-

versal Service, defeated the League of Nations, crusaded against narcotics.

Hearst was as alive as when, while building San Simeon he campaigned against the Power Trust, demanded veterans' bonus, battled for repeal of the Volstead Act, and made Governor Franklin D. Roosevelt, President.

Now he attacked the NRA, advocated the sales tax, asked for enough inflation to overcome deflation, demanded that the navy be built up, that aeroplanes be manufactured for the protection of America. Home markets should be protected, home products, home materials. He insisted that the Government purchase American made goods for government projects. He asked that motion pictures be criticized for slaughtering animals to make dramatic scenes. He flayed the excessive income tax. He attacked the Communists for fomenting the general strike at San Francisco. With all his resourcefulness and vigor of expression and concern for his country he warned America against the evils of Communism.

Within the business-executive Hearst, within the architect Hearst, within the art collector Hearst, within the statesman Hearst, within the far-sighted, powerful editor Hearst, within the crusading American, lives another Hearst seen by few—a Hearst with a religion of his own formulated for himself from all the religions of the world, a religion never discussed by him, that makes him seem detached, remote. He has a large collection of Bibles, and his knowledge of Biblical history is wide. Mrs. Hearst says that he always has a Bible close to his bedside. Once when he was ill a friend entered the room and found an embossed prayer on the table. Casually the visitor said, "No one should die without a prayer on his lips."

Hearst answered, "No one should live without a prayer on his lips."

William Randolph Hearst expressed his philosophy of life not long ago at a dinner at San Simeon. He seemed preoccupied and deserted conversation. He began scribbling what apparently were notes for an article. He was really questioning life's to-morrow. When he finished he handed to Fremont Older the following:

THE SONG OF THE RIVER

The snow melts on the mountain
And the water runs down to the spring,
And the spring in a turbulent fountain,
With a song of youth to sing,
Runs down to the riotous river,
And the river flows to the sea,
And the water again
Goes back in rain
To the hills where it used to be.
And I wonder if Life's deep mystery
Isn't much like the rain and the snow
Returning through all eternity
To the places it used to know.

For life was born on the lofty heights
And flows in a laughing stream,
To the river below
Whose onward flow
Ends in a peaceful dream.
And so at last,
When our life has passed
And the river has run its course,
It again goes back,
O'er the selfsame track,
To the mountain which was its source.

So why prize life
Or why fear death,
Or dread what is to be?
The river ran its allotted span
Till it reached the silent sea.
Then the water harked back to the mountaintop
To begin its course once more.

So we shall run the course begun
Till we reach the silent shore,
Then revisit earth in a pure rebirth
From the heart of the virgin snow.
So don't ask why we live or die,
Or whither, or when we go,
Or wonder about the mysteries
That only God may know.

WILLIAM RANDOLPH HEARST *scripsit,*
Poeta nascitur, non fit.

INDEX

565

572 INDEX

574   INDEX

(1)

CPSIA information can be obtained at www.ICGtesting.com
Printed in the USA
BVOW081605280911

272358BV00014B/152/P